THE
OXYRHYNCHUS PAPYRI
VOLUME LXXII

THE
OXYRHYNCHUS PAPYRI
VOLUME LXXII

EDITED WITH TRANSLATIONS AND NOTES BY

N. GONIS

and

D. COLOMO

WITH CONTRIBUTIONS BY

A. BENAISSA   L. CAPPONI   W. E. H. COCKLE

J. DE JONG   C. MELIADÒ   A. NODAR

A. SYRKOU   J. D. THOMAS

Graeco-Roman Memoirs, No. 92

PUBLISHED FOR
THE ARTS AND HUMANITIES RESEARCH COUNCIL
BY THE
EGYPT EXPLORATION SOCIETY
3 DOUGHTY MEWS, LONDON WC1N 2PG
2008

TYPESET BY THE STINGRAY OFFICE, MANCHESTER
PRINTED IN GREAT BRITAIN
BY THE CHARLESWORTH GROUP, WAKEFIELD
AND PUBLISHED FOR
THE ARTS AND HUMANITIES RESEARCH COUNCIL
BY THE EGYPT EXPLORATION SOCIETY
(REGISTERED CHARITY NO. 212384)
3 DOUGHTY MEWS, LONDON WCIN 2PG

Graeco-Roman Memoirs

ISSN 0306-9222

ISBN-10 0 85698 181 8
ISBN-13 978 0 85698 181 4

PREFACE

Part I continues publication of our New Testament papyri with fragments from two codices of *Corinthians*, the earlier assignable to the fourth century. Part II offers otherwise unknown hexameter poetry, much of it on traditional mythological subjects. The most substantial fragment, **4850**, combines Homeric language and pathetic rhetoric in a way typical of Late Epic. Two lost poets are rescued from oblivion: **4853** Arius (?), author of a *Theogamia* of which we have only the title; **4851** Ausonius, whose *Herm[es?]* apparently celebrated Hermes and Thoeris side by side, clearly a local product and perhaps connected with the Gymnasium of Oxyrhynchus. Part III contains substantial fragments of two rhetorical handbooks. **4854** overlaps with the first *Techne* attributed in the medieval tradition to (Aelius) Aristides, but with substantial omissions, additions and shuffling of sections: the history of this text was clearly even more complex than editors of the medieval version have believed. **4855** contains the end of a summary *Techne* closely related to the progymnasmatic tradition, but with novelties of detail and of structure. Both pieces illustrate the popularity and fluidity of such works, which no doubt circulated both as substantive texts and in a variety of redactions and selections put together by teachers for their immediate purposes.

All but two of the thirty-five documentary texts in Part IV, dated to the second and early third centuries, relate to giro transfers of private grain-stocks within and between state granaries. These are part of a larger group of documents relating to *sitologoi* in the villages around Oxyrhynchus that for some reason came to be discarded, all together, on a rubbish dump in the capital. The group illustrates in detail the day-to-day functioning of the currency-in-kind which played a central part in the micro-economy. In Part V, **4893–4922** belong mostly to the late fourth and fifth centuries; they are chosen for their contribution to the chronology of consulates and post-consulates and to the prosopography of soldiers and officials from both civil and military establishments. Palaeographers will note that **4895**, dated to 380, was written on the back of **4892**, dated 236 or 237. **4923–30** are documents of the sixth and seventh centuries, all relating to the 'glorious house' of the Apions: they attest supplies of meat to soldiers (on behalf of the state, or for private services to the Apions?), and supplies of bread from a monastic bakery to villagers of the estate.

The contributions of Dr Colomo and Dr Nodar originally formed part of their doctoral theses, supervised at Oxford University by Professor Parsons; those of Dr Syrkou derive from her doctoral thesis supervised by Professor Maehler at University College London. A generous grant from the Leverhulme Foundation enabled Dr Gonis to re-catalogue and transcribe the hexameter texts of which this volume publishes a further selection.

Professor Thomas gratefully acknowledges the help and advice of the Revd. Professor David Parker. Dr Gonis records his thanks to Dr N. Litinas, Dr F. Morelli, Professor B. Palme, Professor D. W. Rathbone, Dr J. L. Rowlandson, and Professor E. Wipszycka, who read parts of the documentary sections.

Dr Claudio Meliadò indexed Parts II and III, and Dr Amin Benaissa Parts IV and V; both contributed important corrections to the original script and to the proofs. Dr Daniela Colomo collated texts and images, removing several inaccuracies, and read the entire proof with her customary care and precision.

The Editors are as always indebted to Dr Jeffrey Dean for his expert and resourceful type-setting, and to The Charlesworth Group for efficient production. The continuing publication of the Oxyrhynchus papyri would be impossible without the moral and financial support of the Arts and Humanities Research Council and the British Academy.

January 2008

A. K. BOWMAN	N. GONIS
R. A. COLES	D. OBBINK
J. R. REA	P. J. PARSONS
J. D. THOMAS	*General editors*
Advisory Editors	

CONTENTS

TEXTS

INDEXES

TABLE OF PAPYRI

I. NEW TESTAMENT

II. HEXAMETER POETRY

III. RHETORICAL TEXTS

IV. DOCUMENTS OF THE ROMAN PERIOD

AB = A. Benaissa   WEHC = W. E. H. Cockle   NG = N. Gonis   AS = A. Syrkou
LC = L. Capponi   DC = D. Colomo   CM = C. Meliadò   JDT = J. D. Thomas
           JDJ = J. De Jong   AN = A. Nodar

LIST OF PLATES

NUMBERS AND PLATES

NOTE ON THE METHOD OF
PUBLICATION AND ABBREVIATIONS

The basis of the method is the Leiden system of punctuation; see *CE* 7 (1932) 262–9. It may be summarized as follows:

αβγ	The letters are doubtful, either because of damage or because they are otherwise difficult to read
. . .	Approximately three letters remain unread by the editor
[αβγ]	The letters are lost, but restored from a parallel or by conjecture
[. . .]	Approximately three letters are lost
( )	Round brackets indicate the resolution of an abbreviation or a symbol, e.g. (ἀρτάβη) represents the symbol ⲧ, cτρ(ατηγός) represents the abbreviation cτρ∫
⟦αβγ⟧	The letters are deleted in the papyrus
`αβγ´	The letters are added above the line
⟨αβγ⟩	The letters are added by the editor
{αβγ}	The letters are regarded as mistaken and rejected by the editor

Bold arabic numerals refer to papyri printed in the volumes of *The Oxyrhynchus Papyri*. The abbreviations used are in the main identical with those in J. F. Oates *et al.*, *Checklist of Editions of Greek Papyri and Ostraca* (*BASP* Suppl. no. 9, ⁵2001); for a more up-to-date version of the *Checklist*, see http://scriptorium.lib.duke.edu/papyrus/texts/clist.html.

I. NEW TESTAMENT

4844–4845. CORINTHIANS

The following two texts are from papyrus codices, one containing a fragment of I Corinthians and the other of II Corinthians. In each case only part of a leaf is preserved. The texts have been collated against Nestle–Aland, *Novum Testamentum Graece*[27] (2001) and K. Junack et al. (edd.), *Das Neue Testament auf Papyrus*, ii: *Die Paulinischen Briefe, Teil 1* (Berlin 1989) = *NTPap.*, and the *apparatus criticus* is taken from these two works. I have also consulted Reuben J. Swanson, *New Testament Greek Manuscripts: I Corinthians* and *II Corinthians* (Pasadena 2003–5).

I am grateful for help regarding these texts from the Revd Professor David Parker.

4844. I Corinthians xiv 31–4; xv 3–6

49 5B.102/F(1–2)   7.5 × 6.5 cm   Fourth century
$\mathfrak{P}^{123}$ Plate I

A fragment of a papyrus codex survives, incomplete on all sides except the top. As it is broken on both sides, the restorations at right and left are arbitrary. The original codex will have had approximately 36 letters to the line, which suggests about 14 lines lost between ↓ and →, making *c*.21 lines to the page. The space between the lines is 0.7 cm, with a margin at the top of 1.6 cm. This points to a written area of *c*. 9 × 16 cm and a page of *c*. 11 × 19 cm. This is closest to Turner's Group 8 (*Typology* 20–21). As ↓ precedes →, we are probably dealing with the first half of a codex, if this is a single-quire codex (*Typology* 66). The only other papyrus in which these verses are (mostly) extant is $\mathfrak{P}^{46}$ = P. Chester Beatty II (Fasc. III Suppl., ed. F. G. Kenyon). In $\mathfrak{P}^{46}$, which has approximately 25 letters per line and 27 lines to the page, I Corinthians occupies 45 pages. In **4844** it is likely to have occupied some 40 pages.

The papyrus is written in a slightly right-sloping majuscule, which is neat and competent, but has no pretensions to elegance. It is mostly bilinear except for ρ and φ (ψ does not occur); there is one instance (→ 4, οτι) of long ι. μ has a deep bow and ω is rounded. ο is tiny. ε and c have a noticeable hook at the foot of the curve. This hook and many of the letter-forms generally are similar to those in P. Herm. 4 = *GBEBP* 2a, which is datable to *c*.320. The general impression of **4844** is different from P. Herm. 4, largely because **4844** is more bilinear, but it can be placed in the fourth century with some confidence and probably in the earlier part of the century. There are no lectional signs in the part preserved, and the only *nomen sacrum* preserved is $\overline{\pi\nu\alpha}$ (↓ 2).

On the text Parker remarks 'it seems rarely to agree with the DFG form of the text (the Graeco-Latin bilinguals) in their distinctive readings'. See G. Zuntz, *The Text of the Epistles* (London 1953), especially the Table at the end of the volume.

↓	μα]νθανωϲιν κ[αι παντεϲ	xiv 31
	παρ]ακαλωντ[αι και] π̄ν̄ᾱ προφητων [προφηταιϲ	32
	υ]ποταϲϲεται ου γαρ εϲτι[ν α]καταϲ[ταϲιαϲ ο θ̄ϲ	33
	αλλ ειρ]ηνηϲ ωϲ εν παϲαιϲ τα[ιϲ εκκ[ληϲιαιϲ	
5	των αγι]ων αι γυναικεϲ εν [ταιϲ εκκληϲιαιϲ	34
	ϲιγατωϲαν ου γα]ρ επιτρεπ[εται αυταιϲ λαλειν	
	]...[	

. . . .   . .

→	υ]μιν εν πρωτοι[ϲ ο και παρελαβον οτι	xv 3
	χ̄ϲ απεθα]νεν υπερ των α[μαρτιων ημων κατα	
	ταϲ γραφ]αϲ και ο[τ]ι εταφη και [οτι] εγηγερτα[ι τη	4
	ημερα τη τριτ]η κα[τα] ταϲ γραφαϲ και οτι ωφ[θη κηφα	5
5	ειτα τοιϲ δωδεκα επειτα] ωφθη επανω πεν[τ]α	6
	κοϲιοιϲ αδελφοιϲ εφαπαξ ε]ξ ων οι πλ[ειονεϲ	
	μενουϲιν εωϲ αρτι τινεϲ δε εκο]ιμ[ηθηϲαν	

. . . .   . .

↓ 2 π̄ν̄ᾱ. 𝔓⁴⁶ reads πνευματα without abbreviation, as do A B L and several minuscules according to Swanson; he records ℵ Ψᶜ 049 056 and most minuscules as reading π̄ν̄ᾱτ̄ᾱ, and D F G K Ψ* (*NTPap.* adds 0151) and a few minuscules as reading π̄ν̄ᾱ; for π̄ν̄ᾱ Nestle–Aland²⁷ adds 1241ˢ ar b vgᵐˢˢ syᵖ. **4844** presumably intended the singular by π̄ν̄ᾱ. However, A. H. R. E. Paap, *Nomina sacra in the Greek Papyri* (P. L. Bat. 8: 1959) 82–3 and 102–3, regards π̄ν̄ᾱ as an acceptable abbreviation for the plural, along with π̄ν̄ᾱτ̄ᾱ or π̄ν̄τ̄ᾱ.

προφητων om. 0285*.

3 υ]ποταϲϲεται: υποταϲϲονται L.

4844 did not agree with A, which has the order ο θ̄ϲ ακαταϲταϲιαϲ. It may have read ο θ̄ϲ, with ℵ A B D and most other MSS, or just θ̄ϲ, with 𝔓⁴⁶ F G.

4 In 𝔓⁴⁶ Kenyon read/restored εν παϲαιϲ τα]ιϲ εκκληϲιαιϲ, commenting 'ταιϲ fortasse omittendum propter spatium'. *NTPap.* gives the reading of the papyrus as εν παϲα]ιϲ εκκληϲιαιϲ, commenting 'ταιϲ om. 𝔓⁴⁶'; this is surely correct. Perhaps ταιϲ was omitted through homoioteleuton.

5 Spacing proves that **4844** did not add διδαϲκω after αγιων with F G and some minuscules, nor διαταϲϲομαι with 0150.

4844 did not follow D F G ar b vgᵐˢ Ambst in placing verses 34–5 after verse 40. On this order of verses, see Zuntz, *The Text of the Epistles* 17.

αι γυναικεϲ εν: so 𝔓⁴⁶ᵛⁱᵈ ℵ A B Ψ 0150 0243 33 81 104 365 1175 1241ˢ 1739 1881 2464 *al* lat co: αι γυναικεϲ υμων εν D F G K L 049 056 0142 0151 𝔐 (ar b) sy Cyp. (Ambst).

6 επιτρεπ[εται: so ℵ A B D F G K 0243 33 365 630 1175 1241ˢ 1739 *al* lat(t): επιτετρεπται L: επιτετραπται Ψ 049 056 0142 1881 𝔐 Mcionᴱ. 𝔓⁴⁶ is lost at this point.

7 ℵ A B 0150 33 81 365 (1175) 1241ˢ 2464 *pc* Epiph. read αλλ(α) υποταϲϲεϲθωϲαν; D F G K L Ψ

049 056 0142 0151 0243 1739 1881 𝔐 lat(t) sy read αλλ(α) υποτασσεσθαι, both followed by καθως (𝔓⁴⁶ is lost before καθως). The traces in **4844** are too slight to permit a firm decision between these readings, but υποτασσεσθω]ςαν may be possible.

→   1 Spacing proves that **4844** did not omit ο και παρελαβον with b Ir^lat Ambst.

2 χ̅ς̅. This is the more common form of the abbreviation and was probably what **4844** read; 𝔓⁴⁶ reads χ̅ρ̅ς̅.

3–4 Verse 4, και οτι εταφη . . . γραφας, is omitted by 056 0142 0243 618 1175, no doubt owing to homoioteleuton.

οτι before εγηγερται is omitted by Ψ.

τη ημερα τη τριτ]η. Sufficient of the eta survives to make it almost certain that **4844** had this reading, along with 𝔓⁴⁶ ℵ A B D 048^vid and several minuscules, as against τη τριτη ημερα, the reading of F G K L P Ψ 049 0150 0151 and most minuscules.

5 ειτα: so 𝔓⁴⁶ B D² L P Ψ 056 0142 0150 0243 1739 1881 𝔐 Or.; but επειτα, the reading of ℵ A K 049 0151 33 81 614 1175 *pc*, is also possible. Spacing proves that **4844** did not read και μετα ταυτα with D* F G lat.

5–6 𝔓⁴⁶ is lost between ειτα τ[οις and πλειονες (inclusive of πλειονες). The room available suggests it read φ̅ rather than πεντακοσιοις.

6 ε]ξ ων: εν ων 0142.

πλ[ειονες: so ℵ A B D F G 048^vid 0150 0243; but **4844** could equally well have had the contracted form πλειους, with K L P Ψ 049 056 0142 0151 and most MSS.

7 εκο]μ[ηθησαν. Since mu would appear to be a good reading (there is no other undamaged mu for comparison), the reading is very probable. If it is right, **4844** is likely to have read τινες δε before it, with 𝔓⁴⁶ ℵ* A^vid B D* F G 0243 6 630 1739 1881 *pc* latt sy^h Or., rather than τινες δε και, with ℵ² A^c D² L P Ψ 048 049 056 0142 0150 and most MSS. (The reading of 𝔓⁴⁶ is mistakenly given as δ εκοιμηθησαν in the edition; *NTPap.* gives the correct reading δε εκοιμηθησαν.)

J. DAVID THOMAS

4845. II Corinthians xi 1–4; 6–9

3B.6/IV 𝔓¹²⁴	13.5 × 14.5 cm	Sixth century Plates II–III

Part of a leaf from a papyrus codex survives, incomplete on all sides except the right on ↓ and the left on →. The gap below the last surviving line is slightly larger than that between the lines elsewhere, suggesting that we may have on both sides the bottom line of the page; but the papyrus itself is certainly incomplete at the foot. It is written in a brown ink, in a large, upright, elegant majuscule. Apart from the elegance and size of the script, the huge margins of 5–6 cm at the sides, no doubt matched by similar margins at the top and bottom, prove that we have the remains of a de luxe codex. There are approximately 19 letters per line, which suggests that some 11 lines have been lost between the two sides, if we assume a normal text. This suggests 26 lines to the page. Since the space between the lines is about 1 cm, this would amount to a written of area of *c.* 13 × 25 cm; when we add in the margins, this suggests a page size of *c.* 24 × 38 cm, which would fall into Turner's Group 1 (*Typology* 14).

The script can be classified as 'Alexandrian Majuscule'. This style presents two variants; see *GBEBP* p. 23. One, which has ε θ ο c in their narrow form, is anchored to a certainly dated example, the famous Paschal letter of 577 (*GBEBP* 37). The other, with ε θ ο c in the circular form familiar from Biblical Majuscule, has no such anchor; it is represented by *GBEBP* 8e and 38a–b, all assigned by editors to the middle or later sixth century. **4845** belongs with this latter group. The cross-bar of ε is high (as it is in н and θ), so that the top half of the letter can appear to be a closed semi-circle; the cross-bar of θ does not project outside the circle. π and н are broad; in κ the two strokes at the right are long and slightly hooked. There are also small hooks at both left and right in γ and x. ρ is noteworthy, since the loop is tiny and the letter does not descend below the line. The script is therefore entirely bilinear apart from the large φ (no doubt also ψ , but where it occurs, → 5 and 9, it is only partially preserved). Letter-forms apart, **4845** shows a more modest use of finials, and a lighter contrast between thick and thin strokes, than some similar hands, and it could be argued that this points to a relatively early date. However, we have not enough dated specimens to show that these features represent a diachronic development, rather than the taste of individual copyists. Provisionally, therefore, I assign **4845** to the sixth century.

There are one or two instances of inorganic diaeresis and at least one medial point (→ 5; cf. ↓ 10 n.). The *nomen sacrum* for *Χριστός* is in the form $\overline{χc}$ (↓ 7, 13).

Most of the text preserved in **4845** is also extant in $\mathfrak{P}^{46}$ = P. Chester Beatty II. There is a partial overlap with $\mathfrak{P}^{34}$ = SPP XII no. 191, p. 246 (ed. C. Wessely). The papyrus covers three of the 'Teststellen' discussed in Kurt Aland (ed.), *Text und Textwert der griechischen Handschriften des Neuen Testaments*, ii: *Die Paulinischen Briefe, Band II* (Berlin/New York 1991); see the notes.

The most interesting feature is the use of *paragraphi* to divide the text and the way the text is set out so that a new section begins at the start of a new line (note the blank spaces in ↓ 7 and 13). Parker noted that it would be particularly interesting if this layout were to correspond to the sense-divisions marked in some MSS containing the Euthalian apparatus. On this point I have consulted Dr Simon Crisp, and I am grateful to him for a thorough examination of the possibility. On the positive side he notes that **4845**↓ may show correspondence in this respect with 015 (6th cent.), the earliest and best example of a MS showing the Euthalian text division *per cola et commata* (unfortunately this MS is not extant for **4845**→). However, his further exploration of the question leads him to have serious doubts whether **4845** can have any Euthalian connection, in particular because of the high degree of coincidence between the sense breaks in **4845** and those in A = 02 and especially ℵ = 01, which cannot be Euthalian. He concludes that, while the possibility should not be ruled out altogether, he does not think that the evidence he has collected is sufficient to posit a Euthalian connection with any degree of confidence.

↓   .   .   .

].̣.̣.̣[

] α̣φρο̣[cυνης   xi 1

αλλα και ανε]χεϲθ̣[ε μ]ο̣[υ

ζηλω γαρ υ]μαϲ θ̅υ̅ ζηλ̣[ω   2

5   ηρμοϲαμ]ην γαρ ϋμαϲ ε̣ν̣ι̣

ανδρι παρθ]ενον αγνην

παραϲτηϲ]α̣ι τω χ̅ω̅   *vac.*

φοβουμαι δ]ε̣ μηπωϲ ωϲ   3

ο οφιϲ εξη]π̣α̣τηϲεν ευαν

10   εν τη πανου]ρ̣χ̣ια αυτου φθα

ρη τα νοηματα] ϋμων απο

της απλοτητο]ϲ και της αγνο

τητοϲ της ειϲ το]ν χ̅ν̅   *vac.*

ει μεν γαρ ο ερχο]μ̣̣[εν]ο̣ϲ αλ   4

15   λον ι̅η̅ν̅ κηρυϲϲει ον ουκ] εκη

→   .   .   .

].̣.̣.̣[

τε̣[ϲ εν π]αϲιν [ειϲ υμαϲ   *vac.*   6

η [αμαρτι]αν επ[οιηϲα εμαυ   7

τ̣[ο]ν̣ τ̣απεινω[ν ινα υμειϲ

5   υψ̣ω̅θητε· οτ[ι δωρεαν

τ̣ο του θ̅υ̅ ευαγγ[ελιον ευ

ηγγελ[ι]ϲαμη[ν υμιν   *vac.*

α̣λλα̣ϲ εκκλη[ϲιαϲ εϲυλη   8

ϲα λαβων οψ̣[ωνιον προϲ

10   τ̣ην ϋμων [διακονιαν   *vac.*   9

και παρων̣ [προϲ υμαϲ

και ϋϲτερη[θειϲ ου κατε

ναρκηϲ[α ουθενοϲ το

γα[ρ υϲτερημα μου προϲ

15   αν[επληρωϲαν

     .   .

↓   1–2 The traces surviving in line 1 are too slight to permit a definitive reading; but in view of the way the text is set out one can be confident that Chap. XI began at the start of line 1. This would suggest some 26 letters lost before αφροϲυνης. This is consistent with the reading of ℵ B D Ψ 0121 0243 33 1739 1881 *pc*: οφελον ανειχεϲθε μου μικρον τι αφροϲυνης; 𝔓⁴⁶ agrees except that it omits μου. F G 81 630 1175 *pc* replace τι with της. H K L 049 056 075 0142 0150 0151 𝔐 read τη instead of τι and αφροϲυνη instead of αφροϲυνης (which is of course a possible reading in **4845**).

5 The traces after ϋμα are very slight but do not conflict with the expected reading.

6–9 These lines are lost in 𝔓⁴⁶.

7 παραϲτης]αι: παραϲτηναι 056 0142. Also the bilingual glossary to Pauline letters, *Chester Beatty Codex AC 1499*, ed. Alfons Wouters (Leuven/Paris 1988), has παραϲτηναι: *exhibere* (l. 1204, p. 116).

8 **4845** did not omit δε with L.

μηπωϲ: so most MSS. μηποτε F G 630 1505 1611 1739 1881 2495 vg^ms: μη D* lat JulC^Cl: μητε 0243.

ωϲ om. L.

9 εξη]πατηϲεν εϋαν: so ℵ¹ B F G H P 0121 0150 0243 0278: εϋαν εξηπατηϲεν D K L Ψ 049 056 075 0142 0151: εξηπατηϲεν υμιν ℵ*.

10 There may be a medial point after αυτου (cf. → 5).

10–11 αυτου φθα[ρη: so 𝔓⁴⁶ ℵ B D* F G H P 0150 33 81 1175 r JulC^Cl Cl Lcf: αυτου ουτω(ϲ) φθαρη D¹ and all other Greek witnesses (cf. Aland, *Text u. Textwert* 685–7) lat sy Ambst.

11–13 απο [της απλοτητο]ϲ και της αγνο[τητοϲ. This is the reading of 𝔓⁴⁶ ℵ* B F G 0150 33 81* 104 206 330 429 451 459 1398* 1509* 1719 1735 1962 2110 2400 2492 2799 2805 ar r sy^h** co Pel. For αγνοτητος D reads απλοτητος (preceded by της αγνοτητος D²); και της αγνοτητος om. ℵ² H K L P Ψ and other Greek witnesses (cf. Aland, *Text u. Textwert* 687–90) b f* vg sy^p JulC^Cl.

13 το]ν χ̅ν̅: so 𝔓⁴⁶ B D H K L P Ψ 049 056 0142 0150 0151 33 𝔐 JulC^Cl Cl Epiph.: τον om. ℵ F G 075 0121 0243 365 630 1175 1505 1739 1881 and other minuscules listed in Swanson, *New Testament Greek Manuscripts* 142.

→ 2 τε[ϲ. See Aland, *Text u. Textwert* 690–93. **4845** had either φανερωϲαντες with ℵ* B F G 0121 0243 33 2736 or φανερωθεντες with 𝔓³⁴ ℵ² D² K L P Ψ 049 056 075 0142 0150 0151 0278 𝔐 r (vg^ch); not φανερωθειϲ, D* (lat Ambst), nor φανερωϲαντες εαυτουϲ, 0121 0243 630 1739 1881 *pc*. 𝔓⁴⁶ omits αλλ εν παντι φανερωϲαντες εν παϲιν ειϲ υμαϲ.

F G omit εν παϲιν.

3 **4845** did not add μη after η with F G.

6 There is unexplained ink above the first gamma of εϋαγγ[ελιον (it is too far to the left to be taken as a diastole of the kind placed between double consonants).

6–7 εϋηγγελ[ι]ϲαμη[ν. 𝔓³⁴ reads εϋηγελιϲαμην.

10–11 There may be a *paragraphus* between these lines.

12 και before υϲτερηθειϲ omitted in 𝔓⁴⁶.

J. DAVID THOMAS

II. HEXAMETER POETRY

4846. HEXAMETERS ON PELEUS

95/73(a)   3 × 4.8 cm   First century BC or AD
                                                                              Plate I

A scrap from the lower part of the column, with parts of seven lines and 2.3 cm of the lower margin. The writing is with the fibres and the back is blank.

The text is written in a round hand with a late Ptolemaic/early Roman look, comparable to *GLH* 8a (99 BC), 9b (late I BC) and 10a (early I AD), and generally reminiscent of the so-called 'epsilon-theta' style; cf. also IV **659** = *GMAW*² 21 (I BC; assigned). A is in the capital form; ε, made in three movements, has its cross-bar small and detached from the back; z has a curved base; ʍ is angular; the top of c closes in towards the base. Serifs are attached to the feet of uprights and obliques; they are often large, and accentuate the bilinear impression, which is disturbed only by the stem of φ. All in all, the hand looks amateurish rather than professional: the scribe strove to create a calligraphic appearance, but the result is somewhat crude (φ, for example, is hardly a success).

No lection signs occur. Iota adscript is written in the only place that requires it (5). ἐν is written as ἐμ before mu.

What little survives is heavily dependent on Homer and Hesiod. Peleus was loved by Zeus and was given a goddess, Nereus' daughter, as a wife, although he was a mortal. There is nothing of note except for the Doric vocalizations in 5 and (probably) 6. It may be worth comparing P. Köln VIII 328, a first-century scrap of unknown provenance with 'Doric' hexameters. The editor did not pronounce on the subject matter; I would hazard the guess that this may be dying Achilles addressing his psyche; there are references to Thetis, to a Centaur sometime in the past, and to Paris (Achilles' killer) in a context of destruction. It might not be a co-incidence that we have poems on related subjects in 'Doric', or rather, in Lobel's words, 'a veneer of perfunctory Doric' (XXX **2524** introd.), though I do not wish to imply that the two fragments come from the same work. According to the editor, P. Köln 328 may be a product of the Hellenistic age, as suggested by its versification and apparent originality. Another 'Doric' hexameter papyrus of about the same date is P. Haun. I 4 (M–P³ 1788), which may well transmit a Hellenistic composition. The banality of the subject and Homeric tincture in **4846** might suggest that this is the work of a contemporary local poet, but it would be too hazardous to pronounce when so little is preserved. After all, Dorisms were parts of the epic *Kunstsprache* before the Hellenistic period, found e.g. in Antimachus and Choerilus.

```
  ] . [ . ] ε . [
  ] . αρο . . . . . [                αὐ]τὰρ ὃ Πηλε . [
  ] . κοϲεμμεγ . [                  Αἰ]ακὸϲ ἐμ μεγά[ροιϲ(ι)
  ]νδεζευϲεφ[                       τὸ]ν δὲ Ζεὺϲ ἐφ[ίληϲε
5 ] . ιθνα . ωιε . [                καί] οἱ θνατῶι ἐό[ντι
  ] . ρειοϲκουρ . [                 Ν]ηρεῖοϲ κούρα[
```

1] . , right-facing serif on line, if not foot of oblique sloping from left to right   . [, foot of oblique rising to right   2] . , foot of upright seriffed to left   . . . . . [, curved upright topped by horizontal slightly extending to left, gap, speck at line level (π suggested); foot of upright curved to left or of oblique rising from left to right; speck at line-level, gap, foot of oblique sloping from left: ⲁ or λ (not м, given the position of previous trace); base of curved letter; trace of upright, if not serif, at line-level   3] . , trace at one-third height touching oblique sloping from left   5] . , right-hand curve   α . , left-hand tip of high horizontal   6] . , lower part of oblique descending from left or left-leaning upright   . [, lower part of oblique rising from left

2 αὐ]τὰρ ὃ Πηλε . [. *Il.* 21.599 begins αὐτὰρ ὃ Πηλεΐωνα, but the reference to 'Aeacus in the palace' in 3 speaks against reading Πηλεΐ[ωνα here; it is hard to associate Achilles with his grandfather Aeacus in a domestic context, since the latter had expelled Peleus from Aegina (see Ps.-Apollod. 3.161; Ant. Lib. 38.2; Paus. 2.29; etc.), let alone that Achilles did not grow up ἐν μεγάροιϲ(ι). It would be easier to assume that Aeacus is mentioned as the father of Peleus, in which case read Πηλέα [; ὅ would look forward to Αἰακόϲ in the next line (cf. e.g. *Il.* 1.488). γείνατο might have followed at some point.

3 Αἰ]ακὸϲ ἐμ (*l.* ἐν) μεγά[ροιϲ(ι). See previous note. There are several references to births ἐν μεγάροιϲι in Hesiod (*Th.* 383 f., *Cat.* fr. 26.28, 33a.8, 70.32, 10(a).51, etc.), but the subject is always the mother. ἐν μεγάροιϲ(ιν) often occupies the same *sedes* in Homer, AR, Theocritus, QS.

4 τὸ]ν δὲ Ζεὺϲ ἐφ[ίληϲε. Cf. Hes. *Cat.* fr. 240.6 τὴν δὲ Ζεὺϲ ἐφίληϲε (Dodone); 211.3 Πηλεὺ]ϲ Αἰακίδηϲ, φίλοϲ ἀθανάτοιϲι θεοῖϲιν.

5 καί] οἱ θνατῶι ἐό[ντι. Cf. *Il.* 24.537 καί οἱ θνητῷ ἐόντι θεὰν ποίηϲαν ἄκοιτιν: Achilles tells Priam about Peleus, that the gods gave him a goddess as wife although he was a mortal. If the verse followed the *Iliad* closely, the next line would elaborate on θεάν.

6 Ν]ηρεῖοϲ κούρα[ν is probable: it would be in apposition to an accusative that would have stood in the lost part of the previous line; cf. *Il.* 24.537, cited above. κούρα (or κούρα[ι) is less likely, since it is not easy to account for a nominative; this also tells against reading Ν]ήρειοϲ, a rare adjective. For the collocation, cf. Hes. *Th.* 1003 Νηρῆοϲ κοῦραι (κ. N. QS 3.734; Νηρῆοϲ θυγάτηρ Matro 33.33 Olson–Sens). On genitives in -εῖοϲ of proper names ending -εύϲ, a feature of Hellenistic poetry, see E. Magnelli, *ZPE* 146 (2004) 30.

N. GONIS

4847. HEXAMETERS ON A TROJAN SUBJECT

19 2B.80/A(1)b   3.4 × 4.5 cm   Second century
                                                                                      Plate I

A scrap with middle parts of lines from the top of a column, with upper margin extant to 1 cm. Back blank.

The text is written in a rounded semi-cursive hand, assignable to the second century, earlier rather than later. Elision is effected but not marked. A correction in 4 (a letter added above the line) might be due to a second hand. There is an itacistic error in 5.

References to Priam (1), a helmet or clubs (2), a spear (3), and walls (6) suggest a battle scene at Troy. A lexical item suggests a date in the Imperial period (see 3 n.). The parts preserved come from immediately after the caesura (masculine in 1, 2, 3, 6, ?7, 8; feminine in 5). The preponderance of the masculine caesura, even if the sample is small, is remarkable; it has been associated with 'less skilful versifiers' of the Imperial age (West, *Greek Metre* 177). This is in line with the breach of Naeke's law in 5. It is likely that this is a local composition on a traditional subject.

]ριαμοϲμε‚[	Π]ρίαμοϲ μεγ[
]ορυναϲ…[	κ]ορυναϲ…[
]ογχηϲω‚[	λ]όγχηϲω‚[
]‚ʼνδαμφ‚‚[‚]‚[	]‚ν δʼ ἀμφ‚‚[‚]‚[
5]‚ειγαντωνη[	] γειγάντων η[
]πιτειχεϲι‚[	ἐ]πὶ τείχεϲι‚[
]‚ντωγερα‚[	
]‚αιδυϲμ[	] καὶ δυϲμ[
]‚‚‚‚[	

1 ‚[, upright joining left-hand part of horizontal at the top, Γ suggested, though τ is not entirely ruled out   2 …[, upper part of circle (ο rather than ε); upright; thickened letter-top followed by top of upright (N?)   3 ‚[, (lower part of?) upright joining thick horizontal at mid-height   4]‚, lower left-hand arc   ‚‚[, base of curved letter (ο?); speck on line   ]‚[, trace below line level (part of descender?)   5]‚, trace at mid-height   6 ‚[, upper left corner of Γ or π   ει written over something else   7]‚, top of short oblique rising to right, and trace below (γ? κ ruled out by context)   ‚[, upright   8]‚, upper part of upright followed by (upper part of) oblique rising to right   9]‚‚‚‚[, letter tops (third, of curved letter)

1 Π]ρίαμοϲ μέγ[αϲ? So *Il.* 7.427, 24.477, AG App. *Epigr. sep.* 113.1, always immediately after the caesura. It is less likely that the papyrus had μετ[ά, which may be paralleled, though the context is different (*Il.* 3.303, 24.777 Πρίαμοϲ μετὰ μῦθον ἔειπε).

2 κ]όρυν αϲ- or κ]ορύναϲ. If the latter, the form occurs also in AR 2.99 and Nonn. *D.* 47.169

(Homer does not use the plural); there is no way of telling whether *v* was scanned short or long (if the latter, we would have a violation of Naeke's law, but cf. 5).

3 λ]όγχης ω.[, λ]όγχη cω.[, or λ]όγχη cω.[. The word is not used in epic earlier than the Imperial period.

4 ἀμφοτ[ε]ρ[-?

5 γειγάντων, l. γιγάντων. The point of the reference is unclear (apparently not related to the walls in 6, since these are presumably of Troy). Claudio Meliadò suggests that this may be a mythological paradigm for a battle between people of extraordinary power. In epic poetry the word almost always occupies the end of the verse; it occurs in the same *sedes* as here in [Orph.] *Hymn.* 32.12, *Argon.* 429, and Eudoc. *de Mart. s. Cypr.* 2.102.

6 ἐ]πὶ τείχεϲι.[. This collocation, always positioned after the caesura, also occurs in QS 11.425, Triph. 443, 509, Paul. Sil. 686.

7].ντωγερα.[. Probably ϲ]ὺν τῷ; then γερα.[, γε ρα.[, γ' ἐρα.[.

N. GONIS

4848. Hexameters

71/59(a)   11.7 × 2.1 cm   Second/third century
                                                        Plate I

The ends of two lines, which allow no guess about the subject matter; we only hear of a sea passage (1), and something (fem. plural) that brings gains (gains from seafaring? cf. e.g. Hes. *Op.* 631–4). The interest resides in the *addendum lexicis* in line 2: ἀμοίβιμα.

The text is written in a medium-to-large informal rounded hand of the late second or early third century; for a description of a similar hand and parallels, see LXX **4760** introd. Elision in 2 is effected but not marked.

The right-hand margin is extant to 1.8 cm. The writing runs with the fibres; the back is blank.

].̣.υϲιμεϲονποροναμφιτ..[.]..   ].̣ουϲι μέϲον πόρον Ἀμφιτρί[τ]ης

].̣ταμοιβιμακερδεαγουϲαι   κ]ατ' ἀμοίβιμα κέρδε' ἄγουϲαι

1].̣.̣, low speck, gap, small lower curve; top and right-hand part of θ ο ω .̣.[, lower part of short descender hooked to right; foot hooked to right].̣.̣, low trace; foot hooked to right followed by low oblique trace   2 .̣τ, high loop, as of ⋏; crossbar and top of stem only

1].̣ουϲι. Professor Parsons suggests τε]μ̣ο̣ῦϲι (τέμ]ν̣ο̣υϲι is difficult to read), the subject being 'ships', even if this would be against Meyer's first law. For such a use of τέμνω, see LSJ s.v. VI.3, citing passages from earlier literature, but there are several examples also in later poetry; cf. in particular *AP* 14.129.1–2 εἶπε κυβερνητῆρι πλατὺν πόρον Ἀδριακοῖο τέμνων νηί.

μέϲον πόρον Ἀμφιτρί[τ]ης. Cf. Dion. Perieg. 134 ἕτερος πόρος Ἀμφιτρίτης. The collocation μέϲον πόρον first occurs in A. *Pers.* 505.

2 κ]ατ' ... κέρδε' ἄγουϲαι. κ]αταμοίβιμα, an unattested word, does not have a plausible ring;

it is preferable to read κ]ατ᾽ . . . ἄγουcαι (tmesis), 'bringing home, gaining' (LSJ s.v. κατάγω 7); for the construction somewhat comparable is Thgn. 1.86 ἔπι κέρδοc ἄγει. The subject of the participle may well be the same as of the verb in the previous line: *νῆεc*?

In Homer, κέρδοc in the plural means 'cunning arts, wiles', (LSJ s.v. II), but here it clearly has the sense of 'profits, gains', as already in Hes. *Op.* 352.

ἀμοίβιμα. The word is not recorded elsewhere, though cf. *h. Merc.* 516 ἐπαμοίβιμα ἔργα; ἀμοιβιμαῖον, attested in an inscription from Lydia (IGR IV 1348), presupposes it. The concepts of gain and compensation are juxtaposed in a number of authors of the Imperial age: Sopat. *Διαίρεcιc ζητημάτων* 8.320.5 ποῖον κέρδοc τῆc ἀμοιβῆc;; Jo. Chrys. *Exp. in Psalm.* PG 55.462.41–3 ἀμοιβὴν . . . τῷ δὲ εἰcφέροντι τὴν ἀμοιβὴν τὸ κέρδοc φέρουcαν; *in Joann.* PG 59.80.45–6 ἀμοιβαῖc, αἳ πάλιν εἰc ἡμᾶc τὸ κέρδοc περιcτήcουcιν ἅπαν.

N. GONIS

4849. HEXAMETERS ON NEOPTOLEMUS(?)

96/33(a)   3.7 × 4.7 cm   Second/third century
                                                                      Plate II

A scrap of a codex preserving line-ends on the ↓ side and middle parts of lines on the →. The upper margin measures 1–1.3 cm. It is written in a smallish round hand, which I would assign to the first half of the third century, though without excluding a slightly earlier date. The bilinear impression is breached, as expected, by the stem of ϕ and occasionally the descender of ρ. α, in a single sequence and with looped top, has a tail that often makes contact with the next letter; the base of α extends rightwards; the tails of α and λ start from a hook above the junction; the cross-bar of є is fairly high and is usually elongated; the cross-bar of ө likewise projects to the right (but not to the left). The feet of uprights occasionally are thickened or carry half-serifs. Somewhat comparable are VIII **1100** = *GLH* 20b (206), XLII **3076** (*c.*225) and III **412** = *GLH* 23a (mid III).

There are many lectional signs, apparently all added by a second hand: acute (→1, 3, 6, 7, 8, ↓1, 3, 4) and grave (→2, 9, ↓6) accents, circumflexes (→4, 5), smooth (→9) and rough (→2) breathings (Turner's Form 1), an inorganic diaeresis (→5), apostrophes marking elision (→1, ↓2, 6), high points (↓1, 2), and long marks of quantity (↓1, 6). Iota adscript is written in the only place that requires it (↓8).

The diction is Homeric, and there are significant affinities with Quintus of Smyrna (see →2 n., 6 n.). References to Helenus (↓5) and Neoptolemus (?↓7; 'son of Achilles', →5) indicate that we are dealing with some story of the Posthomerica. We hear of a corpse (→2), a pyre (→4), 'many pigs' (→6), and Neoptolemus is mentioned in this context. It is difficult to identify the scene. One possibility (but not more than that) is that these parts refer to the Neoptolemus' death and funeral, and the subsequent marriage of Andromache to Helenus (see ↓5 n.); in that case, the → side will have come before the ↓.

Although the ↓ side gives line-ends, it is more likely that the parts on the →

side are closer to the middle than the beginning of the lines: we seem to be missing the first foot and second princeps of the hexameter (3–4 syllables); to assume a smaller loss to the left (1 syllable) would lead to serious difficulties with the metre. The feminine caesura is only slightly more prevalent than the masculine, but the sample is small. The two successive elisions in →1, one of which is at the caesura, suggest that this is not the work of a 'polished poet' (cf. West, *Greek Metre* 179). There is a metrical problem in →5, but it may be due to a scribal error, and can be emended away.

→

].τειλ'έντε'επι.[	].τειλ' έντε' ἐπι.[
].ἐρινεκρονόμ[	] περὶ νεκρὸν ὁμ[
]νλαλάγηcανε.[	]ν λαλάγηcαν ε.[
]φιπυρηνχεῦ..[	ἀμ]φὶ πυρὴν χεῦ..[
5]παῖcαχιλληοcϋ[	] παῖc Ἀχι{λ}λῆοc ὑ[
]δεcναcπολέα[c	]δε cύαc πολέα[c
]'δοcλέιηcαπε[	]'δοc λείηc ἀπε[
]ητόc.εφίλον[	]ητόc τε φίλον[
]....τι...ἐ.ν[	

.   .   .

↓

]δῑνήcαντο·	]δινήcαντο·
]ναι·αλλ'ενιμεcc[	]ναι· ἀλλ' ἐνὶ μεcc[
].ρενίοιο	].ρενίοιο
].νατεκέcθαι	τέ]κνα τεκέcθαι
5].ενοιο	Ἑ]λένοιο
]χιδ'αραcτᾱc	ἄγ]χι δ' ἄρα cτάc
].μοιοανακτοc	].μοιο ἄνακτοc
]μφιδεδαφνηι	ἀ]μφὶ δὲ δάφνηι
].[	

.   .   .

→ 1]., trace at mid-height   .[, slightly below line-level, foot of oblique rising to right 2]., right-hand tip of high horizontal sitting on upright   μ[, the first half only   3 ν, the diagonal and upright only, but ʌɪ less likely   .[, top of upright   4 ..[, left-hand curve followed by small horizontal at two-thirds height, then gap, and on the edge the lower half of seriffed upright (where the horizontal belongs is unclear)   5 π, right-hand corner only   8 a horizontal trace at two-thirds height touches η; does this belong to a letter mostly lost in the break or does the horizontal of ʜ extend to the left (not elsewhere in this hand)?   ., upright with horizontal above: τ, unless the left-hand part belongs to the top of c, extended rightwards (then г)   ν, the top junction and remains of the diagonal, then top and foot of upright   9]...., horizontal trace level with letter-tops; upper part of upright joining descending oblique, gap, another upright (N suggested); high speck; top of upright ⸏τι, the upper parts only, but apparently not π ⸏.., upper part of κ or χ; top loop of λ?; upper part of upright ⸏.ν, top of upright with what looks like a right-facing half-serif

↓   3]., high trace and, below, trace at one-third height (H possible)   4]., low semi-horizontal trace   5]., lower part of oblique descending from left (λ rather than χ)   7]., tip of horizontal at mid-height

→   1].τειλ᾽: ἔ]ϲτειλ᾽? A compound such as ἀνέτειλ᾽ cannot be accommodated in the verse as reconstructed in introd. para. 4. If the articulation is correct, one may note the word-end after contracted second biceps, generally avoided unless the word is disyllabic, as may be the case here; see West, *Greek Metre* 178.

2 πὲρι pap. The grave accent indicates that the word should not be accented on the syllable that carries the accent, i.e., one should read περί, not πέρι; see J. Moore-Blunt, *QUCC* 29 (1978) 153.

περὶ νεκρὸν ὁμ[ίλεον? Cf. *Il.* 16.641, 644 περὶ νεκρὸν ὁμίλεον, 'throng about the corpse', in the same *sedes*. One might also consider νεκρὸν ὅμ[ιλον, as in QS 6.264 (the dead in the underworld) and Nonn. *D.* 23.56 (dead Indians lying on the battlefield), but this would cause difficulty with the metre (either Hermann's bridge or Naeke's law would be violated) as well as with the context (see below, 6 n.).

3 λαλάγηϲαν. This may be a reference to birds chirping over the dead. In hexameters, the verb occurs in Theoc. 5.48, used for birds, and 7.139, for cicadas; Greg. Naz. *Carm. mor.* 756.7 and *Carm. q. spect. ad al.* 1539.10 (cicadas); cf. also Dioscorid. 16.15 P. (echo), (Anon.) *AP* 8.129.1 (birds), Marianus Scholasticus *AP* 9.668.11 (nightingales), Leonid. 85.1 P. (swallow).

4 ἀμ]φὶ πυρὴν χεῦ.. [. χεῦεν is suggested by the traces and the accent. For the collocation, cf. *Il.* 7.336 τύμβον δ᾽ ἀμφὶ πυρὴν ἕνα χεύομεν; for the metrical *sedes*, cf. also *Il.* 7.434 and 24.789 τῆμος ἄρ᾽ ἀμφὶ πυρήν. ἀμφὶ πυρήν also occurs in *Il.* 23.256, QS 3.696, Nonn. *D.* 40.222 (always in a funerary context).

5 παῖϲ Ἀχι{λ}λῆος. For the verse to scan, Ἀχιλλῆος should be emended to Ἀχιλῆος (an error of common type). The collocation has no exact parallel in epic (πάϊϲ, not παῖϲ, is the form preferred by Quintus and Nonnus).

ὑ[, ϋ[pap. The diacritical above upsilon might be taken as a circumflex, but the bow is too narrow (and a long vowel would not fit the metre); thus I take it as a diaeresis, written without the scribe lifting his pen.

6 ϲύαϲ. Cf. QS 3.682 ϲὺν δ᾽ ὄιάϲ τε ϲύαϲ τ᾽ ἔβαλον βρίθονταϲ ἀλοιφῇ (pyre of Achilles, on which also Trojans, horses and bulls were thrown). Pigs were not found in pyres described in earlier epic. 'Many' sheep and oxen were slaughtered on the pyres of Patroclus (*Il.* 23.166) and Achilles (*Od.* 24.65 f.); sim. in the pyres described in QS 5.620–22 (Ajax; sheep, bulls, horses), Nonn. *D.* 37.51 (Opheltes; sheep, oxen).

Funeral pyres on which animals are thrown are those of great heroes; this tells against restoring νεκρὸν ὅμ[ιλον, a whole throng of dead, in →2.

7]δοϲ: e.g. ϲτιβά]δοϲ (PJP); cf. *Alcmaeonis* fr. 2 νέκυϲ δὲ χαμαιϲτρώτου ἔπι τείναϲ / εὐρείηϲ ϲτιβάδοϲ, παρέθηκ᾽ αὐτοῖϲι θάλειαν / δαῖτα ποτήριά τε, ϲτεφάνουϲ δ᾽ ἐπὶ κραϲὶν ἔθηκεν.

9 ἔ.ν[. The grave accent may serve a similar purpose to that above in 2, but the reading is uncertain. The damaged letter does not seem to be λ, i.e., not ἐάν; if it is ι, I do not see what word would be meant.

↓   1]δινήϲαντο. This form is known only from Erycius *SH* fr. 407 πάντοϲε παμφαλόωντεϲ ⟨ἐ⟩δινήϲαντο πόδεϲϲι, and QS 5.619 νέκυν πέρι δινήϲαντο.

2]ναι· ἀλλ᾽. ἔμμεναι ἀλλ᾽ occurs in this *sedes* in *Il.* 6.100, 19.96, *Od.* 20.90, and AR 4.239, but in AR 2.148 we have κρινθήμεναι ἀλλ᾽.

ἐνὶ μεϲϲ[: ἐνὶ μέϲϲ[η, μέϲϲ[ηϲ, μέϲϲ[οιϲ, or μέϲϲ[ῳ. For the context, cf. perhaps *Il.* 24.84 f. ἥ δ' ἐνὶ μέϲϲηϲ / κλαῖε μόρον οὗ παιδὸϲ ἀμύμονοϲ (imitated by QS 2.607).

3]. ρενίοιο: -]ηρεν ἴοιο? If so, the reference to ἴον might point to a garland at a feast (cf. e.g. Theoc. 10.28 f.). Cf. δάφνηι below (↓8).

4 τέ]κνα τεκέϲθαι. Cf. *Od.* 22.324, *h. Cer.* 136, Call. *H.* 4.111, Diotim. 4.1 P., etc. (also variations). It usually refers to women; the only woman who could provide a link between Helenus and Neoptolemus is Andromache; see next note.

5 Ἑ]λένοιο stands at verse-end in QS 10.346 and Triph. 49. In QS the references to Helenus are in the context of battles in which Neoptolemus fought, but this need not apply to this passage. Helenus followed Neoptolemus to Epirus after the sack of Troy, and married Andromache after Neoptolemus' death (E. *Andr.* 1245; Paus. 1.11.1, 2.23.6—not the only version of the story).

6 ἄγ]χι δ' ἄρα ϲτάϲ also in *Il.* 24.477, in the same *sedes*, referring to Priam's supplication of Achilles.

ϲτᾱ̀ϲ pap. The placing of a grave accent over a monosyllable, and especially at verse-end, is exceptional; see Moore-Blunt, loc. cit. 159, and C. M. Mazzucchi, *Aegyptus* 59 (1979) 154. The addition of the metrical marker is hard to explain, even if the quantity indicated is correct.

7]. μοιο ἄνακτοϲ. The trace on the edge does not allow reading Πρι]άμοιο. Νεοπτολ]έμοιο (PJP) would be unobjectionable, even if it has not occurred with ἄνακτοϲ elsewhere; for the *sedes*, cf. *Od.* 11.506, QS 7.684, Christod. *AP* 2.1.203.

8 ἀ]μφὶ δὲ δάφνηι. ἀ]μφί, I suppose, is not to be taken with δάφνηι, the latter perhaps being an instrumental dative. For the sense, cf. AR 1.1123 f. ἀμφὶ δὲ φύλλοιϲ / ϲτεψάμενοι δρυΐνοιϲι; Christod. *AP* 2.1.41 f. δάφνη / κοϲμηθείϲ, 367 δάφνη / ϲτεψάμενον. Could it be Helenus the seer crowned with laurel? But cf. above, ↓3, for a possible reference to a garland.

N. GONIS

4850. HEXAMETERS

100/14(b)   4.1 × 16 cm   Third century
                                                    Plate VIII

A fragment of a papyrus codex (upper margin 0.6 cm; lower margin 0.8 cm), or of a single opisthograph sheet, containing remains of a hexameter poem. The → side preserves beginnings of thirty-nine lines (one to two letters are lost to the left), and the ↓ side ends of thirty-five lines (three to five letters are lost to the right). The scribe (perhaps the author himself) used a thick or blunt pen, and wrote in an informal, rapid and forward-sloping hand, to be assigned to the third century; cf. II **222**. The scribe wrote diaeresis (→4; ↓11, 12), and apostrophe to mark elision (→5, 13, 37; ↓5, 15, 24), between double consonants (→7, ?18, 36), and after οὐκ (→?14, 16, 21). οὐκ is not written as οὐχ when aspirated vowels follow. Iota adscript is not written in the only case that requires it (→21). Supralinear additions (→21, 37) are in the same hand as the main text. There is a common phonetic spelling in →9, and possibly in ↓20 (and →18?).

It is difficult to establish the correct sequence of the sides. A speech addressed to a god (Zeus?), in which a woman is involved (→13 ὁρόωϲα), occupies the greatest part of the → side, but I cannot tell whether she is the *persona loquens*. The tragic and mournful situation here described seems to be worsened by a new quarrel (→18; but this is not the only possibility), or a new misfortune that may have something to do with an offence to the gods (→17). Then in →20 f. Zeus is called upon for help. On the ↓ side, someone replies to a previous speech, perhaps that on the → side. It is difficult to identify the theme of the narrative. We may think of an episode of the Theban Cycle (Eteocles and Polynices), or rather of a story from the Trojan Cycle such as the *Hoplôn Krisis*. There are possible references to Ajax or Odysseus in ↓4 (Od.), 10 (Aj./Od.), 15 f. (Aj./Od.), 19 (Aj.). Alternatively, Professor Parsons suggests the possibility of a Muse speaking to Hesiod, who is progressing from the rustic pipe (→36) of *Works and Days* (alluded to in →4–5) to the lyre (→7) with which he will accompany the heroic subject matter of *Theogony* and *Catalogue*, which includes much blood shed by mortal men (→16), war with the immortals (→17), and battle between Zeus and his uncles (→19) the Titans. The same theme of progressing from the rustic to the grandiose, though put in the mouth of Hesiod himself, is treated in L **3537**.

The style is generally Homeric, with a pronounced tragic and pathetic tone, common in late epic (cf. e.g. the repetition of οὐχ ἅλις at →14 and 16). The versification, so far as the text can be reconstructed, seems to observe the educated standards of the Hellenistic-Roman hexameter, with a preponderance of feminine caesuras; one of the two tetrasyllabic endings (↓3), and the two spondeiazontes (↓19, 24), come direct from Homer. Note an apparent breach of Meyer's first law in →17. There is no sign of the accentual limitations observed later by Nonnus.

→

#		
	]ηcε[	]ηcε[
	]π̣.νυμ[	]π̣.νυμ[
	].cτερο.[	] ἀc̣τεροε[
	].ηϊαδαcεκρυψ[	Π]ληϊάδαc ἔκρυψ[ε(ν)
5	].ρυψενδ'υαδαc[	ἔ]κ̣ρυψεν δ' Ὑάδαc[
	].ccατιονπροφε[	τ]οccάτιον προφε[ρ-
	]μωγηφορμιγ.'[	οἴ]μωγὴ φόρμιγ[γοc
	]δεθελειcκαιεχ[	] δὲ θέλειc καὶ εχ[
	]μφοτερεcκαι[	ἀ]μφοτέραιc καὶ[
10	]δεομαιπαραcο.[	]δέομαι παρὰ co.[
	]πουcιδρωοντας[	ἵπ]πουc ἱδρώοντας [
	]δεδε.ηρυccουc.[	]δε δὲ κηρύccουc.[
	]κτει.ωδ'οροωcα[	]κτει.ω δ' ὀρόωcα[
	]καλιcανθρωπου[	οὔ]χ ἅλιc ἀνθρώπου[c
15	]εινομενηνυπο[	κτ]εινομένην ὑπο[
	].'αλιcαιματοcο[	οὔ]χ ἅλιc αἵματοc ο[
	]ανατ.ιcικυδ.[	ἀθ]ανάτο̣ιcι κυδ.[
	].λε̣τερηνεικ[	ἀλ]λ' ἑτέρη νεικ[
	].τροκ.cιγν..[	π]ατροκαc̣ιγνητ[
20	]εμεειcκρονιδ[	ἠρ]εμέειc, Κρονίδ[η,
	].'οραacϲυναρ[	οὔ]χ ὁράαc; ἐπάρ[ηγε
	].εμινεμπλη.[	].ε μιν ἐμπλη.[
	].αcδ.[.].ελεοντα.[	].αcδ.[.].ελεοντας[
	].[...]ντρομε.[	].[...]ντρομε.[
25	].ολε[	].ολε[
	]θο.[	]θο.[
	]αθανα[	] ἀθανα[τ-
	]..οcεcτ[	]..οcεcτ[
	]..φρον[	]..φρον[
30	].πολε[	].πολε[
	].αιτρομ[	].αι τρομ[
	].εγυναι[	].ε γυναι[
	]ατανυκ̣[	κ]ατὰ νύκ[τα(c)
	]μωζω.[	οἴ]μωζω.[
35	].cτηνπ[	].cτηνπ[
	]υριγ'γα̣[	c]ύριγγα[
	]αλλ'οιc̈[	] ἀλλ' οἰόc [

]γνητ[(-)καϲι]γνητ[

] . ϝπο . [   ] . ϝπο . [

2 ̣ν, trace at line-level   3 ̣[, lower part of ε, ϲ   ] ̣, oblique descending from left to right (ᴀ or λ)   4] ̣, oblique descending from left to right (ᴀ or λ)   5] ̣, two oblique and diverging strokes: right-hand part of κ or χ   6] ̣, trace at upper right   10 ̣[, lower part of upright leaning to right   12 ε ̣, foot of upright, break, right-hand extremities of horizontals or obliques at one- and two-thirds height (κ?)   ̣[, trace at lower left   13 ι ̣, letter-foot (upright or ε, ϲ), followed by short blank space and a trace at line-level; the latter is probably the edge of the following ω, but this could be narrow, in which case the traces should be part of the same letter   14]κ, it is unclear whether its upper arm curves downwards or is merged with a diastole   16] ̣, horizontal or flattened oblique sloping down to right   17 τ ̣, traces of round letter   ̣[, left-hand corner of ᴀ, ᴧ, or even ο (angular, as in 15 ϝπο)   18] ̣, high semicircular stroke (diastole?)   19] ̣, right-hand end of medial semi-horizontal   κ ̣, flattish oblique descending to right   ̣[, upright, damaged surface, then high horizontal (two letters)   21] ̣, high and low ink, compatible with the outer extremities of the arms of κ or χ   22] ̣, λ or τ   ̣[, upright with horizontal extending rightwards at top (ᴦ; ɴ, with right-hand upright lost, is less likely)   23] ̣, upright   ̣[̣] ̣, high trace; medial speck   ̣[, trace of upright or oblique at one-third height   24] ̣, high trace of round letter?   ̣[, ο or roundel of ρ   25] ̣, foot of oblique descending to right   26 ̣[, upright   28] ̣ ̣, apparently two horizontals (not ᴈ) followed by upright (ι or ρ)   29] ̣ ̣, two uprights   30] ̣, trace level with tops of letters   31] ̣, the outer extremities of the arms of κ or χ, if not of the cap and crossbar of ε   32] ̣, top of ᴀ or λ   34 ̣[, ᴦ or left-hand part of π   35] ̣, upright possibly joining horizontal at the left (ʜ suggested)   39] ̣, medial horizontal   ̣[, upright

↓

	]πανε[.].[	]πανε[.].[
	].νηδε[.....].[	].νηδε[.....].[
	].νπροσεειπεν[	].ν προσέειπεν [
	]ετισεστεφεμυ.[	]ετις ἔστεφε μύθ[οις
5	].ερινοππστ'εφ.[	]. ἔριν ὁππότ' ἐφῆ[κ-
	]τομηνισαοιδης[	]το μῆνις ἀοιδῆς [
	].λομενηχαριτε[	]λλομενη χαρίτε[σσι(ν)
	]νεωτερηεστιν.[	] νεωτέρη ἐστίν . [
	].εικουρη.ονα.[	]. ει κούρη. ὄναρ [
10	]οσκαικαλλοσοπ.[	]ος καὶ κάλλος οπ.[
	].πτατοκαρτεϊ.[	]ἔπτατο κάρτεϊ.[
	].ινομεν.νενϊ[	].ινομεν.νενϊ[
	].ασκατελεξενο[	]τας κατέλεξεν ο[
	]ψυχησδεμενο[	] ψυχῆς δὲ μενο[
15	]εμοισοιδ'ωπα.[	]εμοισοι δ' ωπα.[
	]ρειοτερονδεμα.[	]ρειοτερονδεμα.[
	]εοτοσσοναρει.[	]εο τόσσον ἀρει.[
	]φροσυνηντεκαι[	]φροσύνην τε καὶ [
	]ελωριοναιχμη.[	π]ελώριον αἰχμητ[άων
20	]νεικησεμαχ..[	] νεικησεμαχ..[
	]εινμεγαν[	]ειν μεγαν[
	].οκι.[.].πε[	].οκι.[.].πε[
	].εο[ ].[.]....[	].εο[ ].[.]....[
	]δ'ηβαι[	οὐ]δ' ἠβαι[όν
25	].εσαια[	].εσαια[
	].ν.νηα[	].ν.νηα[
	]υ[.]τοαμ[	]υ[.]το αμ[
	]ριανη[	]ριανη[
	].ητεραδ[	].ητερα δ[
30	]κηνδια[	]κην δια[
	]ηδιαφε.[	]η διαφε.[
	]αλιζεαι[	]αλιζεαι[
	]ματικ[	]ματικ[
	].γνητ[	(-)κας]ιγνητ[-
35	]εμενα[	]εμενα[

1]., speck at line-level   2]., medial trace and large left-facing arc (not ϴ)   ].[, upright reaching below the line   3]., upright (right-hand part of н?)   4 .[, narrow lower arc   5]., medial speck   .[, lower part of upright   7]., ⱥ or λ   ε, with shorter back than usual and only a trace of the mid-stroke, but є looks better than ⱥ   8 .[, trace at lower left   9]., short upright   η., specks level with letter-tops   .[, the letter looks like ɴ, but the diagonal would be too narrow; the alternative is to read ρ, but the diastole-shaped roundel would be placed rather high and the stem comparatively short   10 .[, evanescent trace   11]., speck on edge at two-thirds height   .[, ascending oblique   12]., tail of ⱥ or λ (м less likely)   ν., ο or ω   13]., top of upright leaning to right topped by horizontal extending to right   15 .[, upright trace   16 .[, curved back   17 .[, ο or ω   19 .[, high horizontal   20 ..[, short upright trace; left-hand tip of high horizontal?   21 μ, ⱥι may also be considered, but would not account for the ink after the putative ι   22]., speck on edge at mid-height   ., upright   ].., upright   23]., short horizontal above short ascending oblique (z?)   ].[, ⱥ or λ   ....[, part of a loop; ο or ω; c?; upright or back of є, c   25]., indeterminate traces (one or two letters)   26]., upright curving to right at foot   ν., ⱥ?   29]., right-hand leg of м?   31 .[, foot of upright rather than of ascending oblique   34]., upright

→   2 Perhaps ἐ]πì νυμ[φ-; not ἐ]πωνυμ[-, unless omega was narrower than usual.

4–5 Π]ληϊάδας ἔκρυψ[ε(ν) . . . / ἔ]κρυψεν δ' Ὑάδας[. Πληιάδας δ' ἔκρυψεν occurs in Pampr. fr. 3.26 Livrea, where it indicates the setting of Pleiades and Hyades between the end of October and the beginning of November, as in Hes. *Op.* 615 f. Πληϊάδες θ' Ὑάδες τε τό τε cθένος Ὠρίωνος / δύνωcιν. One may note the chiasmus.

Π]ληϊάδας ἔκρυψ[ε(ν). The poet may have thought that he could scan -δας long, which would be exceptional. The diaeresis indicates that the Πληϊάδας was not taken as trisyllabic (one could have used the form Πλειάδας—Nonnus uses either form depending on the metre).

6 τ]οccάτιον προφε[ρ-. Cf. Greg. Naz. *Carm. Mor.* p. 538.5 τοccάτιον προφέρουcα γάμου βιότοιό τε δεcμῶν.

7 οἰ]μωγή or οἰ]μωγῇ (the scribe neglects iota adscript). After that, φόρμιγ[γι is also possible. This expression does not occur elsewhere, but may be compared with Diosc. Aphr. fr. 5.18 F. φόρμιγγι πολύcτονι.

8] δὲ θέλεις καὶ εχ[. Perhaps εἰ] (or ἤ])δὲ θέλεις καὶ ἔχ[ειν.

9 α]μφοτερες is a mere phonetic slip for ἀμφοτέραις. This may have referred to χερcίν, which may be posited in the previous line. At the end, e.g. και[νὴν . . . ἔντυνον ἀοιδήν (PJP).

10]δέομαι παρὰ cο.[. Perhaps αἰ]δέομαι or (ἐν)δέομαι. At the end, cοί rather than cοῦ.

11 ἵπ]πους ἱδρώοντας. The same *iunctura* occurs in *Il.* 8.543, 11.597–8, and *Od.* 4.39. Cf. also *Epig.* fr. dub. 6 Bernabè καυχένας ἵππων / ἔκλυον ἱδρώοντας.

12 ὧ]δε δὲ κηρύccουcα?

13]κτει.ω. The letter after κτει could philologically only be ν or c. ν is virtually impossible: there is not enough space for the diagonal and the right-hand upright in the break, while if the trace described in the palaeographical note were taken as part of ɴ and not of ω, part of the diagonal would have been visible. c is not without difficulty either; we would have to assume that its short base curved sharply upwards.

14 οὐ]χ ἅλις ἀνθρώπου[c. Cf. E. *Ph.* 1235 Cπαρτῶν τε λαὸς ἅλις ὅcος κεῖται νεκρόc; cf. also A. *Sept.* 679 f.

16 οὐ]χ ἅλις αἵματος ο[: possible also αἷμα τόcο[ν or even αἷμα τὸ cό[ν. Cf. E. *IT* 1007 ἅλις τὸ κείνηc αἷμα. In Homer, Moschus, and Nonnus always ἦ οὐχ ἅλις; οὐχ ἅλις in Greg. Naz. *Carm. de se*

ipso p. 1386.7; *Carm. quae spect. ad al.* p. 1476.2; *Epigr. AP* 8.242.1; Secund. *AP* 9.301.3. The same repetition οὐχ ἅλις . . . οὐχ ἅλις also occurs in XXX **2514** ii 12–13 (hexameters of the third century).

17　ἀθ]ανάτοιϲι κυδ.[. ἀθ]ανάτοιϲι obliges us to look for a word beginning with κῠδ-: a form of κυδάζω or rather κυδο[ιμός (PJP). In this case, the general sense should be: 'did not enough men die? Was not enough blood shed? Shall we also add the war with the everlasting gods?' A similar offence was the *miasma* caused by the fratricidal struggle between Eteocles and Polyneices (cf. A. *Sept.* 681 f. ἀνδροῖν δ' ὁμαίμοιν θάνατος ὧδ' αὐτοκτόνος, / οὐκ ἔϲτι γῆρας τοῦδε τοῦ μιάϲματος).

18　ἀλ]λ' ἑτέρη νεικ[. At the end a form of νεῖκος or a iotacistic spelling of νίκη (cf. ↓20), but other articulations are possible too: ἑτέρην εἰ κ[, ἑτέρην εἰκ[.

19　π]ατροκαϲιγνητ[perhaps refers to the uncle(s) of Zeus (mentioned in the next line). The word is used of the Cyclopes in Hes. *Th.* 501, likewise in a passage referring to Zeus.

20　For ἠρεμέειϲ followed by a vocative, cf. Nonn. *D.* 20.205, 27.318, 326, always in questions.

21　ἐπάρ[ηγε. The scribe first wrote ϲυναρ[, but later added επ above the line, indicative of a correction or a variant. ϲυναρήγω is a rare compound, previously attested in XXXVII **2814** 8 (Choer. Sam.?), [Greg. Naz.] *Chr. Pat.* 1794, and in Byzantine authors. ἐπαρήγω has an epic patina; it is referred to a god in *Od.* 13.391 πότνα θεά, ὅτε μοι προφράϲϲ' ἐπαρήγοιϲ, Colluth. 178 οὔ ϲοι Ἄρης ἐπάρηξε, and especially *h. Vest.* 10 ἵλαος ὢν ἐπάρηγε. See also VII **1015** 2–3 ἀοιδοπόλῳ δ' ἐπαρήγοιϲ / ἑπτάτονον χείρεϲϲι λύρην πολυηχέα κρούων.

22　At the end, ἐμπλήγ[δην (a Homeric hapax) is one possibility.

23　Perhaps] ας δ' ἀ[γ]γελέοντας.

33　κ]ατὰ νύκ[τα(ϲ). In the same *sedes* in Nonn. *D.* 4.175, Musaeus 207.

37　οἰός [: οἶος, οὖος, ὅιος, or οἰός, but the supscript omicron could be a correction of the kind attested above, in 21, meant to replace one of the letters on the line, e.g. sigma (οιο{ϲ}).

38　(-)καϲι]γνητ[. Cf. →19 π]ατροκαϲιγνητ[; also ↓34.

↓　3　] ν προϲέειπεν [. Perhaps ὑποβλήδ]ην προϲέειπεν, as in AR 3.400 and 1119, or παραβλήδ]ην προϲέειπεν, as in AR 1.835, but also καϲιγνήτ]ην, Λαερτιάδ]ην (D'Alessio), or simply τ]ήν. After προϲέειπεν should begin the answer to a previous speech (that of the → side?).

4　]ετις ἔϲτεφε μύθ[οιϲ. Cf. *Od.* 8.170, where Odysseus in reply to Euryalus says ἀλλὰ θεὸς μορφὴν ἔπεϲι ϲτέφει, and again in 175 ἀλλ' οὔ οἱ χάρις ἀμφὶ περιϲτέφεται ἐπέεϲϲιν. D'Alessio suggests θεός or οὔ ϲ]ε τις or θεός οὔ μ]ε τις, if Ajax is the *persona loquens*.

5　] . ἔριν ὁππότ' ἐφῇ[κ-. E.g. τοῖϲιν μεγάλη]ν ἔριν ὁππότ' ἐφῆ[κε. For the *iunctura* ἔριν ὁππότ', cf. Hes. *Th.* 782 ὁππότ' ἔρις καὶ νεῖκος . . . ὄρηται. The last part of the line may be compared with *Il.* 4.396 τοῖϲιν ἀεικέα πότμον ἐφῆκε, and *Od.* 9.37–8 νόϲτον ἐμὸν πολυκηδέ(α) . . . ὅν μοι Ζεὺς ἐφέηκεν.

6　]το μῆνις ἀοιδῆς [. If we restore ἐρύκε]το, the sense will be 'anger restrains from singing'. μῆνις ἀοιδῆς may be an allusion to *Il.* 1.1. Another possibility would be ὦρε]το (PJP); cf. Hes. *Th.* 782, quoted above.

7　]λλομενη χαρίτε[ϲϲι(ν). Perhaps ἀγα]λλομένη χ., as in Colluth. 250 (-μενος).

8　] νεωτέρη ἐϲτίν. A similar *iunctura* in *Od.* 3.49, but in different *sedes*: ἀλλὰ νεώτερός ἐϲτιν.

9　κούρη . ὄναρ [. Perhaps κούρη δ' ὄναρ [εἶδεν; cf. Nonn. *D.* 8.292 ὄναρ εἶδον.

10　]οϲ καὶ κάλλος οπ . [. Perhaps μέγεθ]ος καὶ κάλλος ὄπα[ϲϲε; cf. *Od.* 18.219 ἐς μέγεθος καὶ κάλλος ὁρώμενος, Nonn. *D.* 22.91 χάριν καὶ κάλλος ὀπάϲϲει.

11　]έπτατο κάρτεϊ . [. Not θ[υμός, as in AR 3.520.

12　] . ινομεν . νενϊ[. φ]αινομένων *vel sim.* ἐνὶ [οἴκῳ, πόντῳ, etc. (D'Alessio).

13　κατέλεξεν ο[. Perhaps ὄ[λεθρον, as in *Od.* 10.250 καὶ τότε τῶν ἄλλων ἑτάρων κατέλεξεν ὄλεθρον.

15　]εμοιϲοι δ' ωπα . [. Perhaps ϲοι δ' ὤπαϲ[αν ὅπλα (D'Alessio); possible also πολ]έμοις, οἵ δ' (PJP).

16–17 At the beginning of 16, χε]ρειότερον or ἀ]ρειότερον, possibly followed by δέμας [εἶναι. In 17, probably in opposition, c]έο τόccον ἄρειο[ν. Cf. Pi. *I.* 4.34–5 (of Ajax) καὶ κρέccον' ἀνδρῶν χειρόνων / ἔcφαλε τέχνα καταμάρψαιc'.

18]φροcύνην τε καὶ [. E.g. ἐν]φροcύνην τε καὶ [ὄλβον, as in *AG* App. *Epigr. dedic.* 314.3, but ἐπι]-φροcύνην or φιλο]φροcύνην are also possible. Cf. also Theoc. fr. 3.1 ἐπαγροcύνην τε καὶ ὄλβον.

19 π]ελώριον αἰχμητ[άων. In *Il.* 3.229 πελώριοc is an attribute of Ajax.] ἐλώριον, 'booty', would also suit.

20] νείκη cε μάχεc[θαι,]νείκηc ἐμάχον[το, ἐν] νείκη cε μάχεc[θαι, or (ἐ)]νείκηcε μαχ . . [. Cf. →18 n. on the ambiguity of νεικ-.

24 οὐ]δ' ἤβαι[όν is restored after a common Homeric clausula.

32]αλιζεαι[. Perhaps μεγ]αλίζεαι, as in Nonn. *D.* 23.243, 47.652 (both times after the caesura).

34 (-)καc]ιγνητ[-. Cf. →19, 38.

C. MELIADÒ

4851. Ausonius, *Herm*[es?]

65 6B.36/H(1–2)b   4.6 × 8 cm   Later third century
Plate VIII

A fragment with remains of the last six lines of a column. Below the last line is a blank space of 2 cm, followed by a single line giving the name of the author and the title of the work, and then the lower margin extant to 2.5 cm. The text runs along the fibres, and the back is blank.

The hand, small sized and careful, is an example of the 'Formal Mixed' or 'Severe Style' of the slanting type. In letter forms as well as in the general disposition of the script, it compares well with P. Lond. Lit. 5 = *GMAW*² 14 ('Harris Homer'), assigned to the later third century. Similar hands are XXVII **2452** = *GMAW*² 27 and *PGB* 33 (*BKT* II pp. 53–4), both assigned to the third century. But our papyrus and, to some extent, the 'Harris Homer' deviate from these more canonical representatives of the style in a way that brings them closer to the earlier specimens of the 'upright pointed majuscule', in spite of the absence of slanting in this latter style: XI **1352** = *GBEBP* 12a, assigned to the early fourth century and regarded as an example of the formative phase of the 'upright pointed majuscule', shares some characteristic features with our script: contrast between broad and narrow letters, but no marked shading or decorative dashes or thickenings; smaller size of o and protrusion of γ below the baseline, among others. I am therefore inclined to suggest the second half of the third century as a date for **4851**.

Diaeresis and acute accent (2, 4) are present, and are due to the main hand. There is a possible case of correction in 4.

What remains seems to be part of the author's concluding address to the subjects of a hexameter poem: Thoeris in the nominative or vocative, and probably Hermes in the vocative, together with the semantic information provided in 5–6, bring our composition closer to a hymn or encomium than to a standard epic. With the exception of Plu. *De Is.* 358c (Θούηρις), Thoeris does not appear elsewhere in Greek literature, but is present in a good number of documents; see W. Clarysse, B. van Maele, J. Quaegebeur, *ZPE* 60 (1985) 217–32. Some of these documents identify Thoeris, an Egyptian hippopotamus-goddess, with Athena. Oxyrhynchus seems to have been her principal cult-centre, and a quarter of the city was named after her temple. Thoeris' presence in these lines is therefore important to understanding the nature of our text, which is very probably the product of local literary activity.

We have the middle portion of lines, with about one foot missing at the line-beginnings. A word-end between two short syllables occurring at approximately the same point in 3–6 may be taken to represent the feminine caesura. Meyer's first law is infringed in 4 and 5.

```
      .    .    .
   ]χα . κεοφ . [ ] . . [                ] χαλκεοφωνο[
   ] . ϋς . φέωνγε . [                   ] ἐϋστεφέων γε . [
   ] . ιςχαριε . . αθ . ω . [            ] . ιϲ χαρίεϲϲα θεῶν [
   ] . αθοηριϲεύϲκοπ[                    ] . α Θοῆρις ἐϋϲκοπ[
5  ] . . . καμοιμιδια . [                ]χρι κάμοιμι διαμ[
   ] . αιγνωτοιϲινα . [                  ] καὶ γνωτοῖϲιν απ[
        (vac.)
   ] . υϲονιου vac. ερ . [               ] Ἀϲονίου Ἑρμ[ῆϲ(?)
```

1 . κ, oblique ascending to right, and from its top another oblique descends to right: ⋀ or ⋋ . [, medial traces of curved stroke facing upwards] . . , trace at line-level; medial traces 2] . , high traces . . φ, first, high traces; below, at line-level, fleck of ink, and to right, high spot of ink; second, remains of vertical or oblique ascending to right; from its mid-height the left-hand end of a horizontal goes to the right; further remains of ink higher in the line, and to the right of the apparent horizontal (ϵ? ρ?) . [, remains of vertical or oblique sharply ascending to right 3] . , a horizontal reaches ι from the left at approximately mid-height; remains of a vertical going down from the left-hand extremity of the horizontal: Γ, τ . . α, first, remains of upright; second, remains of upright or curved stroke facing right; from its lower end another short stroke ascends to the right: tip of upright or lower parts of circular letter? high in the line, fleck of ink . ω remains of upright; above them, remains to the left and right; further remains to the right of the upright, at mid-height . [, upright, from its upper end another stroke seems to go to the right 4] . , top of apparent upright ρ, below its upper circle, remains of ink, as if belonging to the right-hand end of a short stroke going to the right from the vertical of the letter; the stroke would look similar to the lower parts of open circular letters 5] . . . , first, lower end of oblique descending to right; remains of an oblique ascending to right go up from its upper extremity: κ, χ?; second, remains of upright, and from slightly above its mid-height a short stroke gently ascending to right; above, remains of ink; third, lower half of upright . [, oblique ascending to right and joining a descending one 6] . , right-hand end of oblique descending to right; above, right-hand end of oblique

ascending to right: κ, x   .[, low remains touching lower end of right-hand oblique of ⲗ   7].,
long oblique descending to right   .[, upright or oblique sharply ascending to right, with remains
of junction at its top

1 χαλ̣κεοφωνο̣[. χαλκεόφωνος is used in *Il.* 5.785, of Stentor; Hes. *Th.* 311, of Cerberus (also
Dion. Perieg. 789); in an anonymous undated epigram on the Muses, *AP* 9.505.15, of Melpomene;
and in Eudoc. *Homerocentones* 29, for Homer. Eustathius comments on the Iliad passage: φαcὶ δὲ αὐτόν
(= Cτέντορα) τινεc . . . Ἑρμῇ δὲ περὶ μεγαλοφωνίαc ἐρίcαντα ἀναιρεθῆναι (2.201.17). This establishes
a possible link between the adjective here and Hermes, who as the herald of the gods naturally had
a strong voice.

2 ἐϋcτεφέων γε̣ .[. εὐcτεφήc occurs twice in late hexameters: Maximus, περὶ καταρχῶν 529
ἐϋcτεφέοc τ' Ἰοβάκχου; oracle ap. Amm. Marc. 31.1.5 = AG App. *Oracula* 143.2 ἐϋcτεφέαc κατ' ἀγυιάc
(also as a variant in Simias fr. 1.10 Powell). Its semantic equivalent εὐcτέφανοc is much more frequent.
In the singular, it is used mainly as an epithet of gods (especially of Aphrodite, but also of Artemis,
Demeter and even of Dionysus, as in Maximus above), and may also be applied to cities, especially
Thebes. In the plural, it normally modifies nouns denoting sacrifice, altar or the like (πύργοι, πόλειc,
ἀγυιαί, θυμέλαι, θυcίαι).

3].ιc. On the assumption that χαρίεccα refers to Θοῆριc in the next line, and Θοῆριc to Athena, this would be the ending of an epiphet of the goddess. I had first thought of [εὔμη]τιc, which
describes the quality that Athena can give to a child, but this is rather short for the space. One possibility, suggested by Professor Parsons, would be to restore [χρυcαι]γίc, which would also suit Athena
(see LSJ s.v.).

θεῶν. In documentary papyri, Thoeris is usually designated θεὰ μεγίcτη (Clarysse et al., *ZPE*
60 (1985) 225; this is the normal appellation in the Roman period, whereas μεγάλη is attested for the
third century BC). The superlative would agree perfectly with the genitive θεῶν, and fit at the line-end.
We could then supply something like θε̣ῶν [βαcίλεια μεγίcτη (cf. *Orph. H.* 61.1 θεά, βαcίλεια μεγίcτη;
H. Isidor. 1.1 πλουτοδότι βαcίλεια θεῶν).

4 At the beginning, perhaps supply μήποτε; see below, 5 n. After that, e. g. δ]ῖ̣α.

Θοῆριc. Both the shape and position of the short oblique to the right of the descender of ρ suit
the lower elements of c. Perhaps the scribe began to write the final c mistaking the second upright
of н for ι.

ἐϋcκοπ[: e.g. ἐϋcκοπ[έ τ' Ἀργεϊφόντα. Hermes may be hinted at in 1, and his name probably
appears in the title of the poem. There may well be another reference to the god in this line, since
in Homer the epithet ἐΰcκοποc occurs four times in a formula referring to Hermes, *Il.* 24.24 κλέψαι
δ' ὀτρύνεcκον ἐΰcκοπον Ἀργεϊφόντην, etc. The adjective occupies the same *sedes* as here, which suggests that the line might have ended with the same formula but in the vocative to suit the dedicatory
address.

5]χρι κάμοιμι. Traces suggest]κρ̣ι or χρ̣ι, but the latter provides a more plausible word-end:
μέχρι, or ἄχρι, looks most likely. A temporal clause, e.g. '[I shall sing] until I weary', would in principle
require not an optative but the subjunctive with ἄν, in primary sequence. Thus the conclusion is that
μέχρι, or ἄχρι, would best be interpreted as an adverb or preposition. As an adverb, ἄχρι, 'to the ut-
termost', would be possible though pleonastic if διαμ[περέc follows. As a preposition, it would have
to be construed in anastrophe.

Looking at the usual ending of hymns, we find either some sort of petition to the god or simply
a form of salute. The optative may express a desire (at least there is no space for ἄν immediately before or after it). I should therefore think that the author takes up the motif of the poet who prays to
continue singing into his old age; cf. E. *HF* 676 and fr. 369.1 ff.; also Call. fr. 1.37–8 Pf., and Posidipp.
SH 705.24, where the motif is implied. Not to tire of praising the gods is a motif known also from

hymn-texts (*h. Apoll.* 177–8 οὐ λήξω ἑκηβόλον Ἀπόλλωνα / ὑμνέων; *H. Isid.* 1.25 δεσπότι, οὐ λήξω μεγάλην δύναμίν cου ἀείδων). For οὐ/μὴ κάμνω + participle cf. e.g. E. *Or.* 1590 οὐκ ἂν κάμοιμι τὰς κακὰς κτείνων ἀεί; Call. fr. 194.48 μὴ κάμοιμ[ι.

If we restore the adverb διαμ[περές after κάμοιμι, we have 'until . . . let me [not] tire of . . . continually'. For the beginning I suggest [γήραος ἄ]χρι; cf. Bion fr. 16.4 μέχρι γήραος. At the end, a participle with κάμοιμι, e.g. διαμ[περὲς ἔργματ᾿ ἀείδων]. This leaves no room for the necessary negative, so I propose restoring μήποτε at the beginning of 4. (This removes the greeting χαίρετε as a possibility for the beginning of 4, but it should be noted that, although often present in the Homeric and Callimachean hymns, it is rare in the Orphic Hymns and in those in *Papyri Magicae Graecae*.) Another possible supplement would be διαμ[περὲς ἤματα πάντα, as in *Od.* 4.209, *h. Apoll.* 485, *h. Ven.* 209 (cf. also *Il.* 16.499, *h. Ven.* 248), in which case the participle must come towards the end of 6.

6 καὶ γνωτοῖcιν. Since it appears in the dative, it is reasonable to assume that γνωτοῖcιν constitutes the destination of the poet's singing. γνωτός/γνωτή is Homeric, and continues in the epic language; its meaning 'kinsman' is almost always limited to 'brother' or 'sister', which does not seem very appropriate to the context here. I would rather think of 'well-known', and look for a polar expression unknown/known (= everyone), rather than the gender opposition γνωταῖc] καὶ γνωτοῖcιν (cf. *Il.* 15.350), to restore in the lacuna: [ξείνοιc]?

απ[: e.g. ἄπ[ερ κλυτὰ δεῖξατ᾿ ἔμοιγε (if the participle that complements κάμοιμι is given in 5). A further specification of the object of the poet's singing (ἔργματ᾿), insisting on the praiseworthy character of the gods' deeds, seems necessary. It seems that, when it is the gods who are concerned with glorious deeds, they show them, especially to mortals, rather than simply performing or executing them. This is especially evident from the Homeric Hymns: ὃc τάχ᾿ ἔμελλεν / ἀμφανέειν κλυτὰ ἔργα μετ᾿ ἀθανάτοιcι θεοῖcιν, of Hermes (4.15–16); ἀγλαὰ ἔργ᾿ ἐδίδαξεν ἐπὶ φρεcὶ θεῖcα ἑκάcτῃ, of Athena (5.15); ὃc μετ᾿ Ἀθηναίηc γλαυκώπιδοc ἀγλαὰ ἔργα / ἀνθρώπουc ἐδίδαξεν ἐπὶ χθονόc, of Hephaestus (20.2–3); ἐκ cέο δ᾿ ἀρξάμενοc κλήcω μερόπων γένοc ἀνδρῶν / ἡμιθέων, ὧν ἔργα θεαὶ θνητοῖcιν ἔδειξαν, of Helios (31.17–19).

7 Αὐcονίου. RE records no author named Ausonius other than the well-known Latin poet; our fragment does not represent any of his known poems, and in any case this is excluded by the date of the papyrus. The name, however, occurs in several documentary papyri, mostly of the fourth century and later; see A. Coşkun, *APF* 48/2 (2002) 257–66, and N. Gonis, *APF* 51/1 (2005) 88–90. The mention of Thoeris may suggest that he was a native of or resident at Oxyrhynchus. Only one Oxyrhynchite Ausonius has been attested to date, the *hypodektes* in LXIII **4369** 1, 18 (345).

Ἑρμ[ῆc(?). This was the title of poems by Philitas and Eratosthenes. More relevant perhaps is VII **1015** = *GMAW*[2] 50 (Heitsch XVI), a hexameter poem in praise of Theon on a third-century papyrus, possibly the author's own manuscript. This celebrates Hermes and carries the title Ἑρμοῦ ἐγκώμιον, but with Ἑρμοῦ deleted. An alternative, suggested by Professor Parsons, is that the title was Ἑρμ[αθήνη, given the reference to Thoeris-Athena; cf. Cic. *Ad Att.* 1.4.3, where Cicero, on receiving a Hermathena to place in his Tusculan villa, says that Hermes is common to all gymnasia but Athena particularly suited to his own. One could think of Athena and Hermes as patron deities of the gymnasium, and of this poem as written for some similar occasion. However, on the assumption that the end-title was centred with the hexameter lines, Ἑρμ[ῆc may suit the spacing better, although it is difficult to reach a firm conclusion when so much of the text is missing.

A. NODAR

4852. Hexameters on Meleager

18 2B.71/E(4)b   3.5 × 3.3 cm   Third/fourth century
                                                                         Plate III

The lower outside corner of a leaf of a papyrus codex, unless it is an opistho-graph sheet. Of the lower margin 1.7 cm is preserved, a figure probably not far off the original; the left-hand margin on the ↓ side is extant to 0.6 cm. The hand, in-formal to near-cursive, may be assigned to the later third or earlier fourth century; there is some similarity to LXIII **4352**, hexameters written *c.*285.

A diaeresis (organic) is used in ↓2. There is a iotacism in ↓4.

The references to a boar and to Meleager (→2; 5) leave little doubt about the subject matter. The other side preserves parts of a speech, and includes a mention of (the fall of ?) a city (↓4): if this is part of the same poem, which seems plausible, this must be the besieged Calydon. One could think of Cleopatra urging Meleager to abandon his retreat and defend his city.

The possible reference to the fall of a city suggests that this poem is a product of the Imperial age (see ↓4 n.). The story of Meleager and the Calydonian boar will have featured in poems called *Καλυδωνιακά*, said to have been composed by Egyp-tian poets in late antiquity, but now lost. A scholion to Lycophron 486 by Tzetzes refers to *Cωτήριχος ἐν τοῖς Καλυδωνιακοῖς* (p. 175 Scheer); this was Soterichus of Oasis, who flourished at the time of the Tetrarchs, and who has been associated with **4352** and other hexameter texts on papyrus (E. Livrea, *ZPE* 125 (1999) 69–73 and 138 (2002) 17–30—the evidence is suggestive rather than compelling). The better-known Colluthus of Lycopolis, who flourished about two centuries later, in the reign of Anastasius, is also reported to have written *Καλυδωνιακὰ ἐν βιβλίοις ἕξ* (*Suda κ* 1951). That two poets from Upper Egypt are transmitted as authors of epic poems with the same title has a suspicious ring, and one may entertain the thought that Colluthus is a mistake for Soterichus or vice versa; but compare the case of *Βαccαρικά*, title of works by Dionysius and allegedly by Soterichus.

If this fragment came from a codex, this may have been a fairly extensive composition, and perhaps of some ambition, such as Soterichus', for example; but the possibility that this is a single sheet, especially given the informal character of the hand, cannot be discounted.

→   .   .   .

      ].....
      ].εcπεcιοcc.[   ] θεcπέcιοc cὑ[c
      ]αντacολεcθαι[   ]αντac ὀλέcθαι
      ]νανιαιc   ]ν ἀνίαιc
   5]λεαγροc   Mε]λέαγροc

↓   .   .   .

τοιαδιην . . . [τοῖα διην̣ε̣κ̣έ̣[

ωϊομηνϲυδ[ὠϊόμην, ϲὺ δ[

 υϲτατιηϲπ[ὑϲτατίηϲ π[

αϲτυπεϲινκ[ἄϲτυ πεϲ⟨ε⟩ῖν κ[

→   1] . . . ., trace at two-thirds height; foot of upright, space, another upright turning right-wards at the foot, and then trace at two-thirds height (narrow π suggested); short ascending oblique at two-thirds height, space, then medial trace of another such oblique: one or two letters?   2]., upper right-hand arc joining medial horizontal extending to right   .[, high trace

↓   1   . . .[, foot of left-hand arc and to its left part of horizontal at mid height; foot of upright followed by lower part of short oblique descending from left to right; foot of straight-backed left-hand curve

→   2   θεϲπέϲιοϲ ϲῦ[ϲ. In view of the mention of Meleager three lines below, this must be the Calydonian boar; cf. *Il.* 9.539 ϲῦν ἄγριον, a less extravagant description (μέγαϲ ϲῦϲ *Od.* 4.457, 19.439). θεϲπέϲιοϲ, not used for a beast elsewhere, may relate to the fact that the boar was sent by Artemis, un-less it illustrates the 'unspeakable' effect of its presence (cf. LSJ s.v. III; esp. Theoc. 25.70 θεϲπέϲιον δ' ὑλάοντεϲ, for dogs); on this adjective in general, see Campbell on AR 3.443. For the formulation and metrical *sedes*, cf. Nonn. *D.* 14.78 θεϲπέϲιοϲ Πάν, 26.270 πουλυτόκοϲ ϲῦϲ.

3–4 Destruction (3) and grief (4): a description of the devastation caused by the boar.

3 E.g. π]άνταϲ ὀλέϲθαι; cf. *Od.* 2.284, QS 11.269, 14.619 (in the same metrical position in Greg. Naz., *Carm. de se ipso* 978.4, 1274.5).

4 ἀνίαιϲ always occurs at verse-end in hexameters, which with few exceptions also holds for all other cases of this word.

5 Με]λέαγροϲ. The word is often placed at verse-end: *Il.* 2.642, 9.543, [Opp.] *Cyn.* 2.23, Meleag. 2.3 P.

↓   1   τοῖα διην̣ε̣κ̣έ̣[ωϲ? For τοῖα prefacing direct speech (cf. next line), see Campbell on AR 3.24 n. A verb of saying would have followed in the lost part of the line.

2 ὠϊόμην. The uncontracted form of the imperfect with ι short is first found in Greg. Naz. (three times at verse-beginning), but there will have been earlier examples; cf. already AR 1.291 ὠϊϲάμην, in the same *sedes*.

ϲύ: Meleager? We find ϲὺ δ(έ) in the same metrical position, after a verb ending -μην, in AR 3.35, QS 3.473; cf. also Macedonius *AP* 5.247.2 ὠϊϲάμην, ϲὺ δέ μοι πικροτέρη θανάτου (pentameter).

3 ὑϲτατίηϲ. It is unclear whether this is an adjective ('the last') or a noun ('the end'); if the latter, a reference to death is one possibility. The word often occurs in the same *sedes* in QS and Nonn.

4 ἄϲτυ πεϲ⟨ε⟩ῖν. Calydon is called μέγα ἄϲτυ in *Il.* 9.589. The concept of the 'fall' of a city does not appear established before the Imperial period; cf. Jos. *BJ* 5.256, [Luc.] *Philop.* 28, Himer. *Or.* 2.91, Ephr. Syr. *Serm. in Ion. proph.* p. 311.15, 313.14, Jo. Chrys. *Adv. Jud.* PG 48.899.17, 911.8, etc.

κ[: e.g. Κ[αλυδῶνοϲ (suggested by A. Benaissa). Καλυδῶνοϲ occurs in the same *sedes* in Call. fr. 621.

N. GONIS

4853. BOOK-TITLE: AREIOS(?), *THEOGAMIA*

88/105(a)   3.3 × 2.4 cm   Early fourth century
                                                                                    Plate III

The text is written across the fibres and the back is blank; a repair strip was attached to the papyrus before it received writing. The upper edge is straight enough to suggest that it was the original, which would indicate that this was a book-tag (*sillybos*) rather than an end-title (*colophon*); book-tags written across the fibres include II **301** and XLVII **3318**. On book-titles see now M. Caroli, *Il titolo iniziale nel rotolo librario greco-egizio* (2007).

The script is a mature version of the Severe Style, which is commonly assigned to the early fourth century. The lettering is fairly large, as would have been appropriate for a book-title.

The identity of the author, Areios (if this is his name; see 1 n.), is uncertain. We know of three poets of this name with Egyptian links, though none need be identified with our poet:

(i) The author of a four-line Homeric *cento* inscribed on the colossus of Memnon, known from the subscription as Ἀρείου Ὁμηρικοῦ ποιητοῦ ἐκ Μουσείου ἀκούσαντος (*RE* II 624, Areios 7; text in A. & É. Bernand, *Les Inscriptions grecques et latines du Colosse de Memnon* no. 37). He probably flourished under Hadrian.

(ii) A poet mentioned in BGU XIV 2433.5 and 2434.31, Heracleopolite accounts of the first century BC. It may be relevant that Eusebius, *Praeparatio evangelica* 1.10.49, refers to one Ἄρειος Ἡρακλεοπολίτης, who translated a work from the Egyptian (*RE* II 625, Areios 8).

(iii) Areios the 'heresiarch', active in Alexandria in the earlier part of the fourth century (†336); he was the author of *Thalia*, written allegedly in Sotadeans but probably in ionic tetrameters (see M. L. West, *JThS* 33 (1982) 98–105).

The title of the work, Θεογαμία, is not known otherwise. The form in the singular may have been patterned on Hesiod's Θεογονία (cf. the passage from Philo quoted in 2 n.), which might suggest a parody, though this is not necessary. The obvious parallel is the Ἡρωϊκαὶ Θεογαμίαι of Pisander of Laranda, who flourished under Severus Alexander; this was a poem on gods' unions with mortals that spanned almost the entire spectrum of Greek mythology (see R. Keydell, *RE* XIX.1 (1937) 145f., Peisandros 2; Heitsch ii pp. 44–7). The position of the author's name in line 1, if this is Ἀρείου (see 1 n.), suggests that nothing was written in 2 before Θ]εογαμία; otherwise one has to reckon with a composite title, as in the case of Pisander, but such a title (in the singular) does not sound particularly plausible.

Given the date of the papyrus, one ought to consider the question whether the work is Christian; the concept of the 'marriage of/with God' is not uncommon in patristic literature (e.g. Greg. Naz. *Carm. mor.* p. 631.14, Jo. Chrys. *in Matth.* PG 58.651.41). It is questionable, however, whether a title with such pagan connotations would have been considered appropriate.

It would be surprising if a poem on this subject was not in hexameters.

]αρειου	] Ἀρείου
θ]εογαμια	Θ]εογαμία

1 Ἀρείου. One cannot strictly exclude that this is the ending and not the whole name, but the options are very limited: only Δ]αρείου (uncommon) or Καιϲ]αρείου (rare) could really be considered, unless we have an itacistic spelling, e.g. Ἀπολλιν]αρείου. Much depends on the length of the title, on which the author's name is usually centred. If the title was Θεογαμία, Ἀρείου is the best bet; after all, Ἄρειοϲ is a very common name in the papyri. With a longer title, however, we would need a longer name; see introd., last para.

2 Θ]εογαμία. The word in the singular occurs in Phil. *de Decal.* 156.4 κατασκευάζειν οὐκ ἐῶν οὐδ' ὅϲα μύθων πλάϲματα προϲίεϲθαι, θεογαμίαν καὶ θεογονίαν καὶ τὰϲ ἀμφοτέραιϲ ἑπομέναϲ ἀμυθήτουϲ καὶ ἀργαλεωτάταϲ κῆραϲ; but note that the variant θεομαχίαν is also transmitted. It is hardly likely that we should read θεογάμια, the name of a festival in various cities.

N. GONIS

III. RHETORICAL TEXTS

4854. [Aelius Aristides], *Τεχνων Ρητορικων α'*
109, 111, 113, 116, 119, 134–5, 136–7, 165

66 6B.29/J(1–3)c   fr. A 8.9 × 10.4 cm   Late second or early third century
                                                                              Plates IV–V

This text comprises three fragments of leaves of a papyrus codex, none of which is conjugate. These leaves contain sections of the *1st Treatise on Rhetoric* attributed to Aelius Aristides, but the material is placed in a different order. In frr. B↓ and C→ and ↓ there is further material of the same genre that does not survive in the mediaeval tradition.

The text is written in black carbon ink, on papyrus that has apparently been treated in antiquity with *cedrium* to protect it against bookworms (see W. E. H. Cockle, *BICS* 30 (1983) 157 and nn. 129–35). Fr. A has a top margin of 2.9 cm and a surviving outside margin of *c*.2 cm; the written width can be reconstructed as *c*.12 cm, and the page-width as very approximately 16 cm. For comparable widths, see Turner, *Typology* 18. Some codices of this width show page-heights ranging around 28 cm; if our codex belonged to this group, the written height could be estimated at *c*.22 cm or 45 lines.

The script is an informal round hand, 2 mm high and largely bilinear. ι extends well above the line when following τ. β extends above the line, ρ below the line, and φ both above and below. The lettering may be compared with that of BKT IV (P. Berol. 9780) Hierocles, Ἠθικὴ *στοιχείωσις* (republished as CPF I.1** no. 60, with photographs in CPF IV.2 pll. 15–17). This manuscript, which also uses abbreviations like those in **4854**, has been assigned to the later second century. However, such small upright hands are not confined to the second century; see for example LXIII **4352** (hexameters that refer to the accession of Diocletian). On this basis, **4854** could perhaps be dated to the later second century AD, but a date in the first half of the third century is entirely possible.

The copyist uses abbreviations on the system familiar from P. Lond. Lit. 108 (*GMAW*² 60), Aristotle, *Constitution of Athens*, written on the back of estate accounts from near Hermopolis, which date from AD 78–9. It is also found in P. Lond. Lit. 138, *Rhetorical Exercises* of the first century AD, and quite commonly in scholia; see Bilabel in RE II.2 (1923) 2294–7; K. McNamee, *Abbreviations in Greek Literary Papyri and Ostraca* (Ann Arbor 1981); CPF I.1** pp. 276–281. It is interesting that the same style of abbreviation is found in the *Petitions and Grammarian's Complaint* of 253–60 published as P. Coll. Youtie II 66 (text reprinted as XLVII **3366**). It seems that this system was particularly favoured for schoolmasters' texts.

The abbreviations used are κ' = καί; κ` = κατά: δ' = δέ as a particle and in composition (τοδ'); γ' = γάρ; τ' = τ(ήν); τ` = τ(ων); μ' = μέν as a particle and in composition (λεγομ'οις); c' = cύν in composition (c'πληρωcει, c'τομια); π` = παρά as a preposition and in composition (π`cκευην). However, γίνεται and πρός are sometimes written in full. ϩ = αὐτά, αὐτός, ⱶ = γίνεται, / = ἐcτι, and \ = εἶναι are required by the supplements. A suprascript bar may represent ν at line-end (A→ 7 γνωμῆ). Iota adscript is occasionally written. There are no breathings or accents, and no punctuation except *paragraphus* at B→ 2 (end of section) and C↓ 6. A diaeresis is found on ὕπερ.

The extensive use of abbreviations in this papyrus makes it particularly hazardous to propose supplements if there is no parallel from the mediaeval text, since the variation in the number of letters per line is considerable.

Two treatises on rhetoric, ῥητορικαὶ τέχναι, are attributed in the mediaeval manuscripts to 'Aristides', i.e. the famous rhetor Aelius Aristides (117–*c*.187). The manuscripts all descend from P (Parisinus Graecus 1741, a vellum codex of the tenth century); the only independent witness is a mutilated codex (Pc + S) now divided between Paris and Sofia, which includes extracts from these treatises, added in the margins by a hand of the thirteenth/fourteenth century.

The first treatise is περὶ τοῦ πολιτικοῦ λόγου, the second περὶ τοῦ ἀφελοῦς λόγου. It has been generally agreed, since the arguments of Wilhelm Schmid (*RhM* n.F. 72 (1917–18) 113–49, 238–57), that the two treatises are by different authors, and neither by Aelius Aristides. See for an overview M. Patillon, *Pseudo-Aelius Aristide: Arts rhétoriques Livre I* (Budé series, 2002) pp. vii–xxii.

The first treatise itself seems to combines more than one source. After a brief introduction we have (1) §§ 2–128 a systematic discussion of the qualities of style (ἰδέαι), with examples (virtually all from Demosthenes); (2) §§ 129–40 a shorter systematic discussion, with no examples (therefore an abridgement of a fuller text?); (3) §§ 141–86 miscellaneous appendices. Schmid attempted to allot different sections to particular authors from among those now lost who are said to have written περὶ ἰδεῶν before Hermogenes. This enterprise rests on slender grounds, even if the sections could each be treated as self-contained. If, as Patillon argues, some material within his first section (§§ 108, 122.10–11) derives from the second, we need to imagine a more complex redaction. This is now confirmed by **4854**, which shows a variant assemblage of materials circulating at about the same date as that at which the mediaeval version is thought to have been constructed.

4854 comprises three fragments of a codex; the original order of the fragments and their respective sides is uncertain. The fragments contain the material in the following array:

fr. A→ § 134, § 135, § 109, § 111, § 113, and § 116
fr. A↓ § 119, § 165
fr. B→ § 136, § 137

fr. B↓   not in the mediaeval text
fr. C→   not in the mediaeval text
fr. C↓   not in the mediaeval text

Apart from frequent variations in wording, two things are notable. First, A→ combines, in reverse order, material from Patillon's first and second sections; A↓ combines material from the first section and the appendix (an appendix that Patillon guesses to have been added in the fifth century). Second, **4854** omits many of the illustrative quotations (primarily from Demosthenes) that in the mediaeval text characterize the first section as against the second; this makes it necessary to ask whether the examples are all original to the author (in which case **4854** offers an abridgement) or are material added at will by teachers of rhetoric who used this work.

What we seem to have is an elementary work on the art of composition used in the rhetorical schools of the period, whose contents could, to some extent, be transposed and illustrated to suit the need of the individual teacher. The copying of this codex was probably done within the life-time of Aelius Aristides or a generation or so after. That in turn suggests that the original material that appears in both redactions derives from a date substantially earlier than is normally thought.

The content has been compared with the Budé text of M. Patillon (2002), and the Teubner text of Wilhelm Schmid, *Rhetores Graeci* v (1926); references are to the paragraph-numbering introduced by Schmid and adopted by Patillon. I have consulted also Leonard Spengel's *Rhetores Graeci* ii 457–512 (1854); Christian Walz's *Rhetores Graeci* ix 340–409 (1836); and Wilhelm Dindorf's edition of *Aristides* ii 712–68 (1829). Patillon's apparatus reports the readings of P (and where available those of the independent Pc), but only eclectically divergent readings in the apographa of P; Schmid gives a fuller account.

We are indebted for expert advice to Professor D. A. F. M. Russell, Dr D. C. Innes, and Professor M. F. Heath. Dr Cockle's draft was prepared for publication by Parsons, who takes responsibility for any errors and omissions.

Fr. A→

(134) ὅταν τις μεταβαίνων ἀφ' ἑτέρου ἐ]φ' ἕτερον π[ρ]ᾶγμα τοῦ μ(ὲν)

ς(υμ)πληρώςει, τοῦ δ(ὲ)

ἐπαγγελίᾳ χρῆται, κ(αὶ) ὅταν τις c.3] ᾳcεcιν χρῆται, κ(αὶ) ὅταν τις ἀφηγηματικοῖc cχήμαcι χρῆται. (135) κ(ατὰ) δ(ὲ) ἀπαγγελί]αν γίνεται ὅταν τις κοινοτέροιc ὀνόμαcιν χρῆται κ(αὶ) τοῖc cημαντικοῖc τοῖc] cφόδρα κ(αὶ) ἐναργῶc δηλοῦcιν τὰ πράγματα

5   κ(αὶ) ὅταν τοῖc ἰcοδυναμοῦcιν ἥκιcτ]ά τιc χρῆται κ(αὶ) ὅταν τοῖc πραοτέροιc ἀντὶ τ(ῶν) τραχέων.   (109) περὶ cφοδρό]τητος

cφοδρότηc δ(ὲ) γίνεται τριχῶc, κ(ατὰ) γν]ώμην κ(αὶ) κ(ατὰ) cχῆμα κ(αὶ) κ(ατὰ)

λέξιν. κ(ατὰ) μ(ὲν) γνώμη(ν)

οὕτως, ὅταν τις   c.14   ]ς επι[[c.4]] κ(αὶ) ἀνθίστηται, ἢ ὅταν τις ἐνδόξ[ο]ις

προσώποις ἐπιτιμᾶι ἢ ὑπεραγ]ανακτῆι κ(αὶ) ὑπερσχετλιάζηι τοῖς ὀλίγου

10   ἀξίοις, κ(αὶ) (111) ὅταν δ(ὲ) ἀτόπως τις εἰκά]ζηι κ(αὶ) π(αρα)βάλληι. (113) τ[ὸ] δ(ὲ)

μέγιστον εἰδέναι χρή,

ὅτι ὅταν ἦι μὴ ἰσχυρὰ ζητήμ]ατα τὰ ἐξ ἑτέρων τῶν μερῶν, ὑπάρχῃ[ι δ(ὲ) θα-

τέροις μὴ πρόδηλα (αὐτὰ) (εἶναι), ὁ δ(ὲ) ὡς ἐπὶ ὁμολογουμ(έν)ο]ις σχεδὸν τοῖς

ζητήμασιν συνάγε[ι τὸν

λόγον, οἷός ἐστιν ὁ κ(ατὰ) Μειδίου. (116) κ(ατὰ) δ(ὲ)] σχήματα γίνεται σφο[δρότ]ης

οὕτω[ς, ὅταν τις

ἐπιφορικοῖς χρῆται σχήμασι. κ(ατὰ) δ(ὲ)] λέξιν γίνεται σφ[οδρότης ὅταν   c.10

15   c.24   σχ]ήμασίν τις χρῆτα[ι

c.26   ]τα..[.].´....[

·   ·   ·   ·   ·   ·   ·   ·

1 μ΄ς΄πληρωςει, δ΄   2 κ΄   4 κ΄   5 κ΄, τ΄   7 κ΄κ΄, κ΄κ΄, κ΄μ΄γνωμῆ   8 κ΄

9 κ΄   10 κ΄ π̣ βα̣λληι τ[.]δ΄

'[(From the section *On Clarity and Purity*) . . . By figure, clarity and purity are achieved thus . . . when someone, in passing from one topic] to another, completes one [and gives indication] of the other, [and when someone] uses . . . *x* . . ., and when someone [uses] narrative [figures. By dict]ion, clarity is achieved when someone [uses] more ordinary language [and language that is significant,] which brings out the points strongly and vividly, [and when someone makes the minim]um use [of synonyms], and when he uses milder language instead of [harsh.]

'[*On Vehem*]ence. [Vehemence is achieved in three ways, by] thought and by figure and by diction.

'By thought [thus, when someone . . .] . . . and opposes, or when someone [censures persons] held in high repute, or when he [is exceedingly] angry or indignant at people of little [worth, or when someone uses out-of-the-way imag]es and comparisons. But, as the most important point, one must know: [that when the claims] of the other parties [are not strong,] but it is possible [that the claims were not made clear to the other party beforehand, he (Demosthenes) organizes [his speech as if on the basis of] claims [that are almost agre]ed, as in the speech *Against Meidias*.

'[By] figures, vehemence is achieved thus: [when a speaker makes use of impetuous figures.]

'[By] diction. vehemence is achieved [when . . .] a speaker uses . . . figures . . .'

Fr. A→ begins in the middle of §134 περὶ σαφηνείας καὶ καθαρότητος.

2]. ασεςιν χρῆται: not in MSS. Before α a median horizontal descending slightly to the right, compatible with the right hand of λ, μ, ς, or τ. In the break after ἐπαγγελία χρῆται the words κ(αὶ) ὅταν τις (μή) are probably required. There is space for a dative plural third-declension feminine noun ending in -ασις, whose nominative singular is of three syllables, or if μὴ is present of two. κ(αὶ) ὅταν τις μὴ π]λάσεσιν χρῆται 'and whenever a speaker does not use fictions' would fit the space, but other supplements may better suit the context: Professor Heath suggests κ(ατα)ς]τάσεσιν or ἐπα(να)]λήψεσιν, the former associated by Hermogenes (e.g. *Id.* p. 236.17 Rabe) with εὐκρίνεια.

2–3 κ(αὶ) ὅταν τις ἀφηγηματικοῖς | [σχήμασι χρῆται comes after δηλοῦσι τὰ πράγματα in MSS (cf. pap. line 4). This continues into §135, where the mediaeval text has a string of καὶ ὅταν clauses, each of which is not dependent on the preceding: **4854** presents these in a different order without affecting the sense of the paragraph.

3 κ(ατὰ) δ(ὲ) ἀπαγγελί]ạν γίνεται: κατὰ δὲ ἀπαγγελίαν οὕτως MSS.

ὅταν: ο was begun as λ and was then overwritten.

κοινοτέροις ὀνόμασιν: κοινοτέροις τοῖς ὀνόμασι MSS.

4 ἐναργῶς: ἐνεργεστέρως P: ἐναργεστέροις G Vb: ἐναργεστέρως Norrmann and later editors.

5 ἥκιστ]ά τις χρῆται: τις before ἰσοδυναμοῦσιν MSS.

After χρῆται MSS have the gloss τὰ τροπικὰ λέγει καὶ μεταφορικὰ ἰσοδυναμοῦντα τοῖς κυρίοις δηλονότι, deleted by Finckh, Spengel, and most later editors.

6 ff. §136, which follows §135 in the mediaeval text, is found in fr. B→. Here the papyrus moves to §109, with the heading περὶ σφοδρό]τητος. It is strange that τραχέων should be run over into line 6. We should expect the heading, which is centred in mid-line, to stand by itself; compare B→ 3.

7 κ(ατὰ) γν]ώμην κ(αὶ) κ(ατὰ) ϲχῆμα κ(αὶ) κ(ατὰ) λέξιν: κατὰ γνώμην, κατὰ ϲχῆμα, κατὰ λέξιν MSS.

κ(ατὰ) μ(ὲν) γνώμη(ν): καὶ κατὰ μὲν γνώμην MSS.

8]ϲ επι[[c.4]] κ(αὶ) ἀνθίϲτηται, ἤ: not in MSS. There is stray ink above the left hand vertical of π in επι. After επι a blank space with shadows of ink (since the surface seems undamaged, apparently an erasure rather than accidental damage), where the last element may be a high acute representing abbreviation.

9 After ἐπιτιμᾶι the mediaeval MSS continue with quotations from Demosthenes 10.46 and Thucydides 1.69 followed by [Aristides] §§110–11. The papyrus omits these but adds ἢ ὑπεραγ]-ανακτῆι κ(αὶ) ὑπερϲχετλιάζηι τοῖς ὀλίγου | [ἀξίοις, absent from the mediaeval text.

ἢ ὑπεραγ]ανακτῆι: §112 σφοδρότης δέ ἐστι καὶ ὅταν τις ὑπεραγανακτῇ.

ὑπερϲχετλιάζηι is *hapax legomenon*.

9–10 τοῖς ὀλίγου | [ἀξίοις, or perhaps τοῖς ὀλίγου ἀ|[ξίοις. This reconstruction, suggested by Dr Innes and Professor Collard, offers a suitable contrast with ἐνδόξοις. The ink at the end of 9 is vestigial, and might allow τοῖς ὀλίγοις, but that, in the normal sense of 'the few' (oligarchs), seems alien to the context.

10 The papyrus apparently continues with the beginning of §111 καὶ ὅταν δὲ ἀτόπως τις εἰκάζηι, adding κ(αὶ) π(αρα)βάλληι, which is not in the mediaeval text. It then skips to the latter part of §113. The intervening area in the mediaeval text is largely quotation from Demosthenes and Thucydides.

11 ὅταν ᾖι μὴ ἰϲχυρὰ ζητήμ]ατα τὰ ἐξ ἑτέρων τῶν μερῶν: ὅταν ᾖ μὴ ἰϲχυρὰ ζητήματα ἐξ ἑκατέρων τῶν μερῶν MSS. The reconstruction of the papyrus is not certain (but it seems that the first trace does not allow ιϲχ]υρα τα or ιϲχυρ]οτατα): the second τα may be a dittograph.

ὑπάρχη[ι δ(έ): ἀλλ' ὑπάρχη MSS.

12 The supplement at the line-beginning from the mediaeval text of 34 characters is too long for the available space of c.26. Possibly θατέροις was abbreviated at the end of line 11, and ἐπὶ contracted to ε´ (compare McNamee, *Abbreviations* 32). However ἐπί is usually written in full in this papyrus.

13 κ(ατὰ) δ(ὲ) ϲχήματα γίνεται ϲφο[δρότ]ης οὕτω[ϲ: κατὰ ϲχῆμα δὲ οὕτω γίνεται ϲφοδρότης MSS.

13–14 ὅταν τις ἐπιφορικοῖς χρῆται τοῖς ϲχήμαϲιν MSS: in the supplement I have omitted τοῖς for the space.

The papyrus omits the examples that follow in the mediaeval text and moves to the beginning of §116, which the MSS present as κατὰ δὲ ἀπαγγελίαν [τουτέϲτι κατὰ λέξιν secl. Schmid] ϲφοδρότης γίνεται, ὅταν ὑπερβολὰς ποιῇς ἐν τῷ λόγῳ οἷον κτλ.

14–15 A possible supplement is . . . ὅταν ἐν τῷ λόγῳ ὑπερβολικοῖς ϲχ]ήμαϲίν τις χρῆτα[ι, but more is required to fill the available space.

16].´ . . . . [. Tops of letters: the second trace is the high rising oblique of a contraction.

Fr. A↓

(119) λου εἰδέναι χρὴ ὅτι αἱ τρεῖς ἀρεταὶ τοῦ λόγ[ου, ἥ τε cφοδρότηc κ(αὶ) ἡ

ἔμφαcιc κ(αὶ) ἡ τραχύτηc,

εἰ κ(αὶ) τῇ προcηγορίαι διεcτήκαcιν, τῆι γο[ῦν δυνάμει κ(αὶ) cφόδρα ἐπικοινωνοῦcιν

ἀλλήλαιc. (165) τοῦ δ(ὲ) μὴ φορτικῶc ἐπαινεῖ[ν, δύναcθαι δ', ὁποcαχῶc ἂν χρεία γένη-

ται, ἐν τοῖc τρόποιc εἰcὶν οἵδε· πρῶτον ὅ[ταν τιc μὴ ὡc ἐπιβουλεύcαc (αὐτὸc) κ(αὶ) παρα-

5 cκευαcάμενοc, ἀλλ' ὡc cύνηθεc ἐπὶ τ[οῦτο δοκῇ cυνενεχθῆναι· δεύτερον ὅ-

ταν τιc τὰ μὲν ἀποδιώcηται, τὰ δὲ δι[εξίῃ· τρίτοc τρόποc ὅταν πρὶν

εἰπεῖν τι cυγγνώμην

ἐφ' οἷc ἂν μέλλῃ λέγειν αἰτῆται παρὰ [τῶν δικαcτῶν· τέταρτον ὅταν ἐν

τοῖc κοινοῖc τὸν ἔπαινον ἔχηι· πέμ[πτον ὅταν κ(αὶ) αὐτοῖc τοῖc ἀκούουcιν

προcήκειν φάcκηι ἀποδέχεcθαι α[ὐτά· ἕκτον ὅταν κ(αὶ) τοὺc ἀντιδίκουc

10 οἷόc τε ᾖ τιc ἐπιδεικνύῃ ταὐτὸ ποιοῦ[νταc κ(αὶ) δεινὸν εἶναι φάcκηι ἐκεί-

νουc μ(ὲν)] ποιεῖν ὑπὲρ τῆc ἑαυτῶν ὠφ[ελείαc, αὐτὸν δ(ὲ) μή.

4 lines blank

16   ]...[

   ·   ·   ·   ·   ·   ·

2 κ′   3 δ′ or δ/   11 ὕπερ

'[(From the section *On Emphasis*).] It is [of great] importance to know that the three qualities of expres[sion, vehemence, emphasis, and harshness,] even if they are different in name, yet [share much] the same [effect] one with another.

'Among the methods of avoiding offensiveness in praising [but still being able to do so in as many ways as the need ari]ses, are the following: first, when [someone gives the impression of being carried] into [it] [not out of a] preconcerted [plan of his own] but as being normal (?): [secondly when] someone rejects one set of arguments, but [goes] through the other [in detail: the third method is when someone, before speaking,] asks [the jurors their forbearance] for what he is about to say: [fourthly, when] someone receives his praise [in] general terms: fif[thly when (a speaker)] says that it is proper [even for the audience themselves] to accept th[em: sixthly when] someone is able to show [that his opponents too] are doing the same, [and says that it is is dreadful that they] are doing (this) for their own ad[vantage, while he is not.'

Fr. A↓ begins at the start of §119, which in the mediaeval text is headed περὶ ἐμφάcεωc. It omits the rest of §119, and then transmits §165 complete, followed by a blank space of four lines.

1 -]λου εἰδέναι χρὴ ὅτι (e.g. καθό]λου, διό]λου Russell): τρόπον μέν τινα MSS.

2 διεcτήκαcιν: διεcτήκαcι MSS.

3 ἀλλήλαιc ἐπὶ πλείcτοιc, καὶ ἥ τε cφοδρότηc ἐμφαντικὸc λόγοc ἐcτὶν καὶ ἡ τραχύτηc cφοδρό-τητα δύναται· κτλ. MSS. The papyrus continues without a new heading into §165.

Professor Russell observes that this chapter seems originally to have referred not to praising in general but to praising oneself (as in the comparable passage [Hermog.] *Meth.* 25 = 441 ff. Rabe), although the papyrus does not make this any clearer than the mediaeval text.

4 ἐν τοῖc τρόποιc εἰcὶν οἵδε· πρῶτον ὅ[ταν: ἐν τοῖc πολιτικοῖc ζητήμαcιν, τρόποι εἰcὶν οἵδε. πρῶτον μὲν ὅταν MSS. The subject of the sentence that is qualified by τοῦ μὴ φορτικῶc ἐπαινεῖν

is clearer in the mediaeval text. In the papyrus πολιτικοῖς ζητήμασιν seems to have fallen out, and τρόποι been assimilated to the dative.

4–5 παρα]‖ ϲκευαϲάμενοϲ: παραϲκευαϲμένοϲ MSS: παρεϲκευαϲμένοϲ edd.

5 ἀλλ': the cross bar of ⅄ is written twice.

5–6 ἀλλ' ὡϲ ϲύνηθεϲ ἐπὶ τ[οῦτο δοκῇ ϲυνενεχθῆναι· δεύτερον ὅ]ταν τιϲ τὰ μὲν: ἀλλ' ὡϲ ϲυναναγκαϲθεὶϲ καὶ [καὶ del. Norrmann] ἐπὶ τοῦτο δοκῇ ϲυνενεχθῆναι·δεύτερον [P: δεύτερον δὲ cett.] ὅταν τιϲ τὰ μὲν MSS. ὡϲ ϲύνηθεϲ exists elsewhere as a set phrase, 'as usual'. But here it should parallel ὡϲ ἐπιβουλεύϲαϲ in 4. This is syntactically awkward, and in any case the sense seems less suitable to the context than 'by necessity', as in the mediaeval text. (Russell compares [Hermog.] *Meth.* 442.6 ff. Rabe; an alternative contrast would be between 'preparation' and 'spur-of-the-moment invention'; see § 101.)

6 ἀποδιώϲηται pap.: ἀποδιωθῆται MSS: ἀποδιωθῇ Spengel. The sense is the same whether the 3rd sing. Aor. Subj. Mid. or Pres. Subj. Mid. is read.

7 μέλλῃ pap., coni. Spengel: μέλλοι MSS.

10 ἐπιδεικνύῃ: ἐπιδεικνύναι MSS: ἀποδεικνύναι Norrmann. The subjunctive in the papyrus after οἷόϲ τε ᾖ is clearly wrong.

ταὐτό: τὸ αὐτό MSS.

11 ἑαυτῶν: αὑτῶν MSS (according to Schmid): αὐτῶν Spengel.

16 Traces of the tops of letters.

Fr. B→

. . . .

τιϲ τα̣ . . . . [. . .] . [. .] . [

χρῆται κ(αὶ) ὅταν τοῖϲ ἐμφατικοῖ[ϲ

(136) περὶ βρ[αχύτητοϲ καὶ ϲ(υν)τομίαϲ

βραχύτηϲ δ(ὲ) κ(αὶ) ϲ(υν)τομία γίνετ[αι κ(ατὰ) γνώμην, κ(ατὰ) λέξιν. κ(ατὰ)

5   μ(ὲν) γνώμην οὕτωϲ, ὅταν τιϲ τ[οῖϲ ἀναγκαίοιϲ εὐθὺϲ ϲ(υμ)πλέκηται τῶν πραγμάτων κ(αὶ)
ὅταν τιϲ μὴ ἐνδιατρίβηι τοῖϲ ἠπο[ρημ(έν)οιϲ   c.16   κ(αὶ) ὅταν τιϲ μὴ
πᾶϲιν ὡϲ προηγουμένοιϲ χρῆ[ται, ἀλλὰ τοῖϲ μ(ὲν) ⟨ὡϲ⟩ προηγουμένοιϲ τοῖϲ δ(ὲ) μὴ οὕτω.
(137) [κ(ατὰ) λέξιν] δ(ὲ) γί(νεται) [βραχύτηϲ κ(αὶ) ϲ(υν)τομία, ὅταν τιϲ μὴ ταῖϲ
π(αρα)φραϲτικαῖϲ τῶν λέξεων, ἀλλ(ὰ)
[ταῖϲ εὐθείαιϲ χρῆτα]ι, ὅ[ταν μὴ ἐπαγωνίζηται τῇ λέξει τὰ ἰϲοδυναμοῦντα
10   [π(αρα)τιθείϲ,] ἀλλὰ δηλώϲα[ϲ τὸ πρᾶγμα τῇ ϲημαινούϲῃ λέξει εὐθὺϲ ἀπαλλαγῇ
κ(αὶ) ἐν ὀλίγῳ

[c.10   ] . . [

. . . .

2 κ̄'   4 δ̄'ϲ̄'τομια   5 μ̄'   8 δ̄' π̄·

'. . . uses x and when [a speaker uses] striking phases.

'*On Brevity and Conciseness*

'Brevity and conciseness are achieved by thought and by diction.

'By thought thus, when someone immediately engages in the essentials of the matter and when someone does not dwell on the questions in dispute . . . [and when someone does not treat] all points as leading issues but some as leading issues and some not.

'[By diction, brevity and conciseness] are achieved [when someone does not use circumlocutory expressions, but the straightforward ones; when he does not lay stress on the expression by juxtaposing synonyms,] but, having indicated [the matter by the significant expression, straightway moves on and briefly…]'

1–2 These lines are not present in the mediaeval text.

2 τοῖς ἐμφατικοῖ[ς. The mediaeval text has a section (§§ 119–23) περὶ ἐμφάσεως, of which the first sentence appears in fr. A↓ 1–3. Compare [Aristides] τεχνῶν ῥητορικῶν β′ § 133 καὶ τὸ τοῖς ἧττον ἐμφαντικοῖς χρῆσθαι ὀνόμασι καὶ τὰ μικρότερα ἐπὶ τῶν μεγάλων ὀνομάζειν τοῦ εἴδους τῆς ἀφελείας ἐστίν. ἐμφατικός and ἐμφαντικός commonly appear as variants in MSS.

4 § 136 begins. καὶ before κατὰ λέξιν add. Norrmann. The supplement from the mediaeval text is some 24 letters short of those in adjacent lines.

§ 135, which precedes in the mediaeval recension, is found in fr. A→ 2–6.

5 ὅταν τις τ[οῖς ἀναγκαίοις: ὅταν τοῖς ἀναγκαίοις MSS.

6 ὅταν τις μὴ ἐνδιατρίβηι τοῖς ἠπο[ρημ(έν)οις. This clause is not in the mediaeval text. ηπο[is probably from a perfect participle of ἀπορέω. Compare Aristotle Pol. III 1281a 38 ἂν οὖν ᾖ νόμος μὲν ὀλιγαρχικὸς δὲ ᾖ δημοκρατικός, τί διοίσει περὶ τῶν ἠπορημένων;

8–9 The surface fibres are stripped, leaving only occasional traces of ink. The reconstruction is therefore very uncertain. Note that Patillon adds καὶ before ὅταν in 9; the traces would allow this.

11 [c.10]. . [: the damaged letters (first suggests N or perhaps ΔΙ) not obviously reconcilable with the next part of the mediaeval text.

Fr. B↓

3 lines space	
c.36	] π(αρα)σκευὴν τὸ κ(ατὰ) τ(ὴν) ἀπαγγελίαν
c.36	]. ι . ει . ως βούλεται οἵτινες π(αρα)
c.36	]. οιτό τις πολλοῦ ἄξιον, εἰ Διομη-
c.36	]οιως τοῦτο οὔτ[[α]]ως οὖν ποιεῖ
5 c.36	]του ἐνηι προστη.ς.[.].. [
c.36	]δε λέγω ηπ[..].[.] ο [....].[
c.38	]λασιν αγγ[.]λ.ν[.]μ[
c.47	].π.[

1 π`, κ` τ\

The material is not present in the mediaeval text.

The first line stands level with line 3 of fr. B→. Presumably the blank space above separates one section from another, as in A↓ (it cannot belong to an upper margin, since the other side shows no such space).

On the evidence of fr. A↓ c. 36 letters are missing at the beginning of lines 1–6.

Line 1 contains technical terms. The rest might be taken as a quoted example, especially if λέγω is recognised in 6 (compare 3, a possible reference to a Homeric figure; 4 a possible singular imperative).

1 κ(ατὰ) τ(ὴν) ἀπαγγελίαν: 'in respect of style' (Latin *elocutio*), the noun used repeatedly in this work.

2]̣ ι ̣ ει ̣ ωϲ: first, high horizontal ligature joining just below the top of ι (ϲ, ϵ, π?); second, ϲ or perhaps π (second upright not visible); third, π or perhaps ν. ϵ̣ἰπ̣ϵῖν̣ ὡϲ βούλεται would be possible.

οιτ̣ι̣νεϲ: ink above the first ι, possibly on fibres twisted from the recto; of τ the vertical and right-hand crossbar; of the second ι the upper half, perhaps ligature from preceding letter at top left.

3]̣ οιτο: the right-hand side of ζ, κ, μ or χ: e.g. νομί]ζ̣οιτο.

In ἄξιον̣ the ν is faint, but ϲ cannot be read.

Δ̣ιο̣μη- suits the ink better than δὶϲ̣ μὴ; if ϵ̣ἰ is right, we cannot divide διὸ μη(-). Diomedes is used as an example of friendship in Menander *Rhetor* II p. 396.17 (Russell and Wilson), and of temperance ibid. II p. 416.20. But, as Professor Russell suggests, the context (πολλοῦ ἄξιον) might suggest a reference to his proverbial bargain in exchanging his bronze armour for the gold armour of Glaucus (*Il.* 6.234–6). Dr Innes compares the use of Menelaus as an example in §§ 164 and 166.

4]ο̣ιωϲ: of ο̣ the lower curve of a circle, compatible also with θ or μ.

ποιεῖ: or ποίει.

5 ἐνηι: ἐνῆι from ἔνειμι or ἐνίημι, or ἐν ἧι.

πρ̣οϲ̣: minimal traces of ρ; ϲ overwritten, possibly altered to ϵ̣̀ = ἐ(πί).

6 π̣[: τι̣[, τϵ̣[or το̣ [also possible.

7]λ̣α̣ϲιν αγ̣γ̣[̣]λ̣ ̣ ν[: very uncertain. First λ̣ might be δ, γ̣γ̣ might be π,; at end perhaps]λ̣ι̣α̣ν[(αγγ[ϵ]λ̣ι̣α̣ν[?).

8]̣ π̣ ̣[: before π possibly the right-hand half of ω.

Fr. C→

. . . .

*c.*37–40] ̣ ̣ ̣ ̣[
*c.*25–28 "οὐκ ἀγνοῶ μὲν ο]ὖ̣ν ὅτι τὸν Χαρίδημον εὐερ-
γέτην (εἶναί) τινεϲ τῆϲ πόλεωϲ οἴονται" (ἐϲτὶν) ἐν τελικοῦ κ]εφαλαίου εἴδει. εὔνουϲ γ(ὰρ) ϵ̣-
*c.*37–40]̣ α γ(ὰρ) πεπραγμένα δηλοῖ πα̣ν
*c.*37–40]̣ γ(ὰρ) κ(αὶ) πότερον ̣ ̣ θεῶν τοῖ̣ϲ
*c.*37–40]ϲ̣ τοῖϲ ἔργοιϲ ἄλλωϲ ἐν ἐρω̣τη-
*c.*42–45]ϲ̣ κ(αὶ) τοὺϲ εὐφρονοῦνταϲ
*c.*48–51]υ γ̣( ) λεγομ(έν)οιϲ. εὔνουϲ γ(ὰρ)
*c.*48–51] ( ) [̣ ̣ ̣ ̣]ν̣ειδοτ(ων)

. . . .

3 γ′ 4 γ′ 5 γ′ κ′ 7 κ′ 8 γ′ λεγομ′οιϲ, γ̣′ 9] ̀ [, i.e. abbreviation mark visible above lacuna,]ν̣ειδοτ′

The material is not present in the mediaeval text. On the evidence of A→ *c.*37 letters are missing at the beginnings of lines 1–6, on that of B→ *c.*40 letters. The subject matter seems to concern εὔνοια; cf. lines 2, 7, and 8. There is a section περὶ εὐνοίαϲ in Anonymous, προλεγόμενα περὶ τῶν εὑρέϲεων (Walz, *Rhetores Graeci* vii 1, p. 66.11–24). There it forms part of a discussion of prologues, and that may be the context here: Professor Russell notes that [Herm.] *Inv.* p. 99 Rabe uses the same passage of Demosthenes quoted here as an example of 'breaking down good prejudices' in the prologue. Note that the other side of this fragment contains material suitable to a sample prologue.

Dr Innes notes: 'I would suggest a link between the new material (C→ and C↓) and [Aristides] §§ 144–166, the three genres of oratory, encomium, deliberative and forensic. C→ has the τελικὰ κεφάλαια, which are analysed under *deliberative* oratory at §§ 151 ff (even if the actual technical terminology of τελικὰ κεφάλαια is not used). Then C↓ has phrases identifying *forensic* oratory — perhaps all from one model proem, or just "flosculi" to identify the genre. The speech of Demosthenes (23) cited at C→ 2–3 is a prominent exemplar elsewhere in [Aristides], especially §§ 149 ff as a model for mixing elements from the three genres.

'Have we in this papyrus a variant version of [Aristides'] mediaeval tradition, in which the three genres follow after the analysis of individual qualities?'

2–3 Demosthenes 23.6 οὐκ ἀγνοῶ μὲν οὖν ὅτι τὸν Χαρίδημον εὐεργέτην εἶναί τινες τῆς πόλεως οἴονται· ἐγὼ δέ, ἄν περ ἃ βούλομαί τε καὶ οἶδα **πεπραγμέν'** ἐκείνῳ δυνηθῶ πρὸς ὑμᾶς εἰπεῖν, οἶμαι δείξειν οὐ μόνον οὐκ εὐεργέτην, ἀλλὰ καὶ **κακονούστατον** ἀνθρώπων ἁπάντων καὶ πολὺ τἀναντί' ἢ προσῆκεν ὑπειλημμένον. Only the first sentence is quoted here, but the comment may look back to the elements in boldface in what follows.

3 ἐν τελικοῦ κ]εφαλαίου εἴδει. The simplest supplement would be ἐν κ]εφαλαίου εἴδει, 'as a heading' (i.e. to the demonstration of Charidemus' κακόνοια that follows). However, the second sentence of Dem. 23.6 is quoted in the context of τελικὰ κεφάλαια, 'heads of purpose', in a passage attributed to Sopater in σχόλια Συριανοῦ καὶ Σωπάτρου καὶ Μαρκελλίνου εἰς στάσεις τοῦ Ἑρμογένους (Walz, *Rhetores Graeci* iv pp. 757–8) κοινὴ δὲ μέθοδος πάντων τῶν κεφαλαίων τούτων τῶν τελικῶν, ἡ κατὰ ἀντίφασιν εἰσαγωγή· εἰ μὲν γὰρ ἔχοιμεν δεῖξαι, ὅτι δίκαιον ἢ συμφέρον τὸ προκείμενόν ἐστι, τοῦτο κατασκευάσομεν· εἰ δὲ μή, ἐροῦμεν, ὅτι οὐκ ἄδικον ἢ οὐκ ἀσύμφορον· ἔστι δὲ αὐτοῦ τὸ παράδειγμα καὶ παρὰ τῷ ῥήτορι· . . . (p. 757.22) καὶ γὰρ ὁ Δημοσθένης ἐν τῷ κατὰ Ἀριστοκράτους αἰσθόμενος τοὺς ἀντιλέγοντας τὸ κατὰ ἀντίφασιν εἰσάγοντας, ὅτι εἰ καὶ μὴ εὔνους ἐστὶν ὁ Χαρίδημος τῇ πόλει ἀλλ' οὔτε γε δύσνους ἐκ προοιμίων εὐθὺς ἀναιρεῖ τὸ τοιόνδε, καὶ δείξειν ἐπαγγέλλεται κακονούστατον φάσκων, "ἐγὼ δέ, ἄν περ . . . (p. 758.3) καὶ πολὺ τοὐναντίον ἢ προσῆκεν ὑπειλημμένον." On τελικὰ κεφάλαια, see further R. Volkmann, *Die Rhetorik der Griechen und Römer* (²1885) 301; H. Lausberg, *Handbook of Literary Rhetoric* (Leiden 1998) § 375.

4] .α: descending ligature meeting middle left-hand of ∧:] τὰ could be read.

δηλοῖ: Demosthenes shows that all his (Charidemus') actions were disloyal?

5] . : horizontal ink at mid-level and at line-level. Then γ´ i.e. γ(ὰρ) or perhaps τ´ i.e. τ(ων).

πότερον: an example of a question (see 6)? Cf. § 122 εἶτα ἡ ἐρώτησις· πότερον ὑμῖν, ὦ ἄνδρες Ἀθηναῖοι, δοκεῖ μισθωτὸς Αἰσχίνης ἢ ξένος εἶναι Ἀλεξάνδρου; (Dem. 18.52).

. . θεῶν: horizontal ink at mid-level joins and continues through a c-shape with above it an acute accent or abbreviation sign. Perhaps c´ = (ςύν) was the intention, but that does not account for the horizontal ink (something erased? a cancellation stroke?).

θεῶν is more likely than θέων. θεῶν and εὔνοια are linked in Dem. 1.2; 2.22; 11.16 and 18.153, 195.

6 ἄλλως or ἀλλ' ὡς.

ἐν ερωτη-: e.g ἐρωτή[ςει (ἐρωτή[ματι), ἐρωτή[ςεως ςχήματι. Cf. 5 πότερον?

7]c: high curve descending to the right.

8]υ χ´ λεγομ(έν)οιc: if we take the second letter as γ´ and expand it as γ(ὰρ) (as elsewhere in this papyrus), something must have dropped out of the text. If we take it as τ´, it may represent -των (see McNamee, *Abbreviations* 116), e.g. τοῖς περὶ τού]τ(ων) λεγομ(έν)οιc.

9 E.g. τῶ]ν εἰδότ(ων), ςυ]νειδότ(ων). Quotation?

Fr. C↓

```
           .     .    .      .
             ] . [
   ἑτέρους ορωμ . . [ ]εις δικαστη[        c.38
   δι' ἄλλην τινὰ τοιαύτην ἀδι . [         c.38
```

```
      κ(ατ)ηγορήϲαντα τουί. ἐγὼ δ[               c.38
  5   ἢ ὥϲτε αὐτὸ τοὐναντίον . [               c.38
      ἐμοί φημι πρὸϲ τοῦτον ου . [             c.38
      τοῦ παρόντοϲ ἀγῶνοϲ[                     c.41
      ἢ ἑτέρωϲ κ(αὶ) αὐτοὶ ἐν τω[              c.41
      ]μ . ειτο . [
```

    .   .   .

4 κ', ï or ί   8 κ'

The material is not present in the mediaeval text. On the evidence of fr. A↓ *c.* 38 letters are missing at the ends of lines 2–6.

The author of [Aristides], τεχνῶν ῥητορικῶν α', very rarely uses the first person singular in his own exposition. Exceptions are λέγω in § 2 and φημί in § 149. So ὁρῶ (2), ἐγώ and ἐμοί (4 and 6), φημί (6) are probably in quoted speech, and that is confirmed by τοῦ παρόντοϲ ἀγῶνοϲ (7) and by the absence of technical terms. No quotation from Attic oratory has been firmly identified, even allowing for the minor variants that citations of the classics often exhibit in [Aristides]. We may then be dealing with an exemplary composition: the material suggests a model proem. The *paragraphos* below 7 could mark the end of one continuous passage; then ἢ ἑτέρωϲ, 'or alternatively', could introduce a second model.

1] . [: foot of vertical below line, as of ι, ρ, or φ.

2 ορωμ . . [ ]ειϲ: the traces are difficult: ὁρῶμεν (ὁρῶ μὲν) εἰϲ, ὁρῶμαι εἰϲ, ὁρῶ μηδείϲ (μηδ' εἰϲ) seem not to fit. Then e.g. δικαϲτή[ϲ, δικαϲτή[ριον. The overall structure may contrast the behaviour of the speaker with that of others (ἑτέρουϲ . . . (4) ἐγὼ δ[έ).

3 αδι . [: the foot of a vertical. E.g. τοιαύτην ἀδικ[ίαν; cf. Isocrates 15.297.

4 τουί: the interpretation is uncertain. Above the apparent ι two traces that most suggest an acute accent bisected by a patch of damage. Such a stroke might indicate a numeral, or a contraction (although we would expect it to stand further to the right); if the latter, it might be possible to take the 'ι' as a damaged τ, i.e. τουτ' for τούτ(ων). Alternatively, the two traces may represent an asymmetrical diaeresis. In that case we may have a haplography του ï for του⟨του⟩ï. Compare Dem. 23.1 (the speech quoted in C→ 2–3) μηδεὶϲ ὑμῶν, ὦ ἄνδρεϲ Ἀθηναῖοι, νομίϲῃ μήτ' ἰδίαϲ ἔχθραϲ ἐμὲ μηδεμιᾶϲ ἕνεχ' ἥκειν Ἀριϲτοκράτουϲ **κατηγορήϲοντα τουτουὶ** κτλ.

5 αὐτὸ τοὐναντίον: cf. Demosthenes 22.5 ἐγὼ δ' αὐτὸ τοὐναντίον οἴομαι, Dem. 55.17.

. [: horizontal or rising ink at mid-line, compatible with ϒ.

6 . [: low left-hand descending curve, as of ε, θ, ο, ϲ, ω; or possibly, if a further small upright trace level with letter-tops is not delusory, φ.

7 τοῦ παρόντοϲ ἀγῶνοϲ: a phrase from Attic oratory (e.g. Dem. 57.1, in a proem), taken up by rhetoricians of the Roman period (Ael. Arist. Πρὸϲ Πλάτωνα p. 5.22 Jebb; Maximus Rhet. p. 432.13 Rabe; Lib. *Decl.* 13.1, in a proem).

τω[: or το[.

W. E. H. COCKLE

4855. Τεχνη Ρητορικη

112/114 (a) + 115/24 (a)   Fr. 1 10.5 × 23.8 cm   Mid third century
                             Fr. 2 14.9 × 23.9 cm   Plates VI–VII

Two fragments containing a column each, written across the fibres. Although these two fragments come from different boxes, there is clear evidence that they belong to the same roll.

On one side, we have documentary texts written along the fibres, joined in a τόμος cυγκολλήcιμος: on fr. 1, line-beginnings from a sale of land; on fr. 2, line-ends, then a heavy *kollesis* and line-beginnings from another sale of land, written in a different hand. The line-ends on fr. 2 can be seen to belong to the same document as fr. 1: the hand is similar, the wide upper margin of 8 cm is the same, and the name of the same seller, Dioskoros son of Anoubion, occurs in both. The formulas point to a Hermopolite provenance. The date-formula (see P. Bureth, *Les Titulatures impérials dans les papyrus, les ostraca et les inscriptions d'Égypte (30 a.C. – 284 p.C.)* (Bruxelles 1964) 104, third form) in lines 16–17 can be reconstructed across the fragment as follows: ἡ πρᾶcιc κυρία. (ἔτουc) κβ [Αὐτοκράτοροc Καίcαροc Μάρκου Αὐρηλίου Cεουήρου Ἀν]τωνίνου Παρθικοῦ μ[εγίc]του Βρεταν[νικοῦ] | μεγίcτου Γερμανικοῦ μεγίcτου [Εὐcεβοῦc Cεβαcτοῦ (month, day), i.e. 22nd year of Caracalla = 213/14. Thus 45 letters are lost between the right-hand edge of fr. 1 and the left-hand edge of fr. 2. Given that in the preserved beginning of line 17, 26 letters (plus word-spaces) occupy just over 8 cm, we can calculate that the missing 45 letters would require approximately 14 cm of papyrus. The second document has the same distinctive deep upper margin (but in this case filled with writing by a third hand).

Each fragment of the literary text contains one column, and the lacuna of *c.*14 cm in between has precisely enough room for one column plus side-margin. This means that fr. 1 preserves col. i, and fr. 2 col. iii, of the same sequence, while col. ii is lost. Col. iii contains the end of the work and gives the title τέχνη ῥητορική, written in a slightly bigger size. Col. i contains 27 lines, while col. iii contains 20 lines. Col. i has lost a few letters of the beginning and end of individual lines, but it preserves the upper and the lower margin, which are respectively 1.8 cm and 3 cm wide. Col. iii is damaged just at the beginning of individual lines, apart from lines 3–6, but from 2 to 8 its left-hand outside margin is partially preserved and is about 2 cm wide. Its right-hand outside margin is about 1.5 cm wide. Its upper margin is about 1.8 cm wide. After the final title, the rest of the column is blank to a depth of about 6.8 cm. The interlinear space is about 4 mm.

The script, to be assigned to the 'Formal Mixed' type, is upright, basically bilinear (apart from ι, ρ, τ, υ, and φ, whose uprights protrude below the baseline), with occasional ligatures (especially between λ and the following letter and in the diphthong ∈ι) and a remarkable contrast between square and rounded letters. Individual letter-shapes to be noted are: ⲁ, usually in three strokes at a sharp angle, with right-hand diagonal tending to be shorter because of the rapidity of the writing (a feature that may be observed in ⲇ and ⲗ also); ʙ, with triangular lower loop protruding below the baseline (iii 15); ⲙ with broad curve; ɴ, with shorter right-hand diagonal, rapidly written from the lower extremity of the left-hand diagonal without lifting the pen; ο, rather small and lying in the middle or in the upper part of the writing space; ⲫ, with rather flat body; ⲱ, with no separation into two lobes and lying in the upper part of the writing space. The scribe is able to keep an even right edge to the column by enlarging the last letter of the line (see, for instance, the large ɴ in iii, at the end of 3 and 6, and the protrusion of the central stroke of ∈ at the end of 10 in the same column). Although the hand is certainly skilful and competent, the general graphic impression reveals rapidity and irregularity. Occasionally individual words seem to be separated by small blank spaces (see, for instance, i 10, between διάθεϲιν and κἄν; 11, between διαιρεῖται and εἰϲ; iii 6, between γαμεῖν and εἰ; 8, within the sequence ἁπλαῖ μὲν αἱ ζήτηϲιν; 14, between ζ̄ and κατὰ φύϲιν; 15, between βίῳ and βίοϲ). At the same time, there are ligatures between groups of letters belonging to two different words (iii 17, δέ and κατηγορία) and, vice versa, small spaces within a single word (iii 4, within πραγματικαί, where the three final letters are separated from the rest of the word by a slightly wider space; 17, between the two first letters and rest of the word ἐναντίων). Given that the recto provides as a *terminus post quem* the year 213/14, this literary script might be reasonably assigned to the middle of the third century. This is based on the assumption of a minimum time interval of 5–10 years for the reuse of the papyrus; cf. *GMAW*² 19, and M. Lama, 'Aspetti di tecnica libraria ad Ossirinco: copie letterarie su rotoli documentari', *Aegyptus* 71 (1991) 55–120, esp. 87–92. Parallels for this script are: II **223** (pl. I, *GLH* 21a), early iii AD (on the recto: petition of AD 186); I **23** (pl. VI), iii AD (date on the verso: AD 295) + P. Berol. 9766 (= BKT 2.53–4), from the same roll and written in an almost identical hand. Cf. also XXII **2341**, a document dated to 202 (*GLH* pl. 19c), which presents however more cursive elements.

Inorganic diaeresis occurs in i 7 ἰδιώτηϲ, 17 ἴδιαϲ. No accents. Punctuation is marked by means of *paragraphus* below the beginning of the line and *dicolon* within the line (cf. *GMAW*² 8–9). In iii 6, where the end of the sentence coincides with the end of the line, no *dicolon* occurs. In i 21 a superfluous *dicolon* occurs. *Paragraphus* appears not to be marked in i 6 and 27, and iii 8 and 14, whether by a slip or because the ink has completely faded; in iii 10 it is missing probably because of fibre damage.

Scriptio plena occurs in i 4 δεαρρην; 5 ταπανταη; 25 παντααϲαφη; 27 δεοταν; iii 1–2 δεο|ϲαι; 4–5 δε|οϲαι; 10-11 δε|[αι]. Elision occurs in: i 17 επαγοραϲ, επιδιαϲ. Itacistic spelling occurs in i 6 μιρακιο[ν. Corrections occur in: i 3, deletion of a superfluous letter by means of two diagonal strokes, π⟦ρ⟧οτερον; i 20, addition of κακως in the interlinear space in a slightly smaller script, seemingly by the same hand; in the same line correction *currente calamo* in the sequence ηπρου[, where the π has been written on a previous erroneous η.

The bibliological and palaeographical features of **4855**—handbook script equipped with some punctuation and reading marks, the presence of corrections by the scribe himself, and the fact that it is written on reused papyrus—allow us to classify it as a not particularly expensive but still decent copy of a literary text. Therefore it represents a new interesting piece of evidence to contribute to the picture of Oxyrhynchus' book production based on the recycling of documentary rolls drawn by Lama, *Aegyptus* 71 (1991) 94–101, 112.

The content of the two preserved columns offers the classification of πρόcωπον and πρᾶγμα applied to a law (col. i) and the classification of θέcειc (col. iii). In spite of the title τέχνη ῥητορική, the matter in this treatment is presented in a rather summary form. The closest parallel is found in the textbooks called *Progymnasmata*, especially that of Theon on νόμοc and θέcιc, who, however, presents them in reverse order; see pp. 82–102 Patillon–Bolognesi (for editions see the list at the end of this introduction), and concluding remarks after iii 17–18 n. Cic. *Inv.* 1.34–44 offers an earlier detailed treatment (cf. M. C. Leff, 'The Topics of Argumentative Invention in Latin Rhetorical Theory from Cicero to Boethius', *Rhetorica* 1 (1983) 23–44, esp. 27–31).

The πρόcωπον (the agent) and the πρᾶγμα (the action) are the two basic components of every argument, and play an important role in the theory of τόποι/*loci* in Greek and Latin Rhetoric as two of the six elements of the so-called circumstance (περίcταcιc), the other being χρόνοc, τόποc, τρόποc, and αἰτία, as theorized in Herm. *Stas.* pp. 29.7–31.18 and [Herm.] *Inv.* pp. 140.10–147.15. According to Herm. *Stas.* p. 29.7–11, πρόcωπον/agent and πρᾶγμα/action are the two essentials of cτάcιc theory, a theory that 'sought to classify the different kinds of dispute with which speakers have to deal, and to develop effective strategies of argument for handling each kind' (M. Heath, *Hermogenes: On Issues* (Oxford 1995) 2). An account of this treatment is to be found in B. Schouler, 'La Classification des personnes et des faits chez Hermogène et ses commentateurs', *Rhetorica* 8 (1990) 229–54, esp. 233–50; cf. also Heath, *Hermogenes*, esp. 63–6 and 92–5. Our text considers and analyses πρόcωπον before πρᾶγμα, as recommended by Sopater, *RG* 5, p. 40.2–8, in particular 5–7: καὶ λέγομεν, ὅτι προϋφέcτηκε τὸ ποιοῦν τοῦ ποιουμένου, καὶ φύcει τὰ πρόcωπα τῶν πραγμάτων ἐcτίν· οὐ γὰρ πραχθείη πρᾶγμα μὴ προϋφεcτῶτος προcώπου. Each division is subdivided into eight parts. Each part is illustrated by reference to a 'fictional' law: the father-beater should be punished by having his hand cut off.

The θέcιc represents a *progymnasma* that consists of arguing for or against a general proposition, different from the ὑπόθεcιc (= technical term for the sub-

ject of a declamation or a speech) because it does not have the περίcταcιc, i.e.
πρόcωπον, πρᾶγμα, αἰτία, etc., according to Theon, p. 82.14–16 (= 120.14–16),
[Herm.] pp. 24.1–25.2, Aphth. pp. 41.22–42.5, Nicolaus Sophista pp. 71.11–72.6
(cf. Quint. 3.5.7–8). In **4855** θέcειc are classified on the basis of two different cri-
teria. The first subdivision is based on their content and includes three groups:
θέcειc θεωρητικαί (e.g. nature of universe), ἠθικαί, a group unique to **4855** (e.g.
how to treat friends), and πραγματικαί (e.g. should one sail? should one marry?
should one farm?). The other authors of *Progymnasmata* offer a subdivision into two
groups: θέcειc of a theoretical nature—named θεωρητικαὶ by Theon, [Herm.],
and Aphth., and *inspectivae sive intellectivae* by Prisc. *Praeexercitamina* (pp. 47.30–48.1
Passalacqua = p. 559.22–3 Halm), φυcικαί by Nic. Soph. (p. 76.18–20)—and θέcειc
related to an action, a practical activity, named πρακτικαί by Theon, πολιτικαί
by [Herm.] (who also uses as synonym πρακτικαί), Aphth., and Nic. Soph., and
activae by Prisc. (p. 47.30 Passalacqua = p. 559.22–3 Halm). The second subdivision
in **4855** is based on the structure of θέcειc and includes two groups, ἁπλαῖ and
cυγκριτικαί. This corresponds to the subdivision into ἁπλαῖ and διπλαῖ found in
[Herm.] p. 25.16–21. A θέcιc ἁπλῆ concerns the question whether the implementation of an action should be recommended, while a θέcιc διπλῆ concerns the question whether the implementation of an action should be recommended instead of
another action (cf. [Herm.] p. 25.20–21: . . . διπλῆ, δεῖ γὰρ τοῦ μὲν ἀποτρέπειν,
ἐπὶ δὲ τὸ προτρέπειν). Further, Theon (p. 94.5–7 = p. 128.5–7) offers the distinction between θέcειc ἁπλαῖ and cυνεζευγμέναι. The θέcιc cυνεζευγμένη consists of
a composite θέcιc that debates whether the implementation of an action should
be recommended to a particular type of person: for example εἰ βαcιλεῖ γαμητέον.
[Herm.] also mentions this type under a different name, θέcιc πρόc τι, and gives
the same example as Theon (p. 25.19). Not surprisingly themes and wording of individual *theseis* in **4855** share with the other *progymnasmata* texts the echo of popular
wisdom and didascalic approach. Therefore they appears rather distant from an
exclusively technical dimension and in a very broad perspective could be traced
back to Hesiod's didactic poetry: see, for instance, iii 3–4 on children's education
and care for friends, iii 5–6 on sailing, marriage, and farming, and iii 9–10 and
13–14 on engagement in rhetoric and military activity.

    In spite of its closeness to the progymnasmatic tradition, the new text presents
several features that are not exactly paralleled in the extant tradition of *Rhetores
Graeci et Latini*. The following elements/aspects are particular interesting: the variations in the subdivision of πρόcωπον and πρᾶγμα into eight parts (see i 1–2 and
11–24 nn.), the role of the heading τὸ cαφέc in the analysis of the law (see i 24–7 and
24–5 nn., and the final remarks after iii 17–18 n.), the list of headings to be applied
in the θέcιc-exercise (see iii 14ff. and 15–16 nn.), and especially the tripartite classification of θέcειc including the hitherto unattested group of θέcειc ἠθικαί, which
is the most original feature of **4855** (see iii 1–6 n.), Moreover, the presentation of

the material is to be examined in relation to the sequence of the different exercises found in the extant *Progymnasmata* (see final remark after iii 17–18 n.). In any case **4855** contributes further evidence to illustrate how large and diverse was the range of such rhetorical handbooks and their variations of doctrine within this continuously developing teaching tradition (for an updated and detailed survey see M. Heath, 'Theon and the History of the Progymnasmata', *GRBS* 43 (2003/4) 129–60; idem, *Menander: A Rhetor in Context* (Oxford 2004) esp. Part III). τέχναι ῥητορικαί attributed to Rufus (later second century) and Apsines (third century) survive, of which the former as transmitted takes summary form. However, we have no way to tell whether **4855** is a copy or summary of a work that circulated widely, or a local teacher's manual. The fact that the end-title does not name the author tells against the first possibility (but see final remarks after iii 17–18 n.).

Other papyri transmit texts belonging to the *progymnasmata* category. P. Mich. inv. 6 + P. Palau Rib. inv. 155 (*TAPA* 53 (1922) 136–41 and *Aegyptus* 66 (1986) 114-20), part of a miscellaneous codex (M–P³ 2294, LDAB 0552, CPP 0420; cf. Heath, 'Theon' 141), written in an unpractised and irregular majuscule of the third century, contains a definition and analysis of the fable comparable with Theon's account. PSI I 85, *Appunti di retorica*, latest edition by G. Bastianini, in M. S. Funghi (ed.), *Aspetti di letteratura gnomica nel mondo antico* ii (Firenze 2004) 249–63; M–P³ 2287, LDAB 5248, CPP 0357), contains a definition of *chreia* followed by a now lost section on *diegema* (ii/iii AD); its nature as provisional notes is shown by the fact that it is written in a quite inaccurate hand on the verso of a document, and the remaining part of the verso itself has been further used to write a documentary note (see Heath, 'Theon' 141, and Bastianini, loc. cit. 251–4). The structure question/answer of PSI I 85 has a parallel in a papyrus codex of unknown provenance, P. Vindob. G 754 (M–P³ 2288, LDAB 6396, vi AD), a sort of rhetorical catechism dealing with *prooimion, diegesis*, and *staseis*.

4855 adds evidence for the spread of rhetoric in Oxyrhynchus (cf. J. Krüger, *Oxyrhynchos in der Kaiserzeit* (Frankfurt a. M. 1990) 345), where a number of texts of different levels have been found. Apart from the already mentioned PSI I 85, see: III **410**, Rhetorical Treatise in Doric (2nd half of ii AD), containing rather simple and practical instructions for good writing; XVII **2086**v (iii AD), remains of notes on Rhetoric (including a heading περὶ κεφαλαίων); LIII **3708** (ii/iii AD), containing a rather elaborate system of *topoi*; P. Thomas 15, rhetorical handbook dealing with *staseis* and *topoi* (ii AD).

The reconstruction, the interpretation, and the overall assessment of the text have greatly benefited from valuable suggestions and comments by Dr R. A. Coles, Prof. M. Heath, Dr D. C. Innes, Dr T. Reinhardt, and especially Prof. D. A. Russell.

List of editions used for specific authors:

Aphthonius: H. Rabe, *Aphthonii Progymnasmata* (Leipzig 1926)

Apsines: M. Patillon, *Apsinès, Art rhétorique: Problèmes à Faux-Semblant* (Paris 2001) (cf. C. Walz, *Rhetores Graeci*, ix (Stuttgart 1836); L. Spengel, *Rhetores Graeci*, i/2 (Leipzig 1844))

[Augustinus], Iulius Victor, Sulpicius Victor: K. Halm, *Rhetores Latini Minores* (Leipzig 1863)

Consultus Fortunatianus: L. Calboli Montefusco, *Consulti Fortunatiani Ars Rhetorica* (Bologna 1979)

Hermogenes: H. Rabe, *Hermogenis Opera* (Leipzig 1913); [Herm.] = *Progymnasmata*, whose authenticity is doubtful; similarly as [Herm.] *Inv.* I refer to the treatise περὶ εὑρέϲεωϲ wrongly ascribed to Hermogenes

Ioannes Sardianus: H. Rabe, *Ioannis Sardiani Commentarium in Aphthonii* (Leipzig 1928)

Libanius: R. Foerster, *Libanii Opera*, i–xii (Leipzig 1903–23)

Nicolaus Sophista: J. Felten, *Nicolai Progymnasmata* (Leipzig 1913)

Priscianus: K. Halm, *Rhetores Latini Minores* (Leipzig 1863); *Praeexercitamina*: M. Passalacqua, *Prisciani Caesariensis Opuscula*, i (Rome 1987)

Rufus: M. Patillon and L. Brisson, *Longin Fragments: Rufus, Art rhétorique* (Paris 2001) (cf. C. Walz, *Rhetores Graeci*, iii (Stuttgart 1834); L. Spengel, *Rhetores Graeci*, i/2 (Leipzig 1844))

Theon: M. Patillon and G. Bolognesi, *Aelius Théon: Progymnasmata* (Paris 1997) with corresponding pages of the edition by L. Spengel, *Rhetores Graeci*, ii (Leipzig 1853) given in brackets

Sopater: C. Walz, *Rhetores Graeci*, v (Stuttgart 1833)

Syriani, Sopatri et Marcellini, *Scholia ad Hermog. Status*: C. Walz, *Rhetores Graeci*, iv (Stuttgart 1833)

Syrianus: H. Rabe, *Syriani in Hermogenem Commentaria*, i–ii (Leipzig 1892–3)

Fr. 1 (col. i)

top

η̣ ενοϲφυϲιναγωγηνηλικιαν . . . [
ξ . ι . . αθοϲδιαθεϲι . οιονοπατρ . τυ . [
___ . οπειϲθω : γενοϲμ . ν ⟦ρ⟧οτερονθετ[
___ ϲ . . . : φυϲινδεαρρηνηθηλεια : . [
5   . . . ρονυβριϲτηϲταπα̣νταηκα . [
       ] . . . τριοϲ : ηλικιανπαιϲημιρα . ι . [
___ χ . . ¨διωτηϲμονονηκαναρχω . : [
       . [.] . . . . χε . ροκοπηθηϲεταικανηαρ . . . [
___ . . . . ννοκτονοϲ : παθοϲκανπεπηρ[
10   . . . ϲ : διαθεϲινκανευνουϲεξαρχ[
       δ . π . αγ . . διαιρειταιειϲμερηη̄η̄προ[
       αιτιαντοπονχρ . νοντροπογτα . ρο[
       . . . τοϲταεντωπραγματιταμετ . τ[
       . . . . : οιονπροϲωπονεικαιοτην . . [
15   τ . πτηϲαϲχειροκοπηθηϲετα . : αι . [
___ . . . ινομενοϲημ . θυων : . ο . ον . [
___ . . . ωηεπαγοραϲ . επϊδιαϲοικιαϲ : [
       . . νκανπροπολλουηπαραχρημα[
___ . . . νταιϲ . ερϲινηξυλω : τ̣απροτο . [
20   γμ̣ατοϲκανπροακουϲαϲ᾽κακωϲ῾ηπρο . [
___ . . . ιϲ : ταεντωπρ . γματι : ειτυπτ[
___ . . . . ε : ταμετατοπραγμακανε . [
       . [.]ηγωναποθανηεικα . τ . υπατ . . [
       λ[.] . ενουχειροκοπηθη . εταιταυτ̣[
25   πα̣ . ταὰϲαφηκαιαδ . . . : παρανομ . [
       ]αντιοϲηονυνειϲηγουμενοϲτο . [
       ] . κυρωμενοιϲ : αδικοϲδεοτ . . μ . [

foot

1 η . , remains of upright in lower part of writing space, ligature with following ε consisting in short horizontal stroke in upper part of writing space   . . . [, first, tiny traces in horizontal alignment suggesting top horizontal whose centre is in vertical alignment with very tiny mark at line-level; second, extremely faded trace suggesting lower half of upright; slightly farther to left extremely tiny mark lying in upper part of writing space; third, rather blurred traces in roughly diagonal alignment ascending from left to right   2 ξ . , short slightly diagonal stroke ascending from left to right in upper part of writing space   ι . . , first, tiny dot at mid-height; second, remains of top horizontal whose right-hand extremity joins upright   ϲι , lower half of oblique descending from left to right; on its left lower part of stroke slightly slanting to right   ρ . , thick mark at mid-height in vertical

Col. i

　　η̄· γένος, φύσιν, ἀγωγήν, ἡλικίαν, τύχ[ην, πρά-
　　ξεις, πάθος, διάθεσιν. οἷον ὁ πατροτύπ[της χειρο-
　　κοπείσθω. γένος μὲν πότερον θετ[ὸς ἢ γνή-
　　σιος. φύσιν δὲ ἄρρην ἢ θήλεια. ἀ̣[γωγὴν
5　πότερον ὑβριστὴς τὰ πάντα ἢ κἂν̣ [± 5
　　.]. μέτριος. ἡλικίαν παῖς ἢ μ⟨ε⟩ιράκιο[ν. τύ-
　　χην ἰδιώτης μόνον ἢ κἂν ἄρχων. [πρά-
　　ξ[ε]ι̣ς ε̣ἰ χειροκοπηθήσεται κἂν ᾖ ἀριστ[εὺς ἢ
　　τυραννοκτόνος. πάθος κἂν πεπηρ[ωμέ-
10　νος. διάθεσιν κἂν εὔνους ἐξ ἀρχ[ῆς. τὸ
　　δὲ πρᾶγμα διαιρεῖται εἰς μέρη η̄· πρό[σωπον,
　　αἰτίαν, τόπον, χρόνον, τρόπον, τὰ πρὸ [τοῦ πρά-
　　γματος, τὰ ἐν τῷ πράγματι, τὰ μετὰ τ[ὸ πρᾶ-
　　γμα. οἷον πρόσωπον εἰ καὶ ὁ τὴν μη[τέρα
15　τυπτήσας χειροκοπηθήσεται. αἰτ[ίαν κἂν
　　μαινόμενος ἢ μεθύων. τόπον π[ότερον ἐν
　　ἀγρῷ ἢ ἐπ' ἀγορᾶς ἢ ἐπ' ἰδίας οἰκίας. [χρό-
　　νον κἂν πρὸ πολλοῦ ἢ παραχρῆμα. [⟨τρόπον⟩ πότε-
　　ρον ταῖς χερσὶν ἢ ξύλῳ. τὰ πρὸ τοῦ [πρά-
　　　　　　　　　　　　　　　κακῶς
20　γματος κἂν προακούσας ἢ προϋ[βρισ-
　　θείς. τὰ ἐν τῷ πράγματι εἰ τύπτ[ων μὴ τρώ-
　　σειε. τὰ μετὰ τὸ πρᾶγμα κἂν ἐκ [τῶν
　　π[λ]ηγῶν ἀποθάνῃ ⟨ἢ⟩ εἰ καὶ τοῦ πατρὸ[ς μὴ βου-
　　λ[ο]μένου χειροκοπηθήσεται. ταῦτ[α μὲν δὴ
25　πάντα ἀσαφῆ καὶ ἄδηλα̣. παράνομο[ς δὲ ὅταν
　　ἐν]αντίος ᾖ ὁ νῦν εἰσηγούμενος τοῖ[ς ἤδη
　　κ]εκυρωμένοις, ἄδικος δὲ ὅταν μ.̣[

alignment with tiny trace lying in upper part of writing space　　τυ.[, remains of upright whose tip bears tiny trace of joining element to left　　3　.ο, upright, blurred remains of (possible) ascending oblique departing from centre to right　μ.̣, curve, possibly left-hand arc　ν.̣, short stroke approaching to horizontal in upper part of writing space, whose right-hand extremity joins upright; possibly square letter　　4 ς...[, first, upper half of upright; second, thick mark in upper part of writing space; third, left-hand arc　.[, blurred traces suggest tip of triangular letter; to right trace probably representing lower extremity of right-hand oblique of the same triangular letter　　5 ...[, first, upright slightly slanting to right; second, group of three tiny marks very close to each other at mid-height; third, very scanty and scattered traces　.ρ, tiny mark at mid-height; above, ligature with following letter ̣[, faded remains of lower half of two uprights; in between faded and blurred mark at mid-height: square letter? 6]̣ ̣ ̣, first, mark in upper part of writing space in vertical alignment with extremely tiny trace at line-level; further very tiny trace in upper part of writing space in slightly diagonal alignment descending from left to right with the above mentioned mark; second, short oblique trace descending from left to right in upper part of writing space; 2 mm farther right, tiny mark at mid-height; third, extremely tiny and faded marks possibly belonging to top of round letter ρα ̣, lower part of upright joining at mid-height short oblique descending from left to right ι ̣[, mark at mid-height 7 χ ̣ ̣ ̈δ, first, two faded traces in horizontal alignment, 2 mm distant from each other; second, very tiny and faded mark in upper part of writing space, in horizontal alignment with thicker blurred trace 2 mm farther on; third, two tiny marks in vertical alignment lying respectively at mid-height and at line-level χω ̣, two uprights, 2.5 mm apart; in between two very tiny and faded traces at mid-height 8 ̣[, top horizontal whose right-hand extremity joins short oblique slightly descending from right to left that joins at sharp angle at mid-height another oblique ascending from left to right; below, stains at line-level ̣ ̣ ̣, first, two tiny marks in vertical alignment, respectively at mid-height and at line-level; second, traces in upper part of writing space, possibly belonging to left-hand arc; third, very scanty and scattered traces in upper part of writing space ̣χ, two tiny marks very close to each other almost in vertical alignment at line-level ϵ ̣, tiny trace below right-hand extremity of central stroke of preceding ϵ ̣ ̣[, first, lower half of upright; second, two marks roughly in horizontal alignment very close to each other in upper part of writing space, of which the left-hand one is in vertical alignment with thick trace lying in lower part of writing space; third, two very tiny traces very close to each other in horizontal alignment in upper part of writing space 9 extremely scanty and faded remains of *paragraphus* at line-beginning ̣ ̣ ̣ ̣ν, first, left-hand of top horizontal, whose right-hand extremity is in vertical alignment with other tiny traces in lower part of writing space, probably belonging to upright; second, two groups of very tiny traces in horizontal alignment, 1 mm distant from each other, in upper part of writing space; below, a few stains suggesting upright; third, faded and scanty remains of upright in lower part of writing space? fourth, remains of right-hand oblique, bottom stroke and right-hand angle of triangular letter 10 ̣ ̣ς, first, upright whose tip joins oblique descending from left to right and only partially preserved; second, two very tiny marks very close to each other at mid-height and in vertical alignment with tiny trace in upper part of writing space 11 δ ̣, remains of horizontal at mid-height π ̣, lower part of upright protruding below baseline γ ̣ ̣, first, upright followed, a few mm farther on, by lower extremity of oblique descending from left to right; second, left-hand angle of triangular letter, very faded extremity of its right-hand diagonal 12 χρ ̣, left-hand arc τα ̣, upright whose tip joins to right another not preserved stroke 13 ̣ ̣ ̣τ, first, two very tiny marks in vertical alignment lying in upper part of writing space and at line-level respectively; 2 mm farther on, in upper part of writing space, two very tiny marks quite close to each other and in horizontal alignment; second, remains of ascender whose tip joins to right faded curve whose apex lies at mid-height; third, blurred remains of ascendant and bottom stroke of triangular letter τ ̣τ[, scanty remains of obliques of triangular letter 14 faded *paragraphus* at line-beginning ̣ ̣ ̣, first, tip of upright? second, remains of two uprights; in between remains of central element, apparently a curve whose apex lies at mid-height; third, descender in upper part of writing space ν ̣ ̣, first, remains of two uprights of square letter, plus mark close to first upright, probably belonging to central element, possibly μ; second, two very tiny marks in vertical alignment, respectively in upper part of writing space and at line-level 15 very faded *paragraphus* at line-beginning τ ̣, traces of arc in upper part of writing space with apex facing middle of writing space τα ̣, tip of upright αι ̣[, upright protruding below baseline, whose tip bears tiny confused stains; tiny marks to left in upper part of writing space 16 faded *paragraphus* at line-beginning ̣ ̣ι, first, two tiny marks in diagonal alignment descending from left to right in upper part of writing space and at mid-height respectively; 2 mm farther, scanty remains of upright?; second, tip of triangular letter and remains of left-hand oblique   μ̣., short vertical in upper part of writing space, followed, 1 mm farther on, by two tiny marks, approximately in horizontal alignment, at mid-height   .o, blurred remains of upright bearing scanty remains of top horizontal   .ον, uprights belonging to square letter   .[, three marks in vertical alignment 17 very scanty and faded remains of *paragraphus* at line-beginning   ..ω, first, tiny mark at line-level in diagonal alignment ascending from left to right with mark in upper part of writing space; second, very tiny and blurred traces at mid-height suggesting upright; 1 mm farther, tiny trace at mid-height; third, tiny traces in upper part of writing space suggesting top arc, and in lower part of writing space suggesting upright descending below baseline   c̣., lower part of upright?   18 ..ν, first, curve whose convexity lies at mid-height; very reduced trace 1 mm farther to left, below line-level; second, two marks, respectively in lower and upper part of writing space in diagonal alignment ascending from left to right   19 very faded *paragraphus* at line-beginning   .ν, first, upright slightly slanting to right; second, two blurred marks very close to each other in upper part of writing space suggesting top of round letter   .ϵ, three tiny marks in slightly diagonal alignment ascending from left to right in upper part of writing space   το.[, two tiny marks very close to each other in vertical alignment in upper part of writing space   20 ηπ̅, π̅ overwritten on previously written η   ρο.[, upright protruding below line-level whose tip presents projecting serif to left   21 scanty remains of *paragraphus* at line-beginning   .ι, first, right-hand of oval; second, letter completely missing apart from ligature with following ι   πρ̣., short oblique ascending from left to right in lower part of writing space, whose upper extremity is in vertical alignment with vertical trace lying in upper part of writing space   22 scanty remains of *paragraphus* at line-beginning   ...ϵ, first, diagonal trace ascending from left to right in lower part of writing space, whose top is in vertical alignment with trace in upper part of writing space; second, small left-hand arc; third, mark in lower part of writing space   ϵ.[, remains of upright; on its right, a few very tiny stains at mid-height   23 .[, tiny blurred mark in upper part of writing space   κα̣., faded and tiny mark in upper part of writing space   τ̣.υ, two blurred marks in upper part of writing space, very close to each other   ..[, first, upright descending below baseline whose tip bears two tiny marks; second, right-hand arc   24 [.]., blurred triangular shape with vertex in upper part of writing space and obliques departing from middle of writing space   .ϵτ, remains of left-hand arc   25 faded *paragraphus* at line-beginning πα̣., scanty traces in upper part of writing space, perhaps extremity of descender; further mark above its lower extremity   αδ..., first, upright; 2 mm farther, two marks almost in vertical alignment, lying respectively in upper part of writing space and at line-level, possibly belonging to another upright; second, remains of obliques of triangular letter; third, tiny marks in approximately horizontal alignment at mid-height   ομ.[, very tiny mark in upper part of writing space   26 το.[, tiny marks probably belonging to upper part of upright   27].κυ, stroke approximating a horizontal in upper part of writing space; a mark above its left-hand extremity   .μ, first, two very faded and tiny traces at line-level and in upper part of writing space respectively in diagonal alignment ascending from left to right; second, rather blurred tip of upright?   .[, tiny and faded mark at line-level.

Fr. 2 (col. iii)

top

```
      ‸ι ‸ο‸ο[ ‸]αδιοικεικα[ ‸]τοπαν : ηθικαιδεο
       ‸αιηθ‸[‸]καιγνωμηντουακουοντοςω
      φ‸‸ουϲινοιονπωϲτ‸κναπαι‸ευτεον
      ‸‸ωϲφιλοιϲχρηϲτεον : πραγ‸ατικαιδε
   5  οϲαι‸ρ‸[‸]‸[‸]‸ν[‸]ιδαϲκ‸υϲινοιονειχρη
      πλεινειχρηγ‸μει‸ειχρη‸εωργειν
      τωνθεϲεωναιμενειϲιναπλα[‸]αιδεϲυγ
      κρι‸ικ‸ι : απλαιμεναιζητηϲινπερι
      ‸χου‸αιεν‸ϲμονο‸πραγματοϲοιονει
  10  ]ογωνεπιμελητεον : ϲυγκρ‸τικαιδε
      ]δυοκαιπλειονων‸ραγματωνζητη
      ]υπερ‸εχουϲαιοποτερονκρειττονοι
      ]‸π‸τερονεπιμελητεονοπλωνηλο
      ]‸ν : θε‸εωνμερηζ̄καταφυϲινδικ‸‸
  15  ]‸ϲυμφ‸ροντωβιωβιοϲτουμετερχ‸
      ]ενουδυνατονενδοξον‸υγκριϲι[
      ]‸εκατηγοριααποτωνεναντιωνζ̄γ[
      ]εται
```

———   τεχνηρη

τορικη

1 *paragraphus* at line-beginning partially preserved   ι, very scanty traces in upper and lower part of writing space   ο, first, two marks very close to each other in horizontal alignment, in upper part of writing space; of the two, the right-hand one is almost in vertical alignment with a very tiny trace lying at mid-height; second, remains of upright protruding below baseline   ο[, two traces quite close to each other in slightly diagonal alignment descending from left to right; to right very close to them, upper half of upright   2 α, very tiny mark at line-level   ηθ [, thick trace at mid-height   3 φ , first, very scanty and faded traces in vertical alignment in upper part of writing space; second, oblique ascending from left to right   τ , horizontal trace at mid-height; some very tiny marks to left in upper part of writing space   ευ, two traces in diagonal alignment descending from left to right   4 ω, upright whose tip joins remains of (not entirely preserved) cross-bar to left   πραγ , upright whose tip is attached to partially preserved diagonal stroke descending from left to right   5 αι , upright slightly slanting to right   ρ [, remains of triangular letter (top and parts of obliques)   ] , two marks in vertical alignment in upper part of writing space and at line-level respectively   ν, mark in upper part of writing space   κ υ, tiny curve at mid-height, perhaps part of right-hand arc   6 γ , clear remains of triangular letter (right-hand angle and lower extremity of oblique ascending from left to right)   μει , uprights belonging to square letter; the first one is extremely faded   η ε, horizontal trace at mid-height, touching following ε   7 θεϲεωναι,

[Col. ii lost]

Col. iii

εἰ πρόνο[ι]α διοικεῖ κα[ὶ] τὸ πᾶν. ἠθικαὶ δὲ ὅ-
ϲαι ἦθο[ϲ] καὶ γνώμην τοῦ ἀκούοντος ὠ-
φελοῦϲιν· οἷον πῶϲ τέκνα παιδευτέον,
πῶϲ φίλοιϲ χρηϲτέον. πραγματικαὶ δὲ

5   ὅϲαι πρα[.].[.].ν [δ]ιδάϲκουϲιν· οἷον εἰ χρὴ
πλεῖν, εἰ χρὴ γαμεῖν, εἰ χρὴ γεωργεῖν.
τῶν θέϲεων αἱ μέν εἰϲιν ἁπλα[ῖ], αἱ δὲ ϲυγ-
κριτικαί. ἁπλαῖ μὲν αἱ ζήτηϲιν περιέχουϲαι ἑνὸϲ μόνου πράγματοϲ, οἷον εἰ

10   λ]όγων ἐπιμελητέον. ϲυγκριτικαὶ δὲ
αἱ] δύο καὶ πλειόνων πραγμάτων ζήτη-
ϲι]ν περιέχουϲαι ὁπότερον κρεῖττον, οἷ-
ο]ν πότερον ἐπιμελητέον ὅπλων ἢ λό-
γ]ων. θέϲεων μέρη ζ̄· κατὰ φύϲιν, δίκαι-

15   ο]ν, ϲύμφορον τῷ βίῳ, βίοϲ τοῦ μετερχο-
μ]ένου, δυνατόν, ἔνδοξον, ϲύγκριϲι[ϲ.
ἡ] δὲ κατηγορία ἀπὸ τῶν ἐναντίων ζ̄ γ[ί-
ν]εται.

         τέχνη ῥη-
         τορική

between ν and α very short nearly horizontal trace, probably accidental, since the spacing is too narrow to assume that it belongs to *dicolon*   8 κρι., two marks close to each other in horizontal alignment in upper part of writing space   κ.ι, remains of obliques of triangular letter   9 .χ, very tiny traces in lower part of writing space   ου., short stroke approaching to oblique ascending from left to right in upper part of writing space   .ϲ, vertical trace at mid-height   νο., upright descending below baseline, whose tip bears tiny stains (immediately below baseline in correspondence with this sequence accidental traces)   10 ϲυγκρ., very tiny trace in upper part of writing space   11 ν.ρ, very faded and blurred remains of uprights of square letter   12 περ., mark in upper part of writing space   13]., short upright in upper part of writing space curved leftwards at foot   π., left-hand arc   14]., tiny curve in upper part of writing space, possibly right-hand arc   θε., blurred curve, possibly part of left-hand arc   δικ.., first, remains of obliques of triangular letter; second, scanty remains of upright   15]., lower half of upright with thick lower extremity   φ.ρ, round trace in upper part of writing space   χ., mark in lower part of writing space   16 ου., fibres broken; remains of cross-bar in upper part of writing space?   17 .ε, oblique descending from left to right whose lower extremity is linked to left with another not entirely preserved stroke approaching to horizontal   19 some accidental ink above the left extremity of the *paragraphus* preceding the beginning of the final title

'[*On the one hand*, πρόcωπον is divided into] (col. i:) eight parts: birth, nature, way of life, age, fortune, actions, condition, disposition. For instance, "A son who strikes his father shall have his hand cut off." With regard to birth, [we must consider] whether he is son by adoption or by blood. With regard to nature, whether he/she is male or female. With regard to way of life, whether he is violent in everything or [if he will have his hands cut off] even if he is [otherwise?] moderate. With regard to age, a child or a young man. With regard to fortune, whether he is just a private citizen or [if he will have his hand cut off] even if he is in public office. With regard to actions, if he will have his hand cut off even if he is a hero or a tyrannicide. With regard to condition, [if he will have his hand cut off] even if he is [already] mutilated. With regard to disposition even if he was well disposed from the beginning.

'*On the other hand*, πρᾶγμα is divided into eight parts: character, cause, place, time, manner, the events before the act [the preliminaries], what happened during the act, the events after the act [the consequences]. For instance, with regard to character [we must consider] if also the one who strikes his mother will have his hand cut off. With regard to cause, even if he was mad or drunk. With regard to place, whether in the country or in the market place or in his own house. With regard to time, even if [the act took place] long before or just now. With regard to manner, whether [he beat the father] with his hands or with a wooden stick. With regard to "the events before the act", even if he had been previously insulted or treated with contumely. With regard to "what happened during the act", if it could be the case that he hit him without injuring him. With regard to "the events after the act", even if he [i.e. the father] died because of the beating or if he will have his hand cut off even when the father does not wish this. To sum up, all these points are unclear and obscure. But the [law] that is now being introduced is "illegal" when it is contrary to the laws already enacted; it is "unjust" when . . .

'[*Theseis* are divided into speculative, ethical, and pragmatic. Speculative *theseis* are those whose investigation has as its exclusive aim theoretical knowledge: for instance, whether] (col. iii:) divine providence governs the universe as well. Ethical *theseis* are those that benefit the character and the judgment of the listener: for instance, "how should children be educated?" or "how should friends be treated?" Pragmatic *theseis* are those that teach [practical actions?]: for instance, "whether one should sail", "whether one should get married", "whether one should be a farmer". *Theseis* are divided into simple and comparative. Simple *theseis* are those that involve the investigation of a single action: for instance, "whether one should devote oneself to the art of speaking". Comparative *theseis* are those that involve the investigation of two or more actions [in order to establish] which option is better: for instance, "whether one should devote oneself to the art of war or to the art of speaking". The parts of *theseis* are seven: the "according to nature", the just, the expedient for life, the life of the person who puts it into practice, the possible, the honorable, the comparison. The *refutatio* consists of the seven *contraria*.

'HANDBOOK OF RHETORIC'

Col. i

1–25 Subdivision of the πρόcωπον and the πρᾶγμα in eight parts, applied in the case of the law that a father-beater should be punished by having his hand cut off (see introd.).

1–10 Subdivision of the πρόcωπον. The contrast with πρᾶγμα (in 11) and the parallel passages quoted in 1–2 n., show that πρόcωπον must be the subject. Thus η̄ represents the end of a clause of the form τὸ μὲν πρόcωπον διαιρεῖται εἰc μέρη] η̄, corresponding with 10–11.

1–2 These eight subdivisions of the πρόcωπον may be compared to similar lists by other authors in the following table (relevant examples taken from respective texts are written in smaller letters). The table is intended to illustrate the complex of parallel passages, without trying to establish doctrinal or chronological relations among the various authors.

4855	Herm. *Stas.* p. 46.14–18, τὰ ἐγκωμιαστικὰ	Theon, *Prog.* p. 39. 25–7 (= p. 78.25–7) περὶ διηγήματος	Aphth. *Prog.* p. 22. 2–9, περὶ ἐγκωμίου	Rufus, περὶ ἀποδείξεως[a] p. 281 §28
γένος θετὸς ἢ γνήσιος	γένος	γένος	γένος: 1. ἔθνος 2. πατρίς 3. πρόγονοι 4. πατέρες	γένος
φύσις ἄρρην ἢ θήλεια	ἀγωγή	φύσις	ἀνατροφή: 1. ἐπιτηδεύματα 2. τέχνη 3. νόμοι	φύσις
ἀγωγή ὑβριστὴς ἢ μέτριος	παίδευσις	ἀγωγή	πράξεις (= τὸ μέγιστον τῶν ἐγκωμίων κεφάλαιον): 1. ψυχή· ἀνδρεία ἢ φρόνησις 2. σῶμα· κάλλος ἢ τάχος ἢ ῥώμη 3. τύχη· δυναστεία, πλοῦτος, φίλοι	ἀγωγή
ἡλικία παῖς ἢ μειράκιον	ἡλικία	διάθεσις		τύχη
τύχη ἰδιώτης ἢ ἄρχων	φύσις ψυχῆς καὶ σώματος	ἡλικία		ἐπιτηδεύματα
πράξεις ἀριστεὺς ἢ τυραννοκτόνος	ἐπιτηδεύματα	τύχη		πράξεις
πάθος πεπηρωμένος	πράξεις, ὃ καὶ ἰσχυρότατον κεφάλαιον	προαίρεσις		διαθέσεις
διάθεσις εὔνους	τύχη πλούσιος, πένης καὶ τὰ τοιαῦτα	πρᾶξις		
		λόγος θάνατος τὰ μετὰ θάνατον		

[a] = *RG* 3, p. 455.11–13 = Spengel, p. 404.19–21. Rufus, ibid. points out that this subdivision belongs to ἐγκώμια.

Cic. *Inv.* 1.34–36 (cf. 2.28–37)	Quint. 5.10.23–31	Consultus Fortunatianus *Ars Rhetorica* 2.1 (pp. 107.8–108.12)	Sulpicius Victor p. 326.4–5	Iulius Victor p. 395.30–31
NOMEN	GENUS	NOMEN Papirius, Turbo	GENUS	PATRIA
NATURA genus: divinus an humanus sexus: virile an muliebre natio: Graius an barbarus patria: Atheniensis an Lacedaemonius cognatio: quibus maioribus, quibus consanguineis aetas: puer an adulescens commoda/incommoda animi/corporis: valens an imbecillus, longus an brevis, formosus an deformis, velox an tardus, acutus an hebetior, memor an obliviosus, comis an infacetus, pudens, patiens an contra	NATIO barbarus, Romanus, Graecus	NATIO Graecus, barbarus	NATURA	NOMEN
	PATRIA	PATRIA Atheniensis, Lacedaemonius	AETAS	GENUS
	SEXUS	GENUS vel COGNATIO nobilis, ignobilis	DISCIPLINA	CORPORIS HABITUDO
	AETAS	DIGNITAS vir fortis, magistratus	FORTUNA	MORES
	EDUCATIO et DISCIPLINA	FORTUNA dives, pauper	STUDIA	VITA
	HABITUS CORPORIS species libidinis, robur petulantiae	SEXUS masculus, femina	NOMEN	AMICI

Cic. *Inv.* 1.34–36 (cf. 2.28–37)	Quint. 5.10.23–31	Consultus Fortunatianus *Ars Rhetorica* 2.1 (pp. 107.8–108.12)	Sulpicius Victor p. 326.4–5	Iulius Victor p. 395.30–31
	FORTUNA dives, pauper, propinquus amicis, clientibus abundans	AETAS senex, puer	ANTE FACTA	AETAS
VICTUS apud quem et quo more et cuius arbitratu sit educatus, quos habuerit artium liberalium magistros, quos vivendi praeceptores, quibus amicis utatur, quo in negotio, quaestu, artificio sit occupatus, quo modo rem familiarem administret, qua consuetudine domestica sit	CONDICIONIS DISTANTIA clarus an obscurus, magistratus an privatus, pater an filius, civis an peregrinus, liber an servus, maritus an caelebs, parens liberorum an orbus sit	CORPUS validus, longus	HABITUS	INCESSUS
FORTUNA servus an liber, pecuniosus an tenuis, privatus an cum potestate	ANIMI NATURA avaritia, iracundia, misericordia, crudelitas, severitas victus luxuriosus an frugi an sordidus	INSTITUTIO vel EDUCATIO		VULTUS
HABITUS	STUDIA rusticus, forensis, negotiator, miles, navigator, medicus	MORES frugi, luxuriosus, patiens, impatiens		
AFFECTIO laetitia, cupiditas, metus, molestia, morbus, debilitas	QUID AFFECTET QUISQUE locuples an disertus, iustus an potens	VICTUS quibus amicis, ut bonae frugi luxuriosis, quomodo rem suam administret, qua consuetudine domestica sit		

Cic. *Inv.* 1.34–36 (cf. 2.28–37)	Quint. 5.10.23–31	Consultus Fortunatianus *Ars Rhetorica* 2.1 (pp. 107.8–108.12)	Sulpicius Victor p. 326.4–5	Iulius Victor p. 395.30–31
STUDIA	ANTE ACTA DICTAQUE	ADFECTIO equorum armorum canum		
CONSILIA	COMMOTIO ira, pavor	ARS vel STUDIUM medicus, orator		
FACTA	CONSILIA et praeteriti et praesentis et futuri temporis	CONDICIO servus, addictus		
CASUS	NOMEN (this represents an argument only in specific cases)	CONDICIO ALIA quae liberos spectat adoptivus, abdicatus		
ORATIONES		EFFECTUS nupta, vidua		
		HABITUS nitidus, sordidus, obscurus		
		VULTUS laetus, tristis		
		INCESSUS citus, tardus		
		ORATIO gravis, seditiosa		
		ADFECTUS laetitia, ira, morbus, debilitas		

The variety of the tradition in terms of number and order of items and ways of classification is certainly due to the fact that all the *adtributa* of the person (except the *nomen*, which is an accident) belong to the *qualitas*, on the basis of which a *persona* may be considered in an infinite number of aspects; see [Aug.] p. 141.24–9: *Quis significantiam habet personae, quae spectatur duobus modis, ex nomine et qualitate [. . .]. Est autem definita in nominibus, infinita in qualitatibus personarum perspectio, quando in appellationem nihil praeter nomen cadit, in qualitatem et fortuna et aetas et condicio et disciplina et cetera quae sunt infinita numero.* As emerges from the comparative table, there is a close similarity between the subdivision of the πρόϲωπον that is suitable for the judicial genre and that used in the encomiastic genre; cf. H. Lausberg, *Handbuch der literarischen Rhetorik* (Stuttgart 1990³) 205, §376, and L. Pernot, *La Rhétorique de l'éloge dans le monde gréco-romain* i (Paris 1993) 141 n. 60.

1–2 τύχ[ην, πρά]|ξεις. The restoration (compatible with the preserved traces) is suggested by the passages in the table in i 1–2 n.

2–3 ὁ πατροτύπ[της χειρο]|κοπείσθω. This 'law' is quoted, in very similar context, by Theon, p. 97.30–98.36 (= p. 130.30–6): ἡ δὲ παρ' ἔλλειψιν ἀσάφεια γίνεται πολλαχῶς· ⌐ἢ κατὰ αἰτίαν ἢ κατὰ πρόσωπον ἢ κατὰ ἀνάγκην ἢ ἐν τρόπῳ ἢ κατὰ τόπον ἢ κατὰ καιρὸν ἢ κατὰ ποιότητα ἢ κατὰ ποσότητα. κατὰ αἰτίαν┘, οἷον, ὁ πατροτύπτης χειροκοπείσθω· ἐλλείπει γὰρ πότερον καὶ τὸν δι' ἄγνοιαν, ἢ καὶ τὸν ἐπ' εὐνοίᾳ καὶ πάντας ἁπαξαπλῶς. It is alluded to by Heracl. *Alleg. Hom.* 18.7. For a 'case' based on it, see Syriani, Sopatri et Marcellini, *Scholia ad Hermog. Status, RG* 4, pp. 467.29–468.5: οἷον τύραννος ἀνέσπασε τρεῖς παῖδας· τῷ πρώτῳ τὸν πατέρα τυπῆσαι προσέταξεν, οὐ τυπτήσαντα ἀπέκτεινε, καὶ τὸν δεύτερον ὁμοίως· ὁ τρίτος ὑπήκουσεν, ἐσώθη, μετὰ τὴν τῆς τυραννίδος κατάλυσιν κινδυνεύει περὶ τῶν χειρῶν, τοῦτο γὰρ ὁ νόμος ἐκέλευσε· ἐνταῦθα καὶ ἀνθρώπινον προβάλλεται τὸν φόβον· λέγει μέντοι ὁ κατήγορος, ἐχρῆν ἀποθανεῖν μᾶλλον ἢ τυπτῆσαι τὸν πατέρα· ἐν δὲ τῷ ἀπὸ γνώμης στοχασμῷ τοὐναντίον· ὁ γὰρ διώκων προσποιήσασθαί φησι τὸν φεύγοντα μανίαν . . . For Latin declamations based on it, see Sen. *Contr.* 9.4 and [Quint.] *Decl. Min.* 358, 362, 372; cf. also Consultus Fortunatianus, *Ars Rhetorica* I.26, p. 102, and Grillius, *Commentum in Ciceronis rhetoricam*, in J. Martin, *Grillius: Ein Beitrag zur Geschichte der Rhetorik* (Paderborn 1927) p. 76.27 (see 14–15 n.). Of course, ancient morality condemned the πατραλοίας, but we have no actual evidence that such a law existed in historical times; see L. Calboli-Montefusco's note on the passage by Consultus Fortunatianus in her critical edition, p. 336, and S. E. Bonner, *Roman Declamation in the Late Republic and Early Empire* (Liverpool 1949) 96–7, who points out that this law is found outside the Graeco-Roman world in the Code of Hammurabi; see G. R. Driver, J. C. Miles, *The Babylonian Laws* ii (Oxford 1955) 77, §195, and cf. N. Dunbar, *Aristophanes: Birds* (Oxford 1995) on vv. 757–9 and vv. 1337–71.

3 ff. The list is presented in note-form. The accusatives are in apposition to the prefatory μέρη] | ῃ̄, largely missing but restorable from line 10. The details that might be used in arguing the case, sometimes introduced by πότερον '[we must consider] whether', sometimes by κἂν '[we must consider whether he will have his hand cut off] even if / if, as it might be'. Usually this introduces some extenuating circumstance, but in i 22–3 apparently a feature that makes the offense even more disgraceful.

3–4 γνή]|cιος. The restoration has palaeographical support, since the traces at the beginning of 4, although scanty, perfectly fit the required letters. For γνήcιος as the opposite of θετός, see e.g. Philo Judaeus, *De congressu eruditionis gratia* 23.3–4: . . . οἱ θετοὶ παῖδες . . . τοῖς γνηcίοις (*sc.* ἰcοῦνται); idem, *De mutatione nominum* 147.5–6; Arrian, *Bith.* fr. 20.24–9. For the theme of adoption, see Theon p. 98. 36–40 (= p. 130.36–40), which concerns, like our passage, the analysis of a law: ἡ δὲ κατὰ πρόσωπον ἔλλειψις πολυειδής ἐστι· διαφέρει γὰρ δήπου τὰ πρόσωπα καὶ φύσει καὶ ἡλικίᾳ καὶ ταῖς ἐγγυτέρω cυγγενείαις καὶ τύχῃ. οἷον· τῷ προδότῃ cυναναιρεῖσθαι τοὺς παῖδας· οὐ γὰρ διώρισεν ⌐βεβαίως┘, εἰ καὶ τὸν θετὸν καὶ τὴν θήλειαν. Cf. Consultus Fortunatianus, *Ars Rhetorica* 2.1.8 (in the comparative table in i 1–2 n.) *condicione, ut servus, addictus; condicione alia, quae liberos spectat, ut adoptivus abdicatus.* Note also [Quint.] *Decl. Min.* 358 and 372, where *expositi* beat their adoptive fathers, who then claim the same right as the natural fathers to cut off their hand.

5 κἂν [. This is *crasis* for καὶ ἐάν, 'even if / if, as it might be'. The verb is usually omitted in this list, apart from i 8 and 23. The words introduces a case that (all else apart) must be reckoned with. Discussion of the use of κἂν in KG I 244 f., §398 A2, Blass–Debrunner–Rehkopf, *Grammatik des neutestamentlichen Griechisch*[17] §374, A. W. Gomme, F. H. Sandbach, *Menander: A Commentary* (London 1973) 444. Comparable use in Herm. *Stas.* p. 34.12–14: θαυμάζω γάρ, εἴ τις αὐτῆς καταψηφιεῖται, κἂν ἐλεγχθῇ μεμοιχευμένη, δι' ἣν ὁ τύραννος ἀνήρηται.

5–6 We expect here an expression parallel to ὑβριcτὴς τὰ πάντα, since the meaning must be that the accused normally behaves decently and therefore an occasional lapse—i.e. the beating inflicted on the father—deserves leniency. Three possible supplements that suit the space available between the two lines and the sense are: [τὰ πάν]|[τ]ᾳ or [τὰ ἄλ]|[λ]ᾳ / [τἆλ]|[λ]ᾳ or [τὰ πολ]|[λ]ᾴ.

The traces at the beginning of 6 are rather scanty and uncertain, but not incompatible with the required α. For the sense compare Anon. in Arist. *Rh.* p. 77, [b 15] 21–23: μηδὲ ποῖός τις νῦν ἤτοι ὁ λειποτάκτης νῦν ἐστιν, οὐ δεῖ ὁρᾶν, ἀλλὰ ποῖός τις αἰεί, ἤγουν ἠρίστευεν ὡς ἐπὶ τὸ πολὺ καὶ διὰ τοῦτο ϲυγγνωμονητέον αὐτῷ.

6 παῖϲ ἢ μ⟨ε⟩ιράκιο[ν: cf. Sen. *Contr.* 9.4.9.8–9: *quid opus est caveri lege, ne puniatur infans, si pulsaverit patrem?* Age is also considered by Theon in the analysis of the law according to which the sons of the traitor should be executed together with him (quoted in i 3–4 n.), in the part preserved only in the Armenian translation of his *Progymnasmata* of the late sixth-early seventh century (Patillon–Bolognesi, p. 99).

The supplement at the end, consisting of three letters only, is suitable for the space, since the pause after μ⟨ε⟩ιράκιο[ν would have been marked by a *dicolon* preceded and followed by a blank space (cf. i 6, 9–10, and 17–18 nn.).

7 The examples illustrating the heading τύχη may be compared with those of the lists in i 1–2 n., in particular with the fourth heading of Cicero's list, FORTUNA, where the example *privatus an cum potestate* occurs. Consultus Fortunatianus offers a similar example—*vir fortis, magistratus*—under the heading DIGNITAS. For the supplement at line-end in relation to the space, I take into account the blank space following the *dicolon* (see i 6, 9–10, and 17–18 nn.).

8 ἀριϲτ[εύϲ is compatible with the traces, and the restoration is supported by parallel passages where the ἀριϲτεύϲ appears associated with the τυραννοκτόνοϲ, or even identified with him: Theon p. 62.9–10 (= p. 106.9–10): περὶ τόπου· . . . ὁ δέ τιϲ [*sc.* τόποϲ] ὑπὲρ τῶν χρηϲτόν τι διαπεπραγμένων, οἷον ὑπὲρ **τυραννοκτόνου**, **ἀριϲτέωϲ**, νομοθέτου; [Herm.] *Inv.* 1, p. 98.5–6; Lib. *Decl.* xliii (vol. vii, pp. 437–74), pp. 440.21–441.1; cf. also Plut. *Adversus Colotem*, 1126 e.19–25.

Given the association/identification of ἀριϲτεύϲ and τυραννοκτόνοϲ we could supply καὶ instead of ἤ at the end of the line.

9 τυραννοκτόνοϲ. The τυραννοκτόνοϲ is one of the most popular types in rhetorical texts: see, for instance, Luc. *Tyr.*, and Lib. vol. viii, pp. 203–8 (here as an example for the *progymnasma* κοινὸϲ τόποϲ); cf. D. A. Russell, *Greek Declamations* (Cambridge 1983) 32–3. Parallels for our passage are found in Sen. *Contr.* 9.4: *tyrannus patrem in arcem cum duobus filiis accersit; imperavit adulescentibus, ut patrem caederent. alter ex his praecipitavit se, alter cecidit. postea in amicitiam tyranni receptus occiso tyranno praemium accepit. petuntur manus eius; pater defendit.* See in particular 9.4.1.10 *praecidetis tyrannicidae manus?* and 9.4.11.25–28 *an tutus sit qui pro patria fecit; an hic pro patria fecerit, id est, an illo iam tempore cogitationem tyrannicidi habuerit et hoc animo ceciderit, ut aditum sibi faceret ad amicitiam tyranni.* The elimination of the tyrant is frequently alleged as a reason for leniency or some other privilege, as in the following texts: Herm. *Stas.* p. 34.8–14, pp. 59.18–60.4; Lib. *Decl.* xliii (see i 8 n.); cf. comparable passages listed in Heath, *Hermogenes*, 103–4.

9–10 πεπηρ[ωμέ]|νοϲ. The supplement, consisting only of three letters, at first glance seems too short. However, we have allowed for the possible enlargement of letters at line-end and their wider spacing; see above introd. Note iii 10, where the final ε remarkably extends its central stroke to maintain an even right edge to the column.

In this context, the participle means 'maimed'. The application of the law is considered under the subdivision πάθοϲ in relation to the actual physical condition of the person; the question is whether the hand should be cut off if the person already has a physical defect, i.e. a mutilation. In other words, a previous mutilation seems to represent a possible reason for leniency. The application *tout court* of a law is discussed in relation to the physical condition of the accused in Theon *Prog.*, περὶ νόμου, in the part preserved only in the Armenian translation (Patillon–Bolognesi, p. 100). Here, the law that the adulterer shall be deprived of his sight is questioned on the basis of the heading δυνατόν (see i 24–7 ff. n.) by hypothesizing a case where the adulterer is actually a person who is already blind and therefore cannot be punished in the way prescribed by the law. πάθοϲ does not appear as such in the other Greek lists in the table above (i 1–2 n.); it corresponds to Latin *affectio* or *affectus*, where the examples given include *morbus* and *debilitas*, but not physical mutilation. However, although I translate πεπηρωμένοc as 'mutilated', the verb can in fact refer to various kinds of disability, including blindness (e.g. Sopater, *RG* 8, p. 317.11–13).

For the supplement at the end of 10 I take into account the space required for an original *dicolon* (cf. i 6, 7, and 17–18 nn.).

11–24 List and illustration of the eight subdivisions of πρᾶγμα. The extant works of Greek and Latin rhetorical theory offer treatments of this subject under the heading μόρια περιcτάcεωc, *partes circumstantiae* (often outlining the distinction between περίcταcιc and θέcιc, cf. introd.). The different classifications found in the tradition are illustrated in the following comparative table (cf. Leff, 'The Topics of Argumentative Invention', 23–44).

4855	Herm. *Stas.* pp. 45.22–46.2	[Herm.] *Inv.* pp. 140.16–141.1	Theon, *Prog.* περὶ μύθου, p. 37.13–14 (= p. 77.13–14); cf. περὶ διηγήματοc, p. 38.18–21 (= p. 78. 18–21)	Syr. *in Hermogen. Commentaria* 2, p. 39.19–20
πρόcωπον	πρόcωπον	τόποc	πρόcωπον	πρόcωπον
αἰτία	πρᾶγμα	χρόνοc	πρᾶγμα	πρᾶγμα
τόποc	τόποc	τρόποc	τόποc	τόποc
χρόνοc	τρόποc	πρόcωπον	χρόνοc	χρόνοc
τρόποc	χρόνοc	αἰτία	τρόποc	αἰτία
τὰ πρὸ τοῦ πράγματοc	αἰτία	πρᾶγμα	αἰτία	τρόποc
τὰ ἐν τῷ πράγματι		ὕλη (additional sub-division added by the philosophers)	τι τῶν τοιούτων	
τὰ μετὰ τὸ πρᾶγμα			Cf. the last three items of the list of 28 τόποι for the analysis of the θέcιc (p. 86.24–6 = p. 122.24–6; see iii 14 ff. n.) 26. ἐκ τῶν πρὸ τοῦ πράγματοc 27. ἐκ τῶν παρ' αὐτὸ τὸ πρᾶγμα 28. ἐκ τῶν μετὰ τὸ πρᾶγμα	

Quint. 3.6. 25–27[a]	Consultus Fortunatianus, *Ars Rhetorica* 2.23 (= pp. 130.6–131.10)	Iulius Victor p. 395.24–28	Martianus Capella 5.557–8
persona	ante rem: a persona a re a causa a tempore a loco a modo a materia	loci qui rem praecedunt: persona causa tempus locus materia modus sive ratio	ante rem: a persona a re a causa a tempore a loco a modo a materia
tempus (Gr. χρόνος)	in re: a toto a parte a genere a specie a differentia per septem circumstantias a proprio a definitione a nomine a multiplici appellatione ab initio a progressione vel profectu a perfectione vel consummatione	loci qui in re ipsa sunt: a toto a parte a genere a specie a differentia a proprio a definitione a nomine	in re: a toto a parte a genere ab specie a differentia per septem circumstantias a proprio a definitione a nomine a multiplici appellatione ab initio a progressione vel profectu a perfectione vel consummatione
locus	circa rem: a simili (exemplum, similitudo, fabula, imago, exemplum verisimile; apologi is added by several people) a dissimili a pari a contrario per positionem et negationem ἀπὸ τοῦ πρός τι ab inter se collidentibus per habitionem et amissionem a maiore ad minus a minore ad maius a precedenti ab eo quod simul est vel a coniunctis vel a consequentibus	loci qui circa rem sunt: a simili a dissimili a pari a contrario a maiore a minore a praecedente ab eo, quod simul est a consequente	circa rem: a simili (exemplum, similitudo, fabula, imago, veri simile; apologi is added by several people) a dissimili a pari a contrario per positionem et negationem ad aliquid ab inter se collidentibus per habitionem et amissionem a maiore ad minus a minore ad maius a praecedenti ab eo quod simul est vel a coniunctis a consequentibus

Quint. 3.6. 25–27[a]	Consultus Fortunatianus, *Ars Rhetorica* 2.23 (= pp. 130.6–131.10)	Iulius Victor p. 395.24–28	Martianus Capella 5.557–8
tempus iterum (Gr. καιρός)	post rem: ab eventu a iudicato	loci qui post rem sunt: ab eventu a iudicatis	post rem: ab eventu a iudicato
actum (Gr. πρᾶξις)			
numerus			
causa			
modus (Gr. τρόπος)			
occasio factorum (Gr. ἀφορμὰς ἔργων, cf. ὕλη)			

[a] Greek equivalents are to be found in Quintilian's text.

The final expression of Theon's list, τι τῶν τοιούτων (together with the definition of the same list given at p. 38.21–2 (= p. 78.21–2) τούτων δὲ ὄντων τῶν ἀνωτάτω cτοιχείων) suggests an open list, without a strictly determined number of items.

12–14 The three final subdivisions may be compared with the last three of the 28 τόποι on the basis of which the θέcιc-exercise is developed in Theon (p. 86.24–6 = p. 122.24–6); see table above.

14–15 ὁ τὴν μη[τέρα]|τυπτήcαc. If the supplement is correct, the text would pose the case 'whether [the son] who strikes his mother, as well as [the son who strikes his father], would have the hand cut off', in other words whether the formulation of the law with the masculine victim is to be applied in the same terms to the other parent. See Consultus Fortunatianus, *Ars Rhetorica* 1.26, p. 102: *A simili quem ad modum? ut 'qui patrem pulsaverit, manus perdat: matrem pulsavit et petitur ad poenam'*. Note that here the law is mentioned as an example to illustrate the *modus a simili* of the *status collectivus, status* that consists of making a syllogism for what is unwritten on the basis of what is written, so that the unwritten can be considered as if it had been written; in very similar context and wording the law is treated by Grillius, *Comm. in Cic. rhet.* p.76.25–8. One cannot help recalling the end of Aristoph. *Nu.* (vv. 1321–1510), focused on both father- und mother-beating, effectively summarized by the *scholia* by Tzetzes (*Schol. in Aristoph.*, ed. W. J. W. Koster and others, iv.2 372, col. 2.18 ff.: καὶ ἀντιλέγων ἐκείνῳ ἱκανῶc ἐπατροτυπτήθη, ἀπεδείκνυ δὲ Φειδιππίδηc, ὅτι καὶ δίκαιόν ἐcτι παρὰ τῶν υἱῶν τὸν πατέρα τύπτεcθαι, προcεπιτούτοιc δὲ καὶ τὴν μητέρα δικαίωc ἔλεγε τύψαι πρὸc παρηγόρημα τοῦ πατρόc, ἀγανακτήcαc ὁ γέρων μετὰ τῶν cὺν αὐτῷ ὁμοῦ πιμπρᾷ καὶ καταβάλλει δικέλλαιc τὸ cωκρατικὸν φροντιcτήριον). Only here violence against one's mother is presented as a worse crime than against one's father (see v. 1444 by poor Strepsiades), while in all other attestations mother- and father-beating seem to share the same degree of criminality (see: Aristoph. *Ra.* 149–150; Pl. *Grg.* 456d, *Phd.* 114a; Lys. x 8; Aesch. i 28.3–4); but cf. K. J. Dover, *Aristophanes: Clouds* (Oxford 1968) on vv. 1443–4, who states that Pl. *Lg.* 881b μητραλοῖαί τε καὶ τῶν ἄλλων γεννητόρων ἀνόσιοι πληγῶν τόλμαι provides some support to Strepsiades' statement.

15–16 αἰτ̣[ίαν κἂν]‖ μαινόμενος ἢ μεθύων. Abnormal mental conditions and/or drunkenness are presented as cause and/or as reason for leniency in a number of passages: Theon p. 98.33–6 (= p. 130.33–6), in relation to the law of the father-beater: ⌜κατὰ αἰτίαν, οἷον· ὁ πατροτύπτης χειροκοπείσθω· ἐλλείπει γὰρ πότερον καὶ τὸν δι' ἄγνοιαν, ἢ καὶ τὸν ἐπ' εὐνοίᾳ καὶ πάντας ἀπαξαπλῶς; cf. the example used by Herm. *Stas.* p. 58.19–21 to illustrate the στοχασμὸς ἀπὸ γνώμης (= conjecture based on intention): . . . οἷον ἐν δόξῃ μανίας μητρυιὰ τὸν μὲν υἱὸν ἔτρωσε, τὸν δὲ πρόγονον ἀπέκτεινε, καὶ ἀνενεγκοῦσα φεύγει φόνου. See also Sopater, *RG* 5, pp. 145.30–146.7: ζητεῖται δὲ, τί διαφέρει ὁ ἀπὸ γνώμης στοχασμὸς συγγνώμης· εἰ γὰρ εἰς μίαν ἀναφέρει, ἴσμεν δὲ ὅτι καὶ ἡ μανία συγγνώμην ποιεῖ, ὡς ὁ ἐν μανίᾳ τὸν πατέρα τυπτήσας καὶ ἀνενεγκὼν καὶ κρινόμενος, τί διοίσει; ἐροῦμεν, ὅτι ἐν συγγνώμῃ ὁμολογούμενόν ἐστι τὸ πάθος, ἐφ' ὃ ἀναφέρει τὴν αἰτίαν, ἐν δὲ στοχασμῷ αὐτὸ τοῦτο ζητεῖται, εἰ ἐμαίνετο, καὶ ἔστι τοῦτο ἀμφίβολον καὶ κατασκευῆς δεόμενον, ὅτι μόνους ὁ τεχνικὸς οἶδεν στοχασμούς; Sen. *Contr.* 9.4.9; [Quint.] *Decl. Min.* 372. 8; Quint. 5.10.34; Sulpicius Victor, *Inst. Or.* pp. 348.37–349.3.

Of course, such conditions could be used in mitigation in actual law-cases. See for example Dem. xxi 38: πρῶτον μὲν γὰρ ὁ τὸν θεσμοθέτην πατάξας **τρεῖς εἶχεν προφάσεις, μέθην, ἔρωτα, ἄγνοιαν** διὰ τὸ σκότους καὶ νυκτὸς τὸ πρᾶγμα γενέσθαι; cf. 73–4, 180; idem, liv 25. This recalls also cases of New Comedy, where for example a similar argument is used in defence of rape in Ter. *Ad.* 470–71: *persuasit nox, amor, vinum, adulescentia, / humanumst . . .*

16–17 π̣[ότερον. The traces suggest an upright. Palaeographically, κ̣[ἂν ἤ would be equally possible. The spacing at the line-end does not decide between the two. There would be a difference of meaning, since πότερον seems to introduce neutrally a list of circumstances whereas κἂν emphasizes that the circumstances are exceptional.

The general sense seems to be that the gravity of the crime of father-beating varies with the place where it took place. If it took place in the ἀγορά, it implies a public humiliation and therefore may be considered particularly serious. If it took place ἐπ' ἰδίας οἰκίας, it is no less serious because it represents an act of ὕβρις against the authority of the *pater familias* perpetrated in his own home. From a general point of view, this interpretation seems to be compatible with the theoretical treatments of this subject, found, for example, in Cic. *Inv.* 1.38: *locus consideratur, in quo res gesta sit, ex opportunitate, quam videatur habuisse negotium administrandum; ea autem opportunitas quaeritur ex magnitudine, intervallo, longinquitate, propinquitate, solitudine, celebritate, natura ipsius loci et vicinitatis et totius regionis; ex his etiam attributionibus: sacer an profanus, publicus anne privatus, alienus an ipsius, de quo agitur, locus sit aut fuerit*; cf. Quint. 3.6.25: *locum, unde controversia videtur, an fas fuerit tyrannum in templo occidere, an exulaverit qui domi latuit* (cf. Lausberg, *Handbuch* §382).

17 ἀγρῷ. The traces seem to fit the base of an ᴀ whose shape is similar to the ᴀs in i 24 παράνομο[ϲ; the traces of the second letter clearly suggest ᴦ; the traces of the third character could belong to the head of ᴘ.

If the reading is right, we could interpret it in the context suggested above: if the beating took place in the isolation of the countryside, away from society (cf. Cicero's *solitudine* in the passage quoted in the previous note), it could be reckoned less serious. I have also considered ναῷ (or atticistic νεῷ), cf. Quintilian's *in templo* (passage quoted in the previous note), and [Quint.] *Decl. Min.* 265 pr 3, 103. In that case, all three items would represent circumstances that make the act more criminal. However, the trace before ω does not seem to suit ᴀ or even ᴇ.

17–18 [χρό]‖ν̣ον. For the supplement at line-end, I take into account that the *dicolon* after οἰκίας would have been followed by a blank space (see i 6, 7, and 9–10 nn.).

[χρό]‖ν̣ον κἂν πρὸ πολλοῦ ἢ παραχρῆμα. The fact that a long time (πρὸ πολλοῦ) has passed since the event had taken place may represent a plausible argument for leniency. Compare Herm. *Stas.*

p. 44.9–11, a case of exception (παραγραφικόν) in relation to time: ἢ κατὰ χρόνον, οἷον δειλοῦ παῖς ἠρίστευσε, καὶ μοιχείας κρίνει τὴν γυναῖκα· τοσούτοις γάρ φησιν ὕστερον χρόνοις μὴ δεῖν κρίνεσθαι.

18–19 According to the list in 12 one is tempted to restore τρόπον πότε]‖ρον, but the space at the end of 18 is not enough, taking into consideration the fact that the *dicolon* should be placed before τρόπον, preceded and followed by a short blank (see i 6 n.). Then one should conclude that τρόπον was accidentally omitted, as the corrected omisson of κακῶς in 20. See Antipho, *Tetr.* 3.2.2, where the accused claims to have defended himself from the attack by the person whom eventually he killed using the same instrument, i.e. the hands: τὸν γὰρ ἄρξαντα τῆς πληγῆς, εἰ μὲν σιδήρῳ ἢ λίθῳ ἢ ξύλῳ ἠμυνάμην αὐτόν, ἠδίκουν μὲν οὐδ᾽ οὕτως — οὐ γὰρ ταὐτὰ ἀλλὰ μείζονα καὶ πλείονα δίκαιοι οἱ ἄρχοντες ἀντιπάσχειν εἰσί — ταῖς δὲ χερσὶ τυπτόμενος ὑπ᾽ αὐτοῦ, ταῖς χερσὶν ἅπερ ἔπασχον ἀντιδρῶν, πότερα ἠδίκουν; Cf. also Luc. *Tyr.* 11.7–10: ἐπεὶ κἀκεῖνο προσεξετάσειν μοι δοκεῖς καὶ συκοφαντήσειν τοὺς εὐεργέτας, εἴ τις μὴ ξίφει, ἀλλὰ λίθῳ ἢ ξύλῳ ἢ ἄλλῳ τῳ τρόπῳ ἀπέκτεινεν.

20–21 προϋ[βρις]‖θείς. The traces after προ fit ϒ, and I print e.g. the supplement προϋ[βρις]‖θείς (the syllabic division between c and θ is the more common usage; see Mayser, *Grammatik* i.1, 222). However, according to a TLG search, this verb is attested only three times: Photius, *Fragmenta in epistulam ad Romanos* 524.32, Eust. *Comm. ad Homeri Iliadem* vol. iii, p. 917.20, and *Scholia in Theocritum* V 120b.3 (p. 181 Wendel). Alternatively the traces can fit two other different letters, so that two other supplements can be proposed. (1) Since the traces of the protrusion of the upright below the baseline are very faded, they may be considered just accidental ink, so that the upright would be shorter and might fit π. We may think of προπ[ηλακις]‖θείς, which follows the usual division into syllables, but it is perhaps too long for the space. (2) The traces can fit a τ. If so, the supplement προτ[υφ]‖θείς may suit the sense: it would indicate a physical offence by contrast with the preceding προακούσας, which indicates a verbal insult. The simple verb also occurs in 21. However, three objections may be raised. (*a*) The supplement does not follow the usual division into syllables (see Mayser, *Grammatik* i.1, 221–2). (*b*) It seems to be too short, although we can assume an enlargement of the letters at line-end and wider spaces left between individual letters (cf. introd.). (*c*) This aorist form of προτύπτω, although attested, is much rarer than the classical form προτυπείς.

21 After πράγματι an erroneous *dicolon* occurs.

21–2 εἰ τύπτ[ων μὴ τρώ]‖ςειε. The use of the optative here, although unexpected, suggests that the possibility is presented as less real than those given by the recurrent κἄν with the subjunctive.

22–3 ἐκ [τῶν]‖ π[λ]ηγῶν ἀποθάνῃ. At the end of 22, the supplement consists of three letters only, but it is certainly acceptable, if we assume an enlarged final ν as in iii 3 and 6. An interesting treatment of death caused by beating is found in Antipho, *Tetr.* 3.2.3–6 and 3.3.2–4.

23 ⟨ἢ⟩ εἰ. The whole sense of the sentence seems to require the insertion of ἢ, which must have been omitted by haplography after the preceding η.

23–4 τοῦ πατρὸ[ς μὴ βου]‖λ[ο]μένου. Compare Sen. *Contr.* 9.4, a case in which the father defends the son who beat him following the tyrant's order (*petuntur manus eius; pater defendit*). A tyrant orders two brothers to beat their father: one of them commits suicide in order to avoid parricide; the other follows the tyrant's order and beats his father; after that he becomes a friend of the tyrant, organizes a plot against him, and kills him. The father defends his son saying that he himself gave him the order to beat: in fact, by beating him, the son became close to the tyrant and able to kill him, i.e. to rise to the role of 'tyrannicide'. See in particular 9.6.1–3: *quoniam usque eo saeculum mutatum est, ut parricidae pater adsit, nos istius advocationi adsumus? defendit quamvis nocentem. ecquid agnoscitis indulgentiam?*

24–7 From these lines it clearly emerges that the analysis of πρόσωπον and πρᾶγμα in col. i is an example of the progymnasmatic exercise called νόμου εἰσφορά. The expression ὁ νῦν εἰσηγούμενος—as explained in detail in i 26 f. n.—is to be referred to the introduction of a law. The most relevant feature that points in this direction is represented by the application of the τελικὰ κεφάλαια comparable to the treatment of this exercise found in *Progymnasmata*; see: [Herm.] p. 27.1–2, who lists τὸ σαφές, τὸ δίκαιον, τὸ νόμιμον, τὸ συμφέρον, τὸ δυνατόν, τὸ πρέπον; cf. Aphth. p. 47.13. Theon p. 95.9–12 (= p. 129.9–12) contains a lists of the corresponding 'opposite' κεφάλαια (with slight variations) to be applied in the *confutatio* of the law (see i 26 ff. n.): τὸ ἀσαφές, τὸ ἀδύνατον, τὸ οὐκ ἀναγκαῖον, τὸ ὑπεναντίον, τὸ ἄδικον, τὸ ἄξιον, τὸ ἀσύμφορον, τὸ αἰσχρόν; see comments in Patillon–Bolognesi, pp. xci–xciii, and cf. iii 14 ff. n. In **4855** i 25 ἀσαφῆ καὶ ἄδηλα corresponds to τὸ σαφές of [Herm.] and ἀσαφές of Theon; παράνομο[c corresponds to τὸ νόμιμον of [Herm.]; ἄδικος of line 27 corresponds to τὸ δίκαιον of [Herm.] and τὸ ἄδικον of Theon. On the passage as a whole Prof. Heath offers interesting considerations, based on the following table of the series of headings contained in [Herm.], **4855** and Theon, which he constructed by converting the heads of **4855** and Theon into the 'positive' terms of [Herm.]:

[Herm.]	**4855**	Theon
1. σαφές	1. σαφές	1. σαφές
2. δίκαιον	3. νόμιμον	5a. δυνατόν
3. νόμιμον	2. δίκαιον	5β. ἀναγκαῖον
4. συμφέρον	?	3. νόμιμον
5. δυνατόν	?	2. δίκαιον
6. πρέπον	?	4. συμφέρον
		6. πρέπον

We see that all three authors place τὸ σαφές in the first position; **4855** has in common with [Herm.] the second and third heading, but in reverse order. From that we could easily infer that **4855** also could have completed the analysis of the law according to (at least) τὸ συμφέρον, τὸ δυνατόν, and τὸ πρέπον, probably using the same syntactic structure already applied for the first two headings, i.e. a conditional clause introduced by the conjunction ὅταν.

24–5 The pair ἀσαφῆ καὶ ἄδηλα concludes what has emerged from the whole previous analysis of the law, focusing on the fact that the actual wording of the law does not provide for special circumstances. This recalls Theon's treatment of law on the basis of the τόπος "τὸ ἀσαφές" (p. 95.9 = p. 129.9; cf. i 24–7 n.) in the section at pp. 95.13–98.40 (= pp. 129.13–130.40), which represents the only treatment of this heading in the proposal of law in the extant *progymnasmata* ([Herm.] simply introduces it with a short quotation from Demosthenes). But the 'qualitative' difference between Theon and **4855** is remarkable. On the one hand, Theon illustrates several aspects of obscure, faulty, ambiguous, and problematic formulation by considering grammatical, syntactical and linguistic aspects (like prosody, homonymy, polysemy, synonymy, archaism, pleonasm, ellipsis) and offers numerous examples from various laws (see the analysis of C. Atherton, *The Stoics on Ambiguity*, Cambridge 1993, 194–9, 480–2), resulting—as Prof. Heath observes—in a pedantic, overelaborated, and unfocused casuistic. In this respect it is noticeable that in Theon the same law of the father-beater is simply one of many examples, being briefly mentioned to illustrate the case of obscurity due to ellipsis κατ' αἰτίαν (see i 2–3 n.). On the other hand, **4855** applies the heading τὸ σαφές in an organic and articulated analysis of a single law offering a quite instructive example of a strategy of analytic argumentation, i.e. a technique indispensable in declamation training, where one has to argue whether and how a law applies in given circumstances. This opens the possibility that the treatment of the law in **4855** is not a *progymnasma tout court* but a post-progymnasmatic exercise (cf. final remarks after iii 17–18).

25–7 παράνομο[c δὲ ὅταν. In reconstructing this passage (and contrasting παράνομο[c of 25 and ἄδικος of 27 with ἀcαφῆ καὶ ἄδηλα of 25) I have taken into consideration the syntactic articulation of the sequence of τελικὰ κεφάλαια found in [Herm.] p. 27. 2–10: . . . τῷ μὲν cαφεῖ, ὡς . . .· τῷ νομίμῳ δέ, ὅταν λέγωμεν ὅτι . . .· τῷ δικαίῳ δέ, ὅταν λέγωμεν ὅτι . . . κτλ. παράνομο[c and ἄδικος both agree with an implied ὁ νόμος, which is the subject of the subordinate clause in 26–7 (see i 26 ff. n.). Therefore I restore δὲ ὅταν to parallel 27 δὲ ὅταν; some such conjunction is required to govern the subjunctive ᾖ in 26 (this η could also be interpreted as ἤ, but this does not seem to make any sense). The difficulty is that we would expect the words ὁ νόμος to appear somewhere, yet there is no room left for them at the end of 25. It is possible that the whole section was headed περὶ νόμου, so that the subject ὁ νόμος could be omitted and easily understood. Alternatively one could think that it has been accidentally omitted at the end of 25, i.e.: παράνομο[c δὲ ⟨ὁ νόμος⟩ ἂν. Cf. [Herm.] p. 27.5–7 (from the passage already partially quoted in this note): τῷ νομίμῳ δέ, ὅταν λέγωμεν ὅτι "παρὰ τοὺς ἀρχαίους ἐστὶ νόμους"· τῷ δικαίῳ δέ, ὅταν λέγωμεν ὅτι "παρὰ τὴν φύσιν καὶ παρὰ τὸ ἔθος".

26 f. The verb εἰσηγέομαι is used here in a technical sense to indicate the proposal/introduction of a law, as in Theon p. 87.29 (= p. 123.29), in Dio Chrys. *Or.* lxxx 3.10 and D. H. *Antiquitates Romanae* 1.76.4 and 2.27.4; the noun εἰcήγηcιc occurs in Theon p. 95.5–6 (= p. 129.5–6), and in Nic. Soph. p. 78.10; the synonym εἰcφέρω in: Theon p. 95.29 (= p. 128.29); [Herm.] *Inv.* 2.3, p. 113.15; Nic. Soph. p. 78.14; the noun εἰcφορά occurs in [Herm.] *Inv.* 2.3, p. 112.13, p. 113.12–13.

The proposal of law—εἰcφορὰ or εἰcήγηcιc νόμου—represents an exercise in the *Progymnasmata*, treated by Theon pp. 95–8 = pp. 129–130; [Herm.] pp. 26–7; Aphth. pp. 46–51; Nic. Soph. pp. 77–9. It consists of two parts, a *confirmatio* and a *confutatio* of the law, slightly differently named by the different authors (καταcκευή/ἀναcκευή by Theon p. 95.4–5 = 129.4–5; cυνηγορία/κατηγορία by Aphth. p. 47.7; εἰcφορά/λύcιc by [Herm.] *Inv.* 2.3, p. 113.13). This exercise was performed through the application of the so-called τελικὰ κεφάλαια (see i 24–7 n.).

In our passage, we have to take into consideration the following participle in the dative τοῖ[c . . . κ]εκυρωμένοις, which clearly indicates something that has been enacted, and therefore it is plausible that it refers to laws. On this basis, I have supplied in the lacuna the adverb ἤδη; cf. Theon p. 95.31 (= p. 128.31) περὶ δὲ τῶν ἤδη κειμένων ⌐νόμων⌐. Alternatively, the adverb πάλαι is equally suitable for the sense and the space; cf. Syrian. *in Hermog. Commentaria* 2, p. 162.26–7 κατὰ δὲ νόμου πάλαι κειμένου κύρωcιν καὶ ἀναίρεcιν. Thus ὁ νῦν εἰcηγούμενος is said to be 'contrary to the (laws) [already] enacted'. This contrast suggests that νόμος is to be supplied with εἰcηγούμενος as subject of the sentence, and that therefore εἰcηγούμενος must be taken as a passive, while in the passages previously mentioned the verb εἰcηγέομαι has the active sense. The passive use seems grammatically possible, although rare and mostly in Byzantine authors (see Theophylactus Simocatta 3.2.7.5; Michael Attaliates, *Historia* 246.16; Anna Comnena, *Alexias* 15.8.4.19). Note J. *AJ* 19.179.1 προεισηγημένα.

27 ὅταν μ. [. If at first glance the space for αν seems slightly narrow, one may compare the sequence ΤΑ in 15 -ceται and the ligature between Α and Ν in 23 -θανη. Of the last letter of the line only a tiny mark is preserved. In any case we need to reconstruct a conjunction that would introduce a subordinate clause parallel to that in 25–7.

The missing part of the text probably defined the case of unjust law through arguments that may have a strict relation with the law of the father-beater. It is worth taking into consideration the discussion by Theon in a passage preserved only in the Armenian translation (see Patillon–Bolognesi, pp. 100–101). Here the examination of the law according to τὸ δίκαιον consists of the question whether the law is just for all citizens or whether it has been introduced for individuals in particular conditions. The example considered is the law that the one who strikes and causes wounds shall pay the amount of 1,000 drachmai, otherwise he shall be charged with ἀτιμία. This law is defined as unjust because it does not take into account the conditions of individuals: in fact, a poor man will be charged with ἀτιμία for not being able to pay this amount. On this basis I propose the following supplement e.g.:

col. i 27   ἄδικος δὲ, ὅταν μί̣[αν τιμω-
col. ii 1   [ρίαν τιθῇ πᾶϲιν ἴϲωϲ οὐδὲν ἄλλο λογιζόμε-
      2 [νοϲ

to be translated as: 'but unjust is [the law] when it establishes the same punishment for all without taking into consideration anything else'. However, one could object that this supplement, although plausible, is too restrictive, i.e. it is only one of a very wide range of possibilities for a law to be unjust. While the heading τὸ ϲαφέϲ is handled in remarkable detail (see i 24–5 n.), the following heading τὸ νόμιμον would be—if this supplement is right—covered in one short sentence. Therefore we can think of a more general formulation, for example something similar to [Herm.] p. 27.6–7 (already quoted in 25–7 n.): τῷ δικαίῳ δὲ, ὅταν λέγωμεν ὅτι "παρὰ τὴν φύϲιν καὶ παρὰ τὸ ἔθοϲ". Since the traces of the last uncertain letter of the line are very scanty, it is also possible to reconstruct at the end ὅτα̣ν μὴ̣[and propose the following supplement e.g.:

col. i 27   ἄδικος δὲ, ὅτα̣ν μὴ [τῇ φύϲει
col. ii 1 [μηδὲ τῷ ἔθει ϲυνέπηται

or, with a slight variation,

col. ii 1 [μηδὲ τοῖϲ κοινοῖϲ πάντων ἀνθρώπων ἔ-
      2 [θεϲι ϲυνέπηται

to be translated as: 'but unjust is [the law] when it complies with neither nature nor custom (or all the customs common to mankind)'.

Col. iii

1–6 Classification of the θέϲειϲ, which must have been introduced in the previous column (col. ii), into three categories: θέϲειϲ θεωρητικαί, ἠθικαί, and πραγματικαί (cf. introd.). As already said above, the θέϲειϲ ἠθικαί as a category are not found in the other authors of *Progymnasmata* but they are very close to the θέϲειϲ πρακτικαί (cf. G. Reichel, *Quaestiones progymnasmaticae* (Leipzig 1909) 99, and H. Throm, *Die Thesis: Ein Beitrag zu ihrer Entstehung und Geschichte* (Paderborn 1932) 81, 84–9, 92–4, 98), especially if we take into consideration the examples offered to illustrate them, which occur in other authors in the group of the practical/pragmatic *theseis* (see below iii 3 and 4 nn. and overall assessment of **4855** after iii 17–18 n.). Note that according to Diogenes Laertius both Chrysippus and Herillus wrote works entitled θέϲειϲ ἠθικαί (see DL 7.199 and 7.166 respectively); on Stoic echos in *theseis* cf. iii 1 n.; on the relationship between *theseis* in rhetoric and *theseis* in philosophy within the so-called doxographical tradition, see J. Mansfeld, 'Doxography and Dialectic: The *Sitz im Leben* of the "Placita"', *ANRW* II.36.4, 3056–229, esp. 3125–6, 3193–205.

1–6 First subdivision of θέϲειϲ illustrated by examples introduced by the conjunction οἷον, as for the other subdivision in 7–14. Content and structure are quite close to Theon's treatment, p. 83. 7–84.15 (= p. 121. 7–15).

1 εἰ πρόνο[ι]α διοικεῖ κα[ὶ] τὸ πᾶν recalls Theon p. 83.8–9 (= p. 121.8–9) οἷον εἰ θεοὶ προνοοῦνται τοῦ κόϲμου, which is introduced as an example of θέϲιϲ θεωρητική as opposed to θέϲιϲ πρακτική. Since the following portion of the text of **4855** contains two other groups of θέϲειϲ, ἠθικαί and πραγματικαί, it is highly probable that this sentence represents an example introduced to illustrate a previous group of θέϲειϲ, which should be the group of θέϲειϲ θεωρητικαί. This first group of the subdivision would have been introduced in the final part of the previous column. Exploiting the wording used for introducing a subdivision in line 7, the definition of θέϲιϲ θεωρητικαί given by Theon (p. 83.7–8 = p. 121.7–8) and the average number of letters for line in **4855**, I conjecturally reconstruct the last three lines of the previous col. ii as follows:

[τῶν θέϲεων αἱ μέν εἰϲιν θεωρητικαί, αἱ δὲ
ἠθικαί, αἱ δὲ πραγματικαί. θεωρητικαὶ μὲν ὅ-

καὶ θεωρίας ἕνεκα μόνον ζητοῦνται· οἷον]
col. iii εἰ πρόνο[ι]α διοικεῖ κα[ὶ] τὸ πᾶν . . .

Here the use of κα[ὶ] implies that πρόνοια governs a more limited sphere (e.g. human life as well as the whole universe).

Elsewhere, Theon offers the development of the θέσις "εἰ θεοὶ προνοοῦνται τοῦ κόσμου", pp. 91.7–94.9 (= pp. 126.3–128.4), which shows a Stoic flavour (as observed by Reichel, *Quaestiones progymnasmaticae* 27–9, 104–5; cf. Throm, *Thesis* 78 n. 2). Compare also Quint. 3.5.6. Similar examples of θέσεις of speculative type are: εἰ σφαιροειδὴς ὁ οὐρανός (Aphth., p. 41.19–20, Nic. Soph., p. 76.18–19 and [Herm.] p. 25.7), εἰ κόσμοι πολλοί ([Herm.] p. 25.8 and Aphth. p. 41.20), and εἰ ὁ ἥλιος πῦρ ([Herm.] p. 25.8).

On the different character of θέσεις speculative and practical/pragmatic, see also Theon pp. 83.10–84.15 (p. 121.10–15); cf. Nic. Soph. p. 76. 21–22 and Patillon–Bolognesi, pp. lxxxiv–lxxxvii.

On the basis of the extant *progymnasmata*, it is very likely that the classification of the type of *theseis* was introduced by a general and short definition of this exercise, possibly preceded by a heading, e.g. περὶ θέσεως.

3 πῶς τέκνα παιδευτέον. As far as I know this thesis is not paralleled in progymnasmatic literature. The topic itself, however, is certainly not new, given the role played by upbringing and education in Greek civilization, especially within philosophical debate. Among the treatises devoted to this topic only Ps.-Plutarch's περὶ παίδων ἀγωγῆς (*Mor.* 1a–14c) has entirely survived, while from others we have only the title and scanty fragments: a περὶ παιδείας by Aristotle (DL 9.53, frr. 62–3 Rose), a περὶ παίδων ἀγωγῆς by Theophrastus (DL 5.50, Theophr fr. 436 no. 10 F), a περὶ παίδων ἀγωγῆς attested in a treatise on Hellenistic monarchs transmitted on papyrus in LXXI **4809** ii 12–13, a περὶ ἀγωγῆς by Cleanthes (fr. 481.27 Armin), a περὶ παιδείας by Clearchus (fr. 13–16 Wehrli), a περὶ παιδείας by Aristippus (DL 2.83–85 = fr. 144 Giannantoni), a περὶ Ἑλληνικῆς παιδείας by Zeno of Citium (frr. 41, 250 Arnim), a work by Chrysippus to which Quint. 1.1.17 refers as *praecepta de liberorum educatione* (frr. 732–738 Armin), παιδευτικοὶ νόμοι by Aristoxenus (frr. 42–43 Wehrli). At Rome Gel. 4.19.2 quotes Varro's *Catus aut de liberis educandis*, a dialogue belonging to the *Logistorici* (fr. 17 Riese). According to Quintilian (first book of the *Institutiones*) upbringing and primary education play a crucial role in the development of the future orator (see in particular 1.1.1–37, 1.2.1–31, 1.3.1–17). Clearly for this topic also the relation between philosophy and rhetoric has to be taken into consideration: cf. iii 1 n. on Stoic echo on *theseis*, and final remarks after iii 17–18 n.; see also Atherton, *Stoics on Ambiguity*, 473–82. Finally note that Men. Rhet. p. 363.30 Spengel, p. 66 RW lists the topic ἡ τῶν παίδων ἀγωγή as a relevant one in the praise of cities.

4 πῶς φίλοις χρηστέον; cf. Cic. *Part.* 18.65, where the *quaestio quibus officiis amicitia colenda sit* is mentioned as an example of *quaestio* whose *propositum* is an *actio*, as opposed to *cognitio*, i.e. it is classified as a practical *thesis* (see above iii 1–18 n.).

For the motif of φίλοι compare Ioan. Sard. p. 232.4–5 ὅτι σπουδαστέον ὑπὲρ πατρίδος ἢ φίλων, which from structural/formal standpoint is a θέσις συγκριτική (see below).

4–5 The definition of θέσεις πραγματικαί of **4855** is not exactly parallelled in the extant rhetorical texts. In 5 the traces do not allow a certain reconstruction of the text. We could restore the verb πρά[τ]τ[ε]ιν, assuming that the lower part of the upright of τ has been abraded and that the ι has a round tip because in ligature with the preceding ε in lacuna. For the 'Attic' spelling -ττ-, see iii 12 n. (the alternative form πρα[σ]σ[ε]ιν would be palaeographically possible, since the two traces visible after the first lacuna may represent the two extremities of the arc of the required σ). At first glance the noun πρά[γμ]α[σ]ιν would paleographically be suitable, assuming that the two traces after the first lacuna belong to the left-hand diagonal of the required ᾱ, which would have then a very slightly inclination; however, the first lacuna is in fact too small to contain the sequence γμ, which in this script occupies at least a space about 2 mm larger; moreover we would have to assume a ι with a blurred 'round' tip. In any case, πρά̣[γμ]α̣[c]̣ιν would produce a syntactically odd construction with the verb [δ]ιδάcκω as a dative plural in the meaning of 'teach in relation to actions (?)'; one would in fact expect an accusative. As said above, the wording of the definition of **4855** is unique, especially for the use of the verb διδάcκω. The closest formulation is Theon p. 83.9–10 (= p. 121.9–10) αἱ δὲ πρακτικαὶ εἴc τινα πρᾶξιν τὴν ἀναφορὰν ἔχουcαι (cf. also Aphth. p. 41.16–17 καὶ πολιτικαὶ μὲν αἱ πρᾶξιν ἔχουcαι πόλιν cυνέχουcαν, οἷον εἰ γαμητέον, εἰ πλευcτέον, εἰ τειχιcτέον).

5–6 εἰ χρὴ| πλεῖν . . . εἰ χρὴ γεωργεῖν. Compare Aphth., p. 41.17. Lib. (vol. viii, pp. 564–6) offers the development of the exercise εἰ πλευcτέον, while Themistius has a rather articulated piece entitled θέcιc εἰ γεωργητέον (vol. ii, pp. 181–6 Downey, Yarnon, Schenkl).

6 εἰ χρὴ γαμεῖν. This θέcιc is mentioned as an example of θέcιc πρακτική by Theon p. 83.10 (= p. 121.10), [Herm.] p. 25.18, Nic. Soph. p. 72.19–20 and pp. 74.15–75.12, Aphth. p. 41.17; cf. Quint. 2.4.24–25 *ducendane uxor*, and 3.5.8. The complete development of the exercise is in Aphth. (pp. 42–6) and Lib. (vol. viii, pp. 550–61).

εἰ χρὴ γεωργεῖν. Compare [Herm.] p. 25.19–20, where agricultural activity represents the second member of the θέcιc διπλῆ entitled εἰ ἀθλητέον μᾶλλον ἢ γεωργητέον.

7–14 Second classification of the θέcειc into two categories, ἁπλαῖ and cυγκριτικαί (cf. introd.)

9–10 εἰ |[λ]όγων ἐπιμελητέον. The topic of this *thesis* may be compared with [Herm.] p. 25.5 εἰ ῥητορευτέον.

10 cυγκριτικαί. As said in introd., this type of θέcειc corresponds to the θέcειc διπλαῖ treated in the other authors of *progymnasmata*. For the use of this term, see Syriani, Sopatri et Marcellini, *Scholia ad Hermog. Status, RG* 4, p. 708.4. Compare also Quint. 2.4.24: *thesis autem quae sumuntur ex rerum comparatione (ut 'rusticane vita an urbana potior . . .').*

12 κρεῖττον. The 'Attic' spelling in -ττ- might indicate the stylistic level aimed at by the writer. Note however that -ττ- is the norm also in documentary papyri from the third century onwards; see Gignac, *Grammar* i 146–7.

13–14 ἐπιμελητέον ὅπλων ἢ λό|[γ]ων. Compare Quint. 2.4.24 *iuris periti an militaris viri laus maior*, who refers to the obvious example of Cic. *Mur.* 19 ff. Individual topics of this double θέcιc, belonging to the military and the rhetorical field respectively, may be compared with two other θέcειc ἁπλαῖ: εἰ τειχιcτέον (mentioned in Aphth. p. 41.17; Lib. contains the development of the exercise, vol. viii, pp. 561–4); εἰ ῥητορευτέον (mentioned in [Herm.], see 9–10 n.). This *thesis* recalls many commonplace reflections on the civil/military antithesis, like e.g. Cicero *cedant arma togae* (*Pis.* 72.8–9, 73.5; *Off.* 1.77.2–3; *Phil.* 2.20.4).

14 ff. List of the seven headings on the basis of which the θέcιc-exercise is to be developed. The headings are called μέρη, like the headings under πρόcωπον and πρᾶγμα in col. i. Theon calls them τόποι, Herm. and Aphth. τελικὰ κεφάλαια, corresponding to *capitula finalia* in Prisc. (p. 40.2 Passalacqua = p. 555.10–11 Halm). Nic. Soph. p. 72.9–12. points out that terminology and headings vary from author to author: οὐ λέληθε γάρ με, ὅτι ἕτεροι καὶ ἑτέροιc τιcὶν ἐχρήcαντο κεφαλαίοιc, οἳ μὲν τοῖc τελικοῖc καλουμένοιc, τινὲc δὲ καὶ ἄλλοιc, καινὰ αὐτοῖc ὀνόματα περιτιθέντεc. In the following table the list in **4855** may be compared with several similar lists found in the other sources.

4855	Theon p. 84.22–3 (= p. 121.22–3, on θέcιc)	Herm. *Stas.* pp. 52.20–53.1	Aphth. p. 42.10	Nic. Soph. p. 72.16–18 (on θέcιc)	Nic. Soph. p. 44.21–2 (on κοινὸc τόποc)	Aps. *Rhet.* p. 73.1–2 (= *RG* 9, p. 527.10–11 = Spengel p. 291.9–10)	Prisc. *Praeexercitamina*, p. 40.2–3 Passalacqua (= p. 555.11 Halm)
κατὰ φύcιν	ἀναγκαῖον	νόμμον	νόμμον	κατὰ φύcιν	cυμφέρον	νόμμον	utile
δίκαιον	καλόν	δίκαιον	δίκαιον	κατὰ νόμον	δίκαιον	δίκαιον	iustum
cύμφορον τῷ βίῳ	cυμφέρον	cυμφέρον	cυμφέρον	κατὰ ἔθοc	νόμμον	cυμφέρον	legitimum
βίοc τοῦ μετερχομένου	ἡδύ	δυνατόν	δυνατόν	κατὰ τὸ ὅcιον περὶ τοὺc τελευτήcαντac	δυνατόν	δυνατόν	honestum
δυνατόν		ἔνδοξον (cf. πρέπον in [Herm.] p. 26.2, on θέcιc)		κατὰ τὸ ὅcιον τὸ περὶ τὴν πατρίδα	ἔνδοξον	ἔνδοξον	similia
ἔνδοξον					ἀναγκαῖον	cαφέc[a]	
cύγκρισιc					ῥᾴδιον		

[a] This is given as optional (. . . εἰ βούλει cαφὲc πρὸc τούτουc).

Variations are found in the same author according to the exercise to which the headings are to be applied, as shown in the table by the two different lists found in Nic. Soph. Similarly, [Herm.] pp. 25.22–26.2, on the treatment of θέcιc, offers a list of 4 items (δίκαιον, cυμφέρον, δυνατόν, πρέπον). Moreover, the conciseness of the treatment and wording itself sometimes suggest that they may be considered open lists, like Priscian's list, which ends with the word *similia* (for similar lists see J. Martin, *Antike Rhetorik: Technik und Methode* (Munich 1974) 169–74, and Lausberg, *Handbuch* § 375.5). For the variety of lists and their relationship with the genres cυμβουλευτικόν and ἐγκωμιαcτικόν, cf. Nic. Soph., pp. 72–3, and Patillon–Bolognesi, pp. lxxxviii–xci. Lib., in his θέcιc-exercises (vol. viii, pp. 550–66), offers examples of the application of the lists found in Herm. and Aphth. Theon, in his treatment of θέcιc, offers a much longer and detailed list of τόποι. This consists of 28 items of which the first 17 may be ascribed to the genre cυμβουλευτικόν, while the rest represent more general τόποι (cf. Arist. *Rh.* 2.23 [1397a.7–1400b.36], where the τόποι ἐκ τοῦ ἐναντίου, ἐκ τοῦ μᾶλλον, and ἐκ τοῦ ἧττον are suitable for a more general application in comparison with the τόποι specific to each oratorical genre, as illustrated in *Rh.* 1.3 [1358b.20–5]). Compare also *Rhet. Alex.* 1421 b 24 ff. (§§ 4–5, p. 6 Fuhrmann), containing a list of eight headings to be applied to the genre cυμβουλευτικόν: δίκαιον, νόμιμον, cυμφέρον, καλόν, ἡδύ, ῥάδιον, δυνατόν, ἀναγκαῖον; and Quint. 3.8.22–32.

14 κατὰ φύcιν. Compare Nic. Soph. p. 72.16 and 20 (and the table above, iii 14 ff. n.). κατὰ φύcιν is also included as the second item of Theon's detailed list (see 14 ff. n.), which is to be identified with νόμιμον according to the definition given at p. 84.28–32 (= p. 121.28–32): δεύτερον δὲ ὅτι κατὰ φύcιν ἐcτὶ καὶ κατὰ τὰ κοινὰ πάντων ἀνθρώπων ἔθη τε καὶ νόμιμα· οὐ γὰρ ἀπόχρη πρὸς τὸ πρᾶξαί τι δυνατὸν αὐτὸ εἶναι, ἐὰν μὴ κατὰ φύcιν καὶ κατὰ νόμον ὑπάρχῃ. In Ioan. Sard. p. 241.21–2, ἀπὸ φύcεωc is a sub-heading of δίκαιον: τὸ δὲ δίκαιον τριχῶc λαμβάνεται· ἀπὸ φύcεωc, ἀπὸ ἔθουc, ἀπὸ ἐγγράφου. δίκαιον, the second item in **4855**, occurs as second in Herm., Aphth., Aps., and Prisc. and as eighth in Theon's detailed list; see 14 ff. n.

15 cύμφορον τῷ βίῳ. The trace may fit the head of ο, or be itself a very small ο, like the one at the very end of line 1; the space, rather narrow, leads me to restore this letter. In the other sources we find the synonymous cυμφέρον (second heading in Herm. and Aphth., a sub-heading under no. 18 ἐκ τοῦ ἐναντίου in Theon's detailed list, see 14 ff. n.). In **4855** there are two palaeographical arguments against reading ε here: (1) space too narrow; (2) no trace of the base of this letter or of the likely ligature with the following ρ (cf. e.g. 14 μερη, 15 μετερχο).

15–16 βίος τοῦ μετερχο|[μ]ένου. In this context, the participle μετερχόμενος is used in the sense of 'go seek', 'pursue', 'to put into practice', and the object to be understood is the πρᾶγμα that is taught by the θέcειc πραγματικαί, as stated in 5. The meaning of βίοc is slightly different from the previous τῷ βίῳ. There it refers to human life in general; here it refers to the life of a category of people pursuing the activity that represents the topic of the θέcιc. With regard to the examples of θέcειc given in 5–6, one should think of the life of the sailor and the farmer; for those in 9–10 and in 13–4, one may think of the life of a rhetor or a student of rhetoric and the life of a soldier. This heading is not in the lists found in the other sources. However, one can compare the following passage, where μέτειμι, a synonym of μετέρχομαι, occurs: [Herm.] p. 24.11–15: ἁπλῶc ταῦτα πάντα ἀφελόντεc τὸ πρᾶγμα ἐφ' ἑαυτοῦ θεωρήcομεν, τῶν προcόντων αὐτῷ τὴν ἐξέταcιν ποιούμενοι, οἷον εἰ ποιητέον τόδε ᾡτινιοῦν διὰ τὸ τοιάδε εἶναι τὰ ἀποβαίνοντα τοῖc μετιοῦcιν. For this 'restrictive' meaning of βίοc we can consider Theon p. 94.13–21 (= p. 128.13–21), and Ioan. Sard. p. 242.2–20. In the development of the *thesis* εἰ γαμητέον, Lib. (vol. viii, p. 554.11–18) offers a passage that may be connected with the heading ὁ βίοc τοῦ μετερχομένου.

16 cύγκριcι[c. Compare the following passages, all related to the treatment of the κοινὸc τόποc: Theon p. 64.3–5 (= 108.3–5); [Herm.] pp. 13.14–14.1; Aphth. p. 17.8–10; Nic. Soph. p. 43.6–14; cf. Ioan. Sard. pp. 99.11–100.19.

17–18 The final sentence introduces the *refutatio* of the *thesis*. In **4855** this is named κατηγορία as in Theon p. 3.13–14 (= p. 61.13–14); [Herm.] p. 26.13; Aphth. p. 47.7; Nic. Soph. p. 78.11 (all these passages refer to the εἰcφορὰ νόμου-exercise). The *refutatio* is alternatively named ἀνακευή (see Theon p. 90.21 = p. 125.21, p. 94.23–4 = p. 128.23–4) as opposed to κατακευή, *confirmatio*, also named cυνηγορία, as in Aphth.'s treatment (cf. Lib. vol. viii, pp. 568–71) or ἀπολογία (see Nic. Soph. p. 78.12). The *pars destruens* based on the opposite headings represents a substantial part of all *progymnasmata* (cf. R. Webb, 'The Progymnasmata as Practice', in Y. L. Too (ed.), *Education in Greek and Roman Antiquity* (Leiden, Boston, Köln 2001) 300; Heath, *Theon*, 143; T. Reinhardt and M. Winterbottom, *Quintilian: Book 2* (Oxford 2006) 76, 98–9). The conciseness and the wording in **4855** is comparable to Theon p. 84.20–3 (= p. 121.20–3): τῶν μὲν οὖν πρακτικῶν θέcεων τὰ ἀνωτάτω κεφάλαια [κατα] λαμβάνεται κατακευάζοντι μὲν ἐκ τοῦ ἀναγκαίου καὶ τοῦ καλοῦ καὶ τοῦ cυμφέροντοc καὶ τοῦ ἡδέοc, ἀνακευάζοντι δὲ ἐκ τῶν ἐναντίων . . .; cf. p. 90.21 (= p. 125.21): ἐκ δὲ τῶν ἐναντίων εὐπορήcομεν εἰc ἀνακευήν; p. 86.39 (= p. 123.39): ἐκ δὲ τῶν ἐναντίων ἀνακευαcτέον; [Herm.] p. 26.6–7: οὕτω κατακευάcειc· ἀνατρέψειc δὲ ἐκ τῶν ἐναντίων. λύcειc δὲ καὶ τὰc εὑρικομέναc ἀντιθέcειc.

I add some general observations about the significance of **4855** and its innovations and originality within the progymnasmatic tradition.

Starting from the most original feature, the classification of the *theseis* (cf. introd. and iii 1–6 n.) into three categories including the hitherto unattested group of ethical *theseis*, one could observe that this tripartite scheme recalls the tripartite classification of the arts as theoretical, practical, and creative/'poetic' by Quint. 2.19. Further, Cic. *Acad.* 2.22 offers a bipartite classification into theoretical and practical arts, which is paralleled by the classification of the *theseis* into practical and theoretical at Quint. 3.5.11 (cf. Reinhardt–Winterbottom, *Quintilian: Book 2*, 353–4). If so, as Dr Innes points out, taking into consideration this parallelism/overlap between the classification of the arts in general and rhetoric in particular, it appears less striking that **4855** introduces a tripartite classification of the *theseis*, although not identical to the tripartite classification of the arts offered by Quintilian.

Dr Innes also brilliantly suggests a possibility of tracing back the 'origin' of the tripartite division of *theseis* (theoretical, ethical, and practical) in **4855** through the analysis of Cic. *Part.* 62–7, who offers subdivisions of each of the two overall distinctions of theoretical and practical *theseis*. In particular (in 67), the practical *theseis* are subdivided into moral duty (*officium*) and emotion (i.e. *ēthos* and *pathos*), the first being illustrated by 'how to behave to parents' (parents together with friends are in fact traditional examples for duty; cf. the longer list of moral *officia*, including moral behaviour to friends and parents, in Hor. *Ars* 312–16). In fact **4855** gives to the moral duty an equal place beside the theoretical and practical *theseis* under the label of 'ethical *theseis*', i.e. it 'upgrades' to a main category what in Cicero is a subdivision.

In the words of Dr Innes (communication of 16 July 2007) 'What may have happened is that the author (no doubt not the first to do so) elevates the moral type to reflect the standard division of philosophy into natural philosophy (e.g. the nature of the universe) and moral philosophy (e.g. how to treat friends). For this ethical type he isolates moral duty. Then whatever is left over goes into the third category, the practical (career-oriented, one's choice of *bios*, e.g. "should one farm?" "should one marry?"). So a pick and mix of traditional components, which nicely happens to be hitherto unattested.'

Moreover, Arist. *Top.* leads me to further reflections. After having defined the *thesis* as πρόβλημα (104b 29 ff.), he offers a tripartite (*sic!*) classification of προτάcειc and προβλήματα (105b 19–25): ἔcτι δ' ὡc τύπῳ περιλαβεῖν τῶν προτάcεων καὶ τῶν προβλημάτων μέρη τρία· αἱ μὲν γὰρ ἠθικαὶ προτάcειc εἰcίν, αἱ δὲ φυcικαί, αἱ δὲ λογικαί. ἠθικαὶ μὲν οὖν αἱ τοιαῦται, **οἷον πότερον δεῖ τοῖc γονεῦcι μᾶλλον ἢ τοῖc νόμοιc πειθαρχεῖν**, ἐὰν διαφωνῶcιν· λογικαὶ δὲ οἷον πότερον τῶν ἐναντίων ἡ αὐτὴ ἐπιcτήμη ἢ οὔ· **φυcικαὶ δὲ οἷον πότερον ὁ κόcμοc ἀΐδιοc ἢ οὔ**. ὁμοίωc δὲ καὶ τὰ προβλήματα. Here the given examples present striking similarities with the examples illustrating the θέcειc θεωρητικαί/φυcικαί, and the type of θέϲειϲ that—as we have seen—are named πρακτικαί in the progymnasmatic texts, and ἠθικαί only in **4855**. Thus **4855**, within its tripartite classification, seems to preserve the 'original' denomination of a type of *theseis* that have later been included in the group of *theseis* πρακτικαί within the bipartite system common to the rest of the progymnasmatic tradition. This point may also be supported by the tradition of Aristotle as the εὑρετήϲ of the *thesis*-exercise involving at the same time training in philosophical debate and development of rhetorical skills (see DL 5.3 πρὸϲ θέϲιν ϲυνεγύμναζε τοὺϲ μαθητὰϲ ἅμα καὶ ῥητορικῶϲ ἐπαϲκῶν; cf.: Theon p. 13.1–2 (= p. 69.1–2); Cic. *Orat.* 14.46; Reichel, *Quaestiones progymnasmaticae* 97–100; Throm, *Thesis* 172–3, 177–9, 182–3; Mansfeld, 'Doxography and Dialectic', 3197–201). Moreover, the classification of *theseis* into three groups attested only in **4855** recalls Aristotle's tripartite classification of προτάϲειϲ and προβλήματα, although it is not identical.

Finally, a remark about the order of the *progymnasmata* in **4855** and the purposes of the work contained in it. We have seen that the exercise in col. i very probably belongs to the category of νόμου εἰϲφορά, while col. iii deals with θέϲειϲ. We have also tried to reconstruct in outline the content of the missing col. ii: it surely included the end of the analysis of the law of the father-beater—probably the treatment according to the headings τὸ ϲυμφέρον, τὸ δυνατόν, and τὸ πρέπον—and the beginning of the section on the *thesis*, consisting of an introductory definition of the exercise followed by the classification that carries on in the preserved col. iii (cf. i 24–7 and iii 1 nn.). From that it is clear that the θέϲιϲ-exercise follows the νόμου εἰϲφορά, a sequence that is unparalleled in the other extant progymnasmatic texts, where the opposite order is found: the θέϲιϲ precedes the νόμου εἰϲφορά in Theon, [Herm.], Aphth., Nic. Soph. (cf. Quint. 2.4.24, 26, and 33, who presents the following series with the law in the last position: *thesis*, question of *voluntas* in the so-called *causae coniecturales*, *legum laus atque vituperatio*). This is at the first sight quite puzzling. On the one hand, it is true that in general terms the order of *progymnasmata* varies from author to author (see Patillon–Bolognesi, pp. xii–xvi and xxviii–xxxi; Webb, *Progymnasmata*, 294–6; Heath, *Theon*, 132, 139, 141, 143–4, 149–51; G. A. Kennedy, *Progymnasmata: Greek Textbooks of Prose Composition and Rhetoric* (Atlanta 2003) xiii; Reinhardt–Winterbottom, *Quintilian: Book 2*, 74–7). Yet on the other hand the sequence θέϲιϲ – νόμου εἰϲφορά is shared by all extant sources and has an obvious rationale: the νόμου εἰϲφορά exercise is the most advanced (Aphth. pp. 46.20–47.6 even points out that it could be considered almost a *hypothesis*, i.e. a declamation) and consequently should come at the end. However, as Prof. Heath suggests, there are some pieces of evidence that may allow us to consider the non-standard order of **4855** only an 'apparent' oddity. (1) The awareness of the variety in the ordering of the *progymnasmata*, especially with regard to the later stages of the *cursus*, is attested by Nic. Soph. p. 67.18ff.: τινὲϲ μετὰ τὴν ϲύγκριϲιν εὐθὺϲ τὴν ἔκφραϲιν τάξαντεϲ οὕτωϲ ἔγραψαν· ἔϲτι μὲν **ἡ τῶν ἐφεξῆϲ προγυμναϲμάτων τάξιϲ ἀδιάφοροϲ** ἄλλων ἄλλωϲ ταττόντων . . . This may point to a certain degree of 'tolerance' for an 'unorthodox' ordering of the exercises. (2) The two exercises θέϲιϲ and νόμου εἰϲφορά are strictly connected through their similarities, as one could infer from an anonymous commentary on Herm. *Stas.*, *RG* 7, p. 620.5–11: here the *progymnasma*, which has no specified circumstances, is opposed to the dimension and role of laws in *hypotheses*, which as such consist of a legal question where the specific circumstances of the case have always to be taken into consideration; the proposal is thus a kind of *thesis*: παντὶ ῥητῷ δεῖ τινα ὑποκεῖϲθαι περίϲταϲιν, εἰ μέλλει ἐν ὑποθέϲει ἀλλὰ μὴ ἐν θέϲει λαμβάνεϲθαι· ὅταν γὰρ αὐτὸ ἐφ' ἑαυτο⟨ῦ⟩ τὸ ῥητὸν ἀμφιϲβητῆται, **θετικὴ** γίνεται ἡ κατ' αὐτὸ ἐξέταϲιϲ **κατὰ νόμου εἰϲφοράν·** οἷον εἰ δημηγορητέον τοῖϲ τὰ πατρῷα κατεδηδοκόϲιν, εἰ πολιτευτέον τοῖϲ ἡταιρηκόϲι; cf. ibid. p. 623.12–17; Syriani, Sopatri et Marcellini, *Scholia ad Hermog. Status*, *RG* 4, p. 778.25–30. These similarities between the two exercises both coming at the end of the progymnasmatic program, may further be supported by Ioan. Sard. p. 267.7–12: commenting on Aphth. 47.13–14 on the proposal of law, he states that two or three proems can be used in this exercise, and reports the opinion of 'many' who say that the *thesis* also could include three proems, on the grounds that it makes sense for a young man completing the *progymnasmata* to use three proems to prepare for proper ζητήματα (subjects of dispute). To sum up, given that the two exercises were 'felt' so similar and both came at the final stage of the *cursus*, an inversion of their order is not so striking. (3) As Dr Innes observes, a logical and didactical reason for the collocation of the *thesis*-exercise at the very end of the *progymnasmata* series may depend on the nature of the *thesis* itself: in fact, with the addition of the circumstances (person, facts, time, space, etc.) a *thesis* becomes a *hypothesis* (cf. introd.), often an exercise on deliberative themes (Lat. *suasoria*) to be practiced before the more complex forensic case (Lat. *controversia*). For example the *thesis* 'should one marry?' becomes 'should Cato marry?' (see Quint. 2.4.25 and 3.5.8–11).

In this direction, an even more 'radical' view about the nature of the *thesis* is expressed by Sopater fr. 8.107–134 (in Aphth. pp. 68–9 = Ioan. Sard. pp. 251.5–252.5), according to which the *thesis* is a complete *hypothesis* with heads of arguments (cf. the definition of the proposal of law by Aphthonius as a 'quasi-*hypothesis*' mentioned above, and Quint. 3.5.8–9's remark that specific references may be given even in a *thesis*: for example, from the simple *thesis an res publica administranda* one could make the more specific and complex formulation *an in tyrannide administranda*, which, although it is not a proper *hypothesis*, implies the consideration both of time and of quality by introducing the figure of the tyrant as a 'hidden person').

From this standpoint, the *thesis*-exercise as the last *progymnasma* may be considered a sort of 'glide' towards the next stage of the rhetorical syllabus including the exercises on deliberative topics (*suasoriae*).

The non-standard order of **4855** could also be explained in slightly different terms: our text may not be *stricto sensu* a treatise on *progymnasmata*, but a treatment very close to this genre, perhaps a post-progymnasmatic work composed for the very first stage of declamation training, and therefore the author could have taken more freedom in distributing and treating his material. An important element in this direction is the role played by the heading τὸ ϲαφέϲ in the analysis of the νόμοϲ, which itself is not directly paralleled in the extant progymnasmatic tradition (cf. i 24–5 n.) and represents, in the words of Prof. Heath, 'a significant and serious contribution to progymnasmatic literature'. The final title τέχνη ῥητορική may also point in this direction.

In any case it has to be observed that the section on *thesis* is comparatively short and concise (lacking any fully worked models) and can be classified as progymnasmatic *tout court*. This fact may (virtually) reflect a 'real' teaching situation (cf. Heath, *Menander*, 218–19, on [Herm.] *Progymnasmata* as originated 'in elementary classroom instruction'). We can imagine a rhetor engaged at the same time in the instruction of students at different levels of progression in need of diversified teaching in different progymnasmatic (and possibly post-progymnasmatic) exercises (but the authorship of the doctrine is not necessarily to be attributed directly to him). Alternatively, in the fluid activity of the classroom, the teacher could have chosen to focus on the νόμου εἰϲφορά and offer a quite detailed and instructive example even going beyond the elementary progymnasmatic level, and to conclude with a cursory revision of the *thesis* in the elementary progymnasmatic format already known to his students. Indeed, the possibility that **4855** has originated from notes taken by students is not to be ruled out. But we have to take into account that the paleographical features—rapidly executed but still professional bookhand script—do not match with what is to be expected from an autograph working copy of a teacher or notes by students, i.e. a text jotted down without particular care, with errors and *lapsus* left uncorrected. Therefore, going back to what has already been said in the introd. about **4855** as an artifact written on recycled papyrus, we can assume that a professional scribe was engaged to write properly the 'original' notes in order to produce a copy that, though unpretentious and inexpensive (as written on recycled material), was still decent (as written in bookhand, equipped with some reading and punctuation marks, and corrected by the scribe himself), a copy to be used as a handy reference work. In other words, **4855** was meant to last beyond the span of time of a single or a couple of ephemeral lectures. At this point one cannot help recalling Quintilian's mention (1.pr.7) of the edition of two works on rhetoric put in circulation under his name by his students: they derived from the notes taken by the students themselves during his lectures and therefore were not yet perfectly structured and polished as expected in the case of a formal and systematic treatise for publication as opposed to an oral exposition in a classroom situation, which is always provisional, at least to some extent (cf. Heath, *Menander*, 225 and 261–3, including comparable episodes).

D. COLOMO

IV. DOCUMENTS OF THE ROMAN PERIOD

4856–4890. Transfers of Credit in Grain

This section publishes thirty-five documents of familiar kind, and peculiar to the Oxyrhynchite nome. All but two carry instructions for giro transfers out of private grain stocks held in state granaries; in one case the instruction is preceded by a notice of transfer (**4887**), while two others carry only such notices of transfer (**4886**, **4890**). For discussions of such texts, see P. Pruneti, *AnPap* 6 (1994) 53–91, and most recently N. Litinas, *ZPE* 160 (2007) 183–202, who offers a full edition of the *descripta* III **615–22** and **628–32**, as well as an analysis of the formulas and related issues.

Forty-four orders for transfer of credit in grain (διαϲτολικά) have been published to date (in a few cases, the papyrus carries more than one order); see the list in Litinas, loc. cit. 198, to which add P. Lips. II 140–41 and SB XXVI 16493. The earliest are LXVII **4588** (33) and XLIX **3486** (c.41); there follows a silence in our evidence for just under eighty years, though there are a several '*sitologus* receipts' of this period which certify grain deposits. **4856** of 118 is now the earliest text in a new series that spans some sixty years (the latest is I **88** of 179). Was the practice of issuing such orders discontinued? By contrast, notices of transfer of credit in grain continue to be issued for another hundred or so years.

With a single exception (**4872**), the papyri in this section were excavated during Grenfell and Hunt's third season at Oxyrhynchus (1903/4); they belong to a larger group of documents relative to activities of *sitologi*, which, to judge from the inventory numbers, were found more or less together. This is the source of many other such texts published hitherto: apart from XXXVIII **2863–71** and LXVII **4587–90**, which concern transfers of credit in grain, this applies to XLI **2958** and **2961–7**, documents referring to the price of πυρὸϲ ϲυναγοραϲτικόϲ, and to LVII **3902–9**, which concern the supply of seed-corn. (In view of their links with documents published here, P. Lips. I 112–17, acquired on the market, may originally have been part of the same group.) These texts refer to *sitologi* of about two dozen granaries, and span a period of over a century (the earliest texts in the group are **3902** and **3907**, both of 11.xi.99; the latest is LXVII **4590** of c.231). Although they are addressed to overseers of village granaries, whose signatures they sometimes bear, or were issued by them, their concentration in the same rubbish dump of Oxyrhynchus shows that they do not come from village granaries. Some of the texts found with them, such as those published in volumes XLI and LVII, are addressed to *strategi*. We may consider whether this 'archive' emanates from a section of the office of the Oxyrhynchite *strategus* that was concerned with grain transactions. The *strategus* was the recipient of accounts and reports of *sitologi* that recorded all activity in the granaries under their supervision (see e.g. the duties of the *sitologus* described in P. Mich. XI 604.16–18 and XXXVI **2769** 15–17). However, it is difficult to see why all these chits should have ended there, unless they were required as a measure for checking the accuracy of the reports.

It has not been my intention to present a comprehensive edition of the 'archive' (this would not be practical at present). I have selected perhaps the majority of those texts that offer significant details for the prosopography of the landowners and generally the agrarian history of the Oxyrhychite nome. Many of these papyri attest Roman citizens and Alexandrians, some of them of very high rank, such as members of the family of Tiberii Iulii Theones or the *archidicastes* Claudius Munatianus; others refer to eminent Oxyrhynchites or individuals known from previously published papyri. These persons held giro accounts in various village granaries, and may be presumed to have had landholdings in the vicinity; several of them employed various managers, indicative of the operation of estates. This information is mostly new, and is of particular interest in the case of the Romans (other than veterans) and Alexandrians, who had previously made a fairly modest appearance in the Oxyrhynchite documentation relative to estates in the earlier second century.[1]

The persons who issued or in general appear in these orders are chiefly metropolites; the great majority have Greek names of the kinds that were favoured by the Oxyrhynchite elite. Although heavily represented in this category of texts, the movements of their accounts were a fraction of the daily business of a granary, which mostly concerned small deposits by villagers. Instructive in this respect is P. Mich. XVIII 786, the only granary account with a fixed second-century date (*c.*167), which records activity in the granary of Tanais; cf. also XLIV **3169** (200–212), taken to indicate that 'the economic importance of metropolitans . . . far exceeds their numbers' (**3169** introd., and cf. Rowlandson, *Landowners and Tenants* 117).

The purpose of these 'private' grain transfers is generally not stated; it is only in the third century when we find explicit references to taxes (see **4890** 6 n.). In some cases we may have payments of rent in kind; in some other cases landlords perhaps transfer wheat into the accounts of their lessees for the latter to pay dues on land. Loans or repayments of loans of wheat also come into play; XLIX **3493–4** (175), two rather peculiar loans of wheat, were found with the *sitologi* documents published here, and one of them (**3494**) bears a docket referring to *sitologi*.

The backs of all are blank except for **4885**, written on reused papyrus, and **4861**. The writing is with the fibres unless indicated otherwise.

---

[1] See I. Bieżuńska-Małowist, 'Les Citoyens romains à Oxyrhynchos aux deux premiers siècles de l'Empire', in J. Bingen et al. (edd.), *Le Monde grec: Hommages à Claire Préaux* (1975) 741–7, esp. 745–6; cf. J. Rowlandson, *Landowners and Tenants* (1996) 107 ff.

All toponyms attested in the papyri published here are well known; for further information, see the repertories of P. Pruneti, *I centri abitati dell'Ossirinchite* (1981), and A. Calderini, S. Daris, *Dizionario dei nomi geografici e topografici dell'Egitto greco-romano* (and supplements), under the names. These standard works are mentioned in the notes only sparingly. Information on Oxyrhynchite granaries, including a list, is given in J. Krüger, *Oxyrhynchos in der Kaiserzeit* (1990) 60–62, but no reference to it will be made in the notes, since the details are in need of serious update and revision.

III **615–22** and **628–32** are cited below without reference to page numbers in *ZPE* 160 (2007); the key is: **615** = pp. 183–4; **616** = pp. 184–5; **617** = p. 186; **618** = pp. 186–7; **619** = pp. 187–8; **620** = p. 189; **621** = p. 190; **622** = pp. 190–91; **628** = pp. 191–2; **629** = pp. 192–3; **630** = pp. 193–4; **631** = pp. 194–5; **632** = pp. 195–6. References to line numbers in III **613** are based on inspection of an image.

N. GONIS

4856. ORDER FOR TRANSFER OF CREDIT IN GRAIN

26 3B.50/B(1)a　　　　　7 × 13 cm　　　　　2 August 118

This is the earliest document of this type dating from the second century (see above, general introd.). It concerns a transfer of sixty-two artabas of wheat within the same granary; this is specified by the use of the term θέμα, which comes at a rather unexpected point (see below, 9 n.).

```
(m. 2?)        cι(τολόγ- ) . . [
(m. 1)     Διονύcιοc Παυc[ιρ-
           Cαραπίωνι cιτολόγῳ λιβὸc
           τοπ(αρχίαc) Cερύφεωc τόπ(ων) χαίρειν.
    5      διάcτειλ[ο]ν ἀφ' ὧν ἔχειc ἐν
           θέματι παρὰ cοὶ πυροῦ γενή(ματοc)
           τοῦ ⟨ἐ⟩νεcτῶτοc δευτέρου
           ἔτουc Ἁδριανοῦ τοῦ κυρίου
           Διοcκόρῳ Διογένουc θέμα
   10      πυροῦ ἀρτάβαc ἑξήκοντα
           δύο, (γίνονται) (πυροῦ) (ἀρτάβαι) ξβ. (ἔτουc) β Ἁδρια[νο]ῦ
           τοῦ κυρίου, Μεcορὴ θ.
```

　1 ct　　4 το϶ (bis)　　6 γεν϶　　11 /χϭ̄, L

(2nd hand?) '*Sitolog-* of . . .'. (1st hand) 'Dionysius son of Pausir— to Sarapion, *sitologus* of the western toparchy, district of Seryphis, greetings. Transfer, from the amount you hold on deposit in your granary, from the wheat-crop of the current second year of Hadrianus the lord, to Dioscorus son of Diogenes, as a deposit, sixty-two artabas of wheat, total 62 art. of wheat. Year 2 of Hadrianus the lord, Mesore 9.'

1 *cι(τολόγ-*) ̣ ̣[. The unread letters should belong to a place name, seat of a granary. *Cϵ[ρύ-φϵωc* has obvious attractions but is difficult to read. I am not aware of a similar annotation in any other text of this kind; it is present in P. Köln III 137.1 (88), an order for grant of seed emanating from a *strategus*.

2 *Παυc[ιρ-*: *Παυc[ίριοc*, *Παυc[ιρίωνοc*, or even *Παυc[ιρίου*.

4 *Cϵρύφϵωc*. Cf. **4875** 11, **4887** 3, **4888** 3. *Sitologi* of Seryphis are attested in XLIV **3163** 5 (72), SB XXVI 16493.2–3 (*c.*123), XXXVIII **2867** 3 (127), **2871** 3 (175/6), I **90** 5 (179/80), XVII **2126** 3 (261/2), XII **1542** 3–4 (307); the granary is also implied in XLI **2968** 18 (190), XLIV **3169** 208 (200–212), and **3170** 87, 104, 153 (III). On the village of Seryphis, in addition to the standard topographical repertories, see LV **3795** 13 n.; Rowlandson, *Landowners and Tenants* 12–13, 18.

6 *παρὰ coί*. See **4861** 5 n.

9 *θέμα*. There is some writing above mu which I cannot explain; a short upright trace is all that is clear enough. The word *θέμα* could have been abbreviated, so that one would have to read *θέματ(οc)* (see below), but the position of the trace, further to the left than one would expect it, does not favour this option.

As established by F. Preisigke, *Girowesen im griechischen Ägypten* (1910) 72, the term *θέμα* refers to a private deposit in a granary. Among orders for transfer of credit in grain, it occurs at this point, i.e., after the name of the payee and before the quantity of wheat to be transferred, in **4856** 9, **4869** 7, and **4884** 5, 8. It is much more at home in (1) notices of deposit and/or (2) transfer of credit, introduced by *μεμέτρη(ται)* and *διεcτάλ(η)* respectively, and in (3) granary accounts. It is absent from most of the earlier texts of the first two categories, and does not seem to consolidate its place before the 170s (see Litinas, *ZPE* 160 (2007) 197 with n. 11). It apparently indicates that a payment was made into a giro account held in the same granary as the payer's. We may tell this from the fact that in other texts we find toponyms in this place: there, the transfer of credit is made to an account held in a different granary from that in which the payer's account is held. In most orders for transfer of credit, the transfer presumably takes place within the same granary, since there is no indication to the contrary. The use of the term *θέμα* in **4869** 7 may be due to the fact that the order concerns two transfers of credit, and one of them is into an account in another granary. The scribe of **4856** may have been particularly precise in matters of detail.

In the categories of texts described in the previous paragraph, the word is usually abbreviated, and is often resolved as *θέμ(ατοc)*: (1) III **518** 5, XLIV **3181** 8; (2) III **614**, XII **1539** 8, 15, **1540** 6, **1541** 4, 6; (3) XLIV **3165** 2, 4, **3169** 49, 50 *et passim*. However, when it is written out in full, it invariably appears as *θέμα*: this is the case apparently here and certainly in **4884** 5. The word appears without abbreviation in (1) XVII **2126** 5, SB XII 11025.7 (see *ZPE* 160 (2007) 197 n. 9); (2) LXXII **4887** 5; (3) XII **1444** 33, 35, **1526** 8, PSI Congr. XXI 12 iv 11, v 4. On the face of it, *θέμα* could be the subject of *μεμέτρη(ται)* or *διεcτάλ(η)*, with *ἀρτάβαι* in apposition; we find the latter (written out in full and) in the nominative in I **90** 5 (also in LXII **4338** 5, though the construction is different; see below). However, as mentioned earlier, *θέμα* occupies a place where we find toponyms, and when declined these are usually in the genitive (see **4874** 11 n.). Further, several texts give the names of the payees in the nominative, which could be taken as the subjects of the introductory verbs; see Litinas, *ZPE* 160 (2007) 197. It would be best not to seek a clear syntactical structure.

A case apart is LXII **4338** 5 (a 'diastolikon-metrema document' in Litinas' classification; see *ZPE* 160 (2007) 201–2, though this text is not discussed there). The text runs *μεμέτρη(ται) ἀπὸ θέματοc . . . Θέωνι τῷ καὶ Πτολεμαίῳ Ἀντιώχου ν(εωτέρου) θέμα(τοc) ἀρτάβαι κτλ*. The papyrus has *θεμα*, with no indication that the word is abbreviated, but cf. 3, where *αποθεμα = ἀπὸ θέμα(τοc)*. I suggest reading *δι(ὰ) θέμα(τοc)*; the abbreviation dubiously interpreted as *ν(εωτέρου)* is that commonly used for δι(ά), even if it is somewhat different from that found in line 3 of the same document. This prepositional construction is otherwise attested only in XII **1530** 4, 9, 11,15, a granary account of 215/16.

N. GONIS

4857. ORDER FOR TRANSFER OF CREDIT IN GRAIN

26 3B.47/B(5–8)b   8.8 × 15.8 cm   26 August 118

An order issued by Achilles, secretary of Iulius Theon, who also issued **4868** some four years later. Iulius Theon, a scion of a well-known Alexandrian family, is a familiar figure in such documents (cf. **4872**). The order concerns transfers of small quantities of wheat into accounts held by a woman in three different granaries; three such transfers are also mentioned in XXXVIII **2867** (127), which likewise emanates from a secretary of Iulius Theon.

```
      Ἀχιλλεὺς γρ(αμματεὺς) Ἰουλίου Θέω(νος)
      Διδύμωι ϲιτολ(όγῳ) Ϲκωι τόπ(ων) χαί-
      ρειν. διάϲτειλον ἀφ' οὗ
      ἔχεις ἐν θέματι τοῦ Ἰουλίο(υ)
  5   Θέωνος πυροῦ γενή(ματος) β (ἔτους)
      Ἰϲαροῦτι Διογένου[ϲ ..]..
      ἀρτάβαϲ τέϲϲαραϲ ἥμιϲυ,
      Ϲοῦιϲ ἀρτάβαϲ δύο ἥμιϲυ
      τέταρτο[ν], Ϲεντω ἀρτάβη⟨ν⟩
  10  μίαν τέταρτο[ν], (γίνονται) ἐπὶ τὸ
      αὐτὸ (πυροῦ) (ἀρτάβαι) η L. (ἔτους) β
      Ἀδρια[νοῦ Καίϲαρο]ϲ τοῦ κυρίου,
      Μεϲορ[ὴ ἐπ]αγο(μένων) γ̄.
```

1 γρ/, θε^ω   2 ϲιτο^λ, το⟩ l. Ϲκω   4 ιουλι°   5 γενηβL   10 /   11 ↗σηL   Lβ   13 [επ]αγο

'Achilles, secretary of Iulius Theon, to Didymus, sitologus of the district of Sco, greetings. Transfer, from the amount you hold on deposit for Iulius Theon, from the wheat-crop of the 2nd year, to Isarus daughter of Diogenes, (for her account) at . . . , four and a half artabas, at Suis, two and a half and a quarter artabas, at Sento, one and a quarter artaba, grand total 8 ½ art. of wheat. Year 2 of Hadrianus Caesar the lord, Mesore epagomenal 3.'

1 Ἀχιλλεὺς γρ(αμματεὺς) Ἰουλίου Θέω(νος). Achilles recurs in **4868** 1, which dates from some four years later. After that, another secretary of Iulius Theon makes his appearance in documents addressed to *sitologi*, viz. Heras, attested in 123 and 124; see **4872** 1 n. Whether Iulius Theon employed a plurality of secretaries in his Oxyrhynchite estate or there was only one such post whose incumbents changed across the years, we cannot tell.

The presence of secretaries in such texts is not unusual. Iulius Sarapion, another member of the family of Iulii Theones, also acts through a secretary (see **4869**). Secretaries represent the lessees of an imperial estate in P. Lips. I 113 (127; see **4878** 4 n.); a victor of the sacred games and ex-*exegetes* in III **516** (160); Dionysia alias Diogenis, a lady apparently of some standing, since she employs an *oikonomos* as well, in III **621** (162/3); and another person in III **627** descr. = SB XII 11167.2 (148) (see D. Hagedorn, *ZPE* 154 (2005) 199). See further below, **4858** 10, **4861** 1, and possibly **4877** 2.

Ἰουλίου Θέω(νος). Cf. **4868** 1, **4872** 1, 9. The identity of this person cannot be established with certainty. An important text is XLIV **3197** (111), a division of slaves of the deceased Ti. Iulius Theon (Theon I), ex-*hypomnematographus* and gymnasiarch (of Alexandria), between his sons Ti. Iulius Theon (Theon II), ex-*strategus* and *archidicastes*, and Ti. Iulius Sarapion, and his grandson Ti. Iulius Theon (Theon III), victor at the sacred games. Sarapion is no doubt the same as the *hypomnematographus* in **2866** and **4869**. The gymnasiarch Theon in **2865** and **2867**, and now also in SB XXVI 16493 and **4872**, was tentatively identified with Theon II, though the possibility that he is Theon III had remained open; see J. D. Thomas, **3197** 1 n. (P. J. Sijpesteijn, P. Theones p. 2, was less sceptical on the identification with Theon II, and even less so were Jones and Whitehorne, *Register of Oxyrhynchites*, under no. 4972). Given that the office of gymnasiarch was not as elevated as those posts Theon II had held by 111, it may be preferable to identify the gymnasiarch with Theon III. The latter went on to hold other high offices; see **3197** 2 n. para. 2. Iulius Theon in **4857** is certainly the same as the gymnasiarch, even though he carries no title (see also **4868**).

2 ϲιτολ(όγῳ) Cκωι τόπ(ων). The granary of Sco, a village in the upper toparchy, is well attested. Without counting abbreviated forms, a plurality of *sitologi* of this granary are mentioned in III **619** 2 (*c*.147), **620** 1–2 (147), XXXI **2588** 5 (148), XXXVIII **2870** 2 (176); possibly also in **627** descr. = SB XII 11167.2 (148) (see PSI Com. 17.10–11 n.—to judge from the image, a conjecture rather than a reading). One *sitologus* again in XVII **2125** 5 (225; see BL VII 144). Further references to the granary: XXXVIII **2840** 5 (75), III **617** 3 (135), XLI **2967** 11 (154), XXXI **2591** 15 (158/9), LXVII **4590** 19 (*c*.231).

The family of Iulii Theones owned a bath-house in the area of Sco; see P. Theones 3.3–4 (156).

6 .].. These must be the remains of a toponym.

8 Cοῦιϲ. This is the first occurrence of this locality in connection with a granary, and one of the very few references to a granary in the lower toparchy in texts of this kind. For the use of the nominative, see **4874** 11 n.

9 Cεντῳ. A village in the middle toparchy, whose granary is mentioned or implied also in P. Erl. 44.1, etc. (11), and III **632** 2 (159 or 160).

11 αὐτό. The reading is largely intuitive.

N. GONIS

4858. ORDER FOR TRANSFER OF CREDIT IN GRAIN

26 3B.49/E(1)b   5.7 × 7.3 cm   12 August 119

The upper part of the text is lost, and we do not know who issued the order and what granary was concerned; we may only infer from the subscription that a secretary was involved. The chief point of interest is the attestation of the village Τυχιναβιτωου (6–7), previously known from III **501** = M. *Chr.* 349.7–8 (186), where it was first read as Τυχινακιτωου (see BL VIII 236).

The writing is across the fibres.

```
                  .        .        .        .
          .] . . . . . . . [
          μου ἐν θέματι πυροῦ
          γενήματος τρίτου (ἔτους)
          Ἀδριανοῦ Καίcαροc
    5     τοῦ κυρίου Cαραπίωνι
          Ἐπιμάχου Τυχιναβι-
          τωου ἀρτάβαc δύο. (ἔτους)
          τρίτου Ἀδριανοῦ Καίcαροc
          τοῦ κυρίου, Μεcορὴ ιθ̄.
(m. 2) 10     c.5 ] . . γρ(αμματεὺс) ἐπήνεγκ(ε) καὶ ἔcτιν
          ] . . . γρ(αμμ- ).

    7 Ⳑ        10 γρᴸἐπηνεγκ       11 ] . . . γρᴸ
```

'. . . on deposit for me, from the wheat-crop of the third year of Hadrianus Caesar the lord, to Sarapion son of Epimachus, (for his account) at Tychinabitoou, two artabas. Year 3 of Hadrianus Caesar the lord, Mesore 19.'

(2nd hand) '. . . secretary, brought (this) and what is written above is his.'

1 It is difficult to match the expected διάcτειλον/διαcτείλατε with the traces.

2 πυροῦ: only traces of uncertain distribution on damaged fibres.

6–7 Τυχιναβιτωου. See above, introd. A check of the original by A. Benaissa has shown that III **501** has Τυχιναβιτωου. This village may have belonged to the eastern toparchy, since in **501** someone originating from this village leases land near Taampemou, a village in this toparchy.

10 γρ(αμματεύc). See **4857** 1 n.

10–11 III **620** 19–20 has ἐπήνεγκ(ε) καὶ ἔcτιν αὐτοῦ τὰ προγεγραμ(μένα). The second part of the formula cannot be read here, though it apparently ends in a form of γράφειν.

The first person singular occurs in III **516** 14 (160), where the payee adds his name followed by ἐπήνεγκα at the foot of the document. We find the same form in III **613** 4–5 (c.155), used by a person who asks that the transfer of credit recorded in the main text be carried over to him. (In SB XII 11025.16 (201), [ἐ]πήνεγκα should probably be read in place of [με]τήνεγκα.)

N. GONIS

4859. ORDER FOR TRANSFER OF CREDIT IN GRAIN

26 3B.48/G(14–17)b   11.7 × 9.7 cm   120/21

This text, **4862**, and **4863** stem from stewards and managers of Claudius Munatianus, a senior Alexandrian office-holder. Thanks to another text of this kind (see **4863** introd.), we already knew that one Claudius Munatianus held an account in the granary of Ophis, and that he employed a steward, indicative of the presence of an estate. The new texts establish the identity of Munatianus with the Alexandrian dignitary of this name, and offer further information on his estate, which will have been of substantial size.

Ἑρμα ̣ υς οἰκονόμος Κλαυδίου Μουνατια[νοῦ
ϲειτολ(όγῳ) Πακερκη ἀπηλιώτου χα(ίρειν). διάϲτειλον ἀφ' οὗ
ἔχειϲ ἐν θέματι τοῦ Κλαυδίου Μουνατια-
νοῦ πυροῦ γενήματος δ (ἔτους) Ἀδριανοῦ
5　　Καίϲαροϲ τοῦ κυρίου Ἡραΐδι τ ̣ ̣ ̣ [c.6
Ϲαραπίωνοϲ ἀρτάβαϲ ὀκτὼ ὄγδ[οον, (γίνονται) (ἀρτάβαι) η γ'.
(ἔτους) ε Ἀδριανοῦ Καίϲαροϲ τοῦ κυρί[ου *month, day*

2 ϲειτο^λ, l. ϲιτολόγῳ　　χ̄　　4, 7 Ꝉ

'Herma–us, steward of Claudius Munatianus, to the *sitologus* of Pacerce Eastern, greetings. Transfer, from the amount you hold on deposit for Claudius Munatianus, from the wheat-crop of the 4th year of Hadrianus Caesar the lord, to Herais . . . of Sarapion, eight (and) one-eighth artabas, total 8 ⅛ art. Year 5 of Hadrianus Caesar the lord, *month, day*.'

1 Ἑρμα ̣ υς. The unread letter is tau (compare the shape of the letter in 5, τοῦ) rather than upsilon. In either case, no known name offers a match, except perhaps for Ἑρμανῶς, well attested in sixth-century Aphrodito.

οἰκονόμος. Cf. **4862** 1, **4870** 1, **4879** 5, **4881** 3. Few οἰκονόμοι had previously occurred in Oxyrhynchite texts of this date; an οἰκονόμος of Ti. Claudius Theon I is attested in XLII **3051** 1 (89), and two others occur in orders addressed to *sitologi*: XXXI **2588** 4 (148), in which the οἰκονόμος represents a former *agoranomus* and gymnasiarch, and III **621** 2, 12 (162/3), where the οἰκονόμος acts for a woman who also employs a secretary. As for the function itself, '[i]n practice . . . it seems that the titles *cheiristes, epitropos* and *oikonomos* did not denote specific functions but were synonyms meaning "manager" or "administrator"' (D. Rathbone, *Economic Rationalism and Rural Society in Third-Century A.D. Egypt* (Cambridge 1991) 62).

Κλαυδίου Μουνατια[νοῦ. There is no reference to an office or other description in any of the *sitologi* documents that mention him, but the amount involved in **4863**, the presence of stewards, and the very name indicate that Claudius Munatianus was an important man, no doubt identical with Munatianus son of Munatianus (the latter a former *archidicastes*), member of the Museum, ex-chiliarch, ex-*strategus* of Alexandria, priest and *archidicastes* in 128; see P. Mil. Vogl. I 26.1 (with BL VII 118), and VI 266.2, 3. **4862** 2, Κλαυδίου Μουνατιανοῦ νεωτ(έρου), indicates that there was a Claudius Munatianus 'senior': these will be father and son. It is of course conceivable that **4859** and **4863** may refer to the father, but this seems less likely. SB XVIII 13156, a record of proceedings that mentions Κλαύδιος Μουνατιανός (8) two lines after a reference to ὁ ἱερεὺς καὶ ἀρχιδ[ικαϲτής (6), confirms the *gentilicium* of the priest and *archidicastes* (father or son), and corroborates the identification of Claudius Munatianus in the granary texts with the Alexandrian dignitary.

2 ϲιτολ(όγῳ) Πακερκη ἀπηλιώτου. Cf. **4860** 3, **4868** 2, **4874** 5. ἀπηλιώτου distinguishes it from the homonymous village in the middle toparchy. This village has occurred in connection with granaries also in XVIII **2185** 3 (92), XXXVIII **2864** 2 (123), VII **1024** 4–5 (129), XXXVIII **2868** 10

(147) (the toparchy is not specified but is probably the eastern), LXVII **4589** 31 (*c.*170), XLI **2968** 18–19 (190), XLIV **3170** 97, 162 (III), **3181** 3 (251/2). A single *sitologus* is mentioned in **2864** and **1024**.

     5 τ . . . [. This must be Herais' patronymic, in which case Cαραπίωνοc would be her papponymic. (τῇ κα[ί does not seem a possible reading, even if eta is not ruled out.)

N. GONIS

4860. ORDER FOR TRANSFER OF CREDIT IN GRAIN

26 3B.48/G(18–21)b   10.1 × 17.2 cm   18 August 122

This document is remarkable (though not exceptional) for its fairly elaborate structure. The person who issued it, orders transfers of credit first into his own accounts in three different granaries, and then into the accounts of two brothers that formerly belonged to their mother, held in two other granaries.

    Ἡρ . . . . . Πτολεμαίου ἀπ' Ὀξυρύγχ(ων) πόλ(εως)
    Φαύcτωι τῷ καὶ Ἀμφίονι cιτολ(όγῳ) ἀπηλ(ιώτου)
    τοπ(αρχίας) Πακερκ(η) τόπ(ων) χαίρειν. διάcτειλ(ον)
    ἀφ' οὗ ἔχειc ʽμού᾽ ἐν θέμ(ατι) (πυροῦ) γενή(ματος) ϛ (ἔτουc)
5   Ἀδριανοῦ Καίcαροc τοῦ κυρίου ὑπὲρ
    μὲν ἰδίου ὀνόματο(c) Πακερκ(η) ἀπηλ(ιώτου)
    (ἀρτάβαc) ἑπτὰ χοί(νικα) μίαν, ὁ αὐτ(ὸc) Ψῶβθ(εωc) ἀπηλ(ιώτου)
    (ἀρτάβαc) ἐννέα τέταρτ(ον) ὄγδοον, ὁ αὐτ(ὸc) Cατύρο(υ)
    ἐποικ(ίου) (ἀρτάβην) μίαν ἥμιcυ τέταρτ(ον) χοί(νικα) μίαν,
10   Ἀπολλωνίωι καὶ Διονυcίωι τῷ καὶ
    Ἀμοιτᾷ ἀμ(φοτέροιc) Ἥρωνο(c) (πρότερον) τῆ(c) μητ(ρὸc) ʽαὐτῶ(ν)᾽ Cινθώ(νιοc)
    Ἀλεξάνδ(ρου) Θώcβ(εωc) (ἀρτάβαc) πέντε ἥμιcυ
    ὄγδοον, τοῖc αὐτοῖ(c) ὁμοί(ωc) (πρότερον) τῆ(c) α(ὐτῆc)
    μητρὸc αὐτῶ(ν) Cινθώ(νιοc) Cενοκώμ(εωc)
15   (ἀρτάβαc) ἓξ ἥμιcυ τέταρτον, (γίνονται) ἐπὶ τὸ α(ὐτὸ)
    (ἀρτάβαι) τριάκοντα ἥμιcυ χοί(νικεc) δύο.
    (ἔτουc) ϛ Αὐτοκράτοροc Καίcαροc
    Τραϊανοῦ Ἀδριανοῦ Cεβαcτοῦ, Μεcο(ρὴ) κε̄.

    1 οξυρυγ^χπο^λ   2 cιτο^λ   2, 6, 7 απη^λ   3 το꒹, το꒹, διαcτει^λ   3, 6 πακερ^κ
4 θε^μᵷγεν^η   4, 17 L   6 ονοματ°   7, 8, 9, 12, 15, 16 ⸀   7, 9, 16 χ^{οι}   7, 8 αυ^τ
7 ψωβ^θ   8, 9 τεταρ^τ   8 cατυρ°   9 εποι^κ   11 α^μηρων꒷ᾱ τ꒷μη꒷   11, 14 αυτ^ωcινθ^ω
12 αλεξαν^δθωc^β   13 αυτ°ομ°ᾱ τ꒷ᾱ   14 cενοκω^μ   15 /, ᾱ   18 μεc°

'Her— son of Ptolemaeus, from the city of the Oxyrhynchi, to Faustus alias Amphion, sitologus of the eastern toparchy, district of Pacerce, greetings. Transfer, from the amount you hold on deposit for me, from the wheat-crop of the 6th year of Hadrianus Caesar the lord, for my own account at

Pacerce Eastern, 7 art. (and) one choen.; the same, at Psobthis Eastern, nine (and) one-quarter (and) one-eighth art.; the same, at the hamlet of Satyrus, one (and) one-half (and) one-quarter art. (and) one choen.; and to Apollonius and Dionysius alias Amoitas, both sons of Heron, (for the account) formerly of their mother Sinthonis daughter of Alexander, at Thosbis, five (and) one-half (and) one-eighth art.; to the same (persons), likewise (for the account) formerly of their mother Sinthonis, at Senocomis, six (and) one-half (and) one-quarter art., grand total thirty and one-half art. and two choen. Year 6 of Imperator Caesar Traianus Hadrianus Augustus, Mesore 25.'

1 Ἡρ.....: Ἡρακλᾶς? For the gender, cf. 7, 8 ὁ αὐτ(ός).

2 Φαύστωι τῷ καὶ Ἀμφίονι σιτολ(όγῳ). Faustus alias Amphion is attested in the same post in XXXVIII **2864** 1–2 (123), which comes from the same 'archive'. In P. Lips. II 141.1–2 of 133 we find him addressing the *sitologus* of Phoboou (see **4883** 4 n.), a village in the same toparchy as Pacerce (only the alias survives but the restoration of his first name seems likely; this text also supplies his patronymic, viz. Ptolemaeus). His son Dionysius is likewise addressing *sitologi* in III **516** of 160; he is described as a victor of the sacred games and a former exegete of Oxyrhynchus. A son who achieved such distinction surely had a father of some standing. The latter's service as *sitologus* must have been a liturgy connected with landownership at Pacerce; he was surely a metropolitan, and most probably an absentee landlord. It would be interesting to know whether he discharged his duties in person at the village or through paid deputies. If these suppositions hold, they offer a picture of the office of *sitologus* which appears to be new (not discussed in the relevant literature at hand, admittedly uneven and out of date). There are some clear parallels with the office of *decaprotus*, whose sphere of competence, however, was much broader.

3 Πακερκ(η). Cf. 6. See **4859** 2 n.

5–6 ὑπὲρ μὲν ἰδίου ὀνόματο(ς). This expression has not been attested in any other document of this kind, though the context must be the same as in the fragmentary BGU III 746.9 (Herm.; 259/60), where it occurs among references to artabas of wheat. It probably means that the transfers are to be made into accounts held by the person issuing the order at the granaries of Pacerce, Psobthis, and Satyrou; the quantities of grain transferred were presumably to be credited against his taxes (cf. **4890**) or rents on land in the area of these villages. Such transfers from an account held at one granary to that held at another are those indicated by the expression δι(ασταλεῖσαι) ἑαυτῷ + name of village, common in granary accounts; see P. Mich. XVIII 786.6, 17, etc., XLIV **3169** 2, 45, etc., PSI Congr. XXI 12 i 6, 12, etc.

7 χοί(νικα) μίαν. Cf. 9. The word has occurred as feminine in some first-century ostraca from Caranis: O. Mich. I 31.3, 33.3, 34.3, 37.3, 41.4, 43.4, 46.4, 49.3.

Ψῶβθ(εως) ἀπηλ(ιώτου). See **4882** 1–2 n.

8–9 Cατύρο(υ) ἐποικ(ίου). This is the first time this hamlet, located in the eastern toparchy, occurs in connection with a granary.

10 One Ἀπολ( ) Ἥρωνος acts for a friend in XXXVIII **2869** 1–2 (c.147).

11 (πρότερον) τῆ(ς) μητ(ρός). Cf. 13–14. References to the previous holders of granary accounts are very few; this is the first time we have members of the same family, which suggests an inheritance. It is more common to find parcels of land described 'formerly of (their) father/mother'.

The same abbreviation was interpreted as (ὀνόματος κληρονόμων) in Theban ostraca; see J. C. Shelton, *ZPE* 20 (1976) 127–35, with the qualifications in P. Brook. 66.4 n. (by Shelton himself), and O. Heid. 66.3–4 n.

12 Θώςβ(εως). See **4873** 3 n.

14 Cενοκώμ(εως). Cf. **4889** 6. *Sitologi* or the granary of this village, situated in the western toparchy, are also mentioned in XXXVIII **2841** 5 (85), **2867** 9 (127), SB XIV 11265.9 (II/III), 12181.4 (III).

N. GONIS

4861. ORDER FOR TRANSFER OF CREDIT IN GRAIN

27 3B.42/H(10)a   c.7 × c.16 cm   28 August 122

This order stems from a secretary of (M.) Antonius Dius, who was known to have served as *strategus* of Alexandria and *neocorus* of the Great Serapeum, and to have had business interests in Oxyrhynchus.

A sheet-join runs 1.9 cm from the left-hand edge. There is a short line of writing on the back, which I have not been able to decipher in full; it starts with γραμ (a form of γραμματεύς? abbreviated?), and ends (δραχμαί) $\overline{A}$, '1,000 drachmas'.

```
     Ἑ]ρμᾶς γραμματεὺς
     Ἀντωνείου Δίου
     ϲιτολ(όγοιϲ) Ϲινκεφα τόπ(ων) χ(αίρειν).
     διαϲτείλατε ἀφ’ οὗ ἔχετε
  5  π]αρ’ ὑμῖν ἐν θέματι
     τ]οῦ Ἀντωνείου Δίου (πυροῦ) γεν(ήματοϲ)
     τοῦ ἐνεϲτῶτοϲ ϛ (ἔτουϲ)
     Ἀδριανοῦ Καίϲαροϲ
     το]ῦ κυρίου Διογένει
 10  τῷ καὶ] Θέωνι Θέωνοϲ
     ἢ οἷϲ ἐ]ὰν αἱρῆται
     (ἀρτάβαϲ) ἑκα]τόν, (γίνονται) (ἀρτάβαι) ρ.
     (ἔτουϲ) ϛ Ἀδρ]ιανοῦ τοῦ κυρίου,
     Μεϲορὴ] ἐπ[αγ]ομ(ένων) ε̄.
```

2, 6 l. Ἀντωνίου   3 ϲιτο^λ, το?χϛ   6 ?γενϛ   7 ϛ   12 /σ̄
14 επ[αγ]ο^μ

'Hermas, secretary of Antonius Dius, to the *sitologi* of the district of Sincepha, greetings. Transfer, from the amount you hold on deposit in your granary, for Antonius Dius, from the wheat-crop of the current 6th year of Hadrianus Caesar the lord, to Diogenes alias Theon, son of Theon, or to whomever he chooses, one hundred artabas, total 100 art. Year 6 of Hadrianus the lord, Mesore epagomenal 5.'

1 γραμματεύϲ. See **4857** n.

2 Ἀντωνείου Δίου. This person was previously attested in I **100** 1–2 (133) as Μᾶρκοϲ Ἀντώνιοϲ Δεῖοϲ καὶ ὡϲ χρηματίζω, ϲτρατηγήϲαϲ Ἀλεξανδρείαϲ, νεωκόροϲ τοῦ μεγάλου Ϲαράπιδοϲ; he owned property in the city of Oxyrhynchus. SB VIII 9904.5–7 (154), Καιϲαρείου τοῦ κατα|ϲκευαϲθέντοϲ ἐν τῇ Ἀντινόου πόλει | ὑπὸ Ἀντωνίου Δείου, could refer to the same individual, since the building of this Caesareum must have taken place in the 130s. It is also possible that the same Marcus Antonius Dius is to be recognized in P. Köln II 98.16 (II), a land register of unknown provenance (not necessarily Oxyrhynchite).

3 ϲιτολ(όγοιϲ) Ϲινκεφα τόπ(ων). Cf. **4867** 8, **4880** 2. *Sitologi* and/or the granary of this village,

situated in the upper toparchy, have occurred in P. NYU II 52.3, etc. (see **4889** 16 n.) (early II), P. Lips. I 116.10 (123), 113.3 (127; see **4878** 4 n.), III **517** 6 (130), **515** 2 (134), PSI XII 1262.23, 25, 27 (137), XXXIII **2676** 36 (151); see also XLIV **3170** 71, 106, 127 (III).

5 π]αρ' ὑμῖν. Cf. **4856** 5. Another occurrence in P. Lips. I 113.4 (127).

11 ἢ οἷς ἐ]ὰν αἱρῆται. Cf. **4862** 7, **4873** 8. The same collocation occurs in P. Lips. I 116.6 (123) (see BL X 96), XLVII **3337** 5 (c.142), and III **628** 5–6 (159).

13 The putative κυρίου is very cursively written, but seems inescapable after τοῦ.

N. GONIS

4862. ORDER FOR TRANSFER OF CREDIT IN GRAIN

27 3B.42/H(8)d   9.3 × 13.3 cm   122

An order issued by another manager (οἰκονόμος), possibly a freedman (see 1 n.) of Claudius Munatianus (see **4859** introd.).

   Κλαύδιος Γερμαν[ὸς] οἰκονόμος
   Κλαυδίου Μουνατιανοῦ νεωτ(έρου)
   cειτολ(όγῳ) Ὤφεως χαί(ρειν).
   διάcτειλον ἀφ' οὗ ἔχεις τοῦ
5   προγεγραμμένου Κλαυδ(ίου)
   Μουνατιανοῦ θέματος
   Δημητρίωι ἢ οἷς ἐὰν αἱρῆται
   πυροῦ γενήμ(ατος) ϛ (ἔτους) Ἀδριανοῦ
   Καίcαρος τοῦ κυρ[ί]ου ἀρτάβας
10   τριάκοντα [τέ]ccαρας ἥμιcυ τέταρτ(ον)ʹ, (γίνονται) (ἀρτάβαι) λδ.
   (ἔτους) ϛ Ἀδριανοῦ Κ[αίcαρος τ]οῦ κυρίου
   month day] *vac.*

2 νεω^τ   3 cειτο^λ; l. cιτολ(όγῳ)   χαι^c   5 κλαυ^δ   8 γενη^μ   8, 11 L
10 τεταρ^τ, /—σ

'Claudius Germanus, steward of Claudius Munatianus the younger, to the *sitologus* of Ophis, greetings. Transfer, from the amount you hold on deposit for the aforesaid Claudius Munatianus, to Demetrius or to whomever he chooses, from the wheat-crop of the 6th year of Hadrianus Caesar the lord, thirty-four (and) a half (and) one-quarter artabas, total 34 art. Year 6 of Hadrianus Caesar the lord, *month, day*.'

1 Κλαύδιος Γερμαν[ὸς] οἰκονόμος. P. Erl. 38.6 Κλαύδιος Γερμανὸς ὁ καὶ [(?; II) need not refer to the same man. That an estate steward bore the same *gentilicium* as the landowner makes it likely that he was a freedman (I owe this observation to Professor Rathbone).

2 Κλαυδίου Μουνατιανοῦ νεωτ(έρου). See **4859** 1 n. para. 3.

3 Ὤφεως. Cf. **4865** 2, **4867** 2, **4869** 2, **4870** 4, **4871** 3, **4884** 2. Other references to the granary of this village, situated in the eastern toparchy, are P. Lips. I 112.1 (122), XXXVIII **2869** 2 (c.147); cf.

also XLIX **3497** 6 (216?), XLIV **3170** 59, 169 (III). On the village of Ophis in general, in addition to the standard repertories, see LXIII **4397** 22 n.; Rowlandson, *Landowners and Tenants* 13 n. 24; P. Köln X 415 introd.

7 *Δημητρίωι*. The absence of the patronymic is remarkable.

ἢ οἷς ἐὰν αἱρῆται. See **4861** 11 n.

10 The papyrus is very damaged at the end of the line, but it seems that the quantity of three-quarters of an artaba, added above the line, was not included in the total.

11 (*ἔτους*) ς̄. Of the L-shaped year symbol, only the base survives. A short semi-horizontal stroke above it, slightly sloping downwards, may be taken as the base of s(t)igma or zeta. I have hesitantly opted for sigma because zeta (not attested elsewhere in this text) would not have had such a long base.

N. GONIS

4863. ORDER FOR TRANSFER OF CREDIT IN GRAIN

27 3B.42/H(11–12)a   12 × 18 cm   26 September 122

An order for a transfer of 700 artabas of wheat out of the account of Claudius Munatianus, effected through a steward (*ἐπίτροπος*). A sister piece, on which the restorations here are based, is P. Lips. I 112, which concerns the payment of 383 ½ art. 3 choen. out of the same account and to the same person as **4863**, and may date from one day later than **4863** (see below, 7 n.). The amounts of wheat transferred are very large (700 art. is the highest figure found in such documents), and imply farming on a grand scale. The reasons behind the transactions are unclear.

The hand is an elegant cursive, the work of a professional scribe who could have penned important official documents. Elegant scripts are not unknown among texts of this kind; **4869** and **4876** are also written in a formal cursive script, though nothing compares with P. Lips. I 117 (175/6), written in a hand of the 'Severe Style'.

Κλαύδιος Μουνατιανὸς [*ϲιτολόγωι* Ὤ*φεωϲ* (?) *τόπ*(*ων*) *χαίρειν.*
διάϲτειλον ἀφ' οὗ ἔχειϲ [*μου θέματοϲ πυροῦ γενήματοϲ*
τοῦ διελθόντοϲ ς (*ἔτουϲ*) Ἀ*δρ*[*ιανοῦ Καίϲαροϲ τοῦ κυρίου*
Διδύμῳ Πτολεμαίου τοῦ [*Πτολεμαίου μητρὸϲ Πρίμαϲ*
5   *ἀρτάβαϲ ἑπτακοϲίαϲ,* [[(*γίνονται*) *ἀρτάβαι* ψ. *ἔτουϲ* ζ
Αὐτοκράτοροϲ Καίϲαροϲ Τρα[*ϊανοῦ Ἀδριανοῦ Ϲεβαϲτοῦ,*
Θὼθ κ̄θ̄. (*m.* 2) *Λεοντᾶϲ τοῦ π*[*ρογεγραμμένου Κλαυδίου Μου-*
νατιανοῦ ἐπίτροποϲ ϲεϲημεί[*ωμαι τὰϲ προκειμέναϲ ἑπτα-*
κοϲία⟨*ϲ*⟩, (*γίνονται*) (*ἀρτάβαι*) ψ. *χρόνοϲ ὁ αὐτόϲ.*

3 ϲ   9 /σ̄

'Claudius Munatianus to the *sitologus* of the district of Ophis(?), greetings. Transfer, from the amount you hold on deposit for me, from the wheat-crop of the past 6th year of Hadrianus Caesar the lord, to Didymus son of Ptolemaeus, grandson of Ptolemaeus, mother Prima, seven hundred artabas, total 700 art. Year 7 of Imperator Caesar Traianus Hadrianus Augustus, Thoth 29.' (2nd hand) 'I, Leontas, overseer of the aforesaid Claudius Munatianus, have countersigned the aforementioned seven hundred, total 700 art. The same date.'

1 [*cιτολόγωι* Ὄφεωc (?) *τόπ*(ων). Restored after P. Lips. 112.1, but it is also possible that **4863** was addressed to the *sitologus* of some other granary.

4 *μητρὸc Πρίμαc* is restored after P. Lips. 112.6 [*μητρ*]*ὸc Πρείμαc*, a suggestion by Viereck, recorded in BL I 215. Wilcken, ibid., countered that parallel texts made no reference to metronymics, but this only reflects the state of the evidence at that time. The addition of the mother's name is rare but not inexistent; cf. e.g. **4869** 6 and **4889** 7.

5 The line as restored seems short; possibly there were no abbreviations, or *ἑβδόμου* was written instead of ζ.

7 *Θὼθ* κ̄θ̄. P. Lips. 112.8, after BL I 215, is said to read [. . . .] λ; the on-line image indicates that [*Θὼ*]*θ* λ would suit space and trace.

7–8 *Λεοντᾶc τοῦ π*[*ρογεγραμμένου Κλαυδίου Μου*]*νατιανοῦ ἐπίτροποc*. The word order is unusual; P. Lips. 112.8–9 has *Λεοντᾶc ἐπίτροπ*(*οc*) *το*[*ῦ*] *προγ*[*εγ*]*ραμμένου Κλαυδίου* [*Μουν*]*ατιανοῦ*. Jones and Whitehorne, *Register of Oxyrhynchites* no. 2640, identify the overseer with Leontas son of Didymus in XXXVIII **2863** 1 (123), who orders the transfer of 130 artabas out of his private account; but this is not inescapable.

8 *ἐπίτροποc*. Preisigke, *Girowesen* 112, thought this term referred to a guardian, but this is ruled out by what we now know of Claudius Munatianus.

8–9 *τὰc προκειμέναc ἑπτα*]*κοcία*⟨*c*⟩, *scil.* ἀρτάβαc, also omitted from P. Lips. 112.9.

N. GONIS

4864. ORDER FOR TRANSFER OF CREDIT IN GRAIN

27 3B.42/G(3–4)a   3.9 × *c.*12 cm   4 October 122

The papyrus has lost the upper part, so that we do not know who issued the order and to which granary it was addressed. The text refers to the smallest quantity of wheat, 4 choenices, attested in a document of this kind (**XXXI 2591** 11 also records the transfer of 4 choen., but this is not the only such transfer recorded there).

       .   .   .

   ..[*c.*8   χ]α̣[ίρ]ε̣ι̣ν.
   διάcτειλο[ν] ἃc ἔχειc
   ἐν θέματι ἐπ᾽ ὀνόματο(c)
   τοῦ ἀδελφοῦ μου Διονυ-
5   cίου πυροῦ γενήματοc
   ἕκτου ἔτουc Ἁδειανοῦ
   τοῦ κυρίου Ἀπίωνι γραμ-
   μα̣τε̣ῖ πρακτόρων Cενε-

κελαιου χ[ο]ίνιγκας
10 τέccαραc. ἔτουc ζ̄
Ἀδριανοῦ τοῦ κυρίου, Φαῶφι̅ ζ̄.

3 ονοματ°   6 l. Ἀδριανοῦ   9 l. -κελεου χοίνικαc

'. . . greetings. Transfer the (artabas) you hold on deposit in the name of my brother Dionysius, of the wheat-crop of the sixth year of Hadrianus the lord, to Apion, secretary of *praktores*, (for his account) at Seneceleu, four choenices. Year 7 of Hadrianus the lord, Phaophi 7.'

3–4 ἐν θέματι ἐπ' ὀνόματο(c) τοῦ ἀδελφοῦ μου. This expression is new in this context; elsewhere, for third-party deposits we find a simple genitive. ἐπ' ὀνόματοc, however, is no stranger to such texts: cf. III **613** 5 (*c*.155).

7–8 γραμματεῖ πρακτόρων. This is the earliest reference to such a γραμματεύc. There is little point in speculating on the possible remit of these πράκτορεc.

8–9 Cενεκελαιου most probably refers to the granary in which Apion holds an account (see **4881** 4 n.), and is not to be taken with πρακτόρων (in that case, we would expect e.g. ἀργυρικῶν or cιτικῶν to have come before the name of the village).

9 χ[ο]ίνιγκαc. For the spelling, cf. XLIV **3163** 21–2 (72) χοίνιγκεc.

N. GONIS

4865. ORDER FOR TRANSFER OF CREDIT IN GRAIN

27 3B.42/H(11–12)b   7.8 × 12 cm   6 October 122

An order issued by the beneficiary of **4863** (and P. Lips. I 112) ten days after the transaction described in **4863** took place; cf. also **4866**. In all these cases the same granary was involved. Such transfers were clearly made only 'on paper'.

Δίδυμοc Πτολεμαίου τοῦ Πτολεμαίου
Διογένει cιτολ(όγῳ) ἀπη(λιώτου) τοπ(αρχίαc) Ὤφεωc τόπ(ων) χ(αίρειν).
διάcτειλον ἀφ' οὗ ἔχειc μου ἐν θέματι
πυροῦ γενήματοc τοῦ διελθόντοc ἕκτου
5 ἔτουc Ἀδριανοῦ Καίcαροc τοῦ κυρίου
Θέωνι Cιρίωνοc πυροῦ ἀρτάβαc
πεντήκοντα τέταρτον
χ]οίνικαc ὀκτώι, (γίνονται) (πυροῦ) (ἀρτάβαι) ν δ χ(οίνικεc) η.
ἔτουc ἑβδόμου Αὐτοκράτοροc Καίcαροc
10 Τ]ραϊανοῦ Ἀδριανοῦ Cεβαcτοῦ, Φαῶφι θ̅.

2 cιτο^λαπ^ητο?ωφεωcτο?χϨ   8 l. ὀκτώ /ϩ̅δ̅, χ^η

'Didymus son of Ptolemaeus, grandson of Ptolemaeus, to Diogenes, *sitologus* of the eastern toparchy, district of Ophis, greetings. Transfer, from the amount you hold on deposit for me, from the wheat-crop of the past sixth year of Hadrianus Caesar the lord, to Theon son of Sirion, fifty (and) one-quarter artabas (and) eight choenices, total 50 ¼ art. 8 choen. of wheat. Year seventh of Imperator Caesar Traianus Hadrianus Augustus, Phaophi 9.'

1 Δίδυμος Πτολεμαίου τοῦ Πτολεμαίου. Cf. **4863** 4, **4866** 1.

2 Διογένει ϲιτολ(όγῳ). Cf. **4869** 2. A Diogenes, *sitologus* of Phoboou (also in the eastern toparchy), occurs in XXXVIII **2863** (22.viii.123); this could be a namesake, but we might consider whether one person was responsible for more than one granary. See **4872** introd. para. 2.

Ὤφε(ωϲ). See **4862** 3 n.

N. GONIS

4866. ORDER FOR TRANSFER OF CREDIT IN GRAIN

27 3B.42/G(3–4)b   *c.*10.5 × 14 cm   122/3

An order issued by the same person as **4865**, and possibly written in the same hand. Unlike **4865**, the transfer is made into an account held at a different granary.

Δίδυμ]οϲ Πτολεμαίου τοῦ Πτολεμαίου ϲιτολ(όγῳ) [ἀπη(λιώτου) (?) τοπ(αρχίαϲ)
Ὤφεωϲ (?) τόπ(ων)] χαίρειν. διάϲτειλον ἀφ᾽ οὗ ἔχειϲ μ[ου ἐν θέματι
πυροῦ γε]νήματοϲ τοῦ διελθόντοϲ ἕκτου [ἔτουϲ
Ἀδριανοῦ Καί]ϲαροϲ τοῦ κυρίου Δημητρίωι Διογέν[ουϲ
5   *c.*4 Φοβ]ωου πυροῦ ἀρτάβαϲ τριάκοντα [*c.*5?
     *c.*6] ἔτουϲ ἑβδόμου Ἀδριανοῦ Καίϲαροϲ τοῦ [κυρίου, *month day*

1 ϲιτο^λ

'Didymus son of Ptolemaeus, grandson of Ptolemaeus, to the *sitologus* of the eastern(?) toparchy, district of Ophis(?), greetings. Transfer, from the amount you hold on deposit for me, from the wheat-crop of the past sixth year of Hadrianus Caesar the lord, to Demetrius son of Diogenes(?), . . . (for his account) at Phoboou, thirty . . . artabas of wheat. Year seventh of Hadrianus Caesar the lord, (*month, day*).'

1–2 The supplements for the end of 1 and the beginning of 2 are based on **4865**, and are by no means certain.

4 Δημητρίωι Διογέν[ουϲ. A Demetrius son of Diogenes issued another order of this kind in 133 (P. Lips. I 115).

5 Φοβ]ωου. On this village, see **4879** 1 n. It is not clear what is lost immediately before it. It could be a word describing the payee (some letters could have been lost also after Διογέν[ουϲ in 4); it is less likely, though it cannot strictly be excluded, that it is another toponym, a village sharing the same granary with Phoboou.

5–6 Further numbers (and a reference to a number of choenices) will have stood at the end of 5 and the beginning of 6.

N. GONIS

4867. ORDER FOR TRANSFER OF CREDIT IN GRAIN

26 3B.48/G(3–6)b   6.5 × 9 cm   122/3

This transfer concerns a small quantity of wheat from the granary of Ophis to that of Sincepha; the order was issued by the brother of the 'payer'.

Δίδυμος οττίωνος
cι(τολόγοις) Ὤφεως τόπ(ων) χαίρειν.
διαστείλατε ἃς ἔχετε̣
μου ἐν θέματι (πυροῦ) γενή(ματος)
5   τοῦ διελθόντος ἕκ[του
ἔτους Ἁδριανοῦ
τοῦ κυρίου Ἀπίωνι [.].[
νος Cιγκεφα τόπων ἀρτάβ(ας)
τρεῖς χοί(νικας) τέσαρας, (γίνονται) (ἀρτάβαι) γ χ(οίνικες) δ.
10   (ἔτους) ζ Αὐτοκράτορος Καίσαρος
Τρ]αϊανοῦ Ἁδριανοῦ Cε[βα]c[τοῦ,

       .   .   .   .

2 c̣τ, το⟩   4 ⸍γεν^η   8 αρτα^β   9 χοι, /⸍σ, χ^δ   l. τέccαραc   10 L

'Didymos son of –ottion, to the *sitologi* of the district of Ophis, greetings. Transfer, from the (artabas) you hold on deposit for me, from the wheat-crop of the past sixth year of Hadrianus the lord, to Apion son of —n, (for his account) at the district of Sincepha, three artabas (and) four choenices, total 3 art. 4 choen. Year 7 of Imperator Caesar Traianus Hadrianus Augustus, (month, day).'

   1 ̣οττίωνος. I have tried to read Κοττίωνος, a rather rare name, but kappa is very difficult; the letter looks like a large beta. *Βοττίων is not attested, though one may compare the name Βόττος (cf. Κοττίων and Κόττος).
   2 Ὤφεως. See **4862** 3 n.
   7–8 [Θέω]νος suits the space better than e.g. [Ἀπίω]νος (the trace at the end of 7 is too small).
   8 Cιγκεφα τόπων. See **4861** 3 n. τόπων indicates that the granary is meant, a detail not usually supplied at this point; I have found it only in III **630** 10, XXXI **2591** 15, P. Lips. I 114.4, 116.7, 14.

                                                                N. GONIS

4868. ORDER FOR TRANSFER OF CREDIT IN GRAIN

27 3B.42/H(8)a   c.8 × 15 cm   122/3

The left part of another order issued by Achilles, secretary of Iulius Theon; cf. **4857**, which seems to be the work of the same scribe as **4868**. The address to the *sitologus* of Pacerce implies that Theon held land in the area of the village; this information is new (see further 2 n.). Two transfers are apparently requested, into accounts held in granaries about which we know little.

Ἀχιλ(λεὺς) γρ(αμματεὺς) Ἰουλ(ίου) Θ[έωνος cιτολ(όγῳ)
ἀπη(λιώτου) τοπ(αρχίας) Πακ[ερκη τόπ(ων) χ(αίρειν). διάcτ(ειλον)
ἀφ᾽ οὗ ἔχεις ἐν [θέματι τοῦ
Ἰουλίου Θέων[ος (πυροῦ) γενή(ματος)
5   ἕκτου ἔτους ...[
Ἰωνθι.[
Τοου [ἀρτάβας
(γίνονται) τεccα[ρ-
(ἔτους) ζ Ἀδ[ριανοῦ

1 αχιˡγρſιουˡ   2 απ⁽ᵗᵒ⁾   8 /   9 L

'Achilles, secretary of Iulius Theon, to the *sitologus* of the eastern toparchy, district of Pacerce, greetings. Transfer, from the amount you hold on deposit for Iulius Theon, from the wheat-crop of the (past?) 6th year, to ... at(?) Ionthis ... at(?) Toou ... artabas ..., total four (or: forty) ... Year 7 of Hadrianus ...'

1 cιτολ(όγῳ). I have restored the form in the singular after 3 ἔχεις. XXXVIII **2864** 1–2 (123) and VII **1024** 3 (129) also refer to a single *sitologus*. There is no room for positing a name in the lacuna.

2 Πακ[ερκη. On this village, see **4859** 2 n. The mysterious Arsinoe daughter of Theon, who had a connection with Iulius Theon, also had dealings with the granary of Pacerce; see **4872** para. 2.

4 There does not seem to be enough space for restoring τοῦ διελ(θόντος) at the end of the line.

5 After ἔτους, we expect Ἀδριανοῦ τοῦ κυρίου; the payee's name would have followed, at the end of the line or in the next, and then the patronymic. A toponym begins the next line; this means that either there was no reference to the emperor, and the payee's name was written in 5, or that there was no reference to a payee, and the transfers were to be made into accounts held by Iulius Theon in other granaries. However, there is no exact parallel to the latter possibility among texts of this kind; the wording in **4860** is different, while P. Lips. I 116 (175/6) refers to a transfer of what remains of a deposit without specifying the beneficiary.

6 Ἰωνθι.[. The scribe may have written Ἰωνθιc, though the trace is too small to confirm this; for the use of the nominative in this context, see **4874** 11 n. The village of Ionthis is mentioned immediately after Pacerce in XLI **2968** 19 (190), in a context that implies the presence of a granary there. For further references to the village, see P. Hamb. IV 253.7 n.

7 Τοου. This may be the village in the eastern toparchy of the Oxyrhynchite nome, attested in PSI IX 1036.3 (192) as Τοου ἀπηλιώτου. Other villages of this name were located close to the Heracleopolite and Hermopolite borders; see Pruneti, *I centri abitati dell'Ossirinchite* 206–7, with P. Wash. Univ. II 78 ii 14 n. The possibility exists, however, that τοου here is the end of the toponym; cf. Τυχιναβιτωου in **4858** 6–7.

8 What I have taken as the symbol for (γίνονται) may be the extension of the upright part of the symbol for (ἔτους). After that, read τέccα[ρεc or τεccα[ράκοντα. The symbol for the artabas was apparently not written.

N. GONIS

4869. ORDER FOR TRANSFER OF CREDIT IN GRAIN

26 3B.52/D(1–3)b　　　　　　9. 3 × 11.5 cm　　　　　　28 June 123

An order issued by Sarapion, secretary of Iulius Sarapion, another scion of the family of Theones. A sister piece is **XXXVIII 2866**, which is closely contemporary (it refers to the same wheat-crop of year 7), and is written in the same hand as **4869**. Unlike **2866**, **4869** is complete; it concerns transfers to two different payees; one of them held an account in the same granary as Iulius Sarapion, as the use of the term θέμα implies (see 7 n.).

The text offers a new, if unexceptional, *dies Augusta* of Hadrian; see 10 n.

Cαραπίων γρα(μματεὺc) Ἰουλίου [Cα]ραπίω(νοc) ὑπομ(νηματογράφου)
Διογένει cιτολ(όγῳ) ἀπηλ(ιώτου) τοπ(αρχίαc) Ὤφε(ωc) τόπ(ων)
χα(ίρειν). διάcτειλον ἀφ' οὗ ἔχειc ἐν θέ-
ματι πυροῦ γενή(ματοc) τοῦ ἐνε(cτῶτοc) ζ (ἔτουc) Ἀδριανοῦ
5　Καίcαροc τοῦ κυρίου τοῦ Ἰουλ(ίου) Cαραπ(ίωνοc)
Cαραπίωνι Cαραπίω(νοc) μη(τρὸc) Ταυcίριοc
Cεφω (ἀρτάβαc) ἕξ, Θέωνι Ὀννω(φρίου) θέμ(α)
(ἀρτάβαc) δώδεκα, (γίνονται) ἐπὶ τὸ α(ὐτὸ) (ἀρτάβαι) ιη.
(ἔτουc) ἑβδόμου Ἀδριανοῦ Καίcαροc τοῦ
10　κυρίου, Ἐπεὶφ δ̄, Cεβαcτῇ.

1 γρα, [cα]ραπι‾ῳυπο‾μ　2 απη‾λτο⸾ωφ‾το⸾　3 χ‾α　4 γεν‾η̣, εν‾ζ⸗　5 ιου‾λcαρα⸾
6 cαραπι‾ῳ μη　7 ‾ο‾, ονν‾ωθε‾μ　8 ‾ο‾, ⸍, ᾱ‾ο‾　9 ⌐

'Sarapion, secretary of Iulius Sarapion, *hypomnematographus*, to Diogenes, *sitologus* of the eastern toparchy, district of Ophis, greetings. Transfer, from the amount you hold on deposit for Iulius Sarapion, from the wheat-crop of the present 7th year of Hadrianus Caesar the lord, to Sarapion son of Sarapion, mother Tausiris, (for his account) at Sepho, six artabas; and to Theon son of Onnophris, (as a) deposit, twelve artabas, grand total 18 artabas. Year seventh of Hadrianus Caesar the lord, Epeiph 4, *dies Augusta*.'

1 = XXXVIII **2866** 1–2.
Ἰουλίου [Cα]ραπίω(νοc) ὑπομ(νηματογράφου) = Jones and Whitehorne, *Register of Oxyrhynchites* no. 4280; see further XLIV **3197** 2 n. He was a brother of 'Theon II', on whom see above, **4857** 1 n.
2 Διογένει cιτολ(όγῳ) ἀπηλ(ιώτου) τοπ(αρχίαc) Ὤφε(ωc) τόπ(ων). See **4865** 2 n.
5 τοῦ Ἰουλ(ίου) Cαραπ(ίωνοc). As in **2866** 7, this part is misplaced; it should have come after ἔχειc (3) or after θέματι (4).

6 μη(τρὸς) Ταυσίριος. See **4863** 4 n. The addition of the metronymic, not given for the second payee, might have served to distinguish this Sarapion son of Sarapion from a namesake.

7 Cεφω. Cf. **4875** 14. This village, in the Thmoisepho toparchy, has occurred in connection with a granary in PSI X 1121.6 (236/7) and XLIV **3170** 13, 34, 233 (iii).

θέμ(α). In view of the reference to Sepho, we would expect a village name here, but no Oxyrhynchite toponym beginning Θεμ- has been attested. The alternative, which I have adopted, is to resolve θέμ(α): the transfer would be made into Theon's account in the granary of Ophis; see above, **4856** 9 n. No other document of this kind attests anything comparable, referring first to an outward giro transfer and then to a transfer inside the home granary.

10 Ἐπεὶφ δ̄, Cεβαcτῇ. The fourth day of a month was regarded as a *dies Augusta* on account of the birthday of Titus; see W. F. Snyder, *Aegyptus* 18 (1938) 223–4, and *Aegyptus* 44 (1964) 162. Snyder knew of no example from the reign of Hadrian; now there are three, all of them occurring in Oxyrhynchite documents of the same kind: **4869** 10; P. Lips. I 113 (28.vii.127; see **4878** 4 n.), Caesarius (= Mesore) 4 (at the end of l. 9, *ed. pr.* read cεc(ημειώμεθα), but the on-line image allows reading Cεβα(cτῇ)); and P. Lips. II 140.7 (1.ix.133), Thoth 4. One or two other *dies Augustae* of the reign of Hadrian have been attested in papyri: PSI I 40.16 (10.ii.129), Mecheir 16; and possibly P. Strasb. IV 250b.3 (2.xi.137), Hathyr 6, after BL V 140, but contrast P. Customs p. 148 (no. 144).

N. GONIS

4870. Order for Transfer of Credit in Grain

27 3B.42/H(7)a　　　　　　　　7.6 × c.14 cm　　　　　　　　c.122–3?

An order issued by the steward of a woman known from a text dating some thirty years later. The date has not been preserved, but it may have fallen in year 6 or 7 of Hadrian, like most other texts addressed to the *sitologus* of Ophis in this group (P. Lips. 112, **4862**, **4865**, **4867**, **4869**, and possibly **4863** and **4866**; the exceptions are **2869** of c.147 and **4884** of 157).

Εὔφημος οἰκονόμος
Ἀγαθοκλείας τῆς καὶ
Ἀπολλωνίας Ἰcχυρίω(νος)
cιτολ(όγῳ) Ὤφεως χαίρειν.
5　διάcτειλ(ον) ἃc ἔχειc μου
ἐν θέματι (πυροῦ) γενή(ματος) [.] (ἔτους)
Ἀδριανοῦ τοῦ κ[υ]ρ[ίου
Ἀπολλω[-
...[

.　　.　　.　　.

3 ιcχυρι^ω　　4 cιτο^λ　　5 διαcτει^λ　　6 ʒγεν^η, L

'Euphemus, steward of Agathocleia alias Apollonia, daughter of Ischyrion, to the *sitologus* of

Ophis, greetings. Transfer the (artabas) that you hold on deposit for me, from the wheat-crop of the ... year of Hadrianus the lord, to Apollo— ...'

1 *Εὔφημος*. The name has not occurred in any other papyrus, but is well attested outside Egypt.

οἰκονόμος. See **4859** 1 n.

2–3 *Ἀγαθοκλείας τῆς καὶ Ἀπολλωνίας Ἰσχυρίω(νος)*. Agathocleia had been attested in XXXI **2564** = C. Pap. Gr. II.1 44.3 ff. (153), in which she declares the death of a slave of hers, with her son Ischyrion son of Theon acting as her guardian.

4 *Ὤφεως*. See **4862** 3 n.

6 The year may be 6 ([ϛ]) or 7 ([ζ]); see above, introd.

N. GONIS

4871. ORDER FOR TRANSFER OF CREDIT IN GRAIN

26 3B.48/G(7–10)b   9.3 × 5.1 cm   *c.*122–3?
                                                Plate XIV

Only the upper part of the text survives; the date is lost, but in view of the papyri found in its immediate vicinity it must date from some time in the reign of Hadrian (the hand looks early enough) or Antoninus Pius. For the argument for placing it in the period 122–3, based on the address to the *sitologi* of Ophis, see **4870** introd. Needless to say, the dating is extremely uncertain.

The *gentilicium* of the lady who issued the order and the presence of a steward (*φροντιστής*) indicate that she was of some standing; nothing else is known of her.

        Οὐαλερία Ἀρτεμιδώρα δι' Ἐ-
        παφροδίτου φροντιστοῦ σιτολ(όγοις)
        ἀπηλιώτου τόπων Ὤφεως τόπων
        χαίρειν. διαστείλατε ἀφ' οὗ
    5   ἔ]χ[ε]τέ μου ἐν θέματι πυροῦ
        γε]νήματ[ος το]ῦ διελθόντο{ι}ς

2 ϲιτο^λ   3 ἀπηλιώτου τόπων: l. ἀ. τοπαρχίας

'Valeria Artemidora through Epaphroditus, steward, to the *sitologi* of the eastern toparchy, district of Ophis, greetings. Transfer, from the amount you hold on deposit for me, from the wheat-crop of the past (*n*th year) ...'

1–2 *Ἐπαφροδίτου φροντιστοῦ*. Cf. **4879** 5, where we find an *οἰκονόμος* of this name in the service of of another lady. The name suggests that he was a slave or freedman. An Epaphroditus, freedman, is attested in P. Genov. II 62.1 (Oxy.; 98). Freedmen are no strangers to managerial posts; cf. e.g. below, **4881** 2–3.

3 τόπων written for τοπαρχίαϲ: cf. XLI **2964** 13 ≈ **2965** 13 ≈ **2966** 12 (154) ἄνω τόπων, followed by Μονίμου τόπων.

Ὤφεωϲ. See **4862** 3 n.

N. GONIS

4872. ORDERS FOR TRANSFER OF CREDIT IN GRAIN

45 5B.57/G(1–2)a   10 × 17.3 cm   2 September 124
                                                                 Plate IX

Two orders issued by Heras, secretary of Iulius Theon, and addressed to *sitologi* of two different village granaries. The first concerns 591 artabas 3 choenices, the third largest amount of wheat attested in a text of this type (see **4863** introd.), close to the 600 art. paid out of the same account in XXXVIII **2865**. The beneficiaries include Arsinoe daughter of Theon, a lady well represented in such texts; see below, 5 n. There are two other such orders by Heras, written by the same scribe as **4872**, **2865** and SB XXVI 16493, both dating from about a year earlier (they both refer to the crop of Year 7 of Hadrian).

The orders are written on the same sheet, one after the other; it would be a reasonable assumption that they never reached their destination (note that this papyrus does not stem from the 'archive' that has produced all the other texts published in this section). A comparable item is P. Lips. I 116, which likewise carries two orders for transfer of credit, out of accounts held possibly by the same person (see Preisigke, *Girowesen* 123), and into accounts of Arsinoe daughter of Theon. The two orders are addressed to *sitologi* of different granaries; the *sitologi* bear the same name (Theagenes, rare in this period), and we may be dealing with one person holding both posts (the editor thought that the two orders are the products of two different hands, but it seems to me that the 'second hand' is only a more cursive version of the 'first', and I would associate them both with the same scribe). The *sitologi* in **4872** are not mentioned by name, which leaves the possibility open (cf. also **4865** 2 n.).

    Ἡρᾶ[ϲ] γραμματεὺϲ Ἰουλ(ίου) Θέ[ωνο(ϲ) γυμνα(ϲιάρχου)
    ϲιτολόγ(ῳ) ϛ[κ]ῳ χ(αίρειν). διάϲτ[ειλον
    ἀ[φ'] ο(ὗ) ἔχειϲ ἐν θέματι τοῦ Ἰουλ(ίου) Θ[έωνο(ϲ)
    (πυροῦ) γενή(ματοϲ) η (ἔτουϲ) Ἀδριανοῦ Καίϲαροϲ τοῦ κυρίου [
5 .].ρ( ) ϲαραπ(ίωνοϲ) καὶ Ἀρϲινό(η) Θέω(νοϲ) ... ἀρτάβ(αϲ) πεντακ[ο-
    ϲί[α]ϲ ἐνενήκοντα μίαν χοί(νικαϲ) τρεῖϲ,
    (γίνονται) [(ἀρτάβαι)] φϙα χ(οίνικεϲ) γ. (ἔτουϲ) θ Ἀδριαν[ο]ῦ Καίϲαροϲ
    τοῦ κυρίου, Θὼθ ε̄.
        (*vac.*)

Ἡρᾶc γραμματεὺc Ἰουλ(ίου) Θέω[ν]ọ(c) [γυ]μνạ(cιάρχου)

10   cιτολ(όγοιc) Cενεπ(τα) χ(αίρειν). διαcτείλατ[ε ἀφ᾿ οὗ ἔχετε

τοῦ Ἰουλ(ίου) Θέωνο(c) ἐν θέματι (πυροῦ) γ[ενή(ματοc) η (ἔτουc)

Ἀδριανοῦ Καίcαροc τοῦ κυρίου Διδυ[μ-

Θέωνοc το(ῦ) Ἀθηνα(ίου) ἀρτάβ(αc) ἑξ⟨ήκ⟩οντα τέτ[αρτον

χοί(νικαc) τρεῖc, (γίνονται) (ἀρτάβαι) ξ δ χ(οίνικεc) γ. (ἔτουc) θ Ἀδριανοῦ

15   Καίcαροc τοῦ κ[υρ]ίου, Θὼθ ε̄.

1, 3, 9, 11 ιου^λ   2 cιτολο^γ   2, 10 χ͞ʃ   3 α[φ]^ο   4, [11] ⸗γεν^η   5].ρ́cαρα⸌,

αρcιν°θε^ω   5, 13 αρτα^β   6 χ^οι   7, 14 /⸍σ, χ^γ L   9, 11 θεων°   10 cιτο^λ cενε⸌

13 τ°αθην^α

'Heras, secretary of Iulius Theon, gymnasiarch, to the *sitologus* of Sco, greetings. Transfer, from the amount you hold on deposit for Iulius Theon, from the wheat-crop of the 8th year of Hadrianus Caesar the lord, to . . . son of Sarapion and to Arsinoe daughter of Theon . . . five hundred ninety-one artabas (and) three choenices, total 591 art. 3 choen. Year 9 of Hadrianus Caesar the lord, Thoth 5.

'Heras, secretary of Iulius Theon, gymnasiarch, to the *sitologi* of Senepta, greetings. Transfer, from the amount you hold on deposit for Iulius Theon, from the wheat-crop of the 8th year of Hadrianus Caesar the lord, to Didym— son/daughter of Theon, grandson/-daughter of Athenaeus, sixty (and) one-quarter artabas (and) three choenices, total 60 ¼ art. 3 choen. Year 9 of Hadrianus Caesar the lord, Thoth 5.'

1 Ἡρᾶ[c] γραμματεύc. This is the third secure reference to Heras, after XXXVIII **2865** and SB XXVI 16493 (see above, introd.). A secretary makes his appearance also in XXXVIII **2867** 1 of 127: the edition prints [. . .] . . γραμματεύc, but the lacuna is not as large as indicated; [Ἡρ]ᾶc can be neither confirmed nor excluded.

Sijpesteijn, P. Theones p. 2 n. 7, entertained the suspicion that Ἥρων γραμματεύc in XLIV **3197** 6 (111), a slave who was part of the share of Theon II, and the only γραμματεύc in that document, might have been the same as Ἡρᾶc. It seems more likely, however, that Ἡρᾶc is a diminutive of a name beginning Ἡρακλ- than of Ἥρων.

Ἰουλ(ίου) Θέ[ωνοc γυμνα(cιάρχου). Cf. 9. On this person, see **4857** 1 n. The resolution γυμνα(cιάρχου) is suggested by XXXVIII **2865** 2 (*c*.123) and **2867** 2 (127), in which the word is written out in full.

C[κ]ω. See **4857** 2 n.

5].ρ( ): perhaps C]αρ(ᾶτι) or C]αρ(ᾷ), suggested by N. Litinas (not C]αρ(απίωνι): the abbreviation would be unusual).

Ἀρcινό(η) Θέω(νοc). (This note updates and expands the discussion in *AnPap* 13 (2001) 29.) Besides **4872**, Arsinoe daughter of Theon is the recipient of wheat from the crop of the 7th year in three other such documents: XXXVIII **2864** (26.viii.123), where her account at Pacerce is set to be credited; P. Lips. I 116 (123), where further credit transfers are made into an account she holds ἔξω πρακτορείαc Πακερκη τόπ(ων), a singular expression; and SB XXVI 16493 (*c*.123), where the same Iulius Theon as here authorizes a transfer of 75 art. into an account she holds at Seryphis. Apart from Seryphis, Iulius Theon possessed an account with the granary at Pacerce too (see **4868**). I had once suspected that Arsinoe might have been Iulius Theon's daughter, but this cannot be proven; it is a curious coincidence that the payers in **2864** and P. Lips. 116 are also called Theon.

Another question is who her fellow payee, the 'son of Sarapion', was and what was their relationship. This is further hampered by the unread letters in this line (see below). To view them as a married couple is tempting, but the idea of a couple holding a joint account would be anachronistic (the case of LXVII **4590** is too uncertain). Payments made jointly to two persons are recorded in III **619**, XXXVIII **2863** (in both cases, brothers), and perhaps XXXI **2590**.

. . . . This is either part of the description of Arsinoe or of Theon; or a toponym, as in 10. (The first letter may be alpha.)

10 Σενέπ(τα). (Σενοπ(ώθεως) is less likely.). The granary of Senepta, a village in the middle toparchy, is referred to explicitly in XXXVIII **2866** 3 (123), PSI XII 1262.21 (137), and probably SB VI 9088.12 (III). References to payments of grain into accounts held in this granary are also mentioned in **4888** 7 and perhaps XXXVIII **2867** 10, where the edition prints Σεν . ( ) but Σενέπ(τα) seems acceptable; cf. also III **517** 2, which seems to refer to a payment made out of Senepta. In addition, there are numerous entries in the account XLIV **3169** (200–212). (Note that in **3169** 46 the papyrus does not have Σενέπ[τ]α, as reported in XLVII p. xviii, but Σέννεως, as read in *ed. pr.* (one might wish to dot the two nus). It is entirely possible, however, that this is a scribal error, as suggested in *ZPE* 30 (1978) 186 n. 1.)

12 Διδυ[μ-: Διδύ[μῳ, Διδύ[μῃ, Διδυ[μᾶτι, Διδυ[μίωνι, etc.

N. GONIS

4873. ORDER FOR TRANSFER OF CREDIT IN GRAIN

26 3B.48/G(3–6)d   4.4 × 9.5 cm   132/3

An order for the transfer of 100 artabas addressed to the *sitologi* of Thosbis. The upper part is lost, carrying away the names of the person who issued the order and of the first *sitologus*.

```
              ·   ·   ·
        c.4 ] . χ . [        c.15
     καὶ Π]απόντῶ[τι σιτολόγοις
     Θ]ώσβεως τόπων [χ(αίρειν). διαστείλα-
     τε ἀφ' οὗ ἔχετέ [μου ἐν θέμα-
5    τι] πυροῦ γενή[ματος τοῦ ἑκκαι-
     δεκάτου ἔτους Ἁ[δριανοῦ τοῦ
     κυρίου Φανίαι . [        c.10
     ἢ ο]ἷς ἐὰν αἱρῆται π[υροῦ ἀρτάβας
     ἑκ]ατόν, γείνοντ[αι (ἀρτάβαι) ρ. ἔτους
10   ἑπτακαιδεκάτου Ἁ[ὐτοκράτορος Καίσαρος
     Τραϊανοῦ Ἁδριανοῦ [Σεβαστοῦ, month
     κη̄.
```

9 l. γίνονται

'. . . and Papontos, *sitologi* of the district of Thosbis, greetings. Transfer, from the amount you

hold on deposit for me, from the wheat-crop of the sixteenth year of Hadrianus the lord, to Phanias
... or whomever he chooses one hundred artabas of wheat, total 100 art. Year seventeenth of Imperator Caesar Traianus Hadrianus Augustus, *month* 28.'

3 Θ]ώϲβεωϲ. Cf. **4860** 12. The granary of this village, situated in the middle toparchy, was
previously known from III **614** (179/80).
5–6 ἐκκαι]δεκάτου. ἑπτακαι]δεκάτου seems to be excluded by the space.
7 Φανίαι ̣[: or Φανίᾳ Ṭ ̣[.
8 ἢ ο]ἷϲ ἐὰν αἱρῆται. See **4861** 11 n.
11–12 The earliest possible date is 25 September (Thoth 28) 132.

N. GONIS

4874. Order for Transfer of Credit in Grain

26 3B.48/G(7–10)d   11 × 12.4 cm   25 July –23 August 135

This order is issued by an Alexandrian, member of the Euthenodotean tribe
(not among the commonest in papyri), represented by a cousin. The beneficiaries
are a woman and another Alexandrian (but of a different tribe).

Ἀλέξανδροϲ Δημητρίου Εὐθηνο-
δότειοϲ ὁ καὶ Ἀλθαιεὺϲ διὰ Θέωνοϲ Θέωνοϲ ἀνεψι[οῦ] Ἀπολλοφάνει καὶ Εὐαγγέλῳ ϲειτολόγ(οιϲ) [ἀπη]λιώτου τοπαρχίαϲ
5   Πακερκη τόπ(ων) χαίρ[ε]ιν. διαϲτείλατε ἀφ' οὗ ἔχετέ μου ἐν θέματ(ι)
(πυροῦ) {(ἀρτάβαϲ)} γενήμ(ατοϲ) ιθ (ἔτουϲ) Ἀδριανοῦ τοῦ κυρίου
Τρωϲίλλει Ἁρμιύϲιοϲ Ϲενεψαυ (ἀρτάβαϲ) κ,
Διονυϲίῳ Διονυϲίου Ϲωϲικοϲ-
10 μείῳ τῷ καὶ Ἀλθ(αιεῖ) διὰ Ζωίλ(ου) Γεμίνο[υ
ἡ α(ὐτὴ) κώμ(η) (ἀρτάβαϲ) ϛ, (γίνονται) (ἀρτάβαι) κϛ. (ἔτουϲ) ιθ
Αὐτοκράτοροϲ Καίϲαροϲ Τραϊ[ανοῦ
Ἁδριανοῦ Ϲεβαϲτοῦ, [Μεϲορ]ὴ ̣.

3–4 l. Εὐαγγέλῳ   4 ϲειτολοⁿ; l. ϲιτολόγοιϲ   5 πακερκη: ρ corr. from κ   τοⁿ
6 θεμαᵀ   7 ϛϲγενηᵘιθL   8 ϲ   10 l. -μίῳ   αλᶿ, ζωιᶩ   11 ηᾱκωᵘϲ c /ϲ

'Alexander son of Demetrius, of the Euthenodotean tribe and the Althaean deme, through
Theon son of Theon, (my) cousin, to Apollophanes and Euangelus, *sitologi* of the eastern toparchy,
district of Pacerce, greetings. Transfer, from the amount you hold on deposit for me, from the wheat-
crop of the 19th year of Hadrianus the lord, to Trosilla daughter of Harmiusis, (for her account) at
Senepsau, 20 artabas, (and) to Dionysius son of Dionysius, of the Sosicosmian tribe and the Althaean
deme, through Zoilus son of Geminus, (for his account) at the same village, 6 artabas, total 26 art.
Year 19 of Imperator Caesar Traianus Hadrianus Augustus, Mesore *n*.'

1–2 Εὐθηνοδότειος ὁ καὶ Ἀλθαιεύς. On the Euthenodotean tribe, see P. J. Sijpesteijn, *APF* 41 (1995) 184 with n. 5 (the text published there is SB XXII 15327); in all its occurrences it is combined with the same demotic as here. Another Alexandrian is among the payees; see 9–10. Other such texts attesting Alexandrians are **4880** (144) (payer), III **623** descr. = SB XII 11165 (*c*.144) (payer), and **632** 4 (159 or 160) (payee).

5 Πακερκη. See **4859** 2 n.

8 Τρωcίλλει. This is no doubt a version of the Roman name Drusilla, rare in the papyri (most references are to the well-known lady involved in a protracted legal case). Her Egyptian patronymic (Ἀρμιύcιοc) would have been truly remarkable had it not been for XLIV **3169** 146 Δρωcίλλα Πετcείριο[c.

Cενεψαυ. This was a village in the western toparchy; the presence of a granary there is implied by this passage, **4876** 12, and **4889** 11.

9 Διονυcίῳ Διονυcίου. Persons of this name but with no further description issued similar orders to the *sitologi* of Syron (western toparchy) in 133 (P. Lips. I 114) and of Sco (upper toparchy) in 147 (III **620**).

9–10 Cωcικοcμείῳ τῷ καὶ Ἀλθ(αιεῖ). This is the commonest combination of Alexandrian tribe and deme names.

11 ἡ α(ὐτὴ) κώμ(η) = Cενεψαυ. ἡ α(ὐτή), referring to 'the same village' (κώμη is usually not written), is common in granary accounts; see XLIV **3169** 29 n., and L. C. Youtie, *ZPE* 30 (1978) 182 (the text published there is SB XIV 12181). More recent examples include PSI Congr. XXI 12 ii 31 *et passim* (261), an account, and LXVII **4590** 22 (*c*.231), a notice of transfer of grain.

When the name of the village is written out in full, it mostly appears in the genitive; see **2867** 9 (127), P. Strasb. 127.6 (135), **4878** 7 (*c*.135), **623** descr. = SB 11167.6 (148), **629** 9, 14 (159/60), **622** 11, **630** 11 (both 161), **2871** 5 (175/6); **4867** 8 (122/3), which adds τόπων after the name of the village, may offer another example. It is given in the nominative in **4874** 11 and **4876** 8; also in **2839** 3 (64), **2840** 6 (75), and SB 12181.8 (if correctly read; the genitive is used in l. 4).

(ἔτουc) ιθ. Only ink flecks are visible, but a later date is not likely, since it would imply that the grain was more than one year old; see **4878** 4 n., last para.

N. GONIS

4875. Order for Transfer of Credit in Grain

26 3B.51/J(1–3)a   7.5 × 17.5 cm   23 August 135

This and the following item (**4876**) are orders issued by Dius son of Acusilaus through representatives (here, his son Acusilaus). Both are addressed to *sitologi* of the same granary, and concern transfers of credit to two different giro accounts.

Dius was a member of an affluent Oxyrhynchite family, previously known from the activities of his father and of his son; see further 1 n.

Δῖος Ἀκουcιλάου διὰ Ἀ-
κουcιλάου υἱοῦ cιτο-
λόγοιc Κερκεθύρεωc
χαίρειν. διαcτείλατε

```
 5    ἀφ’ οὗ ἔχετέ μου ἐν θέ-
      ματι πυροῦ γενήματος
      τοῦ ἐννεακαιδεκάτου
      ἔτους Ἀδριανοῦ Καίσαρος
      τοῦ κυρίου Cυντύχῃ
10    ἀπελευθέρᾳ Cαραπιάδος
      Διονυσίου Cέρυφις ὀκτὼ
      τέταρτον χοίνικες
      ἑπτά, Ἡρακλήῳ τῷ καὶ
      Ἀπίωνι Ἀ[πίω]νος Cεφω
15    δύο ἥμισυ τέταρτον
      χοίνικας τρεῖς, (γίνονται) ἐπὶ τὸ
      αὐτὸ (ἀρτάβαι) ια δ. (ἔτους) ιθ Αὐτοκράτορος
      Καίσαρος Τραϊανοῦ
      Ἀδριανοῦ Cε[βα]cτοῦ,
20    Μεσορὴ λ̄.
```

12 l. χοίνικας   16 /   17 ⸂, L

'Dius son of Acusilaus, through Acusilaus, (my) son, to the *sitologi* of Cercethyris, greetings. Transfer, from the amount you hold on deposit for me, from the wheat-crop of the nineteenth year of Hadrianus Caesar the lord, to Syntyche, freedwoman of Sarapias daughter of Dionysius, (for her account) at Seryphis, eight (and) one-quarter (artabas) (and) seven choenices, (and) to Heracles alias Apion son of Apion, (for his account) at Sepho, two (and) one half (and) one-quarter (artabas) (and) three choenices, grand total 11 ¼ art. Year 19 of Imperator Caesar Traianus Hadrianus Augustus, Mesore 30.'

1–2 Δῖος Ἀκουσιλάου διὰ Ἀκουσιλάου υἱοῦ. This and **4876** are the only texts in which Dius appears in the first person. His father occurs in P. Lips. I 120 = M. *Chr.* 230.2 (after 89) Διον( ) τοῦ καὶ Ἀκους[ι]λ(άου) Δίου τοῦ Διον( ) [τ]οῦ καὶ Ἀμόϊτ[ο]ς, in which he tries to secure repayment of a debt of 1000(+) drachmas. III **494** = M. *Chr.* 305 = Jur. Pap. 24 = Sel. Pap. I 84.3 (156), attests Dius' son and refers to his lineage, which helps establish the name of the grandfather (Dionysius): Ἀκουσίλαος Δείου τοῦ Διονυσίου τοῦ καὶ Ἀκουσιλάου μητρὸς Διονυσίας Θέωνος. (This latter detail escaped Mitteis' notice, as well as of Jones and Whitehorne, who list Dionysius in *Register of Oxyrhynchites* 69 (no. 1280) as DION( ).) In view of this family's tendency for grandsons to take the name of their paternal grandfathers, it is likely that the grandfather of Dionysius alias Acusilaus was also called Dionysius (it is unclear whether this putative Dion(ysius) alias Amois is related to those recorded in *Register of Oxyrhynchites* under nos. 1311 or 1354).

494 is Acusilaus' will, made when he was 48 years old; it was opened in 165. 'The testator, after conferring freedom upon five of his slaves . . . leaves his son Dius heir to his propery [including additional slaves], subject to a life-interest reserved for Aristous, the wife of Acusilaus' (**494** introd.). Acusilaus' wife was also his cousin, daughter of his paternal uncle Heraclides. If Acusilaus was 48 years old in 156, in our text he is (around) 27. His father Dius will have been in his fifties.

The following stemma summarizes what we know of this family:

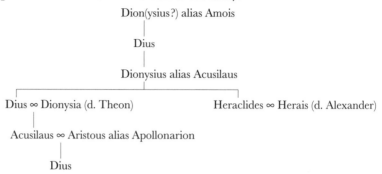

διὰ Ἀκουϲιλάου υἱοῦ. A son acts for his father in LXVII **4590** 11 (*c.*231). (δι(ὰ) τ(οῦ) παι(δὸϲ) Ϲαραπ(ίωνοϲ) is read in XXXI **2591** 8, but I have doubts about τ(οῦ) παι(δὸϲ).)

3 *Κερκεθύρεωϲ.* The granary of this village, situated in the western toparchy, was previously attested only in **4590** 10.

9 *Ϲυντύχη.* The name is rare in the papyri, but not uncommon outside Egypt. The only other papyrus that attests it is P. IFAO I 7.1 (I BC). (There is a gap between sigma and upsilon, probably because of a hole that was already there in antiquity.)

11 *Ϲέρυφιϲ.* For the village, see **4856** 4 n. It was situated close to Cercethyris; see Rowlandson, *Landowners and Tenants* 12, and cf. LXIX **4747** 6–8 (296). For the use of the nominative, attested also in **4876** 8, see **4874** 11 n.

13 *Ἡρακλήῳ.* This is a dative of *Ἡρακλῆϲ* rather than *Ἡράκλειοϲ*, though the latter possibility cannot be excluded; see Youtie, *Scriptiunculae* ii 819, and Gignac, *Grammar* ii 71.

14 *Ϲεφω.* See **4869** 7 n. Unlike Seryphis, this village was not located in the vicinity of Cercethyris.

17 The grand total indicates that the artaba of 40 choenices was used (8 ¼ art. 7 choen. + 2 ½ ¼ art. 3 choen. = 11 art. 10 choen. = 11 ¼ art.).

Αὐτοκράτοροϲ is written in *Verschleifung.*

N. GONIS

4876. Order for Transfer of Credit in Grain

27 3B.42/H(10)c   9.2 × 20.1 cm   24–29 August 135

An order issued by the same person and addressed to the same *sitologi* as **4875**, a few days later. This time Dius is represented through a secretary. The hand is an elegant professional cursive.

     Δῖοϲ Ἀκουϲιλάου διὰ Διογένουϲ
     γραμμ(ατέωϲ) ϲιτολ(όγοιϲ) Κερκ[ε]θύρεωϲ
     χαίρειν. διαϲτείλ[α]τε
     ἀφ’ οὗ ἔχωι ἐν θέματι πυροῦ
5   γενήμ(ατοϲ) τοῦ ἐνεϲτῶτοϲ ιθ (ἔτουϲ)

Ἀδριανοῦ Καίcαροc τοῦ κυρ[ίου
Πτολεμαίῳ Πτολεμαίου ̣ ̣
Κερκευρα ἀρτάβαc ὀκτώι,
(γίνονται) (ἀρτάβαι) η, Θ ̣ ̣ ̣ ̣ ̣ει Νεοπτολ(έμου)
10   διὰ Ἁρμιύcι[ο]c καὶ Ἡρᾶτοc
γεωργῶν Cενεψαυ ἀρτάβαc
ἑπτά, (γίνονται) (πυροῦ) (ἀρτάβαι) ζ, (γίνονται) ἐπὶ τὸ α(ὐτὸ) (ἀρτάβαι) ιε.
(ἔτουc) ιθ Αὐτοκράτοροc Καίcαροc
Τραϊανοῦ Ἀδριανοῦ Cεβαcτοῦ,
15   Μεcο[ρὴ] ἐπαγ(ομένων) ̣ ̣

| 2 γραμμˀcιτο^λ | | 4 l. ἔχω | 5 γενη^μ, ʃ | 8 l. ὀκτώ | 9 /▱, νεοπτο^λ |
| 12 /ᒿ▱ζ/επιτοā▱ιε | | 13 ↳ | 15 επαγ | | |

'Dius son of Acusilaus, through Diogenes, secretary, to the *sitologi* of Cercethyris, greetings. Transfer, from the amount I hold on deposit, from the wheat-crop of the current 19th year of Hadrianus Caesar the lord, to Ptolemaeus son of Ptolemaeus, (for his account) at Cerceura, eight artabas, total 8 art., (and) to Th— son(?) of Neoptolemus, through Harmiysis and Heras, farmers, (for his(?) account) at Senepsau, seven artabas, total 7 art. of wheat, grand total 15 art. Year 19 of Imperator Caesar Traianus Hadrianus Augustus, Mesore epagomenal *n*.'

2 γραμμ(ατέωc). See **4857** 1 n.

Κερκ[ε]θύρεωc. See **4875** 3 n.

8 Κερκευρα. This was a village in the middle toparchy; the granary is mentioned in III **631** 3 (158) (coupled with Petne), XXXVI **2766** (305); cf. also XXXVIII **2839** 3 (64), **2840** 6 (75), XII **1531** 20 (III), XLIV **3170** 37, 197 (III). Κερκευρώcεωc τόπων occurs in III **625** descr. = SB XII 11168.4 (158), and this has led to the resolution Κερκευ(ρώcεωc) in **516** 5 (160); this is not necessary. It is likely that Cerceura and Cerceurosis refer to one and the same village; see S. Daris, *StudPap* 19 (1980) 117–18.

For the use of the nominative, see **4874** 11 n.

9 Perhaps Θεογένει. Abrasion makes reading difficult.

10–11 διὰ . . . γεωργῶν. For the expression, cf. P. Mich. XVIII 786.10–12, etc. (*c*.167), XXXVIII **2871** 5 (175/6), XLIV **3169** 49–50, etc. (200–212), XII **1526** 9 (222/3), PSI Congr. XXI 12 v 4, 5, etc. (261), etc.

11 Cενεψαυ. See **4874** 8 n.

N. GONIS

4877. ORDER FOR TRANSFER OF CREDIT IN GRAIN

27 3B.42/H(6)a   11.7 × 10.5 cm   13 September 135

This order is issued through an intermediary, possibly a secretary (see 2 n.), and concerns a transfer to take place within the same granary.

The writing is across the fibres.

Ἀγα[θὸ]c Δαίμων Δίου διὰ Cαραπίωνος

   *c.*6]˳εωc cι(τολόγοιc) Μονίμ(ου) χαίρειν. διαcτ(είλατε)

ἀφ' ὧ]ν ἔχετε ἐν θέμ(ατι) τοῦ Ἀγαθοῦ Δαίμο(νος)

(πυροῦ) γενή(ματος) το]ῦ ἐννεακαιδεκάτου ἔτους Ἀδριανοῦ

5   Καίc]αρος τοῦ κυρίου Διονυcίωι Φιλίcκου

   *c.*6]˳c ἀρτάβας ἑξήκοντα, (γίνονται) (ἀρτάβαι) ξ. ἔ[τους

εἰκοcτ]οῦ Αὐτοκ[ράτορο]c Καίcαρος Τ[ρ]α[ϊανοῦ

Ἀδριανοῦ] Cεβα[cτοῦ, Θὼ]θ ιε̄.

2 ⳽μονι͙, διαc᷁   3 θε͙, δαιμ°   6 /ⲥ̄

'Agathus Daemon son of Dius through Sarapion . . . , to the *sitologi* of Monimou, greetings. Transfer, from the amount you hold on deposit for Agathus Daemon, from the wheat-crop of the nineteenth year of Hadrianus Caesar the lord, to Dionysius son of Philiscus . . . , sixty artabas, total 60 art. Year twentieth of Imperator Caesar Traianus Hadrianus Augustus, Thoth 15.'

2 *c.*6]˳εωc. The unread letter is lambda or tau. If the latter, read γραμμα]τέωc. Otherwise, we may have Sarapion's patronymic, e.g. Ἀχιλ]λέωc. [ἀπ' Ὀξ(υρύγχων) πό]λεωc would be out of place, let alone that we would expect πόλεωc to be abbreviated too.

Μονίμ(ου). Cf. **4878** 3. There are numerous references to the granary or *sitologi* of Monimou, a 'hamlet' in the upper toparchy: P. Wisc. II 39.2 (*c.*120), P. Lips. I 115.1 (133), III **515** 2 (134), I **89** 5 (*c.*141), III **623** descr. = SB XII 11165.3 (*c.*144), III **624** descr. = SB XII 11166.5 (148; see **4878** 4 n.), XLI **2964** 13, **2965** 13, **2966** 12–13 (all three of 154), III **613** 2 (*c.*155), **628** 2 (159), **629** 2 (159/60), XXXI **2589** 2 (159), **2590** 2 (159), **2591** 7 (*c.*159), XLIV **3170** 40, 148 (III).

6 *c.*6]˳c. This must be the end of a toponym, a village granary in which Dionysius held an account, rather than of an alias of Dionysius (or a papponymic).

6–8 The line-divisions are not entirely certain.

N. GONIS

4878. ORDER FOR TRANSFER OF CREDIT IN GRAIN

26 3B.48/H(8–11)a   12.3 × 8.7 cm   *c.*135

This text stems from a man with an Egyptian name and patronymic, a relative rarity in documents of this sort, where Greek names predominate. The order is addressed to two *sitologi* and their 'associates', which is unexpected in an Oxyrhynchite text of this date (see 2 n.). The transfers of grain requested are destined for accounts held by the payee in two different granaries.

The regnal date clause, which usually closes such documents (though contrast **4883**), was apparently not written. It is less likely that the text is incomplete at the foot, since there is plenty of free space in line 9.

Ὧρος Παυcίριος διὰ Ἀμμωνίου φίλου

Ἀπολλω( ) καὶ Ἁρπαῆϲι καὶ μετόχ(οιϲ) ϲιτολόγ(οιϲ) ἄνω
τοπ(αρχίαϲ) Μονίμου τόπ(ων) χαίριν. διάϲτειλον
ἃϲ ἔχετέ μου ἐν θέματι πυρο[ῦ] γενή(ματοϲ) ιθ (ἔτουϲ)
5   Ἀδριανοῦ Καίϲαροϲ τοῦ κυρίου Ψάμμιδι Ψάμμιδοϲ Μερμέρθ(ων) ἀρτάβαι εἴκοϲι τέταρτον, Ἴϲτρου ἐποικίου ἀρτάβ(αϲ) ἓξ ἥμιϲυ
τέταρτ(ον) [χ]οί(νικαϲ) ἑπτά, (γίνονται) ἐπὶ τὸ α(ὐτὸ) πυρο(ῦ) ἀρτάβ(αι) εἴκοϲι
ἑπτά χοί(νικεϲ) ἑπτά.

2 l. Ἁρπαῆϲει   απολλ ͨ, μετο ˣϲιτολο ͷ   3 το⊃ (bis) l. χαίρειν, διαϲτείλατε   4 γενη ͪιθ§
6 μερμερθ l. ἀρτάβαϲ   7 αρταβ   8 τεταρ ͭ, /, α̅πυροαρταβ   8, 9 χοι

'Horus son of Pausiris through Ammonius, (his) friend, to Apollo— and Harpaesis and their associate *sitologi* of the upper toparchy, district of Monimou, greetings. Transfer the (artabas) that you hold on deposit for me, from the wheat-crop of the 19th year of Hadrianus Caesar the lord, to Psammis son of Psammis, (for his account) at Mermertha, twenty (and) one-quarter artabas, at the hamlet of Istrou, six (and) one-half (and) one-quarter artabas (and) seven choenices, grand total twenty-seven artabas (and) seven choenices of wheat.'

1 φίλου. See XXXVIII **2869** 2 n.; other examples in III **620** 10–12 (147) and **4888** 2.

2 Ἀπολλω( ). Omega is very slightly raised, which implies that an abbreviation was intended. The alternative would be to read Ἀπολλῶ, but it is less likely, since this would be a very early example of this form of the dative of Ἀπολλῶϲ (see Gignac, *Grammar* ii 61). Ἀπολλω(νίῳ) is the likeliest resolution.

μετόχ(οιϲ) ϲιτολόγ(οιϲ). Such μέτοχοι were not previously attested in Oxyrhynchite documents later than 99 (LVII **3905** 2), and there they are always mentioned with a single *sitologus*, not two. They are very common elsewhere, especially in the Fayum.

3 Μονίμου. See **4877** 3 n.

4 πυρο[ῦ] γενή(ματοϲ) ιθ (ἔτουϲ). This is the crop harvested in late spring 135. The text will have been written in the summer of 135 or shortly thereafter, as is the case with all texts in which the crop year is not described as 'current' or 'past'; the latest date I have found is Hadrianus (= Hathyr) 11, year 23 of Antoninus Pius (= 8.xii.159) in XXXI **2589** (there are of course even later dates, but in those cases the reference is to a crop of a 'past year'). In consequence, the dates of several documents assigned by the editors to the full year mentioned in the text (here, this would have been 134/5) need to be revised. Two representative datings that require such slight correction are XXXVIII **2865** and **2866**:

2865 refers to the crop of year 7 of Hadrian; its date clause is lost, and it has been assigned to '*c.* A.D. 122/3'. This should be revised to '*c.*123'. The same applies to SB XXVI 16493, which has the same dating co-ordinates. Cf. also III **623** = SB 11165 (*c.*144, not 143/4), XXXVIII **2869** (*c.*147, not *c.*146/7), XLVII **3337** (*c.*142, not *c.*141/2).

2866 refers to the crop 'of the current seventh year of Hadrian'; its date clause is lost, and it has been assigned to 122/3. But its date 'must fall in [summer of 123] since the document was issued after the harvest of the [seventh] year, which is said still to be current' (quotation from XLIX **3497** 2 n., adapted; *sim.* LXVII **4587** 2 n.). Cf. also P. Lips. I 116 ('current 7th year': 123, not 122/3), III **617** (135, not 134/5), LXII **4338** (183, not 182/3); *sim.* P. Petaus 57 (184, not 183/4), SB XII 11151 (215, not 214/5), XII **1444** (249, not 248/9), **1526** (223, not 222/3).

Some other cases call for more specific comment:

The date of P. Lips. I 113 had long remained uncertain: 127 or 128, the editor having read the year figure in the date clause as ‸ δεκ(ά)του (l. 8). Pruneti, *AnPap* 6 (1994) 62, assigned it to 28.vii.127, 'poiché si parla del raccolto dell'anno 110 di Adriano (e dovrebbe essere l'anno in corso, perché manca la precisazione τοῦ διελθόντος ἔτους'; BL X 96 further added that the reading should be ἑνδεκ(ά)του. This is broadly correct (the on-line image allows reading ἑνδεκάτου), though it rests on an assumption that needs qualification: there are numerous texts dating from the year after that of the crop, although the latter is not specified as 'past' (e.g. **4864**, **4872**, **4877**, **4879**, **4881**, **4885**).

In III **624** descr. = SB XII 11166, the crop is of year 11, but the date is also said to be year 11, Thoth *n*. This is implausible, and in fact the on-line image allows reading (ἔτουϲ) ι⟦α⟧β instead of (ἔτουϲ) ια in l. 12; the date-range is 29.viii.–27.ix.148 (cf. already the description in vol. III: 'Dated in the twelfth year of Antoninus').

PSI Congr. XX 9, a notice of transfer of credit, refers to the crop of year 20 (or 21? the reading is not entirely certain) of Antoninus Pius and carries no other date. It has been assigned to 157–61, the time between the crop of year 20 and the end of the reign of this emperor. This is much too cautious; the text will have dated from within a few months, a year at the most, from the year of the harvest. Wheat a year and a half old is transferred in XLIX **3496**, but there it is explicitly described as such, and it seems to be a special case.

5–6 Ψάμμιδι Ψάμμιδοϲ. Cf. P. Harr. I 72.4 (1/11) Ψάμιϲ Ψάμιδοϲ μη(τρὸϲ) Θερμούθιοϲ (ἐτῶν) κϛ (= Jones and Whitehorne, *Register of Oxyrhynchites* no. 3823).

6 Μερμέρθ(ων). The granary of this village, located in the upper toparchy, is also mentioned or implied in II **276** 11–12 (77), XLIV **3337** 1 (*c.*141), III **619** 14 (*c.*147), **629** 14 (159/60), XLIV **3170** 74, 100, 140 (111), **3179** 2 (248/9).

7 Ἴϲτρου ἐποικίου. The granary of this 'hamlet', situated in the middle toparchy, is mentioned or implied in III **630** 11 (*c.*161), P. Mich. XVIII 786.6, etc. (*c.*167), XII **1444** 22 (249).

N. GONIS

4879. ORDER FOR TRANSFER OF CREDIT IN GRAIN

27 3B.42/G(3–4)e   10.9 × 7 cm   29 August – 27 September 141

The beneficiary of this order is Claudia Ptolema, already known as a land-owner from one or two documents; see below, 4–5 n. As would have been appropriate, Ptolema is represented by an οἰκονόμοϲ. Claudius Chaeremon, who issued the order, is not known otherwise.

A sheet-join runs 4.6 cm from the right-hand edge. The scribe left some space blank in the middle of line 7, before the sheet-join; the reason is unclear (not avoidance of overwriting the sheet-join). A much longer space was left blank in line 8.

Κλαύδιοϲ Χαιρήμ[ων ϲιτ]ο[λ(όγοιϲ) ἀπηλ(ιώτου) τ]οπαρχ(ίαϲ) Φοβωου
τόπων χαίρειν. δι[αϲ]τείλατε ἀφ' οὗ ἔχε-
τέ μου ἐν [θέ]ματι πυροῦ γενήματοϲ (ἔτουϲ) δ
Ἀντωνείνου Καίϲαροϲ τοῦ κυρίου Κλαυδίᾳ
5   Πτολέμᾳ διὰ Ἐπαφροδείτου οἰκονόμου πυροῦ

(ἀρτάβας) εἴκοςι. ἔτους πέμπτου Αὐτοκράτορος
Καίςαρος Τίτου Αἰ   λίου Ἁδριανοῦ
Ἀντωνείνου   Ϲεβαςτοῦ Εὐςεβο̣ῦ̣(ς)
Θὼτ ̣ ̣
(*vac.*)
(*m.* 2)   ̣ Χαιρή̣μ̣[ων] ̣ ̣

3 L   4, 8 l. Ἀντωνίνου   5 l. Ἐπαφροδίτου   6 ⸗   8 ευςεβου
9 l. Θώθ

'Claudius Chaeremon to the *sitologi* of the eastern toparchy, district of Phoboou, greetings. Transfer, from the amount you hold on deposit for me, from the wheat-crop of the 4th year of Antoninus Caesar the lord, to Claudia Ptolema through Epaphroditus, steward, twenty artabas of wheat. Year fifth of Imperator Caesar Titus Aelius Hadrianus Antoninus Augustus Pius, Thoth . . .'

(2nd hand) 'Chaeremon . . .'

1 Φοβώου. Cf. **4866** 5. Further references to this granary are SB XII 11145.3 (65/6), P. Lips. I 116.2 (123), XXXVIII **2863** 2 (123), **2865** 2 (*c.*123), XLI **2956** 3 (148/9), VI **973** (168/9), SB XII 11025.5 (201); cf. also XLIX **3497** 9 (216?), XXII **2346** 17 (III).

4–5 Κλαυδί̣α̣ Πτολέμα̣. This lady is first attested in IV **810** of 134/5, in which she (sub)leases (royal) land near Sinary in the upper toparchy (a full edition of this text is in preparation). There too she acts through an intermediary, viz. a φροντιςτής. A further reference to her may be detected in III **627** descr. = SB XII 11667.5–6 (148), another order for transfer of credit in grain, where the edition prints Κλα[̣ ̣] ̣ ̣ | Πτολεμα(ίου) Ἰςίου Κάτω; the on-line image allows reading Κλα[υδ]ί̣α̣ Πτολέμα̣ (what *ed. pr.* took as an abbreviation sign is a diaeresis: ϊςιου pap.).

XLIX **3497** 6–7 (216?), θέ̣μ̣(ατος) Κλ(αυδίας) | Πτολέμας τῆς κ(αὶ) Δ[, 'is hardly likely to [refer to] the same person [as in **810**] unless her private account was kept up under her name after her death' (note ad loc.); but the latter practice is not otherwise known in documents of this type, unless there is an explicit reference to the 'heirs of so-and-so' (see e.g. below **4890** 6). This latter Cl. Ptolema might be the same as Κλαυδία Πτολέμα in PSI VI 713.8, an Oxyrhynchite tax list assigned to the third century.

5 διὰ Ἐπαφροδείτο̣υ οἰκονόμου. Cf. **4871** 1–2, where a person of this name appears as the φροντιςτής of another woman.

10 It is not clear whether the traces before Χαιρή̣μ̣[ων] belong to an abbreviated version of Κλαύδιος. ςεςημείωμαι, abbreviated in some way, may have stood at the end of the line, but too little survives for any text to be confirmed.

N. GONIS

4880. Order for Transfer of Credit in Grain

26 3B.47/B(9–11)a   8.2 × 12.3 cm   2 September 144

The text of this order is remarkably short, without the elaborate formulas we find in other documents of this kind. It was issued by an Alexandrian, member of the little-attested Nilanabatean tribe.

.ọ.[*c.*8   ]ωνος Νειλαναβάτειος
ὁ καὶ Ἀλθαιεὺς ϲιτολ(όγοιϲ) Ϲιγ(κεφα) τόπων
χαίρειν. διαϲτείλατε Ἀκώρι
Ἱέρακος πυροῦ ἀρτάβας πέντε,
5   (γίνονται) (πυροῦ) (ἀρτάβαι) ε. (ἔτουϲ) η Ἀντωνίνου
Καίϲαροϲ τοῦ κυρίου, Θὼτ ε̄.

2 ϲιτο^λ ϲιγ̄   3 χαιρειν: a large blob over χ (χαι written over something else?)   l. Ἀκώρει
5 /ε̄–σ, L   6 l. Θώθ

'. . . son of —on, of the Nilanabatean tribe and Althaean deme, to the *sitologi* of the district of Sincepha, greetings. Transfer to Hacoris son of Hierax five artabas of wheat, total 5 art. of wheat. Year 8 of Antoninus Caesar the lord, Thoth 5.'

1–2 Νειλαναβάτειος ὁ καὶ Ἀλθαιεύς. This combination was known from P. Lond. II 254 = M. *Chr.* 332.7 (124) and I **100** 3–4 (133); the Nilanabatean tribe also occurs in SB XVI 12526.33 (III).
2 Ϲιγ(κεφα). See **4861** 3 n.
3–4 Ἀκώρι Ἱέρακος. A Hierax son of Hacoris, grandson of Mal—, member of the gymnasial class of Oxyrhynchus, occurs in the census return I **202** descr. = SB XXII 15353 of 146/7. There he is 66 years old, and registers with him his son Hierax. It is possible that this Hacoris is another son of his.

N. GONIS

4881. ORDER FOR TRANSFER OF CREDIT IN GRAIN

26 3B.47/B(9–11)b   6.5 × 13.5 cm   20 September 147

This order was issued through yet another freedman and manager, who added his subscription, in a 'slow' hand. The transfer requested is to be made into an account at Ὥρου ἐποίκιον, a new toponym.

Διονύϲιϲ Ἀντι.[διὰ
Νομερίου ἀπελευθέ[ρου καὶ
οἰκονόμου ϲιτολ(όγοιϲ) λιβὸ[ϲ τοπ(αρχίαϲ)
Ϲενεκελευ τόπ(ων) χαίρειν. δια[ϲ-
5   τείλατε ἃϲ λοιπὰϲ ἔχω
ἐν θέματι πυροῦ γενήματοϲ
ι (ἔτουϲ) Ἀντωνίνου Καίϲαροϲ
τοῦ κυρίου Πνεφερῶτι
Ἑρμίου Ὥρο(υ) ἐποικ(ίου) ἀρτάβαϲ
10   δ.....[ἔτουϲ ἐν-
δεκάτου Αὐτοκράτοροϲ

Καίϲαροϲ Τίτου Αἰλίου
Ἀδριανοῦ Ἀντωνίνου
Ϲεβαϲτοῦ Εὐϲεβοῦϲ, Θὼθ
15   κβ̄. (m. 2) Νεμέριϲ ἀπε-
λεύθεροϲ τοῦ προγ-
εγραμμένου Διο-
νυϲίου ἐπιδέδωκα.

3 ϲιτο^λ   4 το?   7 ⟋   9 ωροεποικ

'Dionysis son of Anti—, through Nomerius, freedman and steward, to the *sitologi* of the eastern toparchy, district of Seneceleu, greetings. Transfer the remaining (artabas) that I hold on deposit, from the wheat-crop of the 10th year of Antoninus Caesar the lord, to Pnepheros son of Hermias, (for his account) at the hamlet of Horus, . . . artabas . . . Year eleventh of Imperator Caesar Titus Aelius Hadrianus Antoninus Augustus Pius, Thoth 22.' (2nd hand) 'I, Nemeris, freedman of the aforesaid Dionysius, have submitted (this).'

2 Νομερίου. Νεμέριϲ in the subscription (15) may suggest that this is the Greek name Νεμέριοϲ rather than the 'Roman' Numerius; on the interchange ε > ο, see Gignac, *Grammar* i 290–92. This, however, is far from certain. We find Νομερίου in SB XX 14248.4, 14, 30, 34, 37 (I/II), but Νεμερίου in 22; this is a list of soldiers from Quseir al-Qadim, and it is tempting to take these forms as versions of the name Numerius (as the editor has done). *o* is often used for *u* in the transcription of Latin names; see Gignac, *Grammar* i 219–21. The form in Νεμ- may be phonetic version of Νομ- rather than a rendering of *Num*-; on ο > ε, see Gignac, *Grammar* i 289–90.

2–3 ἀπελευθέ[ρου καὶ] οἰκονόμου. On οἰκονόμοι, see **4859** 1 n. Another freedman represents the nominal payer in III **630** 1–2 (158). See also **4871** 1–2 n.

4 Ϲενεκελευ. Cf. **4864** 8–9, **4885** 2. *Sitologi* of Seneceleu are also mentioned in LVII **3903** 7 = **3904** 5 (99), P. Lips. II 140.2 (133), IV **740** 26 (c.200–201), and LXVII **4590** 3 (c.231). A plurality are mentioned here, but we find a single *sitologus* in P. Lips. 140 and **4885**.

5 ἃϲ λοιπάϲ. Cf. III **625** descr. = SB XII 11168.6 (158), XXXVIII **2870** 2 (176); also III **613** 3 (c.155) λοιπ(ὸν) θέμ(α) (ἀρτάβη) α.

9 Ὥρο(υ) ἐποικ(ίου). This toponym is new.

10 δ̣ . . . . . [. One would not have much difficulty interpreting the traces as δέ[κ]α̣ (γίνονται) (πυροῦ) (ἀρτάβαι) (of the symbols, the lower parts only), but where we would expect to find ι (= 10), there is the base of a curved letter. This would admit β (U-shaped), which would entail reading δύο̣ at the beginning of the line, but this is not easy. Thus I have preferred to suspend judgement.

18 ἐπιδέδωκα. This verb, common at the close of petitions and declarations to officials, is not found in any other text of this type. We would expect ἐπήνεγκα; see **4858** 10–11 n.

N. GONIS

4882. ORDER FOR TRANSFER OF CREDIT IN GRAIN

26 3B.47/B(1–4)a   10.3 × 9.5 cm   13 August 153

Heraclides son of Heraclides, who issued this order, may have occurred in one or two other texts of this kind; see 1 n. The text is written across the fibres.

Ἡρακλείδης Ἡρακλείδο[υ ϲιτολ(όγῳ)
ἀπηλ(ιώτου) τοπ(αρχίας) Ψώβθεωϲ τόπ(ων) χ[αίρει]ν.
διάϲτειλον ἃϲ ἔχε[ι]ϲ μ[ου] ʼ[ ] ..ʼ ἐν θέ[μ(ατι)
πυροῦ γενήμ(ατοϲ) τοῦ ἐνεϲτῶτοϲ ἑκ-
5   καιδεκάτου ἔτουϲ Ἀντωνείνου
Καίϲαροϲ τοῦ κυρίου Διογένει Ϲαραπίωνοϲ πυροῦ (ἀρτάβαϲ) εἴκοϲι πέντε χ[ο]ίν[(ικαϲ)
τρεῖϲ, Ζωίλῳ Ἡλιοδώρῳ πυροῦ
(ἀρτάβαϲ) δύο, γί(νονται) ἐπὶ τὸ αὐτὸ (ἀρτάβαι) κζ χ(οίνικεϲ) γ. (ἔτουϲ) ιϛ
10   Ἀντωνείνου Καίϲ[αρ]οϲ [τ]οῦ κυρίου,
Μεϲ[ο]ρὴ κ̄.

2 απη^λ, το⟩ (*bis*)   4 γενη^μ   5, 10 l. Ἀντωνίνου   7, 9 ⊤   8 l. Ἡλιοδώρου
9 ᵰϵ⟩, χʼL

'Heraclides son of Heraclides, to the *sitologus* of the eastern toparchy, district of Psobthis, greetings. Transfer the (artabas) you hold on deposit for me, from the wheat-crop of the present sixteenth year of Antoninus Caesar the lord, to Diogenes son of Sarapion, twenty-five artabas (and) three choenices of wheat, (and) to Zoilus son of Heliodorus two artabas of wheat, grand total 27 art. 3 choen. Year 16 of Antoninus Caesar the lord, Mesore 20.'

1 Ἡρακλείδης Ἡρακλείδο[υ. Two other such orders are issued by a person of this name: P. Strasb. III 127 (135), addressed to *sitologi* of the same granary as here; and XXXI **2590** (159), addressed to the *sitologi* of Monimou (upper toparchy). Not all three texts need refer to the same individual.

1–2 ϲιτολ(όγῳ) ἀπηλ(ιώτου) . . . Ψώβθ(εωϲ). Cf. **4860** 7, **4886** 5. The *sitologi* of Psobthis in the eastern toparchy are also mentioned in P. Strasb. 127 (see previous note), XXXVIII **2868** 3 (147), and XLIX **3494** 39 (175). In the two earlier texts, a plurality of *sitologi* are attached to it; here only one. The granary is also implied in XLIV **3170** 84, 179 (III). The *sitologi* mentioned in XLVIII **3408** 7 (IV) may be of this Psobthis (it is less likely they were of Taampemou, as thought by Krüger, *Oxyrhynchos in der Kaiserzeit* 61 n. 72).

3 ʼ[ ] ..ʼ. Too little remains of what was written above the line; it also unclear how much is lost (but part of what is presumably *in lacuna* may survive on some detached fibres). The only word that would suit the context is λοιπ(άϲ) (abbreviated), as in III **625** descr. = SB XII 11168.6 (158) (see also **4881** 5 and n.).

9 γί(νονται). A similar abbreviation, with iota cutting through the horizontal of gamma, occurs in P. Lips. II 141.7 (133), but was interpreted as (γίνεται) (πυροῦ): read γί(νεται).

N. GONIS

4883. ORDER FOR TRANSFER OF CREDIT IN GRAIN

27 3B.42/H(4–5)a   8 × 11.8 cm   *c.*153

This order stems from and is signed by Theon son of Apollonius, a former gymnasiarch of Oxyrhynchus, not known previously. He is presumably the same as the one who authorizes a similar transfer eleven years later, in **4885**.

    Θέων Ἀπολλωνίου τῶν

    γεγυμναςιαρχηκότων

    τῆς Ὀξυρυγχειτῶν πόλεως

    ϲιτολ(όγοιϲ) ἀπηλιώτου τοπ(αρχίας) Τααμπ(εμου)

5   τόπ(ων) χαίρειν. διαϲτείλατε

    Ἀμμωνίῳ Διογένουϲ

    (πυροῦ) (ἀρτάβαϲ) κα ᷋ χ(οίνικαϲ) γ ἀφ' οὗ ἔχε-

    τέ μου ἐν θέματι πυροῦ

    γενήματοϲ ιϲ (ἔτουϲ) Ἀντωνείνου

10   Καίϲαροϲ τοῦ κυρίου. (m. 2) Θέων

    ϲεϲημείωμαι.

   3 l. Ὀξυρυγχιτῶν   4 ϲιτοˡ, τοϿτααμϿ   5 τοϿ   7 ꝣᷓ, χᵞ   9 ʃ
l. Ἀντωνίνου

'Theon son of Apollonius, former gymnasiarch of the city of the Oxyrhynchites, to the *sitologi* of the eastern toparchy, district of Taampemou, greetings. Transfer to Ammonius son of Diogenes 21 ¾ artabas (and) 3 choinices of wheat, from the amount you hold on deposit for me, from the wheat-crop of the 16th year of Antoninus Caesar the lord.' (2nd hand) 'I, Theon, have signed.'

   1–3 See above, introd. There is no way of telling whether XLI **2980** 14 (II), Θέωνο(ϲ) Ἀπολλω( ) τραπεζίτου, refers to the same person (a banker would have had the standing to serve as a gymna-siarch).

   4 Τααμπ(εμου). *Sitologi* of Taampemou are mentioned in PSI Congr. XX 9.2 (*c.*157; see **4878** 4 n.), III **621** 3 (162/3), **626** = SB XII 11244.2 (166/7), and probably **615** 3 (179/80) (see note ad loc.). A further occurrence may be detected in P. Lips. II 141.3 (133), where the on-line image allows reading Ταα̣μ̣π(εμου) (τααμϿ pap.; [. . . .] *ed. pr.*) τόπ(ων). See also above, **4882** 1–2 n.

   9 γενήματοϲ ιϲ (ἔτουϲ) Ἀντωνείνου. This is the crop harvested in late spring 153. On the impli-cations for the date, see **4878** 4 n.

   10–11 Very few such documents bear the signature of the person who issues the order: P. Lips. I 116, III **630**, XLVII **3337**; see also P. Lips. I 112, III **621**, and probably **4858** 10, signed by the intermediaries mentioned in the text.

N. GONIS

4884. ORDER FOR TRANSFER OF CREDIT IN GRAIN

26 3B.48/G(18–21)a   9.8 × 9.2 cm   14 October 157

The order concerns transfers of substantial amounts of grain to two different accounts held in the same granary. The text is of interest for the use of the term θέμα at a certain point (see 5 n.), and for some of the names it attests.

The writing is against the fibres.

Ἀκύτης Ἁροννῶφρις διὰ Θέωνος Θέωνος φίλου ἀπὸ
Ὀξυρύγχων πόλεως σιτολ(όγοις) ἀπηλ(ιώτου) τοπ(αρχίας) Ὤφεως τόπ(ων) χαίρειν.
διαστ(είλατε) ἀφ᾿ ὧν ἔχετέ μου ἐν θέματι (πυροῦ) γενή(ματος) κ (ἔτους) Ἀντωνίνου
Καίσαρος τοῦ κυρίου κληρονόμοις Θέωνος τοῦ καὶ
5   Γαΐου Πετεύριος δι᾿ Ἀκύτου Ἀκύτου γεωργ(οῦ) θέμα
ἀρτάβ(ας) ἑβδομήκοντα δύο καὶ Ταοννώφρει
τῇ καὶ Χαιρημονίδι Διον(υσίου) δι᾿ αὐτ(οῦ) Ἀκύτου γεωργ(οῦ)
θέ(μα) ἀρ(τά)β(ας) ἑβδομήκοντα τέσσαρας, (γίνονται) (ἀρτ.) οδ, (γίν.) ἐπὶ τὸ α(ὐτὸ)
ἀρτάβ(αι) ἑκατὸν τεσσαράκοντα ἕξ.   (ἔτους) κα
10 Ἀντωνίνου Καίσαρος τοῦ κυρίου, Φαῶφι ιζ.

1 1. Ἁροννώφριος   2 σιτο^λ απη^λ το?, το?   3 διασ^τ, ⸦γεν^η, ⸌   5, 7 γεωρ^γ
6, 9 αρτα^β   7 διον̄, αυτ   8 θε̄αρβ, | (bis), ⸉, ᾱ   9 L

'Acytes son of Haronnophris through Theon son of Theon, friend, from the city of the Oxyrhynchi, to the *sitologi* of the eastern toparchy, district of Ophis, greetings. Transfer, from the amount you hold on deposit for me, from the wheat-crop of the 20th year of Antoninus Caesar the lord, to the heirs of Theon alias Gaius, son of Peteuris, through Acytes son of Acytes, farmer, as a deposit, seventy-two artabas, and to Taonnophris alias Chaeremonis, daughter of Dionysius, through the same Acytes, farmer, as a deposit, seventy-four artabas, total 74 art., grand total one hundred forty-six artabas. Year 21 of Antoninus Caesar the lord, Phaophi 17.'

1 Ἀκύτης. Cf. 5, 7. The name in this form is not attested elsewhere. Ἀκοῦς, gen. Ἀκοῦτος, is common. Ἀκούτου is in some cases a heteroclitic genitive, but probably not in BGU IV 1173.3 (5/4 BC?), where it must be the genitive of Ἀκοῦτος, a name attested in various parts of the Greek world (see *LGPN* IIA, IIIB, and IV s.n.).

Ἁροννῶφρις. This is the first occurrence of this name in an Oxyrhynchite text; it is common elsewhere in Egypt.

φίλου. See **4878** 1 n.

2 Ὤφεως. See **4862** 3 n.

4–5 τοῦ καὶ Γαΐου. The Roman *praenomen* Gaius appears as an alias also in P. Mich. V 238.237 (Tebt.; 46), P. Fam. Tebt. 7.17 (Tebt.?; 102/3), PSI V 450.23 (Oxy.; II/III).

5 θέμα. Cf. 8. For the use of the term in this place, see **4856** 9 n.

7 δι᾿ αὐτ(οῦ). Assuming that the reading is correct, we should have had διὰ τοῦ αὐτοῦ; the article is also missing in III **622** 14. A single γεωργός is associated with a plurality of account-holders e.g. in XII **1526** 9–11 (223).

8 ἀρ(τά)β(ας). This kind of abbreviation is unusual at this time, but common from the sixth

century onwards. However, it could be that the scribe omitted τα by mistake; he wrote αρτα^β in 6 and 9.

9 A hole in the papyrus between ἑξ and the year symbol may have already been there when the text was written.

N. GONIS

4885. Order for Transfer of Credit in Grain

27 3B.42/H(6)b   6 × 11.2 cm   24 October 164
Plate X

The person who issued this order, Theon son of Apollonius, is presumably the same as the ex-gymnasiarch in **4883**, even though no function is mentioned; the inventory numbers suggest that the two papyri lay close to each other in the rubbish mound. Still, it is impossible to be certain with names so common among Oxyrhynchites.

The text is written across the fibres on the back of a piece cut from what seems to be a fiscal register mentioning slaves; there are repeated references to a 22nd year and a sum of 7 dr. ½ ob. This 22nd year should be that of Antoninus Pius (158/9).

Θέων Ἀπολλωνίου
cι(τολόγῳ) λιβὸc τοπ(αρχίαc) Cενεκελ(ευ)
τόπ(ων) χαίρειν. διάcτειλ(ον)
ἀφ' οὗ ἔχειc μου ἐν
5   θέματι πυροῦ γενήμ(ατοc)
δ (ἔτουc) τῶν κυρίων Cεβαcτ`ῶν΄
Cαρᾶτι Παυcίριοc διὰ
Ζηνᾶτ .... Cενεκ[ελ(ευ)
ἀρτάβην μίαν, (γίνεται) (ἀρτάβη) α.
10   (ἔτουc) ε Αὐρηλίου
Ἀ]ντωνείνου καὶ Οὐή[ρου
τ]ῶν κυρίων [Cεβαcτῶν,
Φ]αῶφι $\overline{κζ}$.

2 ⳩, τοϽcενεκε^λ 3 διαcτει^λ 5 γενη^μ 6 ſ; cεβαcτ$\overline{ῃ}^{ων}$ pap.   9 /$\overline{σ}$ 10 L
l. Αὐρηλίων   11 l. Ἀντωνίνου

'Theon son of Apollonius to the *sitologus* of the western toparchy, district of Seneceleu, greetings. Transfer, from the amount you hold on deposit for me, from the wheat-crop of the 4th year of the lords Augusti, to Saras son of Pausiris through Zenas . . . , (for his account) at Seneceleu, one artaba, total 1 art. Year 5 of Aurelius Antoninus and Verus, the lords Augusti, Phaophi 27.'

1 Θέων Ἀπολλωνίου. See above, introd.

2 Cενεκελ(ευ). See **4881** 4 n.

6 δ (ἔτους) τῶν κυρίων Cεβαστῶν. The omission of the names of the emperors is unusual; it may be parallelled only by C. Mil. Rec. 76.14.14 (179).

8 Ζηνᾶτ.... One possibility is to read Ζηνᾶ Τ—, Τ— being a patronymic, but I have not been able to match the writing with any name. Alternatively, read Ζηνᾶτος .., but what follows is difficult. I have thought of υἱ(οῦ), but this abbreviation does not seem to have occurred anywhere else, and the last letter resembles sigma more than iota.

Cενεκ[ελ(ευ). The reference to Seneceleu (no other restoration seems possible) is rather unexpected, since in all but one document of this kind (P. Strasb. III 127; the case of **4889** 8 is not comparable) the name of the village granary into which a giro transfer was made is specified only if it is different from the one in which the payers hold their accounts.

10 Αὐρηλίου is a mistake for Αὐρηλίων. We find the same mistake in O. Ashm. Shelton 24.1. (In BGU I 102.5, for Αὐρη[λίου] read Αὐρη[λίων].)

N. GONIS

4886. NOTICE OF CREDIT IN GRAIN

26 3B.51/J(1–3)b   6.7 × 7.4 cm   175/6
                                                                   Plate X

A brief note confirming the deposit of thirteen artabas of wheat. The text is signed by a 'secretary of the *sitologi*' and another person who does not specify his function (wherever else this is stated, it is that of *sitologus*).

This type of document ('metrema receipts') is discussed by N. Litinas, *ZPE* 160 (2007) 196–7; **4886**, as well as **4890** below, displays the same structure as the other six receipts that date from the late second and third centuries.

μεμέτ(ρηται) εἰc τὸ δη(μόcιον) (πυροῦ) γενή(ματοc)
τοῦ διελ(θόντοc) ιε (ἔτουc) Αὐρηλίου
Ἀντωνίνου Καίcαροc
τοῦ κυρίου δι(ὰ) cιτολ(όγων) ἀπηλ(ιώτου)
5   τοπ(αρχίαc) Ψώβθ(εωc) τόπ(ων) Εὐδαίμων
Θέωνοc θέ(μα) ἀρτ(άβ.) δεκα-
τρεῖc, (γίνονται) (ἀρτάβαι) ιγ. Διογένηc
γρ(αμματεὺc) .. cιτολ(όγων) cεcη(μείωμαι) τὰc τοῦ
(πυροῦ) (ἀρτάβαc) ιγ. (m. 2) Χαιρήμων
10   cε]cη(μείωμαι) τὰc τοῦ (πυροῦ) (ἀρτάβαc) ιγ.

1 μεμε⸍, δη̅⸍γεν⸍ͅ   2 διε⸍, ʃ   4 δ̣, απη⸍   4, 8 cιτο⸍   5 το⸍ψωβ⸍θτο⸍
6 θ̅εαρ⸍   7 |⸍σ̅   8 γρ⸍   8, 10 cεc⸍ͅ   9, 10 ⸍⸍σ̅

'Measured into the public granary, of the wheat-crop of the past 15th year of Aurelius Antoninus Caesar the lord, through the *sitologi* of the eastern toparchy, district of Psobthis, Eudaemon son of

Theon, as a deposit, thirteen artabas, total 13 art. I, Diogenes, secretary of *sitologi*, have countersigned the 13 art. of wheat.' (2nd hand) 'I, Chaeremon, have countersigned the 13 art. of wheat.'

1–2 γενή(ματος) τοῦ διελ(θόντος) ιε (ἔτους). The reference is to the crop of 175.

5 Ψῶβθ(εως). See **4882** 1–2 n.

6 ἀρτ(άβ.). See **4890** 6 n.

7–10 Among similar documents of this period, two signatories occur in I **89** (140), LXVII **4587** (179), LXII **4338** (183), P. Köln II 90 (184), SB XII 11025 (201). In all other cases, e.g. **4890**, there is only one signatory.

8 γρ(αμματεὺς) ̣ ̣ cιτολ(όγων). I have not been able to make out the writing between the two abbreviated words. The first trace is a mere blob of ink; the second has an oblique stroke above (it can hardly be a number). I think it less likely that one should read γραμ(ματεύς): the foot of rho continues upwards in a curve, indicating an abbreviation.

The secretary may have been a private employee of a *sitologus*, acting as a deputy or a substitute in the liturgy. The duties of such a secretary are detailed in P. Mich. XI 604 of 223 (see introd. there and 12–13 n.); cf. also XII **1510** (ii/iii), which refers to the payment of a salary to a secretary by the *sitologus*.

N. Lewis, *The Compulsory Public Services of Roman Egypt*[2] (1997) 47, speaks of a liturgic γραμματεὺς cιτολόγων in P. Berl. Leihg. II 46 (136); this was also the view of the editor of the papyrus, but there is nothing in the text to substantiate this (otherwise not implausible) assumption; the γραμματεύς mentioned there has fled following an alleged embezzlement, not because he wished to escape from a liturgical office. Lewis further associates such γραμματεῖc with the liturgies providing assistance to a *sitologus* in P. Ryl. II 90 (iii), but there is no proof for this.

N. GONIS

4887. NOTICE OF AND ORDER FOR TRANSFERS OF CREDIT IN GRAIN

26 3B.52/D(1–3)c   8.5 × 13.7 cm   175/6

Sixty artabas of wheat were transferred to the giro account of Dionysius son of Harthoonis, and of this transaction he received notice. Then Dionysius appended a note ordering that the same amount be transferred to another person. A close parallel is XXXI **2591** (159), which bears a notice of transfer and two successive orders for transfer of credit, and III **630** (c.161), which carries two successive orders, the second issued by the beneficiary of the first; cf. also III **613** (c.155) and **616** (c.162). It has been thought that such documents 'could become negotiable instruments, if endorsed by the payee with his signature and a further order to pay. . . . the documents circulated freely and so functioned almost as a paper currency' (**2588–91** introd.; cf. already Preisigke, *Girowesen* 128–31); contrast N. Litinas, *ZPE* 160 (2007) 200, who argues that all arrangements were made in the office of *sitologi*, which is plausible (**4887** is the work of a single scribe).

διεcτάλ(η) (πυροῦ) γενή(ματος) τοῦ διελ(θόντος) ιε (ἔτους) Αὐρηλίου
Ἀντωνίνου Καίcαρος τοῦ κ[υρίο]υ
δι(ὰ) cι(τολόγων) λιβὸ(c) τοπ(αρχίας) Cερύφε(ωc) τόπ(ων) ἀπὸ θέματος

Φιλοξένο(υ) τοῦ κ(αὶ) Φιλ(ίςκου) Διονύςιος

5 Ἀρθοώνιος θέμα ἀρτάβ(αι) ἑξήκον-

τα, (γίνονται) (πυροῦ) (ἀρτάβαι) ξ. Διονύςι(ος) ςι(τολόγος) ςεςη(μείωμαι).

Διονύςιος Ἀρθοώ(νιος) ὁ προγεγ(ραμμένος). διάςτειλ(ον) Διονυςίῳ

Η . . οὗτος τὰς προκ(ειμένας) ἀρτάβ(ας) ἑξήκοντα,

(γίνονται) (ἀρτάβαι) ξ.

1 διεςτα᾽ϟγεν᾽, διε᾽ιεϛ   3 δϲ⳨λιβ°τοϽϲερυφετο϶   4 φιλοξεν°του῎φι᾽   5 αρτα^β

6 /꜀ϖ, διονυϲιϲ⳨ϲεϲη⁻   7 αρθο^ω, προγεγϛδιαϲτει᾽   8 προ῎αρτα^β   9 /ϖ

'Transferred, from the wheat-crop of the past 15th year of Aurelius Antoninus Caesar the lord, through the *sitologi* of the western toparchy, district of Seryphis, from the deposit of Philoxenus also called Philiscus, to Dionysius son of Harthoonis, as a deposit, sixty artabas, total 60 art. of wheat. I, Dionysius, *sitologus*, have countersigned.

'I, Dionysius son of Harthoonis, the aforesaid. Transfer to Dionysius son of . . . the aforementioned sixty artabas, total 60 art.'

1 διεςτάλ(η). διέςταλ(ται) is another possibility; see Litinas, *ZPE* 160 (2007) 199.

3 Ϲερύφε(ως). See **4856** 4 n.

4 Φιλοξένο(υ) τοῦ κ(αὶ) Φιλ(ίςκου). A Φιλόξενος ὁ καὶ Φιλίςκος Διονυςίου occurs in III **613** 4 (*c*.155), a notice of transfer of credit in grain.

Διονύςιος. We expect the dative, but nominatives occur in three other texts (III **613** 3, XXXVIII **2871** 4, PSI Congr. XXI 9.4); see Litinas, *ZPE* 160 (2007) 199 n. 15.

5 θέμα. See **4856** 9 n.

8 Η . . οὗτος. Though little is missing, we have not been able to read a known name.

J. DE JONG

4888. ORDER FOR TRANSFERS OF CREDIT IN GRAIN

26 3B.52/D(1–3)a   10 × 9.5 cm   16 January 176

Ammonius through his friend Apollonius orders the *sitologi* of Seryphis to transfer small amounts of wheat to the accounts of two other persons, held at the granaries of Athychis and Senepta.

The text is written across the fibres.

Ἀμμώνιος Πρόκλου δι᾽ ἐμοῦ Ἀπολ-

λωνίου Ῥούφου φίλου ϲειτολ(όγοις) λιβ(ὸς) τοπ(αρχίας)

Ϲερύφεω(ς) τόπ(ων) χαίρειν. διαϲτείλ(ατε) ἀφ᾽ οὗ ἔ-

χετέ μου ἐν θέμ(ατι) (πυροῦ) γενή(ματος) τοῦ διελ(θόντος) ιε (ἔτους)

5 Πεκύϲει νεωτ(έρῳ) Παθώθ(ου) Ἀθύχ(εως) (ἀρτάβας) γ

καὶ Δημητρίᾳ Ὥρου διὰ Θέω(νος) Ζωίλ(ου)

Cενεπτα (ἀρτάβην) α d χ(οίνικας) β, (γίνονται) ἀρτ(άβαι) τέccαρεc
τέταρτον χοί(νικεc) δύο, (γίνονται) (ἀρτάβαι) δ d χ(οίνικεc) β. (ἔτουc) ιϛ
Αὐρηλίου Ἀντωνίνου Καίcαροc τοῦ
10   κυρίου, Τῦβ(ι) κ‾.

2 cειτο^λλι^βτο꙳	l. cιτολόγοιc	3 cερυφε^ωτο꙳, διαcτει^λ	4 θεμꙅ ꙅγενη‾, διε^λιεꙅ
5 νεω꙳παθω^θαθυ^χ‾σ	6 θε^ωζωι^λ	7 ‾σ, χ^β/αρ^τ	8 χοι, /‾σ, χ^β, L 10 τυ^β

'Ammonius son of Proculus, through me, Apollonius son of Rufus, (his) friend, to the *sitologi* of the western toparchy, district of Seryphis, greetings. Transfer, from the amount you hold on deposit for me, from the wheat-crop of the past 15th year, to Pecysis the younger, son of Pathothes, (for his account) at Athychis, three artabas, and to Demetria daughter of Horus, through Theon son of Zoilus, (for her account) at Senepta, 1 ¼ art. 2 choen., total one and a quarter artabas (and) two choenices, total 4 ¼ art. 2 choen. Year 16 of Aurelius Antoninus Caesar the lord, Tybi 20.'

2 φίλου. See **4878** 1 n.
2–3 Cf. **4887** 2. See **4856** 4 n.
4 μου should refer to the nominal payee, and sits oddly with ἐμοῦ in 1, used for the intermediary; the scribe used the formula independently of the context.
5 Ἀθύχ(εωc). See **4889** 15 n.
7 Cενεπτα. See **4872** 10 n.

J. DE JONG

4889. ORDER FOR TRANSFER OF CREDIT IN GRAIN

26 3B.47/B(5–8)a   13 × 16.3 cm   176/7
Plate XI

This document is addressed by an Oxyrhynchite to the *sitologi* of Talao in the middle toparchy, a village not known previously. In what is preserved, thirteen giro transfers are mentioned, the highest number of such transfers lumped together in a text of this type (the seven in III **619** is the second highest number; III **616** is a case apart). Among the payees, women make a strong appearance.

Ἀπολλώνιοc ὁ καὶ Εὐδαίμων Εὐδαίμ(ονοc)
ἀπ' Ὀξ(υρύγχων) πόλ(εωc) cειτολόγ(οιc) Ταλαω μέcηc τόπ(ων)
χαίρειν. διαcτείλατε ἀφ' ὧν ἔχετέ μου
(πυροῦ) γενή⟨μα⟩τοc τοῦ διελθόντο(c) ιϛ (ἔτουc) Αὐρηλίου
5   Ἀντωνείνου Καίcαροc τοῦ κυρίου Ἀθηνο-
δώρῳ καὶ Διον(υcίῳ) Cενοκώμεωc (ἀρτάβαc) κ, (γίνονται)
ἀρτάβαι εἴκοcι, Ταχνού[β]ει Ἀμμωνίου μητ(ρὸc)
Ἀράcιοc Ταλ(αω) (ἀρτάβαc) δ, (γίνονται) ἀρτάβαι τέccαρεc,
Κρονοῦτι Νεοπτολέμ(ου) Παώμ(εωc) (ἀρτάβηc) ꝅ, Τήεωc '(ἀρτάβαc)' δ d η',

10 Ἀμμωνᾶτι Ὠφελᾶτος Τή(εως) (ἀρτάβης) ʂ, Ἰσχυρᾶτι
   Ἰσχυρ( ) Cενεψαυ (ἀρτάβας) α η´, (γίνονται) (ἀρτάβαι) ἑπτά, Διδυμ( )
   χρημ(ατίζ.) μητ(ρὸς) Cινθώ(νιος) Θώλ(θεως) μέcη(c) (ἀρτάβας) ε, (γίνονται)
                                                           ἀρτάβ(αι) πέντε,
   Ἀπολλωνίῳ Ἀλεξ(άνδρου) (ἀρτάβας) λη δ χ(οίνικας) β, (γίνονται) ἀρτάβ(αι)
                                                           τριάκοντα
   ὀκτὼ τέταρτον χοί(νικες) δύο, Ἡρῶτι Πτολεμ(αίου)
15 Ἰcείου Νεcλ(α) (ἀρτάβας) α η´, τῇ α(ὐτῇ) Ἀθύχεως (ἀρτάβας) α η´,
   Διονυcίᾳ κ(αὶ) Ταπεκύcει Ἀθύχεως κ(αὶ) Ποΰνεως (ἀρτάβας) α η´ χ(οίνικας) η,
   Ἡ]ρωείτι Ἀρχ( ) Ἀθύχ[εως (ἀρτάβας) δ] δ, (γίνονται) ἀρτάβαι τέccαρες
                                                           τέταρτ(ον)

   C]αραπίωνι ˌαρτ( )[   ] χοίνικ(εc) ὀκτώ,

   ·   ·   ·   ·   ·   ·   ·   ·   ·   ·

   1 ευδαι^μ   2 οˣπο^λcειτολο^γ 1. cιτολόγοιc   4 ϛγενητος, διελθοντ°ιϛʃ   5 1. Ἀντωνίνου
   6 διο̅ν̅   6, 8, 9, 10, 11, 12, 13, 15, 16 ⁻σ⁻   6, 8, 11, 12, 13, 17 /   7, 12 μη^τ   8 ταλʃ
   9 νεοπτολε^μπαω^μ   10 τ^η, ἰcχυρατι   11 ἰcχυρʃ, διδυ^μ   12 χρημʃ, cινθ^ωθω^λμεc^η, αρτ^αβ
   13 αλεξʃ, χ^β   14 χο¹, πτολε^μ   15 ἰcειουνεc^λ, α̅   16 διονυcια^κ, αθυχεως^κποϋνεως, χ^η
   17 1. Ἡρωίδι   αρ^χ, τεταρ^τ   18 ˌαρ̣, χοινι^κ

   'Apollonius alias Eudaemon, son of Eudaemon, from the city of the Oxyrhynchi, to the *si-*
   tologi of the district of Talao Middle, greetings. Transfer, from the amount you hold for me, from
   the wheat-crop of the past 16th year of Aurelius Antoninus Caesar the lord, to Athenodorus and
   Dionysius, (for their account) at Senocomis, 20 art., total twenty artabas; to Tachnubis daughter of
   Ammonius, mother Harasis, (for her account) at Talao, 4 art., total four artabas; to Cronous daughter
   of Neoptolemus, (for her account) at Paomis, ¾ art., (and) at Teis, 4 ¼ ⅛ art.; to Ammonas son of
   Ophelas, (for his account) at Teis, ¾ art.; to Ischyras son of Ischyr—, (for his account) at Senepsau,
   1 ⅛ art., total seven artabas; to Didym— officially known as the son/daughter of Sinthonis, for (his/
   her account) at Tholthis Middle, 5 art., total five artabas; to Apollonius son of Alexander, 38 ¼ art. 2
   choen., total thirty-eight (and) one-quarter artabas (and) two choenices; to Heros daughter of Ptolemaeus, (for her account) at Is(i)eion Nesla, 1 ⅛ art.; to the same (Heros), for (her account) at Athychis,
   1 ⅛ art.; to Dionysia and Tapecysis, (for their account) at Athychis and Poynis, 1 ⅛ art. 8 choen.; to
   Herois daughter of Arch—, (for her account) at Athychis, 4 ¼ art., total four (and) one-quarter artabas; to Sarapion son of ... eight choenices ...'

   2 Ταλαω μέcηc τόπ(ων). This is the first secure attestation of this village. We previously knew
   only of Talao in the upper toparchy.

   3–4 ἐν θέματι ought to have come between μου and (πυροῦ); this may be an inadvertent omission rather than a deliberate variation of the formula.

   6 Διον(υcίῳ). I am not entirely certain that right-hand vertical of nu is there; if not, read sigma,
   i.e., Διος(κόρῳ).

   Cενοκώμεωc. See **4860** 14 n.

   8 Ἁράcιοc. On this name see P. Mich. XVIII 786.12 n.

   Ταλ(αω). Though not called Ταλ(αω) μέcηc, it is more likely that this is the same village as that
   in 2 than the village of the upper toparchy, which also possessed a granary.

9 Παώμ(εως). A village of the Thmoisepho toparchy; further references to its granary are supplied by XXXVI **2670** 4 (127), XII **1541** 3 (192), IV **740** 14 (*c*.200), XLIV **3170** 11.

Τήεως. Cf. 10. Another village of the Thmoisepho toparchy; its granary is mentioned or implied in XLI **2961** 15, **2962** 10, **2963** 15 (154), XLIV **3170** 8, etc. (III).

10 Ὠφελᾶτος. The name appears to be typical of the area of Oxyrhynchus. The Ophelas in SB XVI 12742–3 is a citizen of Antinoopolis but cannot have been born there, since he registers his infant son in 157; like many others, he could have moved to Antinoopolis from Oxyrhynchus.

Ὠφελ(ᾶς) was read in P. Fouad 60.8 (156), a *penthemeros* certificate said to be of unknown provenance, but probably Arsinoite, as suggested by the formula and the name Ψενοβάστεως in l. 6 (Ψενοβιμάχο(υ) or Ψευβςεώχο(υ) ed. pr.; neither name is attested otherwise). Ὠφελ( ) occurs also in P. Ross.-Georg. III 34.3.5, 7, 9 (Ars.; II). Although one cannot exclude that the name is to be resolved as Ὠφελᾶς, Ὠφέλιος or Ὠφελίων may also be considered.

11 Ἰςχυρ( ): Ἰςχυρ(ᾶτος) or Ἰςχυρ(ίωνος).

Cενεψαυ. See **4874** 8 n.

(γίνονται) (ἀρτάβαι) ἑπτά. This is the total of the giro transfers mentioned in 9–11. The reason for lumping them together is unclear.

Διδυμ( ) could be the beginning of either a male or a female name (for a range of options, see **4872** 12 n.). Thus in 12 I have not supplied an ending to the participle.

12 Θώλ(θεως) μέςη(ς). Its granary is mentioned or implied in III **630** 2 (161) and XLIV **3170** 221 (III).

13 Ἀπολλωνίῳ Ἀλεξ(άνδρου). There is no mention of the granary in which Apollonius held an account. This may have been the same as the one mentioned in the previous line, but it is also possible that we have a mere scribal slip.

15 Ἰcείου Νεςλ(α). On the face of it, this is a new locality; there are several Oxyrhynchite villages named after a temple of Isis, and to find yet another would be no great wonder. It could also be that this an alternative name of Nesla, a village in the upper toparchy, owing to the presence of an Iseion in the area. There was in fact an Iseion nearby, which complicates matters: several documents refer to land situated περὶ τὸ Ἰcείον Παγγᾶ ἐν περιχώματι Νέςλα; see Pruneti, *I centri abitati dell'Ossirinchite* 72, 117, and Rowlandson, *Landowners and Tenants* 45 with n. 50. The name of the περίχωμα, 'inundation basin', may be due to its proximity to Nesla; that Is(i)eion Panga lay close to Nesla is also implied by PSI VII 772.

Nesla possessed a granary; see III **622** 12 (161). No granary is attested for Is(i)eion Panga, though it would not be a surprise if there were one; cf. Rowlandson, *Landowners and Tenants* 18–19. Could this be a granary serving both Is(i)eion Panga and Nesla?

Ἀθύχεως. Cf. 16, 17. A village in the upper toparchy; its granary is mentioned or implied in P. Princ. II 42.2, 7, 18, 25, 33, 35, 37, 49 (92/3; see BL VIII 283, X 218), XLI **2958** 12 (99), and LXXII **4888** 5 (176).

16 Διονυcίᾳ κ(αὶ) Ταπεκύcει. κ(αὶ) here and after Ἀθύχεως in the same line is superscript, as is often the case in the abbreviation οˣ = ὁ κ(αί) and the like.

Ἀθύχεως κ(αὶ) Πούνεως. Cf. P. Princ. 42.18 Ἀθύχ(ις) καὶ Πῶ(νις), as read by W. Clarysse, N. Kruit, *ZPE* 82 (1990) 123–4 (= BL IX 218). It is remarkable that Athychis is mentioned on its own in 15 and 17, but with Poynis in 16; P. Princ. 42 offers a similar picture, with Athychis mostly on its own. Perhaps this was a satellite granary of the main one in Athychis, serving some outposts of the village as well as a nearby settlement. But then how to explain that Athychis is combined with Chysis in **2958** 12?

According to Clarysse and Kruit, Πῶ(νις) in P. Princ. 42.18 is a variant of Πούνις (not Πούνις, as the use of the diaeresis here indicates; I do not wish to pronounce on the accent), which occurs in lines 3 and 4 of the same document. The village is also attested in PSI IV 315.8 (136/7; see BL VII 234) as Πω[[.]]νιν; see *ZPE* 82 (1990) 124 = BL IX 313.

Athychis and Po(y)nis also occur in P. NYU II 52 (ed. *ZPE* 149 (2004) 121–3 with Taf. IX) of the early second century, published, as the editors say, chiefly for the occurrence of many Jewish names. They describe it as a 'Private Account' of uncertain import (and provenance). It is in fact a granary account; if it predates the Jewish revolt, it is among the earliest Oxyrhynchite documents of this kind. This new interpretation relies on the entries that come between the column of names and the column with amounts of wheat: these are villages (for the arrangement, cf. e.g. P. Erl. 44 or SB XIV 12181, both Oxyrhynchite granary accounts). ἡ α(ὐτὴ) κώ(μη) in 10 follows after ϲιγκ( ) in the previous line; ϲιγκ( ) was tentatively associated with 'the village Sinkere in the Hermopolite nome or Sinkepha in the Oxyrhynchite nome (but there are also other village names in Σιγκ-)'. ἡ α(ὐτὴ) κώ(μη) recurs in 12; the corresponding entry in 11 was read as χ(όρτου), but this should be a toponym. ἡ α(ὐτή) *tout court* comes in 4–5, 16, and 18–22 after ϲιγκ( ), and in 25 after αθ( ), dubiously related to ἀθήρα, 'wheat porridge'; but this too must be a toponym, and the same applies to πω( ) in 23. Read Ϲιγκ(εφα) in 3, 8, 9, 15, 17; Χ(ῦϲιϲ) in 6, 11, 14; Ἀθ(υχιϲ) in 7, 24; Πῶ(νιϲ) in 23. All these are villages in the upper toparchy of the Oxyrhynchite nome.

17 Ἀρχ( ): perhaps Ἀρχ(ίου), the shortest name starting Ἀρχ-. This could also be a compound, but in that case one would expect a less equivocal abbreviation.

18 ͺαρτ( ). The unread letter may be mu; if so, one may consider reading Μ̣α̣ρτ(ιαλίου) (Μαρτύριοϲ is not a name one expects to find in this period).

N. GONIS

4890. NOTICE OF CREDIT IN GRAIN

27 3B.40/F(1–3)a   13 × 12.8 cm   211
                                                                  Plate XIV

This text records four deposits into the granary of Enteiis by three individuals or groups of individuals (for the erratic use of cases, see 5 n.). The first two deposits were for city dues at Enteiis; the third and fourth, by the same person, were destined for city dues at Enteiis too, but also for the depositor's own account at the granary (for this type of payment, see XLIV **3181** 5 n.). The references to the two latter deposits were subsequently cancelled, and a second hand added that they were meant for municipal dues at Nemera. The original grand total was left uncorrected, but a revised total was appended.

The recording of a plurality of deposits that apparently are unconnected with each other in a single text may be parallelled from XII **1541** (192), which refers to two separate deposits by two persons.

μεμέτ(ρηται) εἰϲ τὸ δημ(όϲιον) (πυροῦ) γενή(ματοϲ) τοῦ ἐνεϲτ(ῶτοϲ)
ι]θ (ἔτουϲ) Μάρκου Αὐρηλίου Ἀντωνίνου
κ]αὶ Πουβλίου Ϲεπτιμίου Γέτα Βρετανικῶν
μεγίϲτων Εὐϲεβῶν Ϲεβαϲτῶν δι(ὰ) ϲιτολ(όγων)
5 ἄνω τοπ(αρχίαϲ) Ἐντείεωϲ τόπ(ων) Ϲαραπιὰϲ Ἀντιόχ(ου)
δι(ὰ) Κορνηλ(ίου) Ἐντείεωϲ πόλ(εωϲ) (ἀρτάβ.) ιζ δ χ(οίν.) β, κλη(ρονόμοι)
                                                                  Ὡρείω-

νος τοῦ κ(αὶ) Βερενικιανοῦ Ἐντείεως πόλ(εως)

(ἀρτάβ.) ε, ⟦Ἀπολλωνίῳ τῷ κ(αὶ) Cαραπάμμωνι⟧

⟦Ἐντείεως πόλεως (ἀρτάβ.) ε 𝌋 χ(οίν.) α, τῷ αὐτῷ Ἀπολλω-⟧

(*m.* 2) Νεμέρων πόλ(εως)

10　⟦νίῳ θέμα (ἀρτάβ.) θ χ(οίν.) θ⟧, (γίνονται) ἀρτ(άβαι) τριάκοντα

ἑπτὰ τέταρτον χοί(νικες) δύο. Ἡρακλείδης ὁ καὶ Ἡ-

ρᾶς cιτολόγος cεcημείωμαι τὰς τοῦ πυροῦ

ἀρτάβας τριάκοντα ἑπτὰ τέταρτον χοί-

νεικας δύο. (*m.* 2) (γίνονται) {(ἀρτάβαι)} (λοιπαὶ) (ἀρτάβαι) κβ 𝈅 χ(οίνικες) β.

---

1 μεμε᾿, δη˝𐅵γε ͜νη¯, ενεc᾿　　2 ∫　　3 l. Βρεταννικῶν　　4 𐅵cιτο^λ　　5 το϶, το϶,
αντιο^χ　　6 𐅵κορνη^λ, κλ^η l. Ὠρίω-　　6, 7, 9 πο^λ　　6, 14 χ^β　　6, 8, 9, 10, 14 ⁻σ⁻
7 του^κ　　8 τω^κ　　9 χ^α　　10 χ^θ/αρ᾿　　11 χοῑ　　14 /, ⌒ l. -νικας

'Measured into the public granary, of the wheat-crop of the present 19th year of Marcus Aurelius Antoninus and Publius Septimius Geta Bretannici maximi Pii Augusti, through the *sitologi* of the upper toparchy, district of Enteiis, Sarapias daughter of Antiochus through Cornelius, at Enteiis, for city dues, 17 ¼ art. 2 choen.; the heirs of Horion alias Berenicianus, at Enteiis, for city dues, 5 art.; ~~Apollonius alias Sarapammon, for city dues at Enteiis, 5 ¾ art. 1 choen.; the same Apollonius, as a deposit, 9 art. 9 choen.;~~' (2nd hand) 'at Nemera, for city dues' (1st hand) 'total thirty-seven (and) one-quarter art. (and) two choen. I, Heraclides alias Heras, sitologus, have countersigned the thirty-seven (and) one-quarter artabas (and) two choenices. (2nd hand) Total (there remain) 22 ¼ art. 2 choen.'

1–2 γενή(ματος) τοῦ ἐνεcτ(ῶτος) [ι]θ (ἔτουc). This was the crop of 211.

5 Ἐντείεωc. The granary of this village is also mentioned in III **616** 3, 14 (*c*.162), LXVII **4589** 37 (171/2), 42–3 (172/3), XLI **2968** 16 (190), and implied in P. Princ. II 42.5 *et pass.* (92/3).

Cαραπιὰc Ἀντιόχ(ου). Cf. 8 Ἀπολλωνίῳ τῷ κ(αὶ) Cαραπάμμωνι; 9 τῷ αὐτῷ Ἀπολλωνίῳ. The use of the cases is confusing; names are given in the nominative and dative with no difference in meaning. Both cases are attested in this context; the nominative is the most common (eg. above, **4886** 5), but the dative occurs in III **517** 9 (130) and **518** 5 (179/80) (the editors' reading was doubted in *ZPE* 160 (2007) 197 n. 8, but the on-line image confirms it).

6 πόλ(εωc). Cf. 7, 9. The opinion generally held is that these are payments for municipal dues, and this I have adopted in the translation, though not without reservations (the issue is too broad to be discussed here). See XLIV **3181** 5 n.; L. C. Youtie, *ZPE* 30 (1978) 178 n. 8; LXVII **4590** 4–5 n.

(ἀρτάβ.). In view of the lax syntax, I have chosen not to supply an ending. We mostly find the accusative, but the nominative too makes an appearance; see Litinas, *ZPE* 160 (2007) 197.

6–7 Ὠρείωνοc τοῦ κ(αὶ) Βερενικιανοῦ. Several papyri refer to this man, first attested as a gymnasiarch and euthenarch and former *exegetes* in VI **908** = W. *Chr.* 426.13–14 of 199; he recurs in P. NYU II 36.13 (= *ZPE* 140 (2002) 148), a land register possibly of 200/1, in which he is represented by a manager (ἐπίτροποc). **4890** offers the earliest posthumous reference; there are two further instances, and both relate to landholdings: L **3565** 22–3 (245), and P. Coll. Youtie II 70.12 (273/4 or 278/9).

10 interlin. Νεμέρων. References to the granary of this village of the middle toparchy are found in XII **1525** 3 (216), XLII **3049** 13 (247), XLIV **3170** 17, 29, 85, 200 (III); cf. also XLI **2960** 24 (100).

10–14 The arithmetic is correct: 17 ¼ art. 2 choen. + 5 art. (+ 5 ¾ art. 1 choen. + 9 art. 9 choen.) = (37 ¼ art. 2 choen.) 22 ¼ art. 2 choen.

14 (λοιπαί). The abbreviation is that commonly used for λοιπαί *et sim.*, on which see A.

Blanchard, *Sigles et abréviations* (1974) 30–31 (for the earlier views, see Youtie, *Scriptiunculae* i 374 with n. 69). However, it has never occurred in a comparable context.

N. GONIS

4891. APPLICATION FOR SEED-CORN

22 3B.19/C(7–8)a　　　　　　　　　9.3 × 23.5 cm　　　　　　28 October–26 November 222

　　What survives, the lower part of an application for seed-corn, follows closely the standard pattern for such documents, which consist of the prescript, request clause, description of the land, amount of seed, purpose, repayment clause, oath, date, and subscription. Its closest parallels are the contemporary P. Hamb. I 19 (225) and VII **1031** = W. *Chr.* 343 (228). The lost upper part of the papyrus will have contained the names of the addressee(s) and applicant, as well as a description of various plots of land and amounts of seed-corn requested. The first ten lines extant carry the application for various amounts of seed-corn to be sown in four different plots of land, specifying the location of the land, its tax rate, the number of arouras, and the number of artabas of seed-corn required. The total of 150 arouras represents the total amount of land for which the applicant requested a loan of 150 artabas of seed-corn (the information that survives concerns 79.5 arouras and an equal number of artabas). Then follows the promise to sow the land (12–15) and to repay an equal amount of corn plus taxes (16–18); the oath (18–21); the date (21–5); and the subscription (25–9), written in a second hand. In this last part, the ink is faded, as if someone tried to rub it off.

　　This document is rich in details on the location of the land, its tenurial history, and the dues imposed on it. Part of the land involved was located in the vicinity of the village of Nemera, in the middle toparchy. The category of the land is not stated (it will have been indicated in the part now lost), but from the tax rates attested (3.5 art.; 3.75 art.; 4 art. 8 choen.) we may surmise that it was royal land, as in most other documents of this kind; for these rates see J. Rowlandson, *ZPE* 67 (1987) 292 (Table III). The amount of seed-corn, 1 art./ar., is the usual one. What is remarkable is the very large amount of land involved, which finds no parallel among documents of this kind. Aurelius Heraclas, who submitted the application, may have been an agricultural entrepreneur, and may have employed other labour for the farming.

　　These applications, of which fourteen (with **4891**) have been published, are one of the three types of documents relative to the government issue of seed-corn to farmers of state land (the other two are the orders to supply seed-corn and the receipts). For a summary of the evidence and analysis of their formal structure, see LVII **3902–6** introd. (also **3907–9** introd., on orders to supply seed-corn). The administrative aspects of the exercise are discussed in detail by Th. Kruse, *Der Königliche Schreiber und die Gauverwaltung* i (2002) 406–63.

].. ι ..[

c.6 (ἀρούρας) ιγ ϛ (ἀρτάβας) ιγ ϛ καὶ περὶ τὴν αὐ(τὴν)

διὰ τῶν ἀπὸ τοῦ Ἡρακλείου (πρότερον) Δημητρί-

ου Παυσίριος καὶ Παάπιος ἐκ τοῦ Ἑρμο-

5 λάου ἀν(ὰ) γ ϛ (ἀρούρας) κ (ἀρτάβας) κ καὶ περὶ Νεμερα

(πρότερον) Πασίωνος Ἀχιλλίωνος ἐκ τῆς ἀπὸ νό-

του καὶ ἀπηλ(ιώτου) μερίδος ἀν(ὰ) γ ϛ (ἀρούρας) ιθ (ἀρτάβας) ιθ

καὶ περὶ τὴν αὐ(τὴν) (πρότερον) Λευκίου Λικινιανοῦ

Μαρτιαλίου ἐκ τοῦ Ἀλεξάνδρου καὶ νότο(υ)

10 καὶ ἀπηλ(ιώτου) μερίδος ἀν(ὰ) δ χ(οίνικας) η (ἀρούρας) κϛ ϛ

(ἀρτάβας) κϛ ϛ, τὰς ἐπὶ τὸ αὐ(τὸ) (ἀρούρας) ρν (ἀρτάβας) ρν,

ἅσπερ κοκκολογή(σας) ἀπὸ κριθῆς καὶ ἔ-

ρης καταθήσω εἰς τὴν γῆν ὑγιῶς

καὶ πιστῶς ἐπακολουθούντων

15 τῶν εἰς τοῦτο προκεχειρισμένων

καὶ ἐγ νέων ἀποδώσω τὰς ἴσας

σὺν τοῖς ἑπομένοις ἅμα τοῖς τῆς

γῆς γνησίοις τελέσμασι. καὶ ὀμνύω

τὴν Μάρκου Αὐρηλίου Σεουήρου

20 Ἀλεξάνδρου Καίσαρος τοῦ κυρίου

τύχην μὴ ἐ[ψεῦ]σθαι. (ἔτους) β

Αὐτοκράτορος Καίσαρος Μάρκου

Αὐρηλίου Σεουήρου Ἀλεξάνδρου

Εὐσεβοῦς Εὐτυχοῦς Σεβαστοῦ

25 (m. 2) Ἀθύρ (vac.) Αὐρήλ(ιος) Ἡρακλᾶς Νε-

χθενίβιος ἐπιδέδωκα καὶ ὤ-

μασα τὸν ὅρκον. Αὐρήλ(ιος) Ἡρακλεί-

δης Ἡρακλείδου ἔγραψα ὑπ(ὲρ) αὐτ(οῦ)

μὴ εἰδότος γράμματα.

---

2 *et passim* ϛ, ⲟ̄   2, 8, 11 αᵛ   3, 6, 8 α/   5, 7, 10 αᵛ   7 απη^λ   9 νοτ°

10 απη^λ   12 κοκκολογη   12–13 l. αἴρης   16 l. ἐκ   21 L   25, 27 αυρη^λ

27 l. -μοσα   28 υᵖαυᵗ

'. . . 13 ¾ arouras, 13 ¾ artabas; and at the same (village), through those from Heracleiou, from the holding of Hermolaus, formerly of Demetrius, son of Pausiris, and Paapis, (taxed) at the rate of 3 ½ (artabas), 20 arouras, 20 artabas; and at Nemera, formerly of Pasion son of Achillion, from the southern and eastern sections, (taxed) at the rate of 3 ¾ (artabas), 19 arouras, 19 artabas; and at the same (village), formerly of Lucius Licinianus Martialis, from the holding of Alexander and the southern and eastern sections, (taxed) at the rate of 4 (artabas) 8 choenices, 26 ¾ arouras, 26 ¾ artabas;

this altogether makes 150 arouras, 150 artabas, which I shall clear of barley and darnel and sow in the ground honestly and in good faith under the supervision of those appointed for this purpose, and I shall repay out of the new crop the equivalent amount with the additional charges, together with the regular dues on the land; and I swear by the fortune of Marcus Aurelius Severus Alexander Caesar the lord that I have not lied. Year 2 of Imperator Caesar Marcus Aurelius Severus Alexander Pius Felix Augustus.' (2nd hand) 'Hathyr. I, Aurelius Heraclas son of Nechthenibis, have submitted (this) and swore the oath. I, Aurelius Heraclides son of Heraclides, wrote on his behalf because he is illiterate.'

3 διὰ τῶν ἀπὸ τοῦ Ἡρακλείου. The people involved were farmers residing there and cultivating royal land in a different village. On the significance of the phrase, see J. Rowlandson, 'The Organisation of Public Land in Roman Egypt', in J. C. Moreno García (ed.), *L'Agriculture institutionnelle en Égypte ancienne: état de la question et perspectives interdisciplinaires* = *CRIPEL* 25 (2005) 192.

τοῦ Ἡρακλείου. This was a village in the middle toparchy; see Pruneti, *I centri abitati dell'Ossirinchite* 52–3. The use of the article implies that it is an ἐποίκιον, as in the official accounts VI **989** descr. (τῷ Ἡρακλείῳ ἐποικίῳ), X **1285** 9, 100, XXIV **2422** 67, and P. Corn. 36.6 (τὸ Ἡρακλεῖον). It is designated a κώμη in X **1260** 12 (286). In the later period, it is called a κτῆμα in XVI **2020** 21 (VI), but a κώμη in XIX **2243a** 11.

4–5 Ἑρμολάου. This *kleros* appears to be new.

5 Νέμερα. On this village of the middle toparchy, see Pruneti, *I centri abitati* 114–15; Calderini and Daris, *Dizionario geografico* ii 331, Suppl. i 204, Suppl. iii 80. See also **4890** 10 n.

Πασίωνος Ἀχιλλίωνος. He is no doubt the same as the (ex-?)gymnasiarch of this name in XII **1540** 5 (187/8).

6–7 ἐκ τῆς ἀπὸ νότου καὶ ἀπηλ(ιώτου) μερίδος. Cf. 9–10 καὶ νότο(υ) καὶ ἀπηλ(ιώτου) μερίδος. In response to our enquiry, Dr Rowlandson notes: 'I have not come across a case quite like this before; other merides I know are (i) early first century AD sub-divisions of (some?) Oxyrhynchite toparchies, or (ii) later, divisions of estates, often named after individuals. But here I would say they refer to parts of the village land of Nemera; if you pay attention to the exact word order, the Southern and Eastern merides have the same status as the *kleros* references, and serve the same purpose, to identify the land. . . . I assume this designates land at Nemera that had never been assigned as *kleroi*, and was therefore divided up differently.'

These details may have serve to indicate which portions of the property within one *kleros* were under lease; cf. Rowlandson, *Landowners and Tenants* 217.

8–9 Λευκίου Λικινιανοῦ Μαρτιαλίου. This person may be related to Licinius Martialis, attested as a banker at the Serapeum of Oxyrhynchus in PSI XII 1262 ii 3–4 (137) and XXXIV **2722** 9 (154); see Jones and Whitehorne, *Register of Oxyrhynchites, 30 BC – AD 96* 136, no. 2699.

9 Ἀλεξάνδρου. A *kleros* of this name is attested in the area of the village of Senepta in the middle toparchy; around Tychinpsalbo in the southern toparchy; and around the *epoikion* of Satyrus in the eastern toparchy. See Pruneti, *Aegyptus* 55 (1975) 166–9; Calderini and Daris, *Dizionario geografico* Suppl. i 23 f. XII **1508** 7–8 (II) mentions a *kleros* of Dorcon and Alexander, formerly of Menon, near Senepta.

10 ἀν(ὰ) (*scil.* ἀρτάβας) δ χ(οίνικας) η. This tax rate is also attested in VII **1044** 15.

12 ἅσπερ κοκκολογή(σας). This clause appears in XLIX **3474** 15 (197), VII **1031** 17–18, and P. Hamb. I 19.21–2. Apart from these 'technical' texts, the verb κοκκολογέω is attested only in one other papyrus, P. Münch. III 65.12 (III).

14–15 ἐπακολουθούντων . . . προκεχειρισμένων. These are the officials who supervised the sowing, a group that may have included the *katasporeus*, the *komogrammateus*, and the *komopraktor*; see LVII **3902–6** introd., sect. E2 (p. 103), **3907–9** introd., sect. C2 (p. 119).

17 cùν τοῖϲ ἐπομένοιϲ. Cf. P. Hamb. 19.20, **1031** 20. These were additional charges to be paid with what had been borrowed. Similar surcharges are described in P. Coll. Youtie I 26.18 (Apoll. Hept.; 156) as τοῖϲ προϲπαραγραφηϲομένοιϲ. J. Rowlandson, *ZPE* 67 (1987) 292 n. 19, queried whether the rates on *basilike ge* also carried the ⅛ supplement levied on private land. These surcharges might represent something similar.

17–18 ἅμα τοῖϲ τῆϲ γῆϲ γνηϲίοιϲ τελέϲμαϲι. The same phrase, with minimal variation, occurs in **3474** 24–5 (without γνηϲίοιϲ), P. Hamb. 19.20–21, and **1031** 21–2, all of which add τοῦ ἐνεϲτῶτοϲ ἔτουϲ. Earlier texts offer slightly different expressions. See **3902–6** introd., sect. F2 (p. 103), **3907–9** introd., sect. D2 (p. 120).

25 Ἀθύρ. The second hand added the name of the month, leaving a blank space, perhaps for the day. It was not necessary to have an exact date. All applications and orders that have one, however, fall in November or December; see **3902–6** introd., sect. H (p. 104), **3907–9** introd., sect. F (p. 120).

25–6 Αὐρήλ(ιοϲ) Ἡρακλᾶϲ Νεχθενίβιοϲ. The Aurelius Heracles son of Nechthenibis in PSI VII 807.33 (280) is certainly not the same person.

26–7 ὤμαϲα, l. ὤμοϲα. For the spelling, see Gignac, *Grammar* ii 296; for the use of the perfect and aorist in the formula ἐπιδέδωκα καὶ ὤμοϲα τὸν ὅρκον, see Mandilaras, *The Verb* 162–3.

L. CAPPONI

4892. Report(?) of Village Scribe

28 4B.57/A(1–5)c   11 × 9.2 cm   17 July 236?

What survives is the lower part (except for the line-ends) of a document, giving the regnal date clause and the subscription of a village scribe through a deputy. For the type of document, cf. the contemporary XLIII **3133** (239), a report submitted to a *strategus* by a village scribe. There are several long strokes in the left-hand margin, as if they belonged to a previous (lost) column.

The interest of this papyrus lies in its reuse. A piece of the original document was reused to carry **4895**, a writing exercise reproducing a loan dated to 380. (It is unclear whether the line-ends had been lost by the time of the reuse, i.e., whether there existed a larger piece than what we have around the year 380.) Such a long time gap between the first and second use of a papyrus is extraordinary. Apart from a very few documents, chiefly from the archive of Heroninus, reused after just over 100 years, only one other text seems to attest a longer interval than we have here, P. Bouriant 41 of 197, a roll reused to form a Christian codex of the fourth/fifth century (P. Bouriant 3 + P. Achmim 1). On the issue of recycled documentary papyri in general, see E. G. Turner, *JEA* 40 (1954) 102–6, and *BASP* 15 (1978) 163–9.

　　·　　　·　　　·　　　　　　·

(ἔτουϲ) [β Αὐτοκρά]τοροϲ Καίϲα[ροϲ Γαΐου
Ἰουλίου [Οὐήρου Μαξιμ]ίνου Εὐϲε[βοῦϲ
Εὐτυχοῦϲ Ϲεβαϲτοῦ καὶ Γαΐου Ἰουλ[ίου Οὐήρου
Μαξίμου τοῦ ἱερωτάτου Καίϲαροϲ Ϲ[εβαϲτοῦ

5   υἱοῦ τοῦ Cεβαcτοῦ, Ἐπεὶφ κγ̄.

───────────

(m. 2)   Αὐρήλιος Παυcανίας κωμογρ(αμματεὺς) Χύcεως δι᾽ ἐμ[οῦ

1 L   2, 3 ϊουλιου   3 γαϊου   6 κωμογρ⳽

'Year 2 of Imperator Caesar Gaius Iulius Verus Maximinus Pius Felix Augustus and Gaius Iulius Verus Maximus the most sacred Caesar Augustus, son of the Augustus, Epeiph 23.'

(2nd hand) 'Aurelius Pausanias, village scribe of Chysis, through me . . .'

1 (ἔτους) [β. It is less likely, though not impossible, that γ is to be restored instead of β: in summer 237 (year 3), we would expect the regnal formula to have included victory titles; see R. Kienast, *Römische Kaisertabelle* (1996²) 184–5.

4 ἱερωτάτου. A version of Lat. *nobilissimus*; see F. Mitthof, *ZPE* 99 (1993) 97–111.

6 Αὐρήλιος Παυcανίας κωμογρ(αμματεὺς) Χύcεως δι᾽ ἐμοῦ. A name and perhaps the verb ἐπιδέδωκα followed in the lost part of the line. For the collocation cf. SB I 4419.5 f. (224) Αὐρήλιος Ἀφροδίcιος κωμογρ(αμματεὺς) | δι᾽ ἐμοῦ τοῦ α . . . ου; XLIII **3133** 20 f. (239) Αὐρήλ(ιος) Ἀκύλας κωμ(ογραμματεὺς) δι᾽ ἐμοῦ | Νι . . [.] . ἐπιδ(έδωκα).

Χύcεως. On this village, see LV **3792** 1 n. (p. 59), with references to further literature; for the later period, see *ZPE* 142 (2003) 117 f.

N. GONIS

V. DOCUMENTS OF THE BYZANTINE PERIOD

4893–4922. MISCELLANEOUS DATED DOCUMENTS

The documents published in this section, which is a sequel to LXVIII **4675–4704**, have been chosen for their chronological and prosopographical interest. They mostly come from the late fourth and fifth centuries, the least well-documented period in the papyri. Many of these texts provide the earliest or latest known dates for the use in Egypt of certain consulates for dating purposes. Several others add to our evidence on the *militia armata* and *militia civilis* at that time.

Abbreviations used:

CLRE = R. S. Bagnall, A. Cameron, S. R. Schwartz, K. A. Worp, *Consuls of the Later Roman Empire* (1987).

*CSBE*² = R. S. Bagnall, K. A. Worp, *The Chronological Systems of Byzantine Egypt*² (2004).

4893. TOP OF DOCUMENT

85/35(c)   10.7 ×7 cm   26 April 375

This scrap, probably of a contract, offers further evidence for the presence of soldiers of the unit of *Mauri scutarii* in Oxyrhynchus in the fourth century.

The back is blank as far as it is preserved. A sheet-join runs *c.*1 cm from the right-hand edge.

> μετὰ τὴν ὑπατείαν τοῦ δεϲπότ]ου ἡμῶν Γρατιανοῦ αἰωνίου Αὐγούϲτου
>   τὸ γ καὶ Φλαουΐο]υ Εἰκυτίου τοῦ λαμ(προτάτου), Π[αχ]ὼν α.
> Φλαουΐῳ name patronymic ϲτρ]ατιώτῃ ἀναφερ[ομέν]ῳ
> εἰϲ τὸν ἀριθμὸν Μαύρων Ϲκυταρίων] τῶν ἐν Λύκῳ[ν πόλ]ει
> 5   διακειμένων   *c.*20   ]ιωτων.[
>   ].[

2 λαμϛ

'After the consulship of our master Gratianus, eternal Augustus, for the 3rd time, and of Flavius Equitius, *vir clarissimus*, Pachon 1.

'To Flavius . . . , soldier seconded to the *numerus* of *Mauri scutarii* stationed in Lycopolis . . .'

1–2 On the consulship, see *CLRE* 282–3 (cf. 284–5); *CSBE*² 189–90. P. Turner 45.9–10 (374), which offers the only other Oxyrhynchite attestation of the formula, likewise has αἰωνίου without the article, but adds κόμιτοϲ after λαμ(προτάτου).

2 Εἰκυτίου, l. Ἐκυτίου. This spelling of the name of Equitius is new; other variant spellings are Ἐκυθίου (BGU XIII 2332.2, SB VIII 9311.2), Ἐκουτίου (P. Turner 45.10), Ἐκυκίου (W. *Chr.* 381 = P. Gen. I 66.22).

4–5 The restorations are based on LXIII **4381** 3–4 (375) ἀρι]θμοῦ | Μαύρων Cκυταρίων τῶν ἐν Λύκων πόλει διακειμένων ὑπὸ Παῦλον πραιπόcιτον, which refers to two members of this unit who owned a camel stable at Oxyrhynchus. Other papyri attesting the presence of *Mauri* in Oxyrhynchus are LX **4084** 6 (339), where we find the wife of a biarch of the *numerus* of *Mauri scutarii comitatenses* who is 'dwelling' in Oxyrhynchus, and perhaps LXVII **4628** (late IV), which refers to *Mauri* in general.

On this unit, see **4381** 3–4 n.; CPR XXIV p. 23 n. 3. Most documents referring to *Mauri* concern the *cuneus* stationed in Hermopolis; apart from **4893** and **4381**, the Lycopolite *cuneus* is attested in BGU XII 2137.4 (426), SB XXVI 16532.3 (535), and some unpublished papyri in the collection of the Académie des Inscriptions in Paris (see J. Gascou, *Pap. Congr. XXII* 542). The *Mauri* in O. Oasis 11 = SEG XXXVIII 1736, and perhaps O. Douch IV 457, may have belonged to the Lycopolite *cuneus*.

5 It is tempting to restore cτρατ]ιωτῶν, and if we supplied γενναιοτάτων before that, we would fill the lacuna. However, cτρατιωτῶν would be otiose after Cκυταρίων, and in any case we do not expect any further description of the unit after διακειμένων other than a reference to the *praepositus*, as in **4381** 4 (cited above).

N. GONIS

4894. PETITION

95/30(a)   17.7 × 8.8 cm   2 August 379

The lower part of a petition from a woman to an official whose name and function are lost. The text furnishes the earliest Egyptian dating by Ausonius and Olybrius coss. 379.

On women's petitions in late antique Egypt, see the study of R. S. Bagnall in J. Gascou, D. Feissel (eds.), *La Pétition à Byzance* (Paris 2004) 53–60.

The back is blank.

```
            .     .   .
              ].[
         ]. υτο καὶ . . . . [ ].[      c.15
       ] τούτου τὰ ἀκόλουθα πράξῃς καὶ . . .[ c.5 ].[.].υ
       ] πέπρακεν Γαΐωνι κα̣ὶ ἐγὼ ἀδικ . . [. .].[
   5   ὑ]πατίας Φλ(αουΐων) Αὐcονίου καὶ Ὀλυβρίου τῶν λαμπροτάτων
           ἐπάρχων,    Μεcορὴ θ.
(m. 2)          Αὐρηλία Μαρία ἐπιδέδωκα.
```

4 γαϊωνι   5 l. ὑπατείαc   φλλ

'. . . that you act accordingly and . . . sold to Gaion and I am wronged (?).
'In the consulship of Fl. Ausonius and Fl. Olybrius, *clarissimi praefecti*, Mesore 9.'
'I, Aurelia Maria, have submitted (this).'

1–4 How much is lost at the beginning of the lines? If 3–4 were aligned with 5, which seems likely, the loss would be minimal; but if 5 was inset, we cannot tell.

4 ἀδικ . [.] . [. ἀδικοῦμαι is expected but is hard to recognize in the traces.

5–6 On the consulship of D. Magnus Ausonius and Q. Clodius Hermogenianus Olybrius, *praefecti praetorio*, see *CLRE* 292–3 (cf. 295), *CSBE*² 190, and *JJP* 33 (2003) 72. It is otherwise attested only in Hermopolite documents, all of which refer to the postconsulate. The formula in **4894** is similar to that in CPR VII 19.1, which however omits *Φλαουίων*. In the other two recorded instances (P. Strasb. VIII 749.1, P. Misc. inv. 179b.1), the name of the other consul is given as Hermogenianus.

N. GONIS

4895. Loan of Money (Writing Practice)

28 4B.57/A(1–5)c   9.2 × 11 cm   14 October 380

On the back of the lower part of a document of 236–7 (**4892**), at 90° and along the fibres, someone penned the beginning of a loan. He stopped half-way through the main body, just before he would have run out of space. This is apparently a writing exercise, which may well be later than the date recorded in its text; another loan contract/writing practice is LXI **4117** (for another writing exercise, see below, **4905**). What is remarkable is the time gap between the two texts; see **4892** introd.

```
     ὑπατείας τῶν δεσποτῶν
     ἡμῶν Γρατιανοῦ τὸ ε// καὶ
     Θεοδοσίου τὸ α// τῶν
     αἰωνίων Ἀγούςτων,
5      Φαῶφι ιζ.
     Αὐρήλιος Φιλόνικο[ς
     Διονυςοδώρου ἀπὸ τ[ῆς
     λαμ(πρᾶς) καὶ λαμ(προτάτης) Ὀξυρυγχ[ι]τ[ῶν
     πόλεως παρὰ Αὐρηλίου
10   Θεοδώρου Δημητρίου ἀπὸ
     τῆς αὐτῆς πόλεως
     χαίρειν. ὁμολογῶ ἐςχηκέ-
     ναι παρὰ coῦ ἐν χρήςι δι-
     ὰ χειρὸς ἐξ οἴκο coυ εἰς ἰδί-
15   αν μου .   (vac.)
```

4 l. Ἀγούςτων   6 l. Αὐρηλίῳ Φιλονίκῳ   8 λαμ∫ (*bis*)   13 l. χρήςει
14 l. οἴκου   ἰδι-

'In the consulship of our masters Gratianus for the 5th time and Theodosius for the 1st time, the eternal Augusti, Phaophi 17.

'To Aurelius Philonicus son of Dionysodorus, from the splendid and most splendid city of the Oxyrhynchites, from Aurelius Theodorus son of Demetrius, from the same city, greetings. I acknowledge that I have received from you on loan, by hand and out of your house, for my own ...'

1–4 For the consulship of Gratianus Aug. v and Theodosius Aug. i coss. 380, see *CLRE* 294–5; *CSBE*[2] 190. Its earliest occurrence in a papyrus dates from three days earlier (P. Flor. I 75 = W. Chr. 433).

6–7 Φιλόνικο[ς] Διονυσοδώρου. The name Φιλόνικος is not very common, and Διονυσόδωρος is rare in this period. It is a curiosity that the only other known bearer of the name Φιλόνικος in Oxyrhynchus at that time is the son of Besammon (VII **1041** 6 of 381), another pagan theophoric name not common in this period.

15 . The scribe wrote an upright, and then stopped. καί was intended.

N. GONIS

4896. Loan of Money

102/166(c)   9.2 × 11 cm   386

The upper right part of a loan, most probably of money (see 8 n.), lent by an assistant of the office of *exactor*. A point of interest is that the consular date clause is phrased somewhat differently from those hitherto known.

A sheet-join is visible at the right-hand edge. The back is blank as far as it is preserved.

ὑπατείας τοῦ δεσπότο]υ ἡμῶν Ὀνωρίου τοῦ
ἐπιφανεστάτου υἱοῦ τοῦ δ]εσπότου ἡμῶν Θεοδοσίου
        Αὐγούστου καὶ] Φλαουΐου Εὐοδίου τοῦ λαμ(προτάτου).
Αὐρηλίῳ ...] . ωνι Κρονίωνος ἀπὸ τῆς
5 Ἡρακλεοπο]λειτῶν βοηθῷ ἐξακτορείας
Αὐρήλιος ...] . ... ος Ἀπφοῦτος ἀπὸ τῆς λαμ(πρᾶς)
καὶ λαμ(προτάτης) Ὀξ]υρυγχιτῶν πόλεως χαίρειν.
ὁμολογῶ ἐσ]χηκέναι παρὰ σοῦ ἐν χρήσι
        c.15   ]ε[ ] .... [ ] . ω .

        .   .   .

3, 6 λαμ𐅵∥   5 l. Ἡρακλεοπολιτῶν, ἐξακτορίας   8 l. χρήσει

'In the consulship of our master Honorius, the *nobilissimus* son of our master Theodosius Augustus, and of Flavius Euodius, *vir clarissimus*.

'To Aurelius —on son of Cronion, from the (city) of the Heracleopolites, assistant to the office of exactor, Aurelius —us son of Apphus, from the splendid and most splendid city of the Oxyrhynchites, greetings. I acknowledge that I have received from you on loan ...'

1–3 On the consulship of Honorius, *nobilissimus Caesar*, and Fl. Euodius, see *CLRE* 306–7 (cf.

308–9); *CSBE*² 191. The text must postdate 26 June 386, when the postconsulate of the previous year was still in use in Oxyrhynchus (SB XVIII 13916); the earliest record of the consuls of 386 dates from 29 August (XXXIV **2715**).

The element υἱοῦ τοῦ δε]cπότου ἡμῶν Θεοδοcίου Αὐγούcτου is not found in any other consular or postconsular clause of 386 or 387, but is comparable to the manner Valentinian is styled in (post) consular formulas of 369–70 (see *CSBE*² 188). It is remarkable that in Honorius' description none of the versions attested in papyri agree with each other (in this too the clauses of 369–70 offer a parallel):

Φλ. Ὀνωρίου τοῦ ἐπιφανεcτάτου (XXXIV **2715** 1);

[τοῦ δεcπότο]υ ἡμῶν Ὀνωρίου τοῦ | [ἐπιφανεcτάτου υἱοῦ τοῦ δ]εcπότου ἡμῶν Θεοδοcίου | [Αὐγούcτου (LXXII **4896** 1–3);

το[ῦ δεcπότου ἡ]μῶν Ὀνωρίου [τοῦ ἐπιφανεcτ]άτου | Καίcαροc (P. Kell. I 45.24–6);

[Φλ.] Ὀ[ν]ωρίο[υ] τ[οῦ] ἐπιφανεcτάτ[ου] | παιδόc (SB XIV 11285.1–2).

4 ...].. ωνι. Apparently not Κρο]νίωνι.

5 Ἡρακλεοπο]λειτῶν suits the space better than Ἑρμουπο]λειτῶν, the only other real alternative.

βοηθῷ ἐξακτορείαc (l. -ρίαc). This is the second earliest attestation of this office, attested exclusively in Oxyrhynchus, after P. Michael. 33.3 (*c.*367–8; see R. S. Bagnall, *CE* 66 (1991) 284–7), which also comes from Oxyrhynchus and refers to βοηθῷ ἐξάκτοροc.

8 ὁμολογῶ ἐc]χηκέναι παρὰ coῦ ἐν χρήcι. This phrase (or *sim.*) is typical of Oxyrhynchite loans of money, but there are exceptions: BGU XIII 2339 (378), a loan of wheat; and I **133** (550) (12 ἐν χρήcει καὶ παραμεμετρῆcθαι) and LXIII **4398** (553), both loans of wheat for seed, and the only such loans from Byzantine Oxyrhynchus published to date.

9 One could read [διὰ χειρὸc ἐξ οἴκου coυ] ε[ἰc], but after that the expected ἰδίαν is not supported by the traces.

N. GONIS

4897. LOAN OF MONEY

40 5B.109/K(6)a   14.2 × 18.3 cm   5 March 391

A loan of one solidus lent by an *optio* to a bread-seller, due to be repaid within eleven days; there is no reference to an interest rate. The text offers some early attestations of certain monetary terms (see 9 n.), and is the latest (and only) record for the postconsulate of Valentinianus Aug. IV and Fl. Neoterius coss. 390.

The spelling is erratic and there are several odd divisions of words between lines (8, 10, 13); the formulas, however, are correctly employed.

μετὰ τὴν ὑπατίαν τοῦ δεcπότου ἡμῶν Οὐαλεντινιανοῦ αἰωνίου Αὐγούcτου τὸ δ καὶ Φλαουΐου
    Νεωτερίου τοῦ λαμπρ(οτάτου), Φαμενὼθ θ̄.
Αὐρήλιοc Νίκω⟨ν⟩ Κυρήλλου καταγινόμενο῀c῀
5 ἐν τῇ Ὀξυρυγχιτῶν πόλει ἀρτωπόλειc
Φλαουΐῳ Μαρκιανῷ ὠψίονι
χαί[ρει]ν. ὁμολογῶ ἐcχηκέναι παρὰ coῦ

ἐν χ[ρ]ήϲει διὰ χιρὸϲ ἐξ οἴκου ϲου εἰϲ ἰδία μου καὶ ἀν-
αγκ[αί]αν χρίαν χρυϲοῦ δόκιμων εὐϲταθμων

10 ν[ομιϲ]μάτιων ἐν καιφαλέου, ἅπερ ἐπάν-
αγκεϲ ἀποδώϲω ϲοι τῇ εἰκάϲι τοῦ ὄντοϲ
μηνὸϲ Φαμενὼθ τοῦ ἐνεϲτῶτοϲ ἔτουϲ
ξζ λϛ ἄνευ τινὸϲ ὑπερθέϲεωϲ καὶ εὑρηϲ-
ιλογίαϲ γιν[ο]μένηϲ ⟨ϲ⟩οι τ[ῆ]ϲ πράξεωϲ

15 π[α]ρά τε ἐμο[ῦ κ]αὶ ἐκ τῶν [ὑπα]ρχόντων
μοι πά]ντων [. .] . . . [. .] . κύριον
τὸ γραμμάτιο]ν ἁπλοῦν γραφὲν [καὶ
ἐπερωτηθεὶϲ ὡμολόγη]ϲα.

        c.20   ] . ἔϲχον ἐν χρ[ήϲει

.   .   .   .   .   .

Back, downwards, along the fibres:

20   . ι( ) Νίκωνοϲ ἀρτωπόλει [

1 l. ὑπατείαν	4 κυρηλλου: ρ corr. from λ; l. Κυρίλλου	5 l. ἀρτοπώλης
6 l. ὀπτίωνι	8 l. χειρός, ἰδίαν 9 l. χρείαν, δόκιμον εὔσταθμον	10 l. νομισμάτιον,
κεφαλαίου, ὅπερ 11 l. εἰκάδι 20 ι/ l. ἀρτοπώλου		

'After the consulship of our master Valentinianus, eternal Augustus, for the 4th time and Flavius Neoterius, *vir clarissimus*, Phamenoth 9.

'Aurelius Nicon son of Cyrillus, resident in the city of the Oxyrhynchites, bread-seller, to Flavius Marcianus, *optio*, greetings. I acknowledge that I have received from you on loan, by hand and out
of your house, for my own and pressing need, one solidus of gold, approved, of full weight, as principal, which of necessity I shall return to you on the twentieth of the present month of Phamenoth of
the current year 67/36 without any delay and subterfuge, you having the right of execution against
both myself and all my belongings. . . . This contract, written in a single copy, is binding, and in reply
to the formal question I assented. . . . I have received on loan . . .'

'. . . of Nicon, bread-seller . . .'

1–3 On this consulship, see *CLRE* 314–5; *CSBE*[2] 191–2. This is its latest occurrence in a papy-
rus. Tatianus and Symmachus, the consuls of 391, are first attested very shortly thereafter, in P. Lips.
I 42, which dates from March/April (Pharmouthi); see R. S. Bagnall, K. A. Worp, *BASP* 17 (1980) 7
= BL VIII 171.

5 ἀρτωπόλεις, l. ἀρτοπώλης. A rather uncommon term; cf. E. Battaglia, *'Artos': Il lessico della
panificazione nei papiri greci* (1989) 171–83. The compounds in -πώλης and -πράτης have received a fair
amount of attention in the literature; see H.-J. Drexhage, *MBAH* 10 (1991) 1–17; 20 (2001) 1–4; 21
(2002) 74–89; and (for the inscriptions) K. Ruffing, *MBAH* 21 (2002) 16–63.

6 ὠψίονι, l. ὀπτίωνι. The spelling is slightly curious (Gignac offers no comparable examples
of τ spelled as ϲ after π; πϲ = ψ), but no other word could have been intended. On *optiones*, see the
literature collected in LXIV **4434** 2 n.; further references have accumulated since: O. Douch IV and
V *passim*, BGU XVII 2715.2, CPR XXIV 2.3, 4.27, SB XXII 15627.2, and possibly P. Sijp. 51.1. Fl.
Marcianus could have been a member of one of the two military units with links to Oxyrhynchus in

the later fourth century, namely the *numerus* of the *Mauri scutarii* (LXIII **4381**, LXXII **4893**) or the *legio I Maximiana* (P. Col. VII 183; LXXII **4900**). The contemporary loan XIV **1712** 3 (394) is addressed ὀπτίονι φαμιλίας ἡ[γεμονικῆς (a civil servant; see note *ad loc.*).

9 δόκιμων εὐςταθμων, l. δόκιμον εὔςταθμον. This is the earliest exactly dated reference to the term εὔςταθμος, and the second earliest (after P. Kell. I 44.7 of 382) mention of the term δόκιμος used for solidi (unless P. Lond. III 985 = W. *Chr.* 466.7, assigned to the fourth century, is earlier).

11 εἰκάςι, l. εἰκάδι. Gignac, *Grammar* i, offers no example for the interchange δ > ς, but refers to transcriptions of prevocalic ςι or ζι as *di* in Coptic texts (75 n. 3), and there are several examples for the interchange of δ and ζ (76), the latter occasionally interchanging with ς before vowels (123). Given the common spelling of δ as τ, perhaps the underlying reason is the same as in ὠψίονι in 6, where *ti* was spelled as *si*.

Phamenoth 20 = March 16.

11–12 There are several short-term loans from the fourth century (see the list in P. Kell. I pp. 115–16), including some to be repaid within a month, but the term specified here, 11 days, seems to be exceptional (O. Montevecchi, *La papirologia* 226, refers to a term of 10 days as the shortest attested, but offers no further details).

13 Oxyrhynchite era year 67/36 = 390/91; see *CSBE*² 139.

16 I do not see what could have stood in the unread part of the line. There is no room for καθάπερ ἐκ δίκης; one may consider reading ὡς πρόκ(ειται), but the traces cannot confirm it.

19 The break at the beginning of the line must have taken away the borrower's name and patronymic. This would suit the space, but the first letter after the break is probably omega; Κυρίλλου could of course be spelled as Κυρίλλω, but it would be hazardous to impose the form here.

20 ̣ι̣( ). I do not see what the word is. The first letter may be sigma, which dips below the baseline to reach the lower part of the putative iota.

N. GONIS

4898. DOCUMENT ADDRESSED TO A *SYSTATES*

102/165(b)   9.1 × 12 cm   391

The upper left corner of a document addressed to an Oxyrhynchite *systates* not known previously, Aurelius Heliodorus son of Muses; see below 2–3 n. The prescript is comparable to LI **3622**, a contract concerning a liturgy.

The back is blank as far as it is preserved.

ὑπατείας Φλαουΐῳ Τατιανῶ κ[αὶ Cυμμάχου τῶν λαμπροτάτων *month, day*
Αὐρηλίῳ Ἡλιωδώρου Μουςέως [ἀπὸ τῆς λαμ(πρᾶς) καὶ λαμ(προτάτης)
                                      Ὀξυρυγχ(ιτῶν) πόλ(εως)
ςυςτάτῃ φυλῆς Δρώμω Γυμναςίο[υ καὶ ἄλλων ἀμφόδων παρὰ Αὐρηλίου
Ἀνικήτου ἀπὸ τῆς αὐτῆς πόλεως [*c.*28

.   .   .   .

1 l. Φλαουΐου or Φλαουΐων, Τατιανοῦ   2 l. Ἡλιοδώρῳ   3 l. Δρόμου

'In the consulship of Flavii Tatianus and Symmachus, *viri clarissimi*, . . .

'To Aurelius Heliodorus son of Muses, from the splendid and most splendid city of the Oxy-rhynchites, *systates* of the tribe of the "Avenue of the Gymnasium" and other quarters, from Aurelius Anicetus from the same city. . . .'

1 For the consuls, see *CLRE* 316–7 (cf. 318–9); *CSBE*[2] 192.

2–3 *Αὐρηλίῳ Ἡλιωδώρου* (l. -ῳ) *Μουσέως* . . . *ϲυϲτάτῃ*. The only *systates* previously attested in Oxyrhynchus between 356 and 386 is Aurelius Muses son of Theon. The very long time-span of Muses' career and other considerations have led to the suggestion that 'the post was a permanent one, not involving reappointment at intervals as previously thought' (LI **3622** introd.). It is conceivable that Heliodorus is Muses' son, and succeeded his father. Heliodorus first occurs in office in the unpublished P. Ashm. inv. 12 of 29 August 384; he will have entered office some time after 381/2 (PSI X 1108), when Muses is still the *systates*. We find Muses again in office in 386 (XXXIV **2715**); it may be that this was a temporary replacement for Heliodorus.

It is tempting to assume that the *systates* Parion son of Heliodorus in **4904** of 417 is the son of Heliodorus the *systates*; if so, it would follow that over six decades three generations of the same family ran the office, which will have lost its earlier liturgical character by that time. (Between Heliodorus and Parion there intervened at least one other *systates*, Hierax, attested in P. Flor. I 39 of 29.viii.396).

A list of Oxyrhynchite *systatai* is given in P. Leid. Inst. pp. 277–81. Besides Heliodorus and Parion, add now Theon, recorded in SB XX 15171 ('iv/v' ed. pr., but the published photograph (*ZPE* 90 (1992) Taf. viia) suggests a date in the fifth century), and Martyrius, attested in SB XXII 15274 ('vi' ed. pr., but Prof. T. Gagos kindly informed me that 'the inv. catalogue lists it as v A.D. and I think that's very plausible').

3 *Δρώμω* (l. -ου) *Γυμνασίο[υ*. On this Oxyrhynchite quarter, see the references collected by S. Daris, *ZPE* 132 (2000) 215 = *Dizionario* . . . Suppl. 3 p. 99. On the tribes of Oxyrhynchus and their relation to the office of systates, see LI **3622** introd. para. 2.

N. GONIS

4899. ACKNOWLEDGEMENT OF RECEIPT

105/51(c)   10.5 × 7.7 cm   27 April 393

Only the upper right corner of the document is preserved. An unknown person addresses a group of heirs and acknowledges receipt and payment. For speculation on the possible nature of the transaction, see 6 n.

The text offers the latest record on papyrus for the postconsulate of Arcadius Aug. II and Fl. Rufinus coss. 392.

A sheet-join runs 3.3 cm from the right edge. The back is blank as far as it is preserved.

> *μετὰ τὴν ὑπατείαν τοῦ δεϲπότου ἡ]μῶν Ἀρκαδίου αἰωνίου*
> *Αὐγούϲτου τὸ β καὶ Φλαουΐου Ῥου]φίνου τοῦ λαμ(προτάτου), Παχὼν β΄΄.*
>   *c.27   -]ίου ἀπὸ τῆϲ λαμπρᾶϲ καὶ*
> *λαμπροτάτηϲ Ὀξυρυγχιτῶν πό]λεωϲ κληρονόμοιϲ*
> 5   *c.25   ]ϲ Αἰατίου Ἀείωνοϲ ἀπὸ τῆϲ*
> *αὐτῆϲ πόλεωϲ χαίρειν. ὁμο]λογῶ ἀπ'εϲχηκέναι καὶ πεπληρῶϲθαι*

c.30   ].[.].[*c*.6]ω . ει

.   .   .   .

2 λαμ∫

'After the consulship of our master Arcadius, eternal Augustus, for the 2nd time and of Flavius Rufinus, *vir clarissimus*, Pachon 2.

'. . . from the splendid and most splendid city of the Oxyrhynchites, to the heirs of . . . Aeatius son of Aeion, from the same city, greetings. I acknowledge that I have received and been paid . . .'

1–2 On the consulship, see *CLRE* 318–19 (cf. 320–21); *CSBE*² 192. This is its latest mention in a text from Egypt; the consuls of the year first appear on 12 October 393 (**4900**).

5]ϲ Ἀιατίου Ἀείωνοϲ. One may think of restoring τοῦ τῆϲ *epithet* μνήμη]ϲ, but there are no parallels for such an expression at this date. One finds τοῦ τῆϲ διαϲημοτάτηϲ/κρατίϲτηϲ μνήμηϲ in a very few second- and third-century documents, used for Roman equestrians, but the Byzantine epithets for the non-senatorial dead do not make their appearance before the fifth century (λαμπρᾶϲ μνήμηϲ first occurs on papyrus in P. Mich. XI 611.3 of 412).

The name Ἀιάτιοϲ may also be attested in P. Vindob. Bosw. 17.9 (ιι/ιιι) Ἀιατ(ίου). Cf. also BGU VII 1719.5 (ιν?) Ἀιατᾶ (gen.).

6 ὁμο]λογῶ ᾽ἀπ᾽εϲχηκέναι καὶ πεπληρῶϲθαι. This collocation is found only three times in DDbDP: XIV **1645** 6 (308), a receipt for the return of 'personal effects' belonging to a deceased person; P. Dubl. 33.8 (513), a sale of a monasterion; and SB I 5320.12 (νιι), a sale of land; see also SPP II p. 34.12 (343), a receipt for payment of transport charges, which reverses the order of the infinitives. Much more common is the collocation ἐϲχηκέναι καὶ πεπληρῶϲθαι, typical of Hermopolite and Antinoopolite sales on delivery. **4899** need not be a sale; the appearance of heirs may suggest a scenario comparable to the story in **1645**, i.e., we may have a receipt of goods and/or money that might have been mistaken for part of the deceased's estate (I owe the observation to Dr Rea).

N. GONIS

4900. Lease of Land

42 5B.75/F(1)a   10 × 11.5 cm   12 October 393
Plate XV

The upper right part of a contract, of interest for its consular date clause and for the attestation of a soldier(?) of the *legio I Maximiana*.

The reference to what seems to be aruras and to a 'ground' (6–7) suggest that this contract refers to land: a sale or a lease. The latter is more likely in view of the arrangement of the text; see below, 3ff. n.

The back is blank as far as it is preserved.

ὑπατείαϲ τοῦ δεϲπότου ἡμῶν] Θεοδοϲίου αἰωνίου Αὐγούϲτου τὸ γ/
καὶ Φλαουΐου Ἀβουν]δαντίου τοῦ λαμπρο(τάτου), Φαῶφι ιε.
ἐμίϲθωϲεν κατὰ μιϲθαποχὴν Α]ὐρήλιοϲ Πτολεμαῖ[ο]ϲ Ἀπφοῦτοϲ
        c.35   ]. Φλαουΐῳ Ἀμμω-
5   νι-   *c*.20   λεγεῶνοϲ πρώτηϲ Μ]αξιμιανῆϲ

c.35] . . ν̣οϲ τὰϲ ὑπαρχούϲαϲ
c.35] . [. .] . [. .] . . ἐδάφουϲ
] . . [. .] . [
] . . υ[

. . . .

2 λαμπρ̣ο   4 φλαουϊω

'In the consulship of our master Theodosius, eternal Augustus, for the 3rd time and of Flavius Abundantius, *vir clarissimus*, Phaophi 15.

'Aurelius Ptolemaeus son of Apphus . . . leased upon prepayment of rent to Flavius Ammoni— . . . of the *legio prima Maximiana* . . . the (aruras) that belong . . . ground . . .'

1–2 On the consulship of Theodosius Aug. III and Fl. Abundantius, see *CLRE* 320–1 (cf. 323); *CSBE*[2] 192. This is its earliest attestation on papyrus. These consuls are also recorded in LXIII **4386**, but no month and day survive there.

3ff. We do not have a prescript of the A-to-B or B-to-A type, but an arrangement in which some text stood before the reference to the contracting party who is the subject of the missing verb. If the document is a lease, it must have been a lease of the private protocol type and not an *epidoche*, common in this period. κατὰ μιϲθαποχήν, restored to fill the space, is modelled on P. Harr. I 82.3 (345) and SB XXVI 16507.2 (475), the two latest Oxyrhynchite leases of the private protocol type and which refer to a μιϲθαποχή (also in the undated, but of the fourth/fifth century, P. CtYBR inv. 1257.3, being edited by A. Benaissa). On μιϲθαποχαί, see P. Münch. III 90 introd.

3 Ἀπφ̣ο̣ῦτοϲ. The putative φ does not look like any other phi in this text, but no other reading suggests itself. It would be easier to read iota, but this would receive support only from the uncertainly read O. Strasb. 577.1 (Theb.; II) Ἀπι̣οῦτοϲ.

4 The break at the beginning of the line must have taken away Ptolemaeus' *origo* (ἀπὸ τῆϲ Ὀξυρυγχιτῶν πόλεωϲ?) and occupation.

5 λεγεῶνοϲ πρώτηϲ Μ]αξιμιανῆϲ. Cf. P. Col. VII 183.7–9 (372) ϲτρατιώτῃ λ̣ε̣γ̣ε̣ῶνοϲ | πρίμα Μαξιμιανῆϲ διακιμέ̣ν̣η̣ϲ̣ ἐν Ὀξυ|ρύγχων. The *legio I Maximiana* was formed under the Tetrarchs, and was stationed in Upper Egypt, to guard the southern frontier. The *Notitia Dignitatum*, whose *pars Orientis* dates from around 400, records that this legion was garrisoned at Philae and was under the command of the *dux Thebaidis* (Or. xxxi 37). The Columbia papyrus implies that the legion was stationed at Oxyrhynchus in 372, but there is no need to assume that the entire legion had moved there. This may have been only a detachment; see D. Hoffmann, *Das spätrömische Bewegungsheer und die Notitia Dignitatum* ii (1970) 175 n. 825 (this text is cited there as SB 9603). On the basis of **4900**, one could think that this unit was in Oxyrhynchus until 393, though this is not the only possible implication. (In 6 there is not enough space to restore διακειμένηϲ ἐν Ὀξυρύγχων in full, but the name of the city may have been abbreviated.) We do not even know whether Fl. Ammoni— was in active service or a veteran. That he seems to be leasing land is not conclusive, especially in view of the increasingly civilian activities of the soldiers at that time; cf. P. Charite 8 (348), in which an *eques* of the *Mauri scutarii* appears to have taken ten aruras on lease.

The first editors of P. Col. 183 offered an elaborate interpretation of the presence of this legion at Oxyrhynchus (*AJPh* 81 (1960) 171–3), which however does not hold. Given that the papyrus comes from Caranis, it was stated in the re-edition that 'nothing here identifies the place as the distant Oxyrhynchos rather than, as reason argues, the nearby village of Oxyrhyncha; the genitive proves nothing, as confusion of genitive and dative is common' (P. Col. 183.8–9 n.). **4900** seems to turn the scales in favour of Oxyrhynchus. The name of the soldier, Ouenaphrios, is typical of the Fayum, and may explain his presence at Caranis.

6] . .voc. The traces are compatible with μηνός, but in that case we would expect the name of the month to be mentioned (e.g., we should have had ἀπὸ νεομηνίας τοῦ ὄντος μηνὸς Φαῶφι).

τὰς ὑπαρχούσας will have been followed by ἀρούρας somewhere in the next line. This must have been arable land.

7 At the beginning of the line, there may have stood αὐτῷ, followed by a reference to the location of the land under lease. ἐδάφους will have been followed by a name + καλουμένου, and then by the number of aruras leased.

N. GONIS

4901. SALE OF WINE ON DELIVERY

63 6B.70/B(1–2)b   14.5 × 14.2 cm   1 June 408

This is the earliest securely dated Oxyrhynchite sale of wine on delivery to be published; see the list in P. Heid. V pp. 296 ff., supplemented in *Laverna* 10 (1999) 152, and *APF* 51/1 (2005) 78. The contract was made between the *domus divina*, through a steward, and a deacon, and concerned the provision of eighty-eight jars of wine.

The deacon originates from a hamlet that belonged to the *domus divina* some time in the sixth century, but later was controlled by the Apions; see below, 4 n. It is likely that the vineyards that would have produced the wine belonged to the *domus divina*, and that the deacon was in its employ. This recalls XLIX **3512** (492), where a *colonus adscripticius* of an Oxyrhynchite *curialis* receives from the latter the price of the wine in advance of delivery.

The scribe had little control over spelling, grammar, and contract formulas. Like the rest of the text, the consular date clause is garbled, referring to Arcadius VII instead of Honorius VII (Arcadius was also dead at that time).

The text is written across the fibres on the back of what seems to be a petition, of which too little remains to warrant publication (it ends]ειν εἰς βοήθειαν).

μετὰ τὴν ὑπατίαν τῶν δεcποτῶν ἡμῶν Ἀρκαδίου
τὸ ζ̄ καὶ Θεοδοcίου τὸ β τῶν αἰωνίων Ἀούcτων, Παῦνι ζ.
τοῖc θειοτάτηc οἰκείαc διὰ Μαρίνου πρ(ονοητοῦ) (vac.)
Αὐρηλίῳ Παμοῦν Μούιτοc ἀπὸ ἐποικίου Κινῆαc
5   διακώνου καθωλικῆc ἐκκληcίαc χαίριν.
ὁμολογῶ ἐcχηκέναι παρὰ coῦ ἀπὸ λόγου τῆc
cυνπεφωνημένηc πρὸc ἀλλήλουc ⟨τιμῆc⟩ οἴνου διπλῶν
μεccτῶν εὐαρέcτον ἐντώπια ὀξυ[ρ]υγχιτικὰ
{διπλᾶ} εὐδοήκοντα ὠκτώ, γί(νονται) δι(πλᾶ) πη μό(να),
10   ἐπὶ τῷ με ταῦτά coι παραcχῖν τῷ Μεcουρὴ μηνὶ

τῆς ἑβδόμη[c ἰν]δικ(τίωνος) ἀνυπερ[θέτω]c καὶ χωρί[c
τιν[ο]c εὑρηcιλο[γίαc,] γιγνομέ[νη]c cοι τῆ[c

.   .   .   .

1 l. ὑπατείαν   2 l. Αὐγούcτων   3 l. τῇ θειοτάτῃ οἰκίᾳ   πρ   4 l. Αὐρήλιοc
5 l. διάκονοc καθολικῆc, χαίρειν   7 l. cυμπεφωνημένηc   8 l. μεcτῶν εὐαρέcτων ἐντοπίων
ὀξυρυγχιτικῶν   9 γε⊄πημ° l. ὀγδοήκοντα ὀκτώ   10 l. παραcχεῖν, Μεcορή   11 l. ἑβ-
δόμηc [ιν]δικ

'After the consulship of our masters Arcadius [*sic*, for Honorius] for the 7th time and Theodosius for the 2nd time, the eternal Augusti, Pauni 7.

'To the *domus divina* through Marinus, steward, (from) Aurelius Pamun son of Muis, from the
hamlet of Cineas, deacon of the catholic church, greetings. I acknowledge that I have received
from you on account of the jointly agreed price of eighty-eight full, satisfactory, local, Oxyrhynchite
double-jars, total 88 double-jars only, on condition that I supply them to you in the month of Mesore
of the seventh indiction without delay and without any subterfuge, you having (the right of execution) . . .'

1–2 'Arcadius VII' is a mistake for 'Honorius VII'; see above, introd. This may be due to the fact
that in 406 Arcadius held his sixth consulship, and documents from the earlier part of 407 (e.g. VIII
1122) were dated by his postcosulship.

This is the latest attestation of the postconsulate of [Honorius] VII and Theodosius II coss. 407,
on which see *CSBE*[2] 193. The consuls of 408 are first attested on 26 September (LXVIII **4677**).

2 Ἀούcτων, l. Αὐγούcτων. For the spelling, see Gignac, *Grammar* i 74.

Παῦνι ζ = June 1. This is a late date for this contract to be made, though there are a couple of
sales of wine which date from July; see the table in CPR XIV pp. 31–2.

3 τοῖc θειοτάτηc οἰκείαc (l. τῇ θειοτάτῃ οἰκίᾳ) διὰ Μαρίνου πρ(ονοητοῦ). A similar address
may have stood in L **3582** 1–2 (442), read as [- - - ἐπι]φανεcτάτηc ἡμῶν δεcποίνηc Ἀρκαδίαc |
[- - -]ι[.]ν δι[ο]ικητοῦ (perhaps read [τῇ θειοτάτῃ οἰκίᾳ τῆc ἐπι]φανεcτάτηc κτλ. | [διὰ Φλαουΐου
Cτρατηγ]ί[ο]υ δι[ο]ικητοῦ).

πρ(ονοητοῦ). This is the earliest reference to a προνοητήc on the employ of the *domus divina*; the
second earliest is in VIII **1134** (421). These were local stewards of the ordinary kind, not administrators of the kind we have e.g. in **4905–6**.

4 Αὐρηλίῳ. On the 'Aureliate' of clergymen, see K. A. Worp, *ZPE* 151 (2005) 145–52, esp. 146–8
for the deacons.

ἐποικίου Κινήαc. Cf. PSI III 196.1 and 197.1 (VI) ὁ θεῖος οἶκος Βίκτορι προν(οητῇ) Κινέαc, which
implies that the hamlet was part of the *domus divina*. The hamlet had passed to the administration or
possession of the Apions by the beginning of the seventh century; this had been implied by XXVII
2479 2 (see J. Gascou, *T&MByz* 9 (1985) 77), and was confirmed by the full publication of I **192** desc.
= SB XXII 15362.4–5 (614/15; 600/615 *ed. pr.*, but Ioannes, who signed for an illiterate, was active in
the 610s; see LXVI **4536** 32–6 n., LXXI **4800** 19 n.). Property lines, however, are not always easy to
draw; XVI **1915** (557 or later; see BL X 144), which refers to this locality twice (ll. 11, 19), shows that
the Apions administered landholdings of the *domus divina*. See further LXVII **4615** 7 n.; T. M. Hickey,
A Public 'House' but Closed (Diss. Chicago 2001) 58–60.

6–7 ἀπὸ λόγου τῆc cυνπεφωνημένηc πρὸc ἀλλήλουc ⟨τιμῆc⟩ οἴνου. Apart from the omission
of τιμῆc, no doubt a scribal error, we have a variation of the formula, which in Oxyrhynchite documents runs τὴν πρὸc ἀλλήλουc cυμπεφωνημένην καὶ ἀρέcαcάν μοι τιμὴν πλήρηc οἴνου; see P. Heid.
V pp. 307–8.

8 ἐντώπια, l. ἐντοπίων. The word is often used for wine; cf. e.g. LVI **3875** 2 (360).

ὀξυ[ρ]υγχιτικά, l. ὀξυρυγχιτικῶν. On 'Oxyrhynchite' jars, see H. M. Cockle, *JRS* 71 (1981) 97.

9 For εὐδοήκοντα = ὀγδοήκοντα, see D. Hagedorn, *ZPE* 67 (1987) 99–101.

10 ἐπὶ τῷ με ταῦτά coι παραcχῖν. This formulation is novel in texts of this type; on the formulas used in other Oxyrhynchite texts, see P. Heid. V pp. 312–13.

11 τῆc ἑβδόμη[c ἰν]δικ(τίωνοc). This indiction 7 ran from 408 to 409; the fiscal indiction (*praedelegatio*) started on 1 May, while the chronological, at Oxyrhynchus, on 29 August. There is no need to assume that this document offers evidence that the latter indiction was already under way (cf. LXVIII **4681** 9–11 n.). Such documents refer to the ῥύcιc of a certain indiction, which is reckoned from the fiscal indiction starting on 1 May; cf. e.g. XLIX **3512** 17–18 (492). But contrast P. Heid. V 358.7–10 (524/5) ἐ[ν] τῇ τρύγῃ τοῦ Με[coρὴ | μηνὸc τοῦ ἐνεcτῶτοc] ἔτουc cα ρο τῆc τρίτη[c ἰν]δι|κτίονοc, οἴνου] ῥύ[c]ε[ωc τ]ῆ[c c]ὺν θεῷ τετάρτη[c | ἐπινεμήcεωc.

ἀνυπερ[θέτω]c. θετω will not fit in the break; the word was probably abbreviated or misspelled.

11–12 χωρί[c] τιν[ο]c εὑρηcιλο[γίαc]. This collocation occurs only in P. Lond. I (pp. 204–7) 113.2.24 (Ars.; VII).

12 The readings in this line are even more uncertain than the dots indicate.

N. GONIS

4902. LOAN OF MONEY

97/198(a)   13 × 22.7 cm   19 October 415

Two fragments giving the top and foot of a loan of one solidus; though there is no reference to Oxyrhynchus in what survives, the text was most probably written there, given the absence from the dating clause of a reference to the indiction. The creditor is a *scriniarius* on the staff of a *comes Aegyptiaci limitis*, which is a novelty in the papyri; see below 5 n. Another point of interest is the consular date clause, the first Egyptian dating by Honorius Aug. x and Theodosius Aug. vi coss. 415.

The text is written in an unpractised hand; the phonetic spellings are numerous. A sheet-join runs 0.3 cm from the right-hand edge. The back is blank.

```
           χμγ
        ὑπατίαc τῶν δεcποτῶν ἡμῶ[ν Ὀνω]ρίου
        τὸ ϊ καὶ Θεοδοcίου τὸ ϛ̄ τῶν αἰωνίων Αὐγούcτῳν̀,
            Φαῶφι κ̄ᾱ.
    5   Φλαουΐῳ Ἀντωνίῳ cκρινιαρίῳ τάξεωc
        τοῦ μεγαλοπρε[π]εcτάτ[ο]υ κόμητοc
        τοῦ Αἰγυπτειακο[ῦ] λιμίτ[ο]υ διὰ Ἰ[ω]άννο[υ
        βωηθοῦ Αὐρήλιο[c Ἄ]μμων Α.[ 2–3 ].. ̣α[
        ἀπὸ γώμηc ..[
   10   νο]μοῦ.[
            ]. ̣α.[
```

]...υ[

·   ·   ·

·   ·   ·

τὸ γραμ[μά]τι[ον ἁπλοῦ]ν γρ[α]φὲν καὶ
ἐπερωτηθεὶς ὡμολόγησα.//
15   Αὐρήλιος Ἄμμων ὁ προγείμενος
ἔσχον ⟨τὸ⟩ τοῦ χρυσοῦ νομισμάτιον
ἓν καὶ ἀποδώσω{ς} ὡς πρόγειτε.
Αὐρήλι[ο]ς Ἰωάννης ἀνακνώσκεις
ἔγραψα ὑπὲρ αὐτοῦ γράμματα
20   μὴ εἰτότος.

2 l. ὑπατείας   6 κόμητος: first ο corr. from ω   7 l. Αἰγυπτιακοῦ   8 l. βοηθοῦ   9 l. κώμης   15 l. προκείμενος   17 l. πρόκειται   18 l. ἀναγνώστης (?)   20 l. εἰδότος

'643. In the consulship of our masters Honorius for the 10th time and Theodosius for the 6th time, the eternal Augusti, Phaophi 21.

'To Flavius Antonius, *scriniarius* of the *officium* of the *magnificentissimus comes Aegyptiaci limitis*, through Ioannes, assistant, (from) Aurelius Ammon son of A—, from the village of . . . of the . . . nome, . . . This deed (is binding), written in a single copy, and in reply to the formal question I assented. I, Aurelius Ammon, the aforesaid, received the one solidus of gold, and I shall return it as aforesaid. I, Aurelius Ioannes, lector (?), wrote on his behalf because he does not know letters.'

1 χμγ. Cf. **4912** 1, **4921** 1. On this Christian symbol, which I take to indicate an isopsephism for Θεὸς βοηθός, see the literature cited in CPR XXIII 34.1 n.

2–3 On the consulship, see *CLRE* 364–5; cf. *CSBE*² 194. It has not been attested in any other papyrus.

5 σκρινιαρίῳ. This is the first attestation of a member of the staff of the *comes limitis Aegypti* in a papyrus. On the *officium* of this *comes*, see B. Palme, *AnTard* 7 (1999) 107–8, 110; on *scriniarii*, see the references collected in CPR XXIV p. 74 n. 2.

This *scriniarius* may have been a landowner, if the *boethos* who represents him in the contract is a private employee, but this is not the only possibility (see 8 n.). Another *scriniarius* and landowner occurs in P. Prag. II 193 (Ars.?; v).

6–7 τοῦ μεγαλοπρε[π]εστάτ[ο]υ κόμητος τοῦ Αἰγυπτειακο[ῦ] λιμίτ[ο]υ. For the formulation, cf. SB VI 9598.3 (427/8 or 442/3; see BL X 201) τοῦ μεγαλοπρεπεσ[τ]άτου καὶ ἀνδριωτάτου κόμιτος τοῦ Αἰγυπτιακοῦ λιμίτου; SPP XX 143.2 (435; see BL VI 196) κόμιτος τοῦ Αἰγυπτιακοῦ λιμήτ[ο]υ. This official, whom the *Notitia Dignitatum* calls *comes limitis Aegypti* or *comes rei militaris per Aegyptum* (Or. xxviii 1–2), was the supreme military commander in Egypt at that time; he had the rank of *vir spectabilis*. See J.-M. Carrié, *AnTard* 6 (1998) 106–11, and F. Mitthof, *Annona Militaris* i (2001) 149–51 (with references to further literature).

8 βωηθοῦ, l. βοηθοῦ. This could have been a functionary of the kind known from the archive of Papnuthis and Dorotheus, and an employee of the *scriniarius*. Alternatively, as Bernhard Palme suggests, βοηθός could be the Greek translation of the official title *adiutor*, who would act as a deputy to the *scriniarius*.

A. [. This is likely to be the beginning of a patronymic, though an occupation may also be considered.

9 γώμης, l. κώμης. For the interchange κ > γ, see Gignac, *Grammar* i 77, 79–80; cf. προγείμενος in 15, and πρόγειται in 17.

At the end of the line, τοῦ Ὀξυρυγχίτου is likely.

13 τὸ γραμ[μά]τι[ον would have been preceded by κύριον in the previous line, now lost.

16 ἔσχον ⟨τὸ⟩ τοῦ χρυσοῦ νομισμάτιον. The omission of the article may be due to haplography. Alternatively, one could think that τοῦ is a mistake for τό, but this would yield a rare formulation; P. Kell. I 45.28 (386), ἔσχον τὸ [χρυσοῦ νομισμά]τιον, seems to be secure by the length of the break (there is no space for τοῦ).

18 ἀνακνώςκεις. I assume the word intended is ἀναγνώςτης. ανακν- for αναγν- is parallelled from P. Mich. V 322a.43 (46), O. Narm. 93.13 (ii/iii), or P. Mich. XIII 667.46 (vi) (see Gignac, *Grammar* i 78), but -κεις for -της is odd. On (church) lectors, see E. Wipszycka, *JJP* 23 (1993) 194–205 = *Études sur le christianisme dans l'Égypte de l'Antiquité Tardive* (1996) 238–48 (204–5 = 247–8 on lectors acting as witnesses or amanuenses).

N. GONIS

4903. LOAN OF MONEY

42 5B.75/K(1–3)c   14.5 × 12 cm   1 August 417

A sausage maker acknowledges a loan of 9,000(+) (?) myriads of denarii from a 'headman', perhaps of the guild of sausage makers; the loan was probably 'interest-free' (see 10 n.). The text offers the latest Egyptian record of the postconsulate of Theodosius Aug. VII and Palladius coss. 416.

There are traces of an earlier document, washed off incompletely.

μετὰ τὴν ὑπατίαν τοῦ δεσπότου ἡμῶν Θεοδοςίου
αἰωνίου Αὐγούςτου τὸ ζ″ καὶ Φλ(αουΐου) Παλλαδίου τοῦ λαμ(προτάτου), Μεςορὴ η.
Αὐρήλιος Εὐφράντιος Φοιβάμμωνος
Ἑρμοπολίτης ἰςικιάριος καταγιγνόμενος ἐν τῇ
5   λαμπρᾷ καὶ λαμπροτάτῃ Ὀξυρυγχιτῶν πόλ[ει
Αὐρηλίῳ Θωνίῳ ἐπιστάτῃ χαίρειν.
ὁ]μολογῶ ἐςχηκέναι παρὰ ςοῦ ἐν χρήςι διὰ χε[ιρὸς
ἐξ οἴκ[ο]υ ςου εἰς ἰδίαν μου κα[ὶ ἀναγκαίαν χρείαν
ἀργυρί]ου μυριάδας ἐνν[ακιςχιλίας (?) *c.*2
10   *c.*10   ] ἀκινδυν.[ ]... ἀπὸ παντὸς [κινδύνου

Back, downwards along the fibres:
γραμμάτιον Εὐφραντ[ίου - - -

1 l. ὑπατείαν   2 φλ, λαμ⳽   4 ἰςικιαριος   7 l. χρήςει

'After the consulship of our master Theodosius, eternal Augustus, for the 7th time and Fl. Palladius, *vir clarissimus*, Mesore 8.

'Aurelius Euphrantius son of Phoebammon, a Hermopolite, sausage maker, residing in the splendid and most splendid city of the Oxyrhynchites, to Aurelius Thonius, headman, greetings. I acknowledge that I have received from you on loan, by hand and out of your house, for my own and pressing need, nine thousand(+) (?) myriads of silver . . . free of all risk . . .'

Back: 'Contract of Euphrantius . . .'

1–2 For the consulship, see *CLRE* 366–7 (cf. 369); *CSBE*² 194. Honorius Aug. xi & Fl. Constantius ii coss. 417 are first attested on 15 November 417 (Pap. Colon. XII, a Hebrew papyrus).

3 Εὐφράντιος. This is not a common name; besides this passage, it occurs in O. Oasis Bahria 6 = SB XX 14889.2 (374/5), P. Dubl. 32.19 (512), SPP X 153.14–15 (vi), P. Prag. II 136.11 (vii).

4 Ἑρμοπολίτης. The term indicates the native of Hermopolis. It is fairly common in papyri of the Roman period, but seems to have fallen out of favour with scribes in later times. This seems to be its latest attestation.

ἰcικιάριοc. This occupation is also attested in SPP XX 85.29 (320/1?), P. Ryl. IV 639.211, 640.10, 641.30 (all three of iv), and P. Strasb. I 46.10 (Antin.; 566), which refers to τὴν τῶν ἰcικιαρίω[ν] χρεί[αν].

καταγιγνόμενος. See LXVIII **4681** 7 n.

6 Θωνίῳ seems to have been inserted, possibly by a second hand, into an inadequate gap.

ἐπιcτάτῃ. That the term is not further specified may suggest that this ἐπιcτάτης was the headman of the guild of ἰcικιάριοι, even though such a guild is unattested. If so, this would become the earliest instance of the title used in this sense; the next earliest is SB XX 14425.3 (443). On such ἐπιcτάται, see J. Gascou, K. A. Worp, *CRIPEL* 10 (1988) 140 (n. l. 3).

9 μυριάδας ἐνν[ακιcχιλίας (?). The use of this currency is exceptional, since practically all other money loans of this period are in gold; only the earlier VII **1041** (381) refers to a loan in myriads of denarii. It may be worth noting, however, that in Oxyrhynchus in that period house rents were often payable in myriads; cf. SB IV 7445 (382), XLV **3203** (400), VII **1037** (444), VIII **1129** (449), P. Yale I 71 (456), LXVIII **4696** (466), XVI **1961** (487), etc.

It is less likely that one has to restore ἐνν[ακοcίας (*sic*). At that time, 9,000(+) myriads of denarii would have had the value of about 2 solidi; see R. S. Bagnall, *Currency and Inflation in Fourth-Century Egypt* (BASP Suppl. 5: 1985) 61–2, and P. Kell. IV p. 225. 900 myriads would correspond to less than one-quarter of a solidus, which is not much. The principal in most late fourth- and fifth-century Oxyrhynchite loans of money is never lower than one solidus, and is rarely very large: 1 sol. in LXXII **4897** (391), **4902** (415), P. Leid. Inst. 66 (427), LXXI **4831** (429), L **3599** (460), P. Wisc. I 10 (468), SB XXVI 16756 (467 or 497?); 2 sol. in P. Select. 1 (454), XVI **1969** (484), VI **914** (486), LXXII **4918** (494–6), BGU XVII 2686 (v); 3 sol. in LXXII **4904** (417); 4 sol. in P. Harr. I 86 (444); 5 sol. in PSI XIII 1340 (420); 6 sol. in XIX **2237** (498); 12 sol. in VIII **1130** (484); 40 sol. in CPR VII 39 (405/6; see BL VIII 112).

10 At the start of the line, perhaps restore [κεφαλαίου]; there is only one but uncertain parallel, P. Mich. XV 728.2.

ἀκινδυν. [ ] . . . ἀπὸ παντὸς [κινδύνου. We ought to have ἀκινδύνους, or ἀκινδύνους οὔcας, to agree with μυριάδας, but this is hard to read. ἀπὸ παντός stands on a separate fragment, and is preceded by letter tops; the first of these might be the tops of υυ, but I am puzzled by what follows. I have toyed with ἀκινδύνων, but the use of the genitive is hard to explain, though one might adduce P. Lips. 13.10–12 ἐφ' ᾧτε | [τ]ούτων [ἀ]κεραίων ὄντων καὶ ἀκινδύνων | [δοῦ]ναί cοι.

The occurrence of the formulation at this point suggests that there was no reference to interest payable on the principal: there is no space for it in 9–10.

10 κινδύνου may well have stood in the next line.

N. GONIS

4904. Loan of Money

41 5B.89/E(1–2)a   *c*.21.5 × 12 cm   7 December 417

A loan of 3 solidi taken by Aurelius Parion son of Heliodorus, *systates* (the latest known holder of the office) and his wife. It is tempting to identify Parion's father with the *systates* Heliodorus, recorded in **4898** of 391, himself conceivably the son of a *systates*.

ὑπατίᾳ τοῦ δεσπότου ἡμῶν Ὁνωρίου τοῦ αἰωνίου Αὐγούστου τὸ ιᾱ
καὶ Φλαουΐ[ου] Κωνϲταντίου τοῦ λαμπρ(οτάτου) τὸ β̄, Χοιὰκ ιᾱ.
Αὐρήλιοι Παρίων Ἡλιοδώ[ρου ϲ]υϲτάτηϲ καὶ ἡ [τ]ούτου γαμετὴ Ἀμμωνοῦ[ϲ
Ϲαραπάμμωνοϲ ἀπὸ τῆ[ϲ λα]μπρᾶϲ καὶ λαμπροτάτηϲ Ὀξυρυγχιτῶν
5   πόλεωϲ Αὐρηλίῳ . . . [.]ερ [Ἰ]ουλίου ἀπὸ τῆϲ αὐτῆϲ πόλεωϲ χ(αίρειν).
ὁμολογοῦμεν ἐξ ἀλ[ληλεγγ]ύηϲ ἐϲχηκέ[ν]αι παρ[ὰ] ϲοῦ ἐν
χρήϲει διὰ χειρ[ὸϲ ἐξ οἴκου ϲο]υ εἰϲ ἰδία[ν] ἡμῶν [καὶ ἀναγκαί]αν
χρείαν χρυϲοῦ ἀπλ[ᾶ δόκιμα] εὔϲταθμα νομιϲμ[άτ]ια τρία, γί(νονται) νο(μιϲμάτια) γ̄
κεφ[α]λαίου, ἅπερ ἀκίν[δυνα ἀπὸ παντὸϲ κι]νδύνου ἐπ[άναγκεϲ
10   ἀπ[οδώ]ϲομεν τ[ῷ-   *c*.12   τοῦ] ε[ἰ]ϲιόντοϲ ἔτουϲ ϟε [ξδ
            c.30   τῆϲ] πράξεω[ϲ

.   .   .   .

Back, downwards, along the fibres:

(*m.* 2) γραμ(μάτιον) Παρίωνοϲ καὶ τῇ[ϲ τούτου γαμετῆϲ Ἀμμωνοῦτοϲ - - -

1 l. ὑπατείᾳ   2 λαμπρ̅   4 ϊδια[ν]   8 τρια: ι corr. from η   Γ⳨Ñ
12 γραμ⳽

'In the consulship of our master Honorius, the eternal Augustus, for the 11th time, and of Flavius Constantius, *vir clarissimus*, for the 2nd time, Choeac 11.

'Aurelii Parion son of Heliodorus, *systates*, and his wife Ammonous daughter of Sarapammon, from the splendid and most splendid city of the Oxyrhynchites, to Aurelius . . . son of Iulius, from the same city, greetings. We acknowledge on mutual security that we have received from you on loan, by hand and out of your house, for our own and pressing need, three solidi of gold, pure, approved, of full weight, total 3 sol., as principal, which, being free from all risk, we shall of necessity return to you . . . of the coming year 95/64 . . . the right of execution . . .'

Back: 'Contract of Parion and his wife Ammonous . . .'

1–2 On the consulship, see *CLRE* 368–9 (cf. 371); *CSBE*[2] 194. This is its second earliest attestation on papyrus, after the Hebrew Pap. Col. XII of 15.xi.417. Constantius' iteration number is not indicated in P. Köln II 102.2, dated by the postconsulate (in CPR X 111.3, which also has a postconsular clause, the part that will have contained the iteration number is lost).

3 Παρίων Ἡλιοδώ[ρου ϲ]υϲτάτηϲ. See above, introd. This now becomes the latest dated reference to the office. (In LV **3796** 3 (412), the name of the office holder is lost in the break, where *c*.25 letters are presumed lost; the sequence Αὐρήλιοϲ Παρίων Ἡλιοδώρου is 23 letters long.)

Another loan made to a married couple is **4921**.

5 ...[.]ϵρ. ọ looks preferable to ω; if the reading is correct, the phonetic spelling looks odd in an otherwise correct text.

10 Considerations of space suggest that the text must have run τ[ῷ *name* μηνὶ τοῦ].

Oxyrhynchite era year 95/64 started on 29 August 418 (see *CSBE*² 141), which means that the loan was to be repaid after nine or more months.

11 τῆϲ] πράξϵω[ϲ would have been preceded or followed by γινομένηϲ ϲοι. The line will have started with an expression meaning 'without delay' or the like; cf. e.g. **4897** 13–14.

N. GONIS

4905. TOP OF DOCUMENT (WRITING PRACTICE)

85/22(b)   16.6 × 8.4 cm   16 October 419
                                                                            Plate XII

All that is written on this sheet is a consular date, which happens to be the earliest Egyptian dating by Fl. Monaxius and Fl. Plinta coss. 419, and a formula of address to Fl. Phoebammon, ex-*protector* and administrator of the *domus divina*. This person was already known from VIII **1134** (421), and recurs in **4906**. The exaggerated lettering in line 4, and the fact that the text comes to an abrupt end after that, indicate that this is a draft or writing exercise.

The back is blank.

ὑπατίᾳ Φλ[αουΐων Μοναξί]ου καὶ Πλ[ί]ντα τῶν λαμπ̣[ρ(οτάτων),
    [   ] Φαῶφι ιη.
Φλαουΐῳ [Φοιβάμμωνι ἀπὸ πρ]ω̣τηκτόρων διοικοῦν[τι
τὰ πράγ[ματα τῆϲ θ]ειοτάτηϲ οἰ̣[κίαϲ
5   Φ[   ] (*vac.*)
            (*vac.*)

1 l. ὑπατείᾳ

'In the consulship of Flavii Monaxius and Plinta, *viri clarissimi*, Phaophi 18.
'To Flavius Phoebammon, *ex protectoribus*, administering the estates of the most divine house ...'

1 Cf. **4906** 1–2. On the consuls, see *CLRE* 372–3 (cf. 374–5); *CSBE*² 194. The postconsulate of 418 was still in use on 6 July 419 (PSI XIII 1365).

3–4 Φλαουΐῳ [Φοιβάμμωνι ἀπὸ πρ]ω̣τηκτόρων διοικοῦν[τι] τὰ πράγ[ματα τῆϲ θ]ειοτάτηϲ οἰ̣[κίαϲ. Cf. **4906** 3–4; VIII **1134** 2–3 (421) Φλάουϊοϲ Φοιβάμμων υἱὸϲ Διογένουϲ ἀπὸ πρωτηκτόρων διοικῶν τὰ πράγματα | τῆϲ θειοτάτηϲ οἰκίαϲ.

ἀπὸ πρ]ω̣τηκτόρων. On the office of *protector*, see LXIII **4367** 2 n.; CPR XXIV 15 introd. (pp. 98 f.).

διοικοῦν[τι] κτλ. XIV **1973** 5 (420) attests a *procurator* (ἐπίτροποϲ) of the *domus divina*, probably a different function from that of διοικῶν. (The man in **1973** was an ex-*praepositus*, which parallels the former officer we have here.) On curators of imperial estates, see R. Delmaire, *Largesses sacrées et res privata* (1989) 218–33; for the few known functionaries of the *domus divina* in Egypt, see Delmaire, *CRIPEL* 10 (1988) 129–31 (nos. 49–55). Another administrator of the *domus divina* may be recognized in the μαγιϲτριανόϲ of P. Wash. Univ. I 24.2 (see BL IX 371; cf. below, **4909** 3–4 n.), though the papyrus breaks off after διοικοῦντι.

5 Φ[. What the scribe intended is not clear.

N. GONIS

4906. LEASE

97/202(a)   11.5 × 13.5 cm   28 July 420

The upper part of a lease that involves on the one hand Fl. Phoebammon, ex-*protector* and administrator of the *domus divina*, and on the other Aurelius Maximinus, from the city of Oxyrhynchus, and another person, originating from a village. All other details of the transaction are lost. In VIII **1134**, of 3 March 421, Phoebammon acknowledges receipt of rents collected by Maximinus in the capacity of *pronoetes*. This offers an indication that **4906** is a lease of land.

There is writing of obscure import above the first line of the document, close to the left-hand edge, possibly a later annotation or addition. The back is blank as far as it is preserved.

μετὰ] τὴν ὑπατίαν Φλαουΐων Μοναξίου καὶ Πλίντα
     τῶν λαμπρο[τ]άτων, Μεϲορὴ δ.
Φλαου]ΐῳ Φοιβάμμωνι ἀπὸ πρῳτη[κτό]ρων δι[οικ(οῦντι)
τὰ πρά]γματα τῆϲ θειοτάτηϲ οἰκί[α]ϲ   (vac.)
5   παρὰ Α]ὐρηλίων Μαξιμίνου [υἱοῦ Ἄμμωνοϲ (?) (+ c.5?)
   ἀπὸ τ]ῆϲ λαμπρᾶϲ καὶ λαμπρ[οτάτηϲ Ὀξυρυγχ(ιτῶν) καὶ
     c.6   υἱ]οῦ Χωοῦτοϲ ἀπὸ κώμ[ηϲ   c.13?
   ἐκουϲίωϲ] ἐπιδεχόμεθα μιϲ[θώϲαϲθαι ἀπὸ
         ].[...].ε.[
           ].[

1 ὑπατιανφλαουϊων; l. ὑπατείαν

'After the consulship of Flavii Monaxius and Plinta, *viri clarissimi*, Mesore 4.
'To Flavius Phoebammon, *ex protectoribus*, administering the estates of the most divine house, from Aurelii Maximinus son of Ammon (?), from the splendid and most splendid city of the Oxyrhynchites, and . . . son of Chôus, from the village . . . We voluntarily undertake to lease from . . .'

1–2 On the consulship, see **4905** 1 n. The postconsulate of Monaxius and Plinta was used for dating purposes as late as 18.xi.420; the consuls of 420 have occurred only in postconsular clauses.

3–4 δι[οικοῦντι | τὰ πρά]γματα τῆς θειοτάτης οἰκί[α]c. See **4905** 3–4 n. Though there is space for further writing in the break, the line seems complete as it stands.

4 Even though the papyrus is not intact, nothing seems to have been written after οἰκί[α]c. VIII **1134** 4 continues ἀπὸ τῆς λαμπρᾶς καὶ λαμπροτάτης Ὀξυρυγχιτῶν πόλεωc.

5 Αὐρηλίων Μαξιμίνου [υἱοῦ Ἄμμωνος (?). The patronymic is restored after **1134** 5.

N. GONIS

4907. LOAN OF MONEY

83/15(a)   fr. 2 14 × 21.8 cm   28 September 422

Two fragments with the very top and the lower part of a loan of three and a half solidi, to be repaid four months later, taken on by a ciγγουλάριoc; the latter's subscription is in the awkward capitals characteristic of a 'slow writer'. There is no reference to an interest rate. The formulas used indicate that the document is of Heracleopolite origin (see 3, 9, 11–12 nn.); cf. SPP XX 90 (415), P. Select. 15 (435), SPP XX 123 (445). The text offers the earliest Egyptian dating by Honorius Aug. XIII and Theodosius Aug. x coss. 422.

ὑπατείας τῶν δεcποτώ[ν ἡμῶν
Ὀνω[ρ]ίο[υ] τὸ ιγ̅ καὶ Θεοδοcί[ου τὸ ι τῶν αἰωνίων
Αὐγούcτων,] Φαῶφι α, ἰν[δικτίωνοc ϛ.
    ]..ο..[.].[

          traces from the ends of two lines

7   c.18   ] χρ[υ]cοῦ νομίcματα
κεφαλ[αί]ου τρὶc ἥμιcυ, γ(ίνεται) χρυcοῦ νο(μίcματα) γ ϛ, ἅπερ
ἐπάναγκεc ἀποδόcω [c]οι τ[ῷ ἐπ]ιόντι μηνὶ
10 Τῦβι τῆc εὐτυχοῦc ἕκτηc ἰνδικ[τί]ονοc ἀνυπερ-
θέτωc καὶ ἄνευ πάcηc ἀντιλογίαc καὶ οὐκ ἐξέcται μοι
ἄλλην προθεcμίαν αἰτήcαcθαι τῆc πράξεώc
cοι οὔcηc καὶ τῆc παρὰ cοῦ ἔκ τ' ἐ[μο]ῦ καὶ τῶν ὑπαρχόντων μοι πάντων. κύριον τὸ γραμμάτιον
15 καὶ ἐπερωτηθεὶc ὡμολόγηcα. (m. 2) Φλ(άουϊοc) Ἄρων ciγ-
γουλάριοc ὁ προκίμενοc cυμ-
φονῖ μοι πάντα ὡc πρό-
κιται.

Back, downwards, along the fibres:

] κεφαλαίου χρυcοῦ νο(μιcμάτων) γ ϛ

8 l. τρία   γ′   8, 19 Ñ   9 l. ἀποδώcω   13 l. τοῖc   16 l. προκείμενοc
17 l. -φωνεῖ   18 l. -κειται

'In the consulship of our masters Honorius for the 13th time and Theodosius for the 10th time, the eternal Augusti, Phaophi 1, indiction 6.

'. . . solidi of gold of principal three and a half, total 3 ½ solidi of gold, which I shall of necessity return to you in the ensuing month of Tybi of the auspicious sixth indiction, without delay and without any objection, and it shall not be possible for me to ask for another deadline, the right of execution being with you and your agents against both myself and all my belongings. This deed is binding, and in reply to the formal question I assented.' (2nd hand) 'I, Flavius Aron, *singularis*, the aforementioned—everything satisfies me as aforementioned.'

Back: '. . . of principal 3 ½ solidi of gold.'

1–3 On the consulship, see *CLRE* 378–9 (cf. 380–81); *CSBE*² 195. It was previously attested only in postconsular formulas of 423. The only other consular date clause of 422 refers to the consuls of the previous year, and dates to 29 August (SPP XX 118), one month earlier than **4907**. The new consuls will have become known in Egypt in September, which is common enough in the fifth century.

3 ἰν[δικτίονοc ϛ. Contrary to notarial practice elsewhere, Oxyrhynchite documents of this date do not normally refer to the indiction at this point. This is a further indication for the provenance of this text.

5–6 Where the papyrus is intact, abrasion is too severe to allow for any textual gain to be made.

7 The reading is to a great extent intuitive.

9 τ[ῷ ἐπ]ιόντι μηνί. A rather rare collocation, mostly found in Heracleopolite documents of the fifth century; see B. Palme in „*Eine ganz normale Inschrift*" . . . *und ähnliches zum Geburtstag von Ekkehard Weber* (2005) 475 (n. l. 6), to whose examples add now P. Vindob. G 15162+20732.6–7, ed. *APF* 51/1 (2005) 76–86 (546/561). It refers to a future month other than the next one in P. Rain. Cent. 123.15, P. Vindob. G 15162+20732.6–7, and apparently here, but not in the earlier and Oxyrhynchite XXXI **2569** 23–4 (265), where ἐπιόντοc is equivalent to εἰcιόντοc.

11–12 καὶ οὐκ ἐξέcται μοι ἄλλην προθεcμίαν αἰτήcαcθαι. Cf. CPR X 39.17–18 (443) καὶ οὐκ ἐξέcται μοι ἄλλην αἰτήcαcθαι | προθεcμίαν περὶ τὴν ἀπόδωcιν; V 14.17–18 (475) οὐκ ἐξέcται κοι|[λαίνειν τὴν] προθεcμίαν περὶ τὴν ἀπόδοcιν.

13 καὶ τῆc (l. τοῖc) παρὰ coῦ. Cf. CPR X 38.17 (420), 39.18–19 (443), SPP XX 90.15 (415), 123.20 (445) (same spelling as here).

15–16 cιγγουλάριοc. This person probably belonged to the *militia officialis*, i.e., he was on the staff of the *praeses Arcadiae*, acting as a 'dispatch rider', rather than to the *militia armata*. See CPR XIV 39.13–17 n.; LVIII **3932** 3 n.; P. Thomas 27.1 n. (para. 6).

N. GONIS

4908. Top of Document

83/91(b)   7 × 4.5 cm   423

This scrap attests the Oxyrhynchite version of the consular formula of 423, which differed from that used in other regions; see 1–2 n.

The back is blank.

ὑπατ]είας Φλαουΐων Ἀσκ[λ]η[πιοδότου καὶ Μαρινιανοῦ
]   τῶν λαμπρ[ο]τ[άτων
].[

.   .   .   .

'In the consulship of Flavii Asclepiodotus and Marinianus, *viri clarissimi*, . . .'

1–2 On the consulship, see *CLRE* 380–81 (cf. 382–3); *CSBE*² 195. It has occurred in three other papyri: SB XII 11023 (424), probably from Oxyrhynchus, which offers the same formula as **4908** (the suggestion to restore Φλ(αουΐων), recorded in *CSBE*², is certain); P. Rain. Cent. 92 (423), of unknown provenance, which calls the consuls τῶν μεγαλοπρεπεστ[ά]|των καὶ ἐ[[ν]]ξοχοτάτω[ν] ἐπάρχω[ν] | τῶν ἱερῶν πρα[ι]τω[ρίων (2–4); and SB XXII 15620 (424), from the area of Antinoopolis, where the consuls are called [τῶν μεγαλοπρεπ]εc[τ]άτων ἐπάρχων τοῦ ἱεροῦ πραιτωρίου.

Both **4908** and P. Rain. Cent. 92 attest consular formulas, but the references to the month and day are lost. They must postdate 24 July 423, when one still dated by the consuls of the previous year (P. Köln III 151). A consular formula is also found in SB 15620, but the indiction implies that ὑπατείας is an error for μετὰ τὴν ὑπατείαν (see BL XI 240), which is very likely, given the generally erratic character of the text.

N. GONIS

4909. TOP OF DOCUMENT

105/72(b)   14 × 6.8 cm   15 October 444

The upper left part of a document of unknown nature, of interest for attesting Fl. Phoebammon, a μαγιcτριανός (*agens in rebus*) not known otherwise.

The back is blank as far as it is preserved.

μετὰ τὴν ὑπ[α]τίαν Φλαο[υΐω]ν Μαξίμου τὸ βϛ κ[αὶ Πατερίου
τῶν λαμπροτάτων, Φα[ῶ]φι ιη. [
Φλαουΐῳ Φοιβάμμωνι τῷ κ[αθωσιωμένῳ μαγιcτριανῷ
τῶν θείων ὀφφικίων υἱῷ Ε..[-   c.15   τῇ
5   λαμπρ]ᾷ κα[ὶ] λα[μπρ(οτάτῃ) Ὀ]ξυρυγ[χιτῶν πόλει

.   .   .   .   .

1 ὑπατιαν; l. ὑπατείαν   3 φλαουϊω   4 υϊω

'After the consulship of Flavii Maximus for the 2nd time and Paterius, *viri clarissimi*, Phaophi 18.
'To Flavius Phoebammon, the *devotissimus magistrianus* of the *sacra officia*, son of E—, . . . in the splendid and most splendid city of the Oxyrhynchites . . .'

1 On the consuls, see *CLRE* 420–21; *CSBE*² 196.
2 Nothing seems to be written after ιη. We would not expect a reference to the current indiction at this point in a text of this date, though cf. LVIII **4688** 3 (442?).

3–4 Φλαουΐῳ Φοιβάμμωνι τῷ κ[αθωϲιωμένῳ μαγιϲτριανῷ] τῶν θείων ὀφφικίων. For the formulation cf. SPP XX 121.3 (439), CPR VI 6.3 (439), X 39.3–4 (443), SB XXII 15461.3 (481), P. Rain. Cent. 108.2–3 (484–6), P. Cair. Masp. II 67126.58 (541). (In P. Wash. Univ. I 24.2, after BL IX 371, restore τῷ καθωϲιωμένῳ before μαγιϲτριανῷ.)

This Fl. Phoebammon is not known from elsewhere. A μαγιϲτριανόϲ whose name is lost occurs in a text dating from less than a year earlier than **4909**, viz. CPR X 39.3–4 (Heracleopolis; 13.xi.443). If there was only one *agens in rebus* in a province at a time (see *CTh* VI 29.2.1 = *CJ* XII 22.4, of 395), one may consider whether this unknown μαγιϲτριανόϲ is Fl. Phoebammon (Φοιβάμμωνι would just fit in the break in l. 3; cf. l. 4 as restored by B. Palme, *Tyche* 10 (1995) 250); but CPR XXV 13 (v/vi) now attests two μαγιϲτριανοί in a Hermopolite context, and one may infer that they both operated in the same province. Another unknown μαγιϲτριανόϲ occurs in the Oxyrhynchite P. Wash. Univ. I 24.2, assigned to 425–50 (the possible dates are 10 May 428–30, 432–3, 435, 437–8, 443–4, or 447–50), but he is probably not to be identified with Fl. Phoebammon, since he had a capacity that Phoebammon apparently did not have, that of the administrator of an imperial estate (see above, **4905** 3–4 n.).

The term μαγιϲτριανόϲ (Lat. *magistrianus*) was a colloquial rendering of *agens in rebus*, an official in the service of the *magister officiorum* (but C. Gloss. Biling. II 9.31 translates μαγιϲτριανόϲ as *magistrianus*). For literature on the office, see B. Palme, CPR XXIV 11.4 n., and 22 introd. nn. 1–4. A list of Egyptian μαγιϲτριανοί is offered by P. J. Sijpesteijn, *CE* 68 (1993) 165–7, updated in CPR XXIV 22 introd. n. 1.

4 γεουχοῦντι ἐν τῇ] is a likely restoration; an indication of residence in Oxyrhynchus, e.g. διάγοντι, is another possibility.

N. GONIS

4910. WORK CONTRACT

105/206(c)   12.3 × 15.7 cm   1 May 447

The upper right part of a contract through which a tradesman agrees to provide services of some sort to a *speculator* on the staff of the *praeses* of Arcadia. This is the first *speculator* explicitly said to be attached to this praesidial *officium*, and the latest attestation of the office of *speculator* in a papyrus, though it no doubt continued to exist long thereafter.

On the back there are exiguous remains of another text written against the fibres, which ends ἀνάλωμαϲ (*sic*) | Φαῶφι α.

μετὰ τὴν ὑπατείαν Φλαουΐ]ων Ἀετίου τὸ τρίτον καὶ Cυμμάχου τῶν λαμ(προτάτων),
        Παχ]ὼν ϛ.

Φλαουΐῳ   c.11   ϲπ]εκουλάτορι τάξεωϲ ἡγεμονίαϲ ἐπαρχίαϲ Ἀρκαδίαϲ
                c.20   ] Αὐρήλιοϲ Φοιβάμμων υἱὸϲ Ἐπιμάχου μητρὸ[ϲ
5   c.16   τὸ ἐ]πιτήδευμα ἀπὸ τῆϲ αὐτῆϲ πόλεωϲ χαίρειν.
ὁμολογῶ διὰ ταύτηϲ μου τῆ]ϲ ἐγγράφο[υ] ἀϲφαλείαϲ ϲυντεθεῖϲθαι
                c.30   ].[.].. ἐν ταῖϲ καταπιϲ[τευ-
ομέναιϲ   c.40   ].[.]..[

        .   .   .   .

1 λαμ, (unless this is a mere extension of μ)

'After the consulship of Flavii Aetius for the third time and Symmachus, *viri clarissimi*, Pachon 6.

'To Flavius . . . , *speculator* of the praesidial office of the province of Arcadia, . . . , Aurelius Phoebammon, son of Epimachus, mother . . . , . . . by profession, from the same city, greetings. I acknowledge through this written bond of mine that I have come to an agreement . . . in the . . . entrusted . . .'

1–2 For the consulship, see *CLRE* 426–7 (cf. 428–9); *CSBE*² 197. It had previously occurred in CPR X 116 (446?) and P. Rain. Cent. 97 (3.xii.447).

3 cπ]εκουλάτορι. On this office, see P. Neph. 20.23 n., pp. 96–9 (list); LIX **4002** 6 n. The *speculator* in **4002**, a private letter of the late fourth or early fifth century, may have been a member of the *officium* of the *praeses Arcadiae*, but this is only an inference.

τάξεως ἡγεμονίας ἐπαρχίας Ἀρκαδίας. On the *officia* of governors in late antiquity, see B. Palme, *AnTard* 7 (1999) 85–133, esp. 100–11. On the appellations of the province of Arcadia, see Palme, *Tyche* 12 (1997) 258.

4 [ἀπὸ τῆς Ὀξυρυγχιτῶν πόλεως] would suit the space (for the omission of the honorific titles of Oxyrhynchus, see **4916** 8 n.), but there could also have stood a phrase indicating (temporal) residence in the city, e.g. ἐνδημοῦντι, as in LIX **3986** 12 (494); still, I consider the former option more likely. What is virtually certain is that there was a reference to Oxyrhynchus: the lack of a reference to the indiction in 2 is typical of Oxyrhynchite documents of this date.

6 ὁμολογῶ . . . cυντεθεῖcθαι. See P. Heid. V p. 152 with n. 40. με πρὸc cέ probably followed in the next line.

7–8 ἐν ταῖc καταπιc[τευομέναιc. The participle has occurred in three Oxyrhynchite work contracts: P. Mil. II 48.11–12 (v/vi) πάντα τὰ | καταπιcτευόμεν⟨ά⟩ μοι παρὰ c[ο]ῦ; I **136** 8–9 (583) ≈ LVIII **3952** 8–9 (610) τῆc καταπιcτευομ[έ]νηc | αὐτῷ προνοηcίαc.

N. GONIS

4911. LEASE

97/220(b)   12.4 × 8.9 cm   24 September 449

This fragment attests a soldier of the *numerus Transtigritanorum*, a unit otherwise attested exclusively in Arsinoite documents or contexts (the Oxyrhynchite SB XIV 11574 refers to *Transtigritani* in the Arsinoite nome). The soldier is a native of Oxyrhynchus. A further point of interest is that the text contains the latest reference to the postconsulate of Zeno and Postumianus coss. 448.

If line 7 is read and restored correctly, the document is a lease; the object of the lease is conceivably city property. Cf. SPP XX 131 (Ars.; 518), where a soldier of this same *numerus* leases a bakery from his brother, who is also a soldier but of another unit.

On the back there are exiguous remains of the endorsement.

μετὰ τὴν ὑπ]ατείαν Φλαουΐων Ζήνωνος καὶ Ποστουμιανοῦ
   τῶν λα]μπροτάτων, Θὼθ κζ/.

Φλά]ουϊος Κωνστάντιος ἀναφερόμενος εἰς τὸν
ἀριθμὸν] τῶν γενναιοτάτων Τρανστριγριτανῶν
5   υἱὸς Ἰωσὴ]φ ἀπὸ τῆ[ς] Ὀξ[υρυγ]χιτῶν πόλεως Αὐρηλίοις
  c.5 -άμ]μωνι ...[....] καὶ Ἄννᾳ θυγατρὶ Ἀχιλ[λ]έ[ω]ς
  ἀπὸ τῆς αὐτ]ῆ[ς πόλεως. ἑκουσίω]ς ἐ[πι]δέ[χομαι

4 l. *Τρανστιγριτανῶν*

'After the consulship of Flavii Zeno and Postumianus, *viri clarissimi*, Thoth 27.

'Flavius Constantius, seconded to the *numerus* of the *fortissimi Transtigritani*, son of Ioseph, from the city of the Oxyrhynchites, to Aurelii —ammon son of . . . and Anna daughter of Achilles, from the same city. I voluntarily undertake . . .'

1–2 On this consulship, see *CLRE* 430–1 (cf. 433); *CSBE*[2] 197. This is its latest record on papyrus. Protogenes and Asturius, the consuls of the year, are first attested in P. Mil. 45 of 7.xi.449. See further **4912** 1–2 n.

4 *Τρανστριγριτανῶν*, l. *Τρανστιγριτανῶν*. It is little surprise that the spelling gave difficulty; cf. SB XIV 11574.4 (406) *Τρανστριγιτανῶν*, 12129.2 (IV/V) *Τρανστριγλιτανῶν*.

On the *numerus Transtigritanorum*, see the discussion and list in B. Palme, CPR XXIV pp. 87–9; a new instance has been furnished by P. Paramone 13.

6 -άμ]μωνι. Presumably Φοιβάμ]μωνι, though in theory there could also have been some other compound.

...[. We expect υἱῷ, but what remains of the first letter does not admit upsilon.

N. GONIS

4912. TOP OF DOCUMENT

83/73(a)   13 × 7 cm   1 October 450

This fragment, probably of a contract, provides the latest instance of the use of the postconsulate of Protogenes and Asturius coss. 449.

The back is blank.

       χμγ
μ]ετὰ τὴν ὑπατίαν Φλαουΐ[ων Πρωτ]ογένους
  καὶ Ἀστο[υ]ρίου τῶν λαμπρ(οτάτων), Φα[ῶ]φι δ.
  Αὐρ]ηλίῳ Δι[ο]νυσίῳ [..].[c.8   τ]ῆς
5   λαμ]πρᾶς καὶ λα[μ]π[ροτάτ]η[ς Ὀξυρυγχ(ιτῶν)] πόλε[ω]ς
       ]..[

2 l. ὑπατείαν   3 λαμπρ

'643. After the consulship of Flavii Protogenes and Asturius, *viri clarissimi*, Phaophi 4.

'To Aurelius Dionysius . . . from the splendid and most splendid city of the Oxyrhynchites
. . .'

2–3 For the consulship, see *CLRE* 432–3 (cf. 434–5); *CSBE*² 197. When the consuls of 450 became known in Egypt, is unclear; they have been attested only once, in a text dated 7.x.451 (CPR IX 40B).

3 Ἀϲτο[υ]ρίου. The same spelling is attested in CPR XIV 12.22 and XXIII 32.17, both from Heracleopolis, but the Oxyrhynchite P. Mil. 45.1 has Αὐϲτουρίου (the details in *CSBE*² should be revised accordingly).

4 [. .] . [: not [υἱ]ῷ; the trace is the top of a tall upright ([υ]ἱ[ῷ] cannot be read either).

The address to an Aurelius in a text of this date seems to suggest that this was the party to a contract rather than the addressee of an official document; if so, read ἀπὸ τ]ῆϲ.

N. GONIS

4913. Sale of Wheat and Barley on Delivery

103/78(b)   fr. 1 7.2 × 16 cm   2 December 462

Two, non-contiguous fragments preserving line ends from the top and lower part of a 'sale on delivery' of wheat and barley. The only other document of this type which involves these two grains and nothing else is SB XVIII 13947 (507). This text too comes from Oxyrhynchus, and refers to a 'buyer' who is in the employ of a *comes*. We find a similar picture in LXII **4349** (504), in which the 'buyer' is a servant (παῖϲ) of a *comes*. It is conceivable that the employees acted on behalf of their ennobled employers, even if this is not explicitly stated.

The text offers the earliest Egyptian record for the consulship of Leo Aug. II cos. 462.

The back is blank as far as it is preserved.

```
        ὑπατείαϲ τοῦ δεϲπότου ἡμῶν Φ]λ(αουΐου) Λέοντοϲ τοῦ αἰωνίου
                Αὐγούϲτο]υ τὸ β̄, Χοιὰκ κϛ, α ἰνδικ(τίωνοϲ).
        Αὐρήλιοϲ - - - υἱὸϲ - - - ἀ]πὸ κώμηϲ Ἰϲίου Παγγᾶ
        τοῦ Ὀξυρυγχ(ίτου) νομοῦ Αὐρηλίῳ] Ϲαμβατίῳ υἱῷ Ϲαμβατίου
5            c.14        τοῦ μεγαλο]πρεπεϲτάτου κόμιτοϲ
            c.10        ἀπὸ τῆϲ λαμπρᾶϲ] καὶ λαμπροτάτηϲ Ὀξυρυγχ(ιτῶν)
        πόλεωϲ χαίρειν.    c.7    ὁμο]λογῶ ἐϲχηκέναι παρὰ ϲοῦ
        ἐντεῦθεν τὴν πρὸϲ ἀλλήλουϲ] ϲυμπ[ε]φωνημένην
        καὶ ἀρέϲαϲάν μοι τιμὴν πλήρηϲ ϲίτ]ου ἀρταβῶν
10      ἑκατὸν καὶ κριθῆϲ ἀρταβῶν τριάκοντα], γί(νονται) ϲί(του) (ἀρτάβαι) ρ καὶ κριθ(ῆϲ) λ,
        ἅπερ γενήματα νέα καθαρὰ κε]κοϲκινευμένα
            c.20        ἐπάν]αγκεϲ ἀποδώϲω
                        ] . [ ] .
```

. . . . . .

].[

15   ].…[

       *c.*22   κύριον τὸ] γραμμάτι-

ον ἁπλοῦν γραφὲν καὶ ἐπερωτηθεὶς ὡμ]ολόγηςα.

Αὐρήλιος *name* υἱὸς *patronymic* ὁ προγεγραμ]μένος

ἔϲχον τὴν τιμὴν πλήρης ϲίτου ἀρταβῶν ρ καὶ] κριθῆς

20 ἀρταβῶν λ καὶ ἀποδώϲω ἐν τῇ προθεϲμίᾳ] καὶ ϲυμ-

φωνεῖ μοι πάντα τὰ προγεγραμμένα ὡς πρ]όκειται καὶ

ἐπερωτηθεὶς ὡμολόγηϲα. Αὐρήλιος *name* υἱὸς - -].υ....

ἀξιωθεὶς ἔγραψα ὑπὲρ αὐτοῦ γράμμα]τα μὴ εἰδότος.

. . . . . .

1 ινδικ//   3 ϊϲιου; l. Ἰϲ(ι)είου   4 υἱω   6 οξυρυγχ〳   10 γι̅ϲι̅τ̅σ̅, κρι^θ

'In the consulship of our master Flavius Leo, the eternal Augustus, for the 2nd time, Choeac 26, indiction 1.

'Aurelius . . . son of . . . , from the village of Is(i)eion Panga of the Oxyrhynchite nome, to Aurelius Sambat(h)ius son of Sambat(h)ius . . . of the *magnificentissimus comes* . . . from the splendid and most splendid city of the Oxyrhynchites, greetings. I acknowledge that I have received from you on the spot the full price jointly agreed and satisfactory to me of one hundred artabas of wheat and thirty artabas of barley, total 100 artabas of wheat and 30 (artabas) of barley; these produces, new, clean, sieved . . . I shall necessarily repay . . . This deed is normative, written in one copy, and in reply to the formal question I assented.

'I, Aurelius . . . son of . . . , the aforewritten, have received the full price of the 100 artabas of wheat and of the 30 artabas of barley, and I shall repay (it) within the deadline, and all the afore-written (terms) are satisfactory to me as aforesaid, and in reply to the formal question I assented. I, Aurelius . . . son of . . . , wrote at his request in his place because he is illiterate. . . .'

1–2 On the second consulship of the emperor Leo I, see *CLRE* 458–9 (cf. 461); *CSBE*² 198. This is its earliest occurrence (it was previously attested only in postconsular clauses). (The text of M. *Chr.* 71 is too uncertain; the date recorded in *CSBE*², '7.x?', stems from a suggestion originally made in a draft of LXVIII **4694** 1–2 n. but later suppressed.) The postconsulate of the previous year was used in Oxyrhynchus as late as 20.ix.462 (PSI III 175).

3 Ἰϲίου Παγγᾶ. See LXXI **4824** 9–10 n.

4 Ϲαμβατίῳ υἱῷ Ϲαμβατίου. This is the latest attestation of this name, which is very common in the Roman period. (The resolution Ϲαμβα(θίου) in CPR VII 23.5 (v/vi) is unwarranted.)

5 The function of Sambatius will have stood at the beginning of the line, but I cannot think of anything that would suit the space and be plausible.

5–6 There are only two *magnificentissimi comites* attested in Oxyrhynchus at that time, Fl. Strategius (I), the forefather of the Apion family, and Fl. Ioannes, attested in LXVIII **4696** of 484 and a number of texts of the 460s and 470s, currently being prepared for publication. Ϲτρατηγίου would suit the space; Ἰωάννου is too short. It should come as no surprise, however, if these were not the only *comites* of this rank in Oxyrhynchus at that time.

7 What is lost between χαίρειν and ὁμολογῶ?

8–11 The supplements are taken from SB XVIII 13947.7–10.

10 ἀρταβῶν is restored in the break only with reservations; it seems rather long for the space, and could have been omitted, as later in the line.

12 What is lost in the break is unclear. SB 13947.11 has μέτρῳ δεκάτῳ δικαίῳ at this point.

13ff. The part lost contained the clause on the repayment of the loan.

19–20 The supplements are modelled on SB 13947.17–19; cf. also XLIX **3512** 23–5 (492), a sale of wine on delivery.

23 εἰδότος. The writing is very compressed, and one might also think that the word was abbreviated.

N. GONIS

4914. Top of Document

1 1B.123/F(a)   18.1 × 6.7 cm   4 February 465
Plate XIII

This fragment, perhaps of a lease, offers the earliest attestation of a Christian priest who is also described as a landowner in Oxyrhynchus; see also **4915**. A further point of interest is the consular date clause, which may be the latest dating by the postconsulate of Fl. Vibianus cos. 463.

On the back, remains of the docket; after traces of what may be a cross, there seems to be a large *M*, which suggests reading μ[ίσθωσις (cf. **4915**).

    μετὰ τὴν ὑπ[ατείαν] Φλ(αουΐου) Βιβιανοῦ τοῦ λαμπρ(οτάτου) καὶ τ[οῦ
        δηλωθησομένου, Μεχεὶρ θ, γ ἰνδικ(τίωνος).
    τῷ εὐλαβεστάτῳ Μαρτυρίῳ πρεσβυτέρῳ τῆς
    ἁ]γίας καθολικῆς ἐκκλησίας υἱῷ τοῦ τῆς ἀ[ρί]ς-
5   τ[η]ς μνήμης Εὐθηρίου γεουχοῦντι ἐν τῇ λ[α]μπρ[ᾷ
    καὶ λαμ]πρ[οτάτ]ῃ ['Οξυρυγχιτῶ]ν πόλει πα[ρὰ] Αὐρη[λί-

   .   .   .   .

1 ὑπ[ατειαν], φλϲ, λαμπρ   4 υϊω

'After the consulship of Flavius Vivianus, *vir clarissimus*, and the consul to be announced, Mecheir 9, indiction 3.

'To the most pious Martyrius, priest of the holy catholic church, son of Eutherius of excellent memory, landowner in the splendid and most splendid city of the Oxyrhynchites, from Aureli—
. . .'

1–2 Vibianus was the consul of 463; see *CLRE* 461 (cf. 463), and *CSBE*[2] 198–9. This is the latest certain dating by his postconsulate, and comes more than a year after the end of his consulship (though SB XVIII 13596, which does not refer to an indiction, could in theory date to 13.iii.465). A second postconsular year is mentioned in VI **902**, which adds τὸ β'. On this basis, **902** has been dated to 20.xi.465 (there is no mention of an indiction), but there are three documents from earlier in the year which are dated by the postconsulate of Rusticius and Olybrius coss. 464: SB I 4821 (Ars.; 3.iv), PSI VII 768 (Herm.; 23.vii), and P. Heid. IV 331 (Oxy.; 16.x). Another problematic text is the Arsinoite P. Prag. I 37, which dates to 14.i.465 (so *ed. pr.*) or 466, depending on the reading of the indiction figure.

It has been suggested that 'in line 2 one can read δ instead of γ as the indiction number, cf. pl. xxxix', which would remove the difficulty of the reference to the 'crops of the fifth indiction' (*CSBE*² 199); however, the plate does not seem to me to confirm the suggested new reading (*ed. pr.* expressed a slight preference for reading γ). Whatever the case, we have to reckon with an anomaly: either that towards the end of 465 one or more scribes reverted to the postconsulate of the previous year, or that in **902** τὸ β′ was used inappropriately, and the text dates from 464, not 465 (contrast *CSBE*² 89).

2 γ ἰνδικ(τίωνος). Of the putative γ only the stem remains; it is not possible to read β.

3–4 τῷ εὐλαβεστάτῳ Μαρτυρίῳ πρεσβυτέρῳ. Even if this may well be a different person, it is worth noting that XLIX **3512** (492) attests Fl. Ioannes, an Oxyrhynchite *curialis* and landowner, said to be the son τοῦ τῆς εὐλαβοῦς μνήμης Μαρτυρίο(υ) (5) (an Oxyrhynchus papyrus of 485, edited by A. Benaissa in his DPhil thesis, refers to another *curialis*, Phoebammon, who is the son of 'the late deacon Martyrius of pious memory': a different person from the one in **4914** but potentially the same as the one in **3512**).

4 ἁ]γίας καθολικῆς ἐκκλησίας. This is the episcopal church of Oxyrhynchus, even if this is not stated explicitly.

4–5 ἀ[ρί]ς|τ[η]ς. I owe this reading to Dr Rea. In documents of this period, the collocation τῆς ἀρίστης μνήμης is used predominantly for deceased fathers of men on government (civil or military) service or holders of municipal office. The fathers too were sometimes former members of the *militia armata* or *civilis*, and in certain cases it was the tenure of office on the part of the deceased that conditioned the choice of this epithet; cf. VI **913** 3–4 (443), where we have a daughter of a deceased *curialis*, and P. Cair. Masp. III 67309.26 (569), which refers to an ex-*scriniarius* of the ducal office of the Thebaid. Cf. next note.

5 Εὐθηρίου. This name is not attested in any other papyrus published to date, and appears to have been rare. There are only three instances in *LGPN*, all in vol. IV, but there are more references in *PLRE*: 4 in vol. I, 2 in II, and 1 in IIIA. These are mostly persons of very high rank (the only one with an Egyptian connection is a fourth-century *praeses* of Augustamnica). Our Eutherius must have been a person of some standing, which tallies with his being described as τῆς ἀρίστης μνήμης (see previous note), and with the reference to his son as a landowner.

γεουχοῦντι. Cf. **4915** 3–4. This implies that Martyrius owned land on a substantial scale, which is unusual. The evidence collected by G. Schmelz, *Kirchliche Amtsträger im spätantiken Ägypten* (2002) 220–32, indicates that, unless they were bishops, the landed clergymen who appear as landowners in the papyri were not among the *magni possessores*; cf. also E. Wipszycka, *Les Ressources et les activités économiques des églises en Égypte du IVᵉ au VIIIᵉ siècle* (1972) 160–71. Certainly there will have been lower-ranking clergymen from relatively well-off backgrounds; cf. the case of Taurinos, a scion of a propertied Hermopolite family, who became a priest after a career in the imperial service (for references, see BGU XVII p. xxxvi; cf. CPR XXIV 10 introd.).

N. GONIS

4915. LEASE OF LAND

97/22(c)   8.5 × 15 cm   10 October 467(?)
Plate XV

A landowning priest leases a plot of three (or more) aruras to two villagers. The priest's name has not survived, but it is tempting to think that he is the same as the one in **4914**; the space does not contradict this hypothesis, and I have ventured to restore the name and patronymic accordingly. The postconsular date clause is also restored; if correct, this would be the latest dating by Fl. Leo Aug. III *e. q. f. n.* coss. 466, and the only consular date of 467 recorded on papyrus.

The back is blank as far as it is preserved.

μετὰ τὴν ὑπατείαν τοῦ δεσπότου ἡμῶν Φ]λ(αουΐου) Λέοντος τοῦ αἰωνίου Αὐγούστου
τὸ γ καὶ τοῦ δηλωθησομένου Φαῶ]φι ιβ, ἀρχ(ῆ) [ϛ] ἰνδικ(τίωνος).
τῷ εὐλαβεστάτῳ Μαρτυρίῳ πρεcβυτ]έρῳ τῆς ἁγ[ί]ας καθολικῆς ἐκκλη-
cίας υἱῷ τοῦ τῆς ἀρίcτης μνήμης Εὐθηρίου γεουχο]ῦντι ἐνταῦθα τῇ λαμπρᾷ
5   καὶ λαμπροτάτῃ Ὀξυρυγχ(ιτῶν) πόλει Αὐρήλιοι *c.*5?] υἱὸς Πέτρου ἀπὸ ἐποικίου
             *c.*35   ἀπὸ] κώμης . . . . . τοῦ Ὀξυρυγχίτου
νομοῦ χαίρειν. ἑκουcίως ἐπιδεχόμεθα μιcθώcαcθαι] ἐξ ἀλληλεγγύης ἀπὸ τοῦ
ἐνεcτῶτος ἔτους ρμδ ριγ cπορᾶc τῆς ἑβδόμης ἰνδι]κ(τίωνος) ἀπὸ τῶν ὑπαρχόντων
             *c.*38   ] . . . ἀρούρας τρεῖς
10   *c.*50   ]ων
             *c.*45   ὑπὲρ] φόρου
             *c.*45   ]α

·   ·   ·   ·   ·   ·   ·   ·   ·   ·

1 φ]λϛ   2 αρ\^χ, ινδιⲕ

'After the consulship of our master Flavius Leo, the eternal Augustus, for the 3rd time and of the (consul) to be announced, Phaophi 12, beginning of 6th indiction.

'To the most pious Martyrius, priest of the holy catholic church, son of Eutherius of excellent memory, landowner here in the splendid and most splendid city of the Oxyrhynchites, we, Aurelii . . . son of Petrus, from the hamlet . . . , and . . . , from the village . . . of the Oxyrhynchite nome, greetings. We voluntarily undertake to lease by mutual security from the present year 144/113, of the crops of the seventh indiction, from the belongings . . . three aruras . . . for rent . . .'

1–2 On the third consulship of the emperor Leo, see *CLRE* 466–7; *CSBE* ² 199.

2 τὸ γ καὶ τοῦ δηλωθηcομένου Φαῶ]φι ιβ, ἀρχ(ῆ) [ϛ] ἰνδικ(τίωνος). The alternative would be to restore τὸ β Φαῶ]φι . . . [β] ἰνδικ(τίωνος), but the length of indentation would be extreme—not impossible, but less likely. Considerations of space in 8 (see n.) also seem to favour the restoration adopted into the text. A reference to the first consulship of Leo (p.c. = 459) or the fifth (p.c. = 474) is excluded by the length of the break in 8. The 'crop indiction' referred to in that line would be the one immediately after the indiction mentioned in the date clause and would have been written out in full. τεccαραcκαιδεκάτηc, i.e. the indiction starting after 459 and 474, would be too long for the break. The fourth consulship (p.c. = 472), held with Fl. Probinianus, is ruled out by chronological considerations; by that time, scribes in Oxyrhynchus would have dated by the consul of 472 (see LXVIII **4695**).

ἀρχ(ῆ) [ϛ] ἰνδ(ικτίωνος). It is late to speak of the beginning of an indiction in the month of Phaophi, but there is a near-contemporary parallel from Oxyrhynchus, VIII **1130** (484); see *CSBE* ² 115.

5 The text restored is indicative rather than certain.

8 ἔτους ρμδ ριγ cπορᾶc τῆς ἑβδόμης ἰνδι]κ(τίωνος). If the document was dated by Leo's second consulship (see 2 n.), the era year would be 140/109 (ρμ ρθ), and the crops would be of indiction 3 (τρίτης). The resulting sequence is slightly shorter than that adopted in the text, which provides a bet-

ter match to the length of lines 1 and 7 as restored. It should be noted, however, that with so much text lost, the argument from the space offers no guarantee.

9 The line may have started τῇ σῇ εὐλαβείᾳ (σοι is less likely), followed by a reference to where the parcel of land was located, e.g. ἐν πεδίοις τῆς αὐτῆς κώμης.

10–12 Several texts suggest restoring εἰς σπορὰν] ὧν | [ἐὰν αἱρώμεθα γενημάτων καὶ τελέσομεν ὑπὲρ] φόρου | [ἀποτάκτου κτλ. (see LXVIII **4687** 10–11 n.), but this will not fill the break in 11.

N. GONIS

4916. TOP OF CONTRACT (LOAN?)

101/130(a)   7.5 × 9 cm   7 March 472

The upper right part of a contract—a loan, if my reconstruction of line 9 holds. The putative borrower is a woman, native of the village of Tinotbe (5), which is not known from elsewhere. The text records a consular formula whose wording is somewhat different from the other clauses of this year.

The back is blank as far as it is preserved.

μετὰ τὴν ὑπατεί]αν τοῦ δεσπότου ἡμῶν Λέοντος αἰωνίου Αὐ]γούς[τ]ου τὸ δ΄ καὶ Φλ(αουίου) Προβινιανοῦ τοῦ λαμ(προτάτου),] Φαμενὼθ ια, ι ἰνδικ(τίωνος).
Αὐρηλία   c.10   -] εἰς θυγάτηρ Σαραπί-
5   ωνος μητρὸς   c.7   ἀπὸ κώ]μης Τινωτβε
τοῦ   c.10   -ίτου νομοῦ] καταμένουσα
      c.18   Αὐρη]λίῳ Ἀιῶνι
υἱῷ   c.14   ἀπὸ τῆ]ς [Ὀ]ξυρυγχιτ[ῶν
πόλεως χαίρειν. ὁμολογῶ ἐσχη]κέ[ν]α̣[ι

          .   .   .   .

2 φλϛ   3 ι·ινδικ   4 θυγάτηρ: θ corr. from ε   7 αἰωνι

'After the consulship of our master Leo, eternal Augustus, for the 4th time, and Flavius Probinianus, *vir clarissimus*, Phamenoth 11, indiction 10.

'Aurelia —is, daughter of Sarapion, mother . . . , from the village of Tinotbe of the —ite nome, residing . . . , to Aurelius Aion son of . . . , from the city of the Oxyrhynchites, greetings. I acknowledge that I have received . . .'

1–3 On this consulship, see *CLRE* 476–7 (cf. 479); *CSBE*² 199. It is attested in three other documents, all three of Hermopolite provenance: P. Lond. V 1793.2–3, P. Rain. Cent. 105.1–2, and P. Strasb. III 148.1–2. These three papyri refer to the consuls as Φλ(αουίου) Λέοντος (or Λέωνος) τοῦ αἰωνίου Αὐγούστου τὸ δ καὶ Προβινιανοῦ. The collocation τοῦ δεσπότου ἡμῶν is also absent from the consular formulas of the Heracleopolite CPR XIV 8 (476?) and P. Rain. Cent. 124 (492).

2 There does not seem to be enough space to restore τοῦ before αἰωνίου (the article is missing from the consular clause in PSI IX 1075.14, of 458).

3 ι·ινδιϙ pap. Was the dot added to distinguish between the two iotas, each of which had a different function?

5–6 ἀπὸ κώ]μης . . . ϙαταμένουϲα. Cf. P. Wisc. I 10.5–6 (468) ἀπὸ κώμης Κέρκε τοῦ ἄνω Θεοδοϲιοπολίτου νομοῦ καταμένοντι ἐνταῦθα τῇ Ὀξυρυγχιτῶν πόλει. ἐνταῦθα τῇ Ὀξυρυγχ(ιτῶν) πόλει would suit the length of the break in 7, but in that case we would expect ἀπὸ τῆϲ αὐτῆϲ πόλεωϲ in 8.

8 ἀπὸ τῆ]ϲ [Ὀ]ξυρυγχιτ[ῶν. In theory we could have had ἀπὸ τῆϲ λαμπρᾶ]ϲ κτλ. (there is no space for καὶ λαμπροτάτηϲ), but this is not necessary; the honorific titles of Oxyrhynchus are not given e.g. in PSI XIII 1365.5–6 (419), LXVIII **4692** 3 (453), **4694** 4 (466), **4698** 5–6 (490).

9 The line as restored suits the space and traces.

N. GONIS

4917. TOP OF DOCUMENT

14 1B.206/F(c)   13.7 × 10.6 cm   13 November 473

This text is addressed to a landowner by someone acting with a guarantor; the presence of the latter suggests that the document concerns a financial transaction involving a risk. The body of the text begins with a reference to a lease, and perhaps the rent to be paid on it (see 10 n.). There are several leases in which lessees appear with guarantors (see 8 n.), but this is not a lease of common type. One may consider whether there was a previous leasing agreement whose terms are qualified or renewed through this document; but I know of no real parallel.

The landowner is the well-known Flavia Cyria, *clarissima femina*; for the latest update on her dossier, which spans the years 469–73, see *Tyche* 17 (2002) 86–8. Another point of interest is that the text offers the first instance of the fifth consulship of the emperor Leo I in a papyrus.

The back is blank as far as it is preserved.

ὑπατείαϲ τοῦ δεϲπότου] ἡμῶν Φλ(αουΐου) Λέοντοϲ τοῦ αἰωνίου
Αὐγούϲτου τ]ὸ ε, Ἁθὺρ ϙζ, ιβ ἰνδικ(τίωνοϲ), ἐν Ὀξυρύγχ(ων).
Φλαουΐᾳ Κυ]ρίᾳ τῇ λαμπροτάτῃ διὰ Παπνουθίου αἰδεϲίμου
      c.4 γεουχο]ύϲῃ ἐντα[ῦθ]α τῇ λαμπρᾷ καὶ λαμπροτάτῃ Ὀξυρυγχιτῶν
5   Αὐρήλιοϲ   c.4] ὁ μέγαϲ υἱὸϲ Θέωνοϲ περιχύτηϲ μετ᾽ ἐγγυη-
      τοῦ τοῦ ἀναδεχο]μένου αὐ[τ]ὸν ἀποπληροῦντα εἰϲ ἅπαντα
            c.13   ]. ἐμοῦ Αὐρηλίου Φοιβάμμωνοϲ υἱοῦ Κολλούθου
            c.12   ἀ]πὸ τῆϲ α[ὐ]τῆϲ πόλεωϲ χαίρειν. μίϲθωϲιν
            c.13   ].[.ο]υ διαφέροντ[ο]ϲ τῇ ϲῇ μεγαλοπρεπείᾳ
10   c.12   ἀ]ποτακτ. καθ᾽ ἕκαϲτον ἐνιαυτὸν ἐπε[ι

1 φλϡ   2 ινδιϙ, οξυρυγχϟ   5 υϊοϲ, εγ᾽γυη   7 υϊου

'In the consulship of our master Flavius Leo, the eternal Augustus, for the 5th time, Hathyr 27, indiction 12, in Oxyrhynchus.

'To Flavia Cyria, *clarissima femina*, through Papnuthius, the most revered . . . , landowner here in the splendid and most splendid (city) of the Oxyrhynchites, Aurelius . . . the elder, son of Theon, bath attendant, having as his surety, guaranteeing that he fulfils (or: pays) in full . . . , me, Aurelius Phoebammon son of Colluthus, . . . , from the same city, greetings. A lease . . . belonging to your magnificence . . . fixed rent(?) for every year . . .'

1–2 On the consulship, see *CLRE* 480–81; *CSBE*² 199. As late as 14 September 473 (SB XVIII 13620, with BL IX 304), Egyptian scribes dated by the postconsulate of Fl. Marcianus and of 'the consul to be announced'.

This indiction 12 = 473/4.

2 ἐν Ὀξυρύγχ(ων). See LXVIII **4701** 2 n.

3 Φλαουΐᾳ Κυ]ρίᾳ τῇ λαμπροτάτῃ. See above, introd. The only other landowning *clarissima femina* attested in Oxyrhynchus at that time is Flavia Isis (LXIII **4390–91**; P. Thomas 26v), daughter of Strategius I, of the 'Apion family'.

4 διὰ Παπνουθίου αἰδεσίμου. Pamuthius' capacity will have been indicated in the next line. One would think he was an administrator of Cyria's estate, e.g. a φροντιστής (the word would have been abbreviated), but the epithet αἰδέσιμος has not been attested with such a functionary. In the fifth century, it is found exclusively with persons of curial rank or civil servants. If a person of this status was in the employ of this *clarissima femina*, she would have been a landowner of a very substantial standing.

5 The text printed assumes that the expected πόλει was not written, which is uncommon though not unparalleled (see *ZPE* 141 (2001) 161 with n. 13), and that ὁ μέγας is an appellation (see P. Wash. Univ. II 93.2 n.; *ZPE* 132 (2000) 196). (Αὐρηλίου in 7 suggests that Αὐρήλιος in 5 was not abbreviated.) Alternatively, one might try reading [πόλει Αὐρήλ]ιο⟨ς⟩ Μέγας υἱὸς κτλ., which would suit the space, but the methodological difficulty is obvious.

περιχύτης. On baths in Oxyrhynchus and the personnel attached to them, see J. Krüger, *Tyche* 4 (1989) 109–18.

6 ἀποπληροῦντα εἰς ἅπαντα or εἰς ἅπαν τά. I have not found an exact parallel. The object of ἀποπληροῦντα must be a word meaning 'requirements' or 'dues'.

8 The line will have begun with the indication of Phoebammon's occupation.

μίσθωσιν. I am not aware of any other document whose main body begins in this fashion. Perhaps the text ran, 'having made (?) a lease of [a property] that belongs to you, and having undertaken to pay as annual rent . . .'.

Leases in which the lessees appear with guarantors include SB XVI 12487 (Herm.; v); P. Cair. Masp. III 67303 (Aphrodite; 553), a lease of agricultural machinery; SB VI 9293 (Ars.; 572) and P. Strasb. V 319 (Herm.; vi/vii), both land leases; P. Ross. Georg. III 51 (Ars.; 631) and SB XVI 12481 (Ars.; 668), both leases of vineyards; P. Cair. Masp. I 67066 (Aphrodite; vi), a letter referring to a land lease; PSI VIII 963 (581) and SB VI 9591 (Herm.; vii), leases of house property.

9 The genitive -]_[_₀]υ modifies μίσθωσιν. The first trace after the break would admit ρ, or φ; λ is also possible though less likely. [ἀμπελικοῦ χω]ρ[ίο]υ would suit but cannot be confirmed. The verb governing μίσθωσιν (a past form e.g. of ποιοῦμαι or τίθεμαι) may have stood at the start of this or the next line.

τῇ σῇ μεγαλοπρεπείᾳ. For the use of this abstract with holders of the clarissimate, see LXVIII **4697** 8 n.

10 ἀ]ποτακτ_ : perhaps ἀ]ποτάκτῳ, in which case ἐπ' ἀ]ποτάκτῳ is a possibility, though the expression seems typical of documents from Aphrodito. It must be a reference to a fixed rent

payable on the property under lease, probably a plot of land (ἀπότακτος is not used for rents of buildings).

ἐπε[ι. Perhaps ἐπε[ὶ (l. ἐπὶ) τῷ, introducing a condition of the lease.

N. GONIS

4918. Loan of Money with Interest in Kind

106/108(a)   18.4 × 15.7 cm   17(?) March 494–6

The upper part of a loan of two solidi made by an Alexandrian tradesman to a native of a Cynopolite village but resident in Oxyrhynchus. The interest is to be paid in flax. The same tradesman occurs in VIII **1130** of 484, another loan of money with interest in kind; this is tow, a flax product.

On loans of money with interest in kind, see LXXI **4831** introd. Apart from **1130**, other loans with interest in tow are P. Rain. Cent. 86 (381) and SB XX 14425 (442). Cf. also **4923**.

μετὰ τὴ[ν ὑπατείαν Φλαουΐου Ε]ὐϲεβίου τοῦ λαμπρ(οτάτου) τὸ β ΄, Φαμενὼθ
κα, [ἰνδικ(τίωνος) η, ἐν] Ὀξυρύγχων πόλει.
Αὐρήλιος Πιηοῦϲ υἱὸϲ Κημ[ ] . μητρὸς Μάρθας ἀπὸ κώμης
Cωουν τοῦ Ἄνω Κυνοπολίτου νομοῦ διάγων ἐνταῦθα τῇ λαμπρᾷ
5   Ὀξυρυγχιτῶν πόλει Αὐρηλίῳ Ἰϲὰκ υἱῷ τοῦ τῆϲ μακαρίας
μνήμης Νίλου γενομένου παλατίνου ἀπὸ τῆς μεγαλοπόλεως
Ἀλεξα[ν]δρείας διαπραγματευομένῳ ἐκ πολλοῦ τοῦ χρόνου
ἐντ[αῦθ]α τῇ αὐτῇ Ὀξυρυγχιτῶν [πό]λει χαίρειν. ὁμολογῶ ἐϲχηκέ[ναι π]αρὰ τῆς σῆ[ϲ ἀρετῆϲ ἐ]ν χρήϲει διὰ χειρὸϲ ἐξ οἴ-
10   κο[υ α]ὐτῆϲ εἰϲ ἰδ[ίαν μου κα]ὶ ἀναγκαίαν χ[ρ]είαν χρυσοῦ
νομ[ιϲ]μάτια ἁπλᾶ [δεσποτικὰ] ε[ὔ]ϲταθμα δόκιμα
ἀρι[θ]μῷ δύο, γί(νονται) χ[ρ(υϲοῦ) νο(μιϲμάτια) β κεφ]αλαίου, ἐπ[ὶ] τῷ με παρα-
ϲχεῖν ϲοι ὑπὲρ δ[ιαφόρου αὐ]τῶν ἄχρι τῆϲ ἑξῆϲ
δηλουμένης [προθεϲμία]ϲ λινοκαλάμης
15   δεϲμ[ίδια   c.10   ]ορ.[c.3].κε.[.]ον.[

Back, downwards, along the fibres:

(m. 2) γρ(αμμάτιον)] Πηηω ἀπὸ Cωουν νο(μιϲματίων) ϐ

1 λαμπρϲ   5 ϊϲακυϊω   6 l. Νείλου   12 γτ   16 Ñ

'After the consulship of Flavius Eusebius, *vir clarissimus*, for the 2nd time, Phamenoth 21(?), indiction *n*, in the city of the Oxyrhynchi.

'I, Aurelius Pieus son of Cem—, mother Martha, from the village of Sooun of the Upper Cynopolite nome, residing here in the splendid city of the Oxyrhynchites, to Aurelius Isac, son of Nilus of blessed memory, former *palatinus*, from the great city of Alexandria, conducting business for a long time here in the same city of the Oxyrhynchites, greetings. I acknowledge that I have received from your excellence as loan, by hand out of your house, for my own and pressing need, two pure, imperial, of full weight, approved solidi of gold, total 2 sol. of gold, as principal, on condition that I shall provide you as interest on them, until the end of the term stated below, . . . bundles of flax . . .'

Back (2nd hand): 'Contract of Peeo [sic] from Sooun for 2 sol.'

1–2 On the second consulship of Fl. Eusebius, held in 493, see *CLRE* 521, 523, 525 (cf. 527); *CSBE*² 201. No consul was recognized in the East in 494–5, so that Eusebius' postconsulate was used during these two years. In Egypt, it is last attested on 15.i.496 (SB VIII 9776, with BL VII 214), but its use may have continued for some time: the only other consular dating from that year, by the p.c. of 495, dates from 22.xi.496 (XVI **1899**). The break in line 2 does not allow establishing the date of this text with certainty; the indiction figure could be one of 2, 3, or 4 (see *CSBE*² 146), and the date would range between 494 and 496. I think it less likely that one has to read κ β [ἰνδικ(τίωνος)]; the letter on the edge is too close to κ not to be part of the same numerical unit.

3 Κημ[ ] . : Κημᾶ? Apparently a new name.

3–4 κώμης Cωουν τοῦ Ἄνω Κυνοπολίτου νομοῦ. This village has not been attested elsewhere.

4–5 τῇ λαμπρᾷ Ὀξυρυγχιτῶν πόλει. See below, **4920** 7 n.

5–7 Aurelius Isac is described in **1130** 5–6 as υἱῷ Νίλω ἀπὸ | τῆς μεγαλωπόλεος Ἀλεξανδρίας πραγματευτῇ.

Other Alexandrian tradesmen resident at Oxyrhynchus occur in XVI **1880–81** (427), and probably LXIII **4392** 9 (479).

6 παλατίνου. On *palatini*, see LXVIII **4693** 3 n.

7 διαπραγματευομένῳ is synonymous to πραγματευτῇ. The word otherwise occurs in XVI **1982** 17 (497), and below, **4922** 7.

ἐκ πολλοῦ τοῦ χρόνου. Cf. **4922** 7. This prepositional phrase also occurs in P. Par. 21bis.4 (592; see BL VII 158) νῦν δὲ πρὸ πολλοῦ τοῦ χρόνου ἐν τῇ κώμῃ Θινός; also P. Ness. III 15.5 (512) ἐκ πολλοῦ χ[ρόνου ἀμφότεροι] τανῦν ἐνταῦθα ἐπὶ τῆς Ῥινοκορουριτῶν ἔχ[ο]ντες.

12 ff. ἐπ[ὶ] τῷ με κτλ. For the clause, see LXXI **4835** 16 n.

14 λινοκαλάμης. On flax, its products, and the terms used for them, see P. Laur. IV 176 introd.; J. Gascou, K. A. Worp, *CRIPEL* 10 (1988) 40; CPR XIV 5 introd. and 10 n.

15 δεϲμ[ίδια (not δέϲμα[ϲ, a term used in earlier centuries for such bundles) is more likely than δεϲμ[ίδιον. The putative delta is of the triangular type, unlike the d-shaped deltas in the rest of the text.

The text will have continued with a reference to the quality of the flax, the number of the bundles, and the indication of the time when the payment of interest was due. But I have not been able to make much out of what remains.

N. GONIS

4919. TOP OF DOCUMENT

102/30(a)   15 × *c.*10 cm   30 August 501

This and the following item add to the meagre number of Oxyrhynchite documents attesting the military unit of *Leontoclibanarii*; see below, 7 n.

Nothing can be said about the nature of document other than that it seems to be a contract between an unknown second party and two brothers, both members of the *numerus* and apparently landowners in Oxyrhynchus. The papyrus is dark, brittle, and shredded in places, in one of which there seems to lurk a new formulation (see 4 n.).

The back is blank.

    † ὑπατείᾳ Φλ(αουΐου) Πομπηίου τοῦ ἐνδοξοτάτου,
         Θὼθ β, ἰνδικ(τίωνος) ι.
     Φλαουΐοις Ἰωάννῃ καὶ Παμουθίῳ τοῖς
      *c.*5?   ἀναφερομένων εἰς τὸν ἀριθμὸν
5   τῶν γενν]α[ι]οτάτων καὶ καθοςιωμένων
     Λεοντοκλιβαν]αρίον υἱοῖς [ ]..η.
      *c.*14   ]. γεου[χοῦσι

. . . . .

1 ὑπατειαφλ∫   2 ινϟ   3 φλαουϊοιϲϊωαννη   5 l. καθωϲιωμένων   6 l. Λεοντοκλιβαναρίων υἱοῖς

'In the consulship of Flavius Pompeius, *vir gloriosissimus*, Thoth 2, indiction 10.

'To Flavii Ioannes and Pamuthius . . . seconded to the *numerus* of the *fortissimi* and *devotissimi Leontoclibanarii*, sons of . . . , landowners . . .'

1–2 On the consulship, see *CLRE* 536–7; *CSBE*² 202. This is its second earliest occurrence in a papyrus, after P. Lond. V 1797 = P. Bingen 129 of 10?.vii.501; a third attestation is offered by BGU XII 2174 (Herm.; 23.ix.501). Pompeius is invariably styled ἐνδοξότατος. Avienus, the Western consul of the year, has apparently occurred only in a postconsular formula of 502 (CPR XXIV 18.1, as restored in *CSBE*² 202).

4 It is unclear whether there was anything written before ἀναφερομένων; the surface is too damaged and dirty to allow certainty. If there was, this could be τῶν, a novel formulation, even if we read {τοῖς} τῶν. One might also think that the genitive is a mistake for a dative; in that case, we could try τοῖς | δυςί ἀναφερομένων (l. -οις) but there are no parallels for this expression from this period.

5 τῶν γενν]α[ι]οτάτων καὶ καθοςιωμένων. γενναιότατος is usually applied to a military unit, while καθωςιωμένος is normally used for individual soldiers; see CPR XXIV p. 89. The two epithets occur together also in **4920** 4–5, P. Warr. 3.5, SB VI 9455.3 (*Leontoclibanarii*); LXVIII **4700** 4–5, (*Pharanitae*); SB XVIII 13620.2–3 (*Mauri scutarii*); and in the earlier BGU IV 1027 = W. Chr. 424.14 (IV), referring to soldiers in general.

6 [Λεοντοκλιβαν]αρίον, l. -ίων. On this military unit, see B. Palme in *Gedenkschrift Ulrike Horak* = P. Horak (Pap. Flor. XXXIV: 2004) 311–32. Not mentioned in the *Notitia Dignitatum*, the unit makes its first appearance under the name of κλιβανάριοι in documents of the fifth century, while the name Λεοντοκλιβανάριοι, probably taken in honour of the emperor Leo I, first occurs in 487. The unit seems to have been stationed in the Heracleopolite Alyi, and members of it mostly occur in Arsinoite papyri. The other Oxyrhynchite documents attesting them are P. Warr. 3 (before 504; see BL VII 93), XVI **1882** (*c.*504) (the reference is to κλιβανάριοι), and below, **4920**.

υἱοῖς. Two other brothers who are both soldiers, though in different units, occur in SPP XX 131 (Ars.; 518).

[ ]..η. . One could try reading [το]ῦ τῆς in 8 (nothing seems to have been written after that in this line), but there is not enough space to restore epithet (e.g. μακαρίας μνήμης) + name in 7. This must therefore be part of the father's name.

7 γεου[χοῦϲι. Cf. **4920** 6 as restored.

N. GONIS

4920. TOP OF CONTRACT

97/201(b)   11.9 × 9.7 cm   Fifth/sixth century

The upper right part of a contract concluded between a soldier of the *numerus* of *Leontoclibanarii*, apparently a landowner at Oxyrhynchus, and a woman from an Oxyrhynchite village.

The back was reused for another text, apparently a letter, of which only line beginnings remain. There is no trace of a docket.

    ✝ τοῖϲ μετὰ τὴν ὑπατείαν Φ[λ(αουΐου) *name* τοῦ *epithet*
        Μεϲορὴ ιε, [ἰνδ(ικτίωνοϲ) n.
    Φλαουΐῳ Μαξίμῳ τῷ καὶ Χρ[- *c.*8 ἀναφερο-
    μένῳ εἰϲ τὸν ἀριθμὸν τῶν [γενναιοτάτων καὶ
5   καθοϲιωμένων Λεοντοκλ[ιβαναρίων υἱῷ
    τοῦ τῆϲ μακαρίαϲ μνήμηϲ [*c.*5 γεουχοῦντι
    ἐνταῦθα τῇ λαμπρᾷ Ὀξυρυγχιτ[ῶν πόλει Αὐρηλία
    Θαηϲία θυγάτηρ Ἀπ μητρὸϲ [*c.*12 ἀπὸ
    κώμηϲ Τακονα τοῦ Ὀξυρυγχί[του νομοῦ

     .   .   .   .   .   .

3 φλαουϊω   5 l. καθωϲιωμένων   8 απ᾽

'Under (the consuls) after the consulship of Flavius . . . , *vir* . . . , Mesore 15, indiction *n.*

'To Flavius Maximus alias Chr—, seconded to the *numerus* of the *fortissimi* and *devotissimi Leonto-clibanarii*, son of . . . of blessed memory, landowner here in the splendid city of the Oxyrhynchites, Aurelia Thaesia, daughter of Ap, mother . . . , from the village of Tacona of the Oxyrhynchite nome . . .'

1 On the τοῖϲ μετὰ τὴν ὑπατείαν formula, see *BASP* 37 (2000) 74–5, with list in n. 3 (add now BGU XVII 2682.1 and CPR XIX 8.1, both of 481 and referring to the second postconsular year of Leo Aug. III cos. 479). Most instances date from the last quarter of the fifth century, the latest being XVI **1891** 1 of 495 (the formula resurfaces in the mid sixth century, in postconsular clauses of Fl. Basilius cos. 541). This tallies with the reference to *Leontoclibanarii*, a unit not attested under this name earlier than 487 (see **4919** 6 n.). The way Oxyrhynchus is described (see below, 7 n.) would admit a date in the early sixth century.

The length of the break indicates that only one consul figured in the formula; however, the candidates are too many to be worth mentioning.

2 Mesore 15 = August 8.

3 Φλαουΐῳ Μαξίμῳ τῷ καὶ Χρ[-. Maximus may have been the name that Chr— took after he joined the army. Another *Leontoclibanarius* with an alias is Fl. Menodorus alias Apaol (P. Rain. Cent.

114.5, SPP XX 139.5), while an alias should perhaps be recognized in the case of Fl. Callinicus Iuvin-nianus (cf. CPR XXIV 18.3 n.).

4–5 See **4919** 5 n., 6 n.

6 γεουχοῦντι is restored on the basis of ἐνταῦθα in 7. In theory, we could also have a participle denoting residence (e.g. καταμένοντι), but the *Leontoclibanarii* were not stationed in Oxyrhynchus. (LIX **3986** 12 ἐνδημοῦντες, used for two *quaestionarii* of the praesidial *officium* in Heracleopolis who were temporarily present in Oxyrhynchus, is too isolated to serve as a parallel.)

7 τῇ λαμπρᾷ Ὀξυρυγχιτ[ῶν πόλει. The omission of the epithet λαμπροτάτη is standard from the early sixth century onwards, but there are such examples already in the fifth century; see D. Hage-dorn, *ZPE* 12 (1973) 290 (several examples have accrued since then).

8 Θαηcία. This name, a late by-form of Θάηcιc, is rare in Oxyrhynchite documents; besides **4919**, it occurs in LXVIII **4681** 6, 15 (419), and (cf. BL XI 172) LXI **4132** 9 (619).

Ἄπ (απ' pap.). This name was previously attested in P. Petaus 116.16, 117.38, 40 (Ars.; 184–7), and P. Mich. XV 734.6 (Oxy.; 572). The diastole, found already in P. Petaus 116.16, signals that the name was indeclinable or 'foreign' (see *GMAW*² p. 11).

9 κώμης Τακόνα. This was a village in the northern part, in the old lower toparchy, of the Oxy-rhynchite nome. It may be relevant that there was a *mansio* in the area of the village (see LX **4087**), and thus there were frequent military visitors. It is surely a mere coincidence that the Thaesia of **4681** (see above, 8 n.) is also a native of Tacona.

N. GONIS

4921. Loan of Money

103/6(f)   12.8 × 10.8 cm   14 July 523

A loan of an unknown number of solidi made to two salt-fish sellers, the two a married couple. The text offers the latest record for the use of the postconsulate of Symmachus and Boethius coss. 522.

The back is blank.

χμγ

† μετὰ τὴν ὑπατείαν Φλ(αουΐων) Ϲ[υμ]μάχου καὶ Βοητίου τῶν
λαμπρο(τάτων), Ἐπεὶφ κ̄, ἰνδ(ικτίων)ο(ϲ) α, ἐν Ὀξυρύγχ(ων).
Αὐρήλιοι Παπνοῦθιϲ υἱὸϲ Ἰωάννου μητρὸϲ Ἡραεΐδοϲ
5   καὶ ἡ τούτου [γ]αμετὴ Χουροῦϲ θυγάτηρ Ἀντωνίου μητρὸϲ
Φιλοξένα[ϲ] ἀμφότεροι ταριχοπῶλοι ἀπὸ τῆϲ λαμ-
π]ρᾶϲ Ὀξυ[ρυγχ]ιτ[ῶ]ν̣ [π]ό[λ]εωϲ Αὐρηλίῳ Δανιηλίῳ
υἱῷ   c.15   ].π.ννοϲ ἀπὸ τῆϲ αὐτῆϲ
πόλεωϲ χαίρειν. ὁμ]ολογ[ο]ῦμεν ἐξ ἀλληλεγγύηϲ
10   ἐϲχηκέναι παρὰ cοῦ ἐν χ]ρήϲε[ι] διὰ χειρὸϲ ἐξ οἴκου
cου εἰϲ ἰδίαν ἡμῶν καὶ ἀναγκαί]α̣ν [χρεί]α̣ν χρυϲοῦ
νομιϲμάτια   c.20   ].α ἰδιωτικῷ
ζυγῷ   c.22   κεφ]α̣λαίου

c.10   ἀκίνδυνα ὄντα ἀπὸ παντὸς] κινδύνου

15   c.30   ] . . . . . ι

.   .   .   .   .   .

2 φλλϛ   1. Βοηθίου   2 λαμπρρ°, ινδ°/, οξυρυγχϛ   4 υϊος   1. Ἡραΐδος
9 αλληλεγ᾿γυης   12 ἰδιωτικω

'643. After the consulship of Flavii Symmachus and Boethius, *viri clarissimi*, Epeiph 20, indiction 1, in Oxyrhynchus.

'Aurelii Papnuthis son of Ioannes, mother Heraïs, and his wife Churus daughter of Antonius, mother Philoxena, both salt-fish sellers, from the splendid city of the Oxyrhynchites, to Aurelius Danielius son of . . . , (mother?) . . . , from the same city, greetings. We acknowledge on mutual security that we have received from you on loan, by hand and out of your house, for our own and pressing need, . . . solidi of gold by private (standard) . . . as principal . . . being free of all risk . . .'

2–3 On the consulship, see *CLRE* 578–9 (cf. 580–81); *CSBE*² 204. This is now the latest attestation of the postconsulate of Symmachus and Boethius, unless SB XVI 13037, which refers to the consulate, dates from 24 October 523, as the indiction indicates. Fl. Maximus, the consul of 523, is first attested in XVI **1984** of 28 October 523 (see BL VII 143; LXVII **4616** 2–3 n.).

5 Χουροῦς. The name appears to be new.

6 Φιλοξένα[ς]. In the later period, the name is exclusively attested in Oxyrhynchite documents, which squares with the fact that most bearers of the name Φιλόξενος occur in documents from this area.

ταριχοπῶλοι. This occupation was known exclusively from literary sources (the resolution ταριχ(οπώλου ?) in P. Bad. IV 97.14 is not inescapable) until it appeared very recently in P. Count. 3.104 (229 BC) and P. Sijp. 30.47, 119, 121 (II); cf. also ταριχοπωλική in P. Graux II 21.8, which corresponds to the more common ταριχηρά. A ταριχοπράτισσα is attested in P. Coll. Youtie II 92.8 of 569 (cited in LSJ from P. Cair. Masp. I 67023, which belongs to the same document). On the compounds in -πώλης, see **4897** 5 n.

ταριχοπῶλοι need not be a mistake for ταριχοπῶλαι. There are a very few compounds in -πῶλος, attested mainly in lexica, e.g. βιβλιοπῶλος, οἰνοπῶλος, προβατοπῶλος.

8] . π . ννος. This must be the ending of Danielius' metronymic.

12] . α. The trace on the edge, a short descending oblique, would admit mu of a shape such as that in 5 [γ]αμετή, but probaly not kappa. [νομισμάτια ἁπλᾶ δεσποτικὰ δόκι]μα would have about the right length, but the resulting sequence is without parallel. Whatever the case,] . α seems to suggest that the loan involved a plurality of solidi.

14 I do not see how to restore the line convincingly.

15 ἐπάναγκες ἀποδώσομεν ἐξ ἀλληλεγγύης probably stood in the lost part of the line.

N. GONIS

4922. LOAN OF MONEY(?)

86/90(a)   19.3 × 9.5 cm   4 May 582

The upper part of what seems to be a loan of money with interest or repayment (a 'sale on delivery') in kind; cf. **4918**. The creditor, Martinus, a dealer in tow, probably recurs in VI **893**, assigned to the sixth/seventh century.

The back is blank.

† βασιλεία]ς τοῦ θειοτάτου καὶ εὐσεβεστάτου ἡ[μῶν δεσπότου μεγίστου
εὐεργέτου Φλαου]ΐου Τιβερίου Κωνσταντίνου τοῦ αἰωνίου Αὐγούστου
καὶ Αὐτοκράτορος ἔτου]ς η̄, ὑπατίας τοῦ αὐτοῦ εὐσεβ(εστάτου) ἡμῶν δεσπότου ἔτους
δ̄, Παχὼν θ̄, ἰνδ(ικτίωνος) τε̄// .

5   τῷ θαυμασιωτάτῳ κυρίῳ Μαρτίνῳ υἱῷ τοῦ τῆς μακαρίας
μνήμης Ἰωάννου Πιλέων στιπποπραγματευτῇ ἀπὸ Τα . . . . .
διαπρα]γματευομένῳ ἐκ πολλοῦ τοῦ χρόνου ἐν κώμῃ Ὤφει
τοῦ Ὀξυρυγχ]ίτου νομοῦ Αὐρήλιος Μηνᾶς υἱὸς Ἀβρααμίου μητρὸς
.α. εἴης ὁρμώ[μ]ενος ἀπὸ κτήματος Λιθίνης τοῦ Ὀξυρυγχίτου
10   νο]μοῦ χαίρειν. ὁμολογῶ διὰ ταύτ[ης μου τῆς] ἐγγράφου ἀσφα[λείας
ἐσ]χηκέναι παρὰ [τ]ῆς σῆς [θαυμασιότητος] ἐντεῦθ[εν ἤδη
. .] . . . [c.7]ε . . . [c.25

fr. 2   fr. 3

] . . ωαλε . . [   ] . [
] . ξ/ καὶ ταῦτα ὁμολογῶ [   ]πεοις εὐαρέστοις κα[

3 l. ὑπατείας   ευσεβ∫   4 ινδ//

'In the reign of our most godly and most pious master, greatest benefactor, Flavius Tiberius Constantinus, the eternal Augustus and Imperator, year 8, in the consulship of our same most pious master, year 4, Pachon 9, indiction 15.

'To the most admirable lord Martinus, son of Ioannes Pileon of blessed memory, dealer in tow, from Ta—, conducting business for a long time in the village of Ophis of the Oxyrhynchite nome, Aurelius Menas son of Abraamius, mother . . . , originating from the holding of Lithine of the Oxyrhynchite nome, greetings. I acknowledge through this written bond of mine that I have received from your admirableness now on the spot . . . (fr. 2) and these I acknowledge . . . (fr. 3) . . . satisfactory . . .'

1–4 On this combination of regnal and consular formulas, see *CSBE*[2] 212; the closest parallel is P. Iand. III 48 (29.v.582).

5 τῷ θαυμασιωτάτῳ κυρίῳ. This collocation otherwise occurs only in in the docket of the letter CPR XXV 18 (vi/vii) (P. Got. 9.3 has τῷ θαυμασιωτάτῳ Κύρῳ; see BL II.2 69, and R. Rémondon, *CE* 41 (1966) 174).

5–6 Μαρτίνῳ . . . στιπποπραγματευτῇ: Μαρίνου στιπποπραγματευτῇ (l. -οῦ) VI **893** 3. This is the only other occurrence of this occupation (and word) in Greek. It is very tempting to think that both texts refer to the same person, even if the writing of the name varies (note that the spelling in **893** is fairly erratic).

6 Πιλέων. This must be an Egyptianized Greek name, formed by the masculine demonstrative article in Egyptian and the Greek name/noun Λέων/λέων (= 'this Leo/lion'), and treated as indeclinable. It does not seem to have occurred elsewhere.

Ta......... I have not been able to read any known toponym in the traces (neither *Ta*(a)μπεμου nor *Ta*(a)μορου can be read). The letter after *Ta* is μ or (less likely?) a; the last letter is ε or c.

7 διαπρα]γματευομένῳ ἐκ πολλοῦ τοῦ χρόνου. See **4918** 7 n.

κώμη Ὦφει. See **4862** 3 n.

9 κτήματος Λιθίνης. This hamlet was part of the Apion estate; see LV **3804** 241 n. **3804** implies that it was situated in the southern part of the Oxyrhynchite nome.

10–11 ὁμολογῶ διὰ ταύτ[ης μου τῆς] ἐγγράφου ἀσφα[λείας ἐc]χηκέναι. This is not a common sequence in Oxyrhynchite documents; I have found it only in XVI **1891** 4–5 (495). It is more at home in documents from the Thebaid.

11 ἐντεῦθ[εν ἤδη. See LXXI **4837** 10–11. This collocation occurs in loans as well as sales on delivery.

fr. 2

1–2 It is tempting to read Ἀλεξα[νδρείας in 1 and Ἀλ]εξ(ανδρείας) in 2, indicating the monetary standard of Alexandria. However, ζυγῶ is difficult to read in 1: it is hard to reconcile the first two traces on the line with ζυ.

2 καὶ ταῦτα ὁμολογῶ. The reference is to the borrowed principal that will have to be repaid; cf. e.g. XVI **1892** 16–17 (581) καὶ ταῦτα ὁμολ[ογῶ] παρασχεῖν τῇ cῇ αἰδεcιμότητι κτλ.

fr. 3

2]πεοιc εὐαρέcτοιc. εὐαρέcτοιc would be part of the description of produce, to be delivered in a 'satisfactory' condition; cf. e.g. BGU XII 2185.10 (512?) ἐν κ]αλάμοιc κ[αλ]οῖc καὶ εὐαρέcτοιc. Given that the creditor is a dealer in tow, the reference could be to tow (or flax), and]πεοιc may be restored as c(τ)ιπ]πέοιc, l. c(τ)ιππ(ε)ίοιc; cf. P. Iand. VI 132.5 (VI/VII) cτιππεα. For the construction cf. PSI V 369.19 (334) [ἐ]ν c[τιππ]ίῳ καθαρῷ εὐα[ρέcτῳ], P. Münch. III 89.20 (339) ἐν cιπ[πίῳ ἐπ]ιτηδίῳ καὶ εὐαρέcτῳ; other passages in which εὐάρεcτον modifies c(τ)ίππιον are P. Herm. 22.17 (394) and VIII **1130** 13 (484).

N. GONIS

4923–4930. Documents from the Dossier of the 'Apion Family'

Most of the documents in this section stem from the archive of the 'Apion estate'. **4923–9** belong to the well-documented period when the estate was under Fl. Apion II, and complement certain documents published in vol. XVI of *The Oxyrhynchus Papyri*. They are receipts and payment orders recording disbursements of meat and bread on behalf of the estate to military personnel and inhabitants of certain settlements respectively. As is often the case with documents of this type, the exact purpose of the payments or the relationship between the estate and the payees and intermediaries of the payments are frustratingly inexplicit (hypothetical contexts are offered below, in the general introductions to the two groups of documents). **4930**, though it does not concern directly the affairs of the estate, attests one of its high-level central administrators.

4923–4925. Receipts for Meat Rations

The following three receipts of meat were issued by Menas, pork butcher (χοιρομάγειρος) in the service of the 'Apion' estate (ἔνδοξος οἶκος; cf. **4923** 1), to various military personnel between 550 and 552. Menas appears in a similar capacity in XVI **2013** (25.vii.551) and **2014** (25.v.551; now fully published by B. Haug, *ZPE* 160 (2007) 217–19), and he may be identical to the χοιρομάγειρος of this name attested as the recipient of a large money payment in the Apionic account XVI **2032** 87, 91 (540/41; see BL VI 105). Menas might conceivably have been an independent butcher, with the Apion estate as his principal customer. It is more probable, however, that he was a central employee of the estate analogous to the οἰνοχειριστής and charged with overseeing the production and distribution of meat within it (on the οἰνοχειριστής see T. M. Hickey, *A Public 'House' but Closed* (Diss. Chicago 2001) 126 ff.). As in the case of the οἰνοχειριστής, there may have been only one χοιρομάγειρος at a time serving the Oxyrhynchite estate. By 561, at any rate, a different butcher appears in this role (XVI **1903** 1).

The recipients, periods of payment, and amounts of meat in the five receipts issued by Menas can be summarized as follows:

4923 (7.ix.550)	10 στρατιῶται	1 month	300 lbs.
4924 (21.xi.550)	5 *buccellarii*	2–8 days	(10–40 lbs.)
2014 (25.v.551)	10 στρατιῶται	1 month	300 lbs.
	+ 'Faustinus'	16 days	16 lbs.
2013 (25.vii.551)	9 στρατιῶται	1 month	270 lbs.
4925 (8.iii.552)	14 στρατιῶται	3 days	42 lbs.

The shorter periods relate to those soldiers said to have come from elsewhere (**4924**, **4925**), whereas the longer ones apply to those 'staying' (παραμένουσι) at the estate. The quantity of meat issued to the soldiers (unpreserved in **4924**) is always equivalent to a daily ration of one pound per person, which is also attested in other military payments recorded in Apionic accounts: XVI **1903** (561); **1920** (after 563; see BL X 145); some of the entries in **2046** (564; see BL X 146; on the variable rations in this account see the analysis of F. Morelli, *Olio e retribuzioni nell'Egitto tardo* (1996) 66–78). The Apionic ration is thus higher than the traditional military *annona* of ½ pound of meat per soldier; cf. F. Mitthof, *Annona militaris: Die Heeresversorgung im spätantiken Ägypten* i (Pap. Flor. XXXII: 2001) 238–45. Like the recipients in **1920** and **2046**, the above soldiers were probably also entitled to rations of bread, wine, and oil.

The functions performed by the soldiers are not stated. The interpretation of the nature of the payments depends to a great extent on the model of the Byzantine 'large estate' adopted and how the relationship between large estates and the imperial government is conceived. Since Jean Gascou's influential thesis that estates such as that of Apions are 'semi-public' institutions (argued most fully in *T&MByz* 9 (1985) 4–90), the view has prevailed that all soldiers receiving rations from the Apion estate are imperial troops: the supply of their *annona* was a public *munus* incumbent upon the estate, and the soldiers served under the latter's authority in the fulfilment of public functions (mostly policing or assisting with the collection of taxes); see J. Gascou, 'L'Institution des Bucellaires', *BIFAO* 76 (1976) 143–56; O. Schmitt, 'Die Buccellarii', *Tyche* 9 (2001) 147–74, esp. 167–8; Mitthof, *Annona militaris* i 244–5. Lately, however, Peter Sarris, *Economy and Society in the Age of Justinian* (2006) 162–75, has revived the idea that at least some soldiers appearing in the Apion archive were 'part-time' retainers illegally recruited from the imperial troops to serve the estate's private ends. Sarris emphasizes the legislation prohibiting this practice and the use of the verb παραμένω in papyri to describe the relation of στρατιῶται, *buccellarii*, and σύμμαχοι to the estate, a verb that he takes to imply a specific contractual relationship (Gascou, 'L'Institution des Bucellaires' 145, also interprets the verb in this manner but does not see it in contradiction with the public function of *buccellarii*; cf. also Haug, loc. cit. 219 [1 n.], for a non-technical understanding of παραμένω). The present receipts, while further illustrating the close association of military forces with the Apion estate, do not help to steer the debate in a particular direction.

4923 and **4924** are written in the same hand, which is also that of **2013** and **2014**, while **4925** appears to be the work of a different scribe. They are written in three lines across the fibres on broad rectangular strips of papyrus. Their backs are blank.

A. BENAISSA

4923. RECEIPT FOR MEAT SUPPLIED TO SOLDIERS

1 1B.120/H(a)   31 × 5.5 cm   7 September 550

A receipt for 300 pounds of meat issued by Menas to 10 soldiers 'staying' (παραμένουσι; see above, general introd.) at the 'glorious house', for their subsistence over one month. It parallels **2013** and **2014**, which likewise concern 'staying' soldiers.

† ἐδόθ(ησαν) δι(ὰ) Μηνᾶ χοιρομαγίρ(ου) (*vac.*) τοῖς ι″ στρατιώτ(αις) παραμένουσ(ι) τῷ
                              ἐνδόξ(ῳ) οἴκ(ῳ) λόγ(ῳ) ἀναλ(ώματος)
τοῦ Θὼθ μη(νὸς) τῆς τεσσαρασκαιδεκάτης ἰνδ(ικτίωνος) κρέως λίτρ(αι) τριακοσίας,
      γί(νονται) κρ(έως) λί(τραι) τ μό(ναι). (*m.* 2) γί(νονται) κρέ(ως) λίτρ(αι) τριακοσίας.
(ἔτους) σκζ ρϙϛ, Θὼθ ι, ἰνδ(ικτίωνος) τεσσαρασκαιδεκάτης. (*m.* 3) γί(νονται) κρ(έως)
                                 λί(τραι) τ μό(ναι).

1 εδο^θ⟨δι, χοιρομαγιϼ (l. -γείρου), στρατιωτ⟩παραμενουσ⟩τωενδοξ⟩οικλογ⟩αναλ   2 μῆ, ἰνꝇ,

λιτρ, γ∈κρ/τμϕ, γ∈κρϵ λιτρ   l. *τριακόсιαι* (*bis*)   2, 3 l. *τεссαρεскαιδεκάτηс*   3 L, ιν꜒,
γ∈κρ/τμϕ

'Given through Menas, pork butcher, to the 10 soldiers who are staying at the glorious house, on account of expenses of the month Thoth of the fourteenth indiction, three hundred pounds of meat, total 300 pounds of meat only.' (2nd hand) 'Total three hundred pounds of meat.'

'Year 227 = 196, Thoth 10, indiction fourteenth.'

(3rd hand) 'Total 300 pounds of meat only.'

1 *Μηνᾶ χοιρομαγίρ*(*ου*). See above, general introd., and below, **4924** 1 n.

стρατιώτ(*αιс*). Cf. **4925** 1. These were soldiers of the regular army, and should not be confused with *βουκελλάριοι*; see O. Schmitt, *Tyche* 9 (1994) 167 n. 175, and B. Palme, *Tyche* 11 (1996) 254. An important text is XVI **2046**, which distinguishes between *стρατιῶται* and *βουκελλάριοι*.

стρατιώτ(*αιс*) *παραμένουс*(*ι*) *τῷ ἐνδόξ*(*ῳ*) *οἴκ*(*ῳ*). Among the receipts issued by Menas, we find the same formulation in **2013** 1 and **2014** 1; cf. also PSI VIII 953.18, 29, etc. (*buccellarii*), XVI **2045** 1 (*сύμμαχοι*).

τῷ ἐνδόξ(*ῳ*) *οἴκ*(*ῳ*). On this designation of the Apion estate, see LXXI **4835** 9–10 n.

λόγ(*ῳ*) *ἀναλ*(*ώματος*). Cf. **2013** 1, **2014** 1, **4924** 2, **4925** 1; see the discussion below, **4924** 2 n.

2 *κρέωс λίτρ*(*αι*). The meat is as a rule pork; see H.-J. Drexhage, *MBAH* 16.2 (1997) 97; Mitthoff, *Annona militaris* i 214–15. 1 pound = 327.4 g; see J. Gascou, 'La Table budgétaire d'Antaeopolis', in *Hommes et richesses dans l'Empire byzantin* i (1989) 287, for other possible conversions.

3 For the conversion of the date to its Julian equivalent, see *CSBE*² 150, 159.

Θὼθ ι. It is remarkable that the date of the payment is ten days later than the beginning of the period covered by the rations.

A. SYRKOU

4924. Receipt for Meat Supplied to *Buccellarii*

97/35(c)   16 × 6 cm   21 November 550
                                                                  Plate XIII

A receipt for meat issued by Menas to five individuals from Cynopolis, no doubt *buccellarii* stationed in this city (see 1–2 n.). The document is incomplete at the right and irregularly damaged at the top. The amount of meat is lost, and the period of payment could range from 2 to 8 days (see 2 n.).

† *ἐδόθ*(*ησαν*) *δι*(*ὰ*)] *Μ*[*ηνᾶ χοι*]*ρ*[*ο*]*μ*[*α*]*γίρ*(*ου*) *vac.* *τοῖс* ε [*βουκελλ*(*αρίοιс*) - - -
ἀπὸ τῆс Κυνῶ(*ν*) *λόγ*(*ῳ*) *ἀναλ*(*ώματος*) *τῶν ἀπὸ μη*(*νὸс*) *Ἀθὺρ κβ ἕωс κ*[*τοῦ αὐτ*(*οῦ*),
                        ἡμερῶν n, κρέωс λίτραι n, γί(*νονται*) *κρ*(*έωс*) *λί*(*τραι*) n.
(*ἔτουс*) *сκζ ρϙϛ, Ἀθὺρ κε, ἰνδ*(*ικτίωνος*) *τεссαραскαιδεκάτη*[ς.

1 -]*γιρ*   l. *χοιρομαγείρου*   2 *κυνωλογ/αναλ, μ̄*   3 L, ιν꜒   l. *τεссαρεскαι-*
δεκάτηс

'Given through Menas, pork butcher, to the 5 *buccellarii* . . . from Cynopolis, on account of the allowance from the 22nd of the month Hathyr to the 2–th of the same (month), (total) *n* days, *n* pounds of meat, total *n* pounds of meat.

'Year 227/196, Hathyr 25, indiction fourteenth.'

1 $M[\eta\nu\hat{a} \; \chi o\iota]\rho[o]\mu[a]\gamma\acute{\iota}\rho(ov)$. The restoration of Menas' name is guaranteed by the identity of the hand in **2013**, **2014**, and **4923**. The list of papyrologically attested $\chi o\iota\rho o\mu\acute{a}\gamma\epsilon\iota\rho o\iota$ by H.-J. Drexhage, *MBAH* 16.2 (1997) 102 n. 23, is incomplete; add XVI **1903** 1 (561), **2032** 87, 91 (540/41; see BL VI 105), **2052** 5 (579); P. Cair. Masp. II 67141.i.35, 36 (VI), 67164.3 (569); P. Ross. Georg. III 18.14 (VI/VII); P. Strasb. I 47.37, 39, 51, 48.8, 10, 49.7, 9, 19, 50.17 (566); SPP III 425.1 (VII). The earliest attestation of the term is in PSI III 202 (338), which mentions an association of pork butchers ($\kappa o\iota\nu\grave{o}\nu$ $\tau\hat{\omega}\nu \; \chi o\iota\rho o\mu\alpha\gamma\epsilon\acute{\iota}\rho\omega\nu$); otherwise the remaining instances are all from the sixth and seventh centuries. P. Prag. I 72 (VII) seems to provide an example of a $\chi o\iota\rho o\mu\acute{a}\gamma\epsilon\iota\rho o c$ in the service of an Arsinoite estate: the butcher David orders the *pronoetes* Menas to issue 15 lbs. of meat (see BL IX 215) to the *notarius* Marianus, which suggests that David worked in the same estate as Menas. $\chi o\iota\rho o\mu\acute{a}\gamma\epsilon\iota\rho o\iota$ are involved in the supply of meat to soldiers also in XVI **1903**, P. Mich. XIII 673, and PSI 938; cf. also P. Lond. III (p. 236) 1254.22 (IV).

1–2 $\tau o\hat{\iota} c \; \epsilon \; [\beta o\upsilon\kappa\epsilon\lambda\lambda(\alpha\rho\acute{\iota}o\iota c) - - -] \; \grave{a}\pi\grave{o} \; \tau\hat{\eta} c \; K\upsilon\nu\hat{\omega}(\nu)$. The recipients are almost certainly a detachment of *buccellarii*, given their provenance; cf. XXVII **2480** 3, 6, 13, 60, 75, 80 and PSI VIII 953.41, which similarly record the issue of wine to *buccellarii* from Cynopolis. On *buccellarii*, irregular state soldiers in the service of a military officer or public official, see the comprehensive treatment of O. Schmitt, *Tyche* 9 (2001) 147–74 (with further bibliography), and cf. the works of Gascou and Sarris cited above, general introd. *Buccellarii* serving under the authority of the Apions' $\H{\epsilon}\nu\delta o\xi o c \; o\mathring{\iota}\kappa o c$ in Oxyrhynchus were garrisoned at Cynopolis, Heracleopolis, and Coma (Heracleopolite nome). A number of Apionic accounts and receipts detail expenditure on their alimentary provision during their stay in the city: I **150** (wine); XVI **1903** (meat); **2046** (bread, meat, wine, oil and wood); XXVII **2480** (wine); PSI VIII 953 (wine); cf. I **156** 1–3. The size of the Cynopolite garrison of *buccellarii* is unknown, but they never exceed 35 in individual account entries and receipts (cf. XXVII **2480** 68, 75, 80). As **2046** 44 ff. shows, *buccellarii* were often paid by *contuberniae*, sub-units of up to seven *buccellarii*, as seems to be the case here; see Schmitt, loc. cit. 165 with n. 150. The rest of line 1 was probably occupied by a generic phrase such as $\grave{\epsilon}\lambda\theta o\hat{\upsilon}c\iota\nu \; \grave{\epsilon}\nu\tau\alpha\hat{\upsilon}\theta\alpha$ (see **4925** 1 with n.).

4924 appears to be the earliest attestation of *buccellarii* in Oxyrhynchus to date. On the impossibility of restoring $\tau o\hat{\iota} c \; [\; . \; . \; \beta o\upsilon\kappa\kappa\epsilon\lambda\lambda\alpha]\rho(\acute{\iota}o\iota c)$ in SB XVI 12608.1 (511), see P. J. Sijpesteijn, *Aegyptus* 68 (1988) 86 = BL IX 287.

2 $\lambda\acute{o}\gamma(\omega) \; \grave{a}\nu\alpha\lambda(\acute{\omega}\mu\alpha\tau o c)$. The phrase is usually associated with expenditure of rations; see Morelli, *Olio e retribuzioni* 26: 'l'espressione è usata spesso con un significato simile a $\upsilon\pi\grave{\epsilon}\rho \; \tau\rho o\phi\hat{\eta} c$ e può quindi essere intesa nel senso di "per le spese, per il consumo, per il bisogno di una certa cosa"' (see also n. 60).

$\grave{a}\pi\grave{o} \; \mu\eta(\nu\grave{o} c) \; '\!A\theta\grave{\upsilon}\rho \; \kappa\beta \; \H{\epsilon}\omega c \; \kappa[\; . \;$ .The time span could range from the 23rd ($\kappa[\gamma$) to the 29th ($\kappa[\theta$) of the month. For the restoration of $\tau o\hat{\upsilon} \; a\mathring{\upsilon}\tau(o\hat{\upsilon})$ (*scil. $\mu\eta\nu\acute{o} c$*), $\mathring{\eta}\mu\epsilon\rho\hat{\omega}\nu \; n$, cf. PSI VIII 953.iv.34, 36 etc. (567/8; see BL V 125), VII **1043** 2 (578). The amount of meat would have been based on the rate of (1 lb. × 5 *buccellarii*) × *n* days; see above, general introd. Thus, assuming that the period of payment runs up to the day of the receipt's issue on 25 Hathyr, one could restore $\grave{a}\pi\grave{o} \; \mu\eta(\nu\grave{o} c) \; '\!A\theta\grave{\upsilon}\rho \; \kappa\beta \; \H{\epsilon}\omega c \; \kappa[\epsilon \; \tau o\hat{\upsilon} \; a\mathring{\upsilon}\tau(o\hat{\upsilon}), \; \mathring{\eta}\mu\epsilon\rho\hat{\omega}\nu \; \delta, \; \kappa\rho\acute{\epsilon}\omega c \; \lambda\acute{\iota}\tau\rho\alpha\iota \; \epsilon\mathring{\iota}\kappa o c\iota, \; \gamma\acute{\iota}(\nu o\nu\tau\alpha\iota) \; \kappa\rho(\acute{\epsilon}\omega c) \; \lambda\acute{\iota}(\tau\rho\alpha\iota) \; \kappa]$. The confirmation of the amount of meat, written in a different hand, would have occupied the end either of this line (cf. **2013** 2, **4923** 2) or of the following line (cf. **4925** 3).

3 The fourteenth indiction as defined by the Oxyrhynchite era numbers 227/196 is the equivalent of the Julian year 29 August 550 to 28 August 551; for the conversion of the date, see *CSBE*[2] 150, 160.

A. BENAISSA

4925. Receipt for Meat Supplied to Soldiers

1 1B.120/H(b)   30 × 4 cm   8 March 552

A receipt for 42 pounds of meat for the supply of 14 soldiers who had come to Oxyrhynchus (ἐλθοῦσιν ἐνταῦθα) for a period of three days.

† ἐδόθ(ησαν) δι(ὰ) Μηνᾶ χοιρομαγίρ(ου) (vac.) τοῖς ῑδ̄ στρατιώτ(αις) ἐλθ(οῦσιν) ἐνταῦθα
                    λόγ(ῳ) ἀναλώμ(ατος) ἡμερ(ῶν) γ̄, ἡμερ[ο]υ(cίωc) κρέωc [λίτ]ραc
δεκατέccαρεc, κρέωc λίτραc τεccεράκοντα δύο, γί(νονται) κρ(έωc) λί(τραι) μβ μόνα.
(ἔτουc) cκη ρϙζ, Φαμενὼθ ιβ, ἰνδ(ικτίωνοc) πέμπτηc ⟨καὶ δεκάτηc⟩.   (m. 2) γί(νονται)
                                        κρέωc λίτραc τεccεράκοντα δύο.

1 εδο⁰ʃδι, χοιρομαγιϱ, cτρατιωτελθ, λοⳁαναλωϟημεϱ, ημε[ρο]υ̸   l. χοιρομαγείρου   1, 2,
3 l. λίτραι   2, 3 l. τεccαράκοντα   2 γικϱ̸   l. μόναι   3 ⌐, ιν⳽, γι

'Given through Menas, pork butcher, to the 14 soldiers who came here on account of expenses of 3 days, at 14 pounds of meat daily, forty-two pounds of meat, total 42 pounds of meat only.
'Year 228 = 197, Phamenoth 12, indiction fif⟨teenth⟩.'
(2nd hand) 'Total forty-two pounds of meat.'

1 ἐλθ(οῦcιν) ἐνταῦθα. The soldiers presumably came from a garrison outside Oxyrhynchus. The phrase recurs in various accounts, receipts, and orders for payment, especially in connection with military personnel: XVI **1888** 2 (488) (cτρατιῶται), **1920** 1 (after 563) (ἄνθρωποι of the *dux* of the Thebaid, including various soldiers and officials), **2046** 1 (564) (βουκκελλάριοι), XXVII **2480** 3–4, etc. (565/6?) (βουκκελλάριοι, νεώτεροι, cταβλῖται, Κρομμυδιῶται), I **150** 1 (590) (βουκκελλάριοι from Heracleopolis and Coma); also SB XVI 12608 1 (511) (recipients uncertain; see BL IX 287). Some of these examples, like **4925**, do not specify the provenance of the recipients. Cf. also **4924** 1–2 n.

3 For the conversion of the date to its Julian equivalent, see *CSBE*² 150, 162.

A. SYRKOU

4926–4929. Orders and a Receipt for the Supply of Bread

4926, **4928**, and **4929** are orders from the 'glorious house' of the Apions to Pamuthius, provost of the monastery of Musaeus, for the delivery of bread to groups of people from various villages. A similar order has been published as XVI **1952**, now to be dated to 21 May 564 (cf. **4927**), where read μοναcτηρ(ίου) Μουcαίου for the editors' μοναcτ(ηρίου) Ὁμοουcίου (first suggested by A. Syrkou in her PhD thesis). **4927** is a receipt by Pamuthius for a similar delivery of bread. The particulars of this group of documents can be summarized as follows:

	Date	Village	ὀνόματα	ψωμία
4926	Pachon 26	Meskanounios and Megalou Choriou	100 (50 × 2)	300
1952	Pachon 26	Tarouthinou	200	600
4927	Pachon 28	Senokomis	213	639
4928	Pachon 2[?]	Theagenous	22	66
4929	Pauni 2	Laura	24	72

The number of recipients is remarkable. Assuming an equal distribution, the quantities of bread imply a ration of three ψωμία per person. In **4927** 2 the purpose of the deliveries is said to be λόγῳ τροφ(ῆς) Παχὼν κη, which suggests a daily ration for sustenance. As the dates of the documents coincide with the peak time of the grain harvest, and most of the settlements named are known to have been part of the Apion estate, one possibility is that the deliveries of bread were intended for the provision of estate labourers involved in the harvest. Compare the free supplies of bread to *epoikiôtai* of the earlier Appianus estate for their extra casual labour in this period; see D. Rathbone, *Economic Rationalism and Rural Society in Third-Century A.D. Egypt* (1991) 161, 181 n. 6, 183. For the later period, cf. the payments of bread (*inter alia*) to vintagers in SB XII 10990 nos. 1–15 (v/vi). These distributions in kind to ὀνόματα from various estate settlements have a close parallel in XVI **2012** (30. ix.590; see BL XI 157), a receipt by an *oinocheiristes* for the issue of wine to a total of 164 individuals from five Apionic hamlets. (The villages in these documents, it may be noted, do not form a geographically coherent group.) If the hypothesis suggested here is correct, it remains unclear whether these labourers were paid for work they performed in their own *epoikia* and villages or in a different part of the estate.

The relationship between the Apion estate and the monastery of Musaeus is not entirely transparent. R. Rémondon, *CE* 47 (1972) 274, interpreted **1952** as an indication that the monastery was under the trusteeship of the estate and was thereby exploited to become a 'centre de distribution de ses aumônes personnelles'. If the bread deliveries were charitable or festal distributions, however, we would expect an expression such as λόγῳ ἑορτικῶν/εὐσεβείας, not λόγῳ τροφῆς in **4927** 2. Furthermore, the only other attestation of the monastery in XVI **2020** 38 (*c.*567–88) suggests that it was administratively and financially independent of the estate, since its (small) fiscal payment in this text is distinct from that of the ἔνδοξος οἶκος (cf. **2020** 15; Rémondon could not have made the connection as he relied on the reading μοναστ(ηρίου) Ὁμοουσίου in **1952**). We may consider whether the monastery ran a commercial bakery, whose services were hired by the Apion estate for the provision of its labourers during times of intensive agricultural work (the estate also possessed at least one bakery of its own, cf. LI **3641** 9–10 (544) κριβανείῳ . . . τῆς ὑμετέρας ὑπερφυείας, but it was probably insufficient when very large quantities of bread were needed). Compare the role of other Oxyrhynchite monasteries in the production of rope for a variety of estate installations: LI **3640** (533), I **148** (556), XVI **2015** (556), SB XVIII 14061–3 (556). The involvement of monasteries in the bread-making trade is not well documented in the papyri, but it is plausible considering that coenobitic monasteries were usually well equipped with mills and ovens; see e.g. H. E. Winlock, *The Monastery of Epiphanius at Thebes* i (1926) 53–4, and cf. XVI **1890** (508); on the trades practiced in monasteries, see generally J. Gascou, in *The Coptic Encyclopedia* v. 1640–41. It is interesting that in a Coptic letter by the ascetic Moses of Abydos (v/vi) to the superior of a convent, he admonishes the nuns for 'baking for lay people'; see E. Wipszycka, 'L'Ascétisme féminin dans l'Égypte de l'Antiquité tardive', in H. Melaerts, L. Mooren (eds.), *Le Rôle et le statut de la femme en Égypte hellénistique, romaine et byzantine* (Studia Hellenistica 37: 2002) 367–8, for references and commentary (we thank Professor Wipszycka for bringing this passage to our attention). The reproach may hint that the practice was not uncommon among some monastic establishments.

4926 and **4928** were written by the same scribe, who also distinguishes himself from the scribes of the other texts by using the terms προεϲτώϲ and μονή for the equivalent ἀρχιμανδρίτηϲ and μοναϲτήριον. The inventory numbers of **4927** and **4929** indicate that these two papyri were found together, but although their hands are similar, they do not appear to be the work of the same scribe (**1952** is in yet another hand). All documents but **4927** are dated by month and indiction only, but the additional use of the Oxyrhynchite era in **4927** 5 allows the others to be assigned to 564.

The papyri are written across the fibres and are blank on the back.

A. BENAISSA

4926. ORDER FOR THE SUPPLY OF BREAD

52 1B.26(C)/D(4)b   14.2 × 6.9 cm   21 May 564

A complete order from the 'glorious house' to Pamuthius for the delivery of bread to a total of 100 people from Meskanounios and Megalou Choriou. It is written by the same scribe as **4928**.

> + τῷ εὐλαβεϲτ(άτῳ) Παμουθίῳ προεϲτ(ῶτι) μονῆϲ Μ[ουϲ]αίου
> ὁ ἔνδοξ(οϲ) οἶκο[ϲ]. παράϲχου τοῖϲ ἀπὸ Μεϲκανούνιοϲ
> ὀνόμ(αϲι) ν καὶ τοῖϲ ἀπὸ Μεγ[ά]λου Χωρίου ὀνόμ(αϲι) ν, γί(νονται) ὀνόμ(ατα) ρ,
> ψωμία τριακόϲια, γί(νονται) ψωμ(ία) τ μό(να). Παχὼν κε,
> 5   ἰνδ(ικτίωνοϲ) ιβ. ⳨⳨⳨

    1 ευλαβεϲτ∫, προεϲτ∫   2 ενδοξ∫   3 ονομ∫ (bis), γϲονομ∫   4 γϲψωμ∫τμⲟ̸
5 ιν⳼

'To the most pious Pamuthius, provost of the monastery of Musaeus, (from) the glorious house. Provide the 50 people from Meskanounios and the 50 people from Megalou Choriou, total 100 people, with three hundred loaves of bread, total 300 loaves of bread only. Pachon 26, indiction 12.'

1 προεϲτ(ῶτι). Cf. **4928** 1. For the term's equivalency to ἀρχιμανδρίτηϲ in certain contexts, see P. Barison, *Aegyptus* 18 (1938) 37, and E. Wipszycka, in *The Coptic Encyclopedia* vi. 2021.

2 Μεϲκανούνιοϲ. For the instances of this *ktema* in relation to the Apion estate, see R. Mazza, *L'archivio degli Apioni* (2001) 182. It is not attested earlier than the sixth century.

3 Μεγ[ά]λου Χωρίου. See Mazza, *L'archivio degli Apioni* 180, for additional attestations of this Apionic *epoikion*.

4 ψωμία. Payments of bread in Apionic documents are usually expressed in (ἄρτων) λίτραι. Presumably one ψωμίον implied a standard weight or amount of grain per loaf of bread. Cf. F. Morelli, *Olio e retribuzioni nell'Egitto tardo* (1996) 101–2; Rathbone, *Economic Rationalism* 308.

A. BENAISSA

4927. Receipt for the Supply of Bread

54 1B.25(A)/D(4)b   15 × 7.5 cm   23 May 564

A receipt for 639 loaves of bread given to the people of Senokomis by Pamuthius 'on account of food'. The receipt implies that Pamuthius received from the administration of the Apion estate an order similar to **1952**, **4926**, and **4928–9**.

+ ἐδόθ(η) δι(ὰ) Παμουθίου ἀρχιμανδρ(ίτου) μοναϲτηρ(ίου) Μουϲαίου
τοῖϲ ἀπὸ Ϲενοκώμε[ωϲ ὀ]νόμ(αϲι) ϲιγ λόγ(ῳ) τροφ(ῆϲ) Παχὼν κη
ἰνδ(ικτίωνοϲ) δωδεκάτηϲ ψωμ(ία) ἑξακόϲια τριάκοντα ἐννέα,
γί(νονται) ψωμ(ία) χλθ μό(να).   ꝛꝛꝛ
5   (ἔτουϲ) ϲμ καὶ ϲθ, Παχὼν κη, ἰνδ(ικτίωνοϲ) δωδεκάτηϲ.

1 εδο^θδt, αρχιμανδρμοναϲτηρ   2 ονομϲϲιγλογϲτροφ   3 ινϪ, ψωμϲ   4 γϲψωμϲχλθμφ
5 Ꝙ, ινϪ

'Given through Pamuthius, archimandrite of the monastery of Musaeus, to the 213 people from Senokomis on account of food for Pachon 29 of the twelfth indiction, six hundred thirty-nine loaves of bread, total 639 loaves of bread only. Year 240 and 209, Pachon 28 of the twelfth indiction.'

2 Ϲενοκώμε[ωϲ. For the connections of this village with the Apion estate, see Mazza, *L'archivio degli Apioni* 185.

λόγ(ῳ) τροφ(ῆϲ). For the resolution of τροφ( ) and parallels, see P. Hamb. III 216.3 n. ('Bei diesen Wendungen handelt sich immer um eine bestimmte Lebensmittelmenge für einen bestimmten Zeitraum'); cf. also F. Mitthof, A. Papathomas, *ZPE* 103 (1994) 61.

5 The twelfth indiction as defined by the Oxyrhynchite era numbers 240/209 is the equivalent of the Julian year 30 August 563 to 28 August 564; for the conversion of the date, see *CSBE*[2] 151, 163.

A. SYRKOU

4928. ORDER FOR THE SUPPLY OF BREAD

53 1B.26(D)F(3)a   15.1 × 4.8 cm   16–24 May 564

A complete order to Pamuthius, presumably from the same 'glorious house' of **4926** 2 and **4929** 2, for the delivery of bread to 22 people from Theagenous. It is written by the same scribe as **4926**.

+ τῷ εὐλαβεϲτ(άτῳ) Παμουθίῳ προεϲτ(ῶτι) μ[ο]νῆϲ Μουϲαίου.
παράϲχου τοῖϲ ἀπὸ Θεαγένουϲ ὀνόμ(αϲι) κβ ψωμ(ία)
ἑξήκοντα ἕξ, γί(νονται) ψωμ(ία) ξϛ μό(να). Παχὼν κ , ἰνδ(ικτίωνοϲ) ιβ.
ϙϙϙ

1 ευλαβεϲτϟ, προεϲτϟ   2 ονομϟ   3 γι̂ψωμϟξ̅ϛ̅μϙ, ιν⳧

'To the most pious Pamuthius, provost of the monastery of Musaeus. Provide the 22 people from Theagenous with sixty-six loaves of bread, total 66 loaves of bread only. Pachon 2–, indiction 12.'

2 Θεαγένουϲ. For the instances of this *epoikion* (8th *pagus*) in relation to the Apion estate, see Mazza, *L'archivio degli Apioni* 186.

A. BENAISSA

4929. ORDER FOR THE SUPPLY OF BREAD

54 1B.25(A)/D(4)c   15 × 7 cm   27 May 564

A complete order to Pamuthius from the 'glorious house' for the delivery of bread to 24 people from Laura.

+ τῷ εὐλαβ(εϲτάτῳ) Παμουθίῳ ἀρχιμανδρίτ(η) μοναϲτιρ(ίου)
Μουϲαίου vac. ὁ ἔνδοξ(οϲ) οἶκοϲ. vac. ⟨παράϲχου⟩ τοῖϲ κδ . ορ(.).( )
ἀπὸ Λαύραϲ ψωμί(α) ἑβδομήκοντα δύο,
γί(νονται) ψωμί(α) οβ. Παῦνι β, ἰνδ(ικτίωνοϲ) ιβ. ϙϙϙ *signs*

1 ευλαβϟ, αρχιμανδριτϟ, μοναϲτιρ̥   l. μοναϲτηρίου   2 ενδοξϟ   3, 4 ψωμ⳺
4 γι̂ψωμ⳺, ιν⳧

'To the most pious Pamuthius, archimandrite of the monastery of Musaeus, (from) the glorious house. (Provide) the 24 . . . from Laura with seventy-two loaves of bread, total 72 loaves of bread. Pauni 2, indiction 12.'

2 . ορ(.).( ). Not ὀνόμ(αϲι) as in the other documents. The first letter, a very tall upright with some scattered traces to the right, is either φ or κ. The final letter is a tall upright undercut by an oblique abbreviation stroke. Some traces to the left suggest the loop of delta, but the loop would be very small compared to other deltas in this hand. What remains of the presumed ρ may also be interpreted as ι with a horizontal join from the right near the top, e.g. ιτ (compare ιτ of ἀρχιμανδρίτ(η) in 1).

3 Λαύρας. This is probably the village of the Cynopolite nome attested in X **1256** 7, 16, 24 (282), on which see N. Litinas, *APF* 40 (1994) 159. XVI **1867** (vii), a letter possibly but not certainly belonging to the Apion archive, mentions two villages by the name of Λαύρας Ἔcω (10) and Λαύρας Ἔξω (16).

A. SYRKOU

4930. Acknowledgement of Debt

65 6B.37/H(1–3)b   12.5 × 34 cm   29 August – 21 November 614
Plate XVI

Victor, headman of the *curialis* Valerius, acknowledges that he owes 4 solidi and 6 carats to Fl. Sergius, *comes* and *dioecetes* of the 'glorious house'; Sergius might supply an example of promotion within the bureaucracy of the estate (see 4 n.). There is no mention of interest. The solidi are said to be 'of 18 carats on the Alexandrian standard', which is new (see below, 13–16 n.).

A blank space of 9 cm separates the main body of the document from the remnants of the notary's signature. The endorsement is in a hand similar to that of the subscription.

εὐεργέτου] Φλ(αουΐου) Ἡρακλείου τοῦ [αἰωνίου
Αὐγούcτου] καὶ Αὐτοκράτοροc ἔ[το]υc
n, month, day] ἰ(ν)δ(ικτίων)ο(c) γ̄.
Φλαο]υΐ[ῳ] Cεργίῳ τῷ περιβλέ(πτῳ) κόμετι
5   καὶ δ]ιοικητῇ τοῦ ἐνδόξου οἴκου υἱῷ
το]ῦ τῆc μακαρίαc {τοῦ τῆc} μνήμηc
Β[ί]κτ[ο]ρ[ο]c ἀπὸ τῆc Ὀξυρυγχιτ(ῶν) πόλεωc
ἐγὼ Βίκτωρ μειζότεροc Οὐαλερίου
τοῦ μεγαλοπρε(πεcτάτου) πολιτευομένου
10   ἀπὸ τῆc αὐτῆc πόλεωc. ὁμολογ[ῶ
ὀφείλειν τῇ ὑμετέρᾳ λαμπρό(τητι)
καὶ χρεωc[τ(εῖν)] καθαρῶc καὶ ἀποκρότ'ωc'
χρυcοῦ νομίcματα τέccερα
καὶ κεράτια ε̄ξ̄ ἕκαcτον
15   ἀπὸ κερατίων δεκαοκτὼ
Ἀ[λ]εξανδρείαc. καὶ ταῦτα
ὁ[μ]ολογῶ διδόναι αὐτῇ ἐν τῇ
εἰκάδι ἕκτῃ τ[ο]ῦ Ἀθὺρ
μηνὸc τῆc παρούcηc
20   τρίτηc ἰ(ν)δ(ικτίων)ο(c) ἀνυπερθέτῳ[c.

κύριον τὸ γραμματεῖον
ἀπλ(οῦν) γραφ(ὲν) καὶ ἐπερ(ωτηθεὶς)
ὡμολόγηςα.+ (*m.* 2) Βίκτωρ
μειζότερ(ος) ςτοιχεῖ μοι
25 τοῦτο τὸ γρ(αμμάτιον) ὡς πρόκ(ειται). Μᾶρκος
ἔγρ(αψα) (ὑπὲρ) αὐτοῦ ἀγρ(αμμάτου) ὄντος.+
(*vac.*)
] . . [1–2 *et*]ε[*liot*]π̅

Back, downwards along the fibres:
(*m.* 2?) + γρα]μ(μάτιον) Βίκτορ(ος) μειζ(οτέρου) Ο]ὐαλερίου τοῦ
μεγαλ(οπρεπεστάτου) πολιτε(νομένου) ἀπὸ τῆς ['Ο]ξ[υ]ρ[υγ]χ[ιτῶν
30 χρ(υςοῦ) Ἀλ(εξανδρείας) νο(μιςματίων) δ κερ(ατίων) ς
ἑκάςτο(υ) ἀπὸ (κερατίων) ιη

1 φλς	3, 20 ἴνᾳ̊	4 περιβλ̅	7 οξυρυγχ̅ι	9 μεγαλοπ̅ρ̣	11 ὕμετεραλαμπ̅ρ̣
22 απλχ̅γραφ, επερ		24 μειζοτερ	25 γρ, προκ̅	26 εγρ̅ς, αγρ̣	29 μεγαλπολιτ̅,
[ο]ξ[υ]ρ[υγ]ˣ	30 χρα̅λ̅Ν̅δ̅κερ̅ςεκαςτ̅απ̅ϛιη				

'. . . benefactor Fl. Heraclius, the eternal Augustus and Imperator, year *n* (= 4 or 5), *month, day,* indiction 3.

'To Flavius Sergius, *vir spectabilis, comes* and *dioecetes* of the glorious house, son of Victor of blessed memory, from the city of the Oxyrhynchites, I, Victor, headman of the most magnificent Valerius, *curialis,* from the same city. I acknowledge that I owe to your splendour clearly and without fail four gold solidi and six carats, each of eighteen carats on the Alexandrian standard. And these I acknowledge to give to you on the twenty-sixth of the month of Hathyr of the current third indiction without delay. The contract, written in a single copy, is binding, and in reply to the formal question I have given my consent.'

(2nd hand) 'I, Victor, headman—this contract is satisfactory to me as aforementioned. I, Marcus, wrote for him as he is illiterate.

'Completed (through me . . .)'

Back: 'Contract of Victor, headman of the most magnificent Valerius, *curialis,* from the (city) of the Oxyrhynchites, of 4 solidi and 6 carats of gold on the Alexandrian standard, each (solidus being) of 18 carats.'

1–3 The restoration is based on regnal formula A 1 in *CSBE*[2] 267, attested in the region of Oxyrhynchus.

3 ἰ(ν)δ(ικτίων)ο(ς) γ. This third indiction began on 29 August 614. The loan was to be repaid on 22 November 614 (see 18–20 n.). Heraclius' regnal year would have been either the 4th or the 5th, depending on whether the text was written before or after 5 October, Heraclius' *dies imperii.* We should rule out the possibility that this indiction 3 was the one starting in 629, since the regnal formula would have been different; the chronological distribution of the Oxyrhynchite documentation and the known dates in the career of the notary Marcus (see 25 n.) also speak against this later date.

4 Φλαο]υΐ[ῳ] Cεργίῳ. This person may be the same as the *spectabilis comes* in P. Heid. V 349.2–3, a work-contract of probable Oxyrhynchite provenance, assigned to the sixth/seventh century; the

fact that Fl. Sergius is not described as *dioecetes* in P. Heid. 349 need not speak against the identification. There is no way of telling whether he is to be identified with Sergius, *chartularius* and *riparius* of
the 'glorious house', in LVIII **3942** 7–8 (606); if that were the case, we would have to reckon with a
promotion within the administration of the Apion estate, which is plausible but not known otherwise.
(P. Heid. 349.2–3 n. relates that a *comes* Sergius occurs in unpublished papyri in the collection of the
Istituto Papirologico 'G. Vitelli'—from which P. Heid. 349 comes—but no further details are given.)

4–5 περιβλέ(πτῳ) κόμετι [καὶ δ]ιοικητῇ. See LXIX **4756** 7–8 n.

8 μειζότερος. See LVI **3871** 3 n.; CPR XXIV 25.7 n.

8–9 Οὐαλερίου τοῦ μεγαλοπρε(πεστάτου) πολιτευομένου. Cf. 28. The epithet μεγαλοπρεπέστατος
is not commonly used for πολιτευόμενοι; it has occurred in this context only in P. Lond. V 1689.5
(527), which is too early to serve as a parallel, SPP XX 218.6 (early VII), in which the πολιτευόμενος is
also styled *comes*, and XVI **1921** 2 (621) τῶν μεγαλοπρε(πεστάτων) πολιτευομ(ένων). It is not inconceiv-
able that Valerius held a *comitiva*, like most persons called μεγαλοπρεπέστατοι in the seventh century,
even if this is not stated. (Οὐαλερίου κόμετος in XVI **2040** probably refers to a different person, given
that **2040** is almost half a century earlier than **4930**.)

11 τῇ ὑμετέρᾳ λαμπρό(τητι). This abstract indicates a lower grade than that of *vir spectabilis*, but
parallels for its use with *spectabiles* are not lacking; cf. e.g. P. Heid. V 349.9, used perhaps for the same
person as the one here.

13–16 This document and another of 605/6 or 620/21 (to be published in a forthcoming volume) refer to solidi of 18 carats on the Alexandrian standard, which is without parallel. Contemporary comparative material from Oxyrhynchus is scarce. I **151** and XVI **2045** (both of 612) attest solidi
of 'minus 4 carats', and P. Amh. II 158 (612) of 'minus 4 ⅛ carats', always on the 'private' standard
of Oxyrhynchus (the rate of deduction is not specified in the important LVIII **3958** of 614). The
latest information on the relationship between the Alexandrian standard and this 'private' standard
comes from the sixth century (*c.*566–90), when the solidi on the standard of Alexandria trailed those
on the 'private' by just under 2 carats; see K. Maresch, *Nomisma und Nomismatia* (1994) 39–43. Thus it
would not be exceptional to have solidi 'of 18 carats', which could also have been expressed as solidi
of 'minus 6 carats', at a time when the rate of deduction in the 'private' standard is minus *c.*4 carats.
Any interpretation of these solidi depends on the view one takes on the 'minus carats' issue, on which
there is no consensus; for the most recent views, see Maresch, *Nomisma und Nomismatia*; J. Banaji, 'Dis-
counts, Weight Standards, and the Exchange-Rate between Gold and Copper', in *Atti dell'Accademia
Romanistica Constantiniana* (1998) 183–202; C. Zuckerman, *Du Village à l'empire* (2004) 57–114.

17 ἐν τῇ. These words are written in different ink, and are probably a later addition.

18–20 Hathyr 26, indiction 3, corresponds to 22 November 614; see above, 3 n.

25 Μᾶρκος. This is the same Marcus who subscribed for illiterates in XVI **1979** 24–5 (614) and
LXX **4802** 19 (VII); see **4802** 19 n.

27]..[1–2 *et*]ε̣[*liot*]ħ̄. It would be reasonable to assume that the notary was Marcus, who signed
on behalf of Victor in 23–6, and whose signature has given difficulties (see LXX **4802** 20 n.). However, the notarial signatures associated with Marcus do not match the remains here. These signatures
end -*thh*, but the second *h* is not written here.

29–30 The docket is written in the 'official cursive hand' common in receipts and accounts; the
ink and pen suggest that it may be the work of Marcus, who used the 'current style' when he signed
for Victor.

A. SYRKOU

INDEXES

Letters in raised type refer to fragments, small roman numerals to columns. Square brackets indicate that a word is wholly or substantially restored by conjecture or from other sources, round brackets that it is expanded from an abbreviation or a symbol. An asterisk denotes a word not recorded in LSJ or its *Revised Supplement*. The article and (in the documentary sections) καί have not been indexed.

I. HEXAMETER POETRY

ἀγάλλεςθαι [**4850** ↓7?]
ἀγγέλλειν [**4850** →23?]
ἄγχι [**4849** ↓6]
ἄγειν **4848** 2?
ἀθάνατος **4850** →17, 27
Αἰακός [**4846** 3]
αἰδεῖςθαι [**4850** →10?]
αἷμα **4850** →16
αἰχμητής **4850** ↓19
ἅλις **4850** →14, 16
ἀλλά **4849** ↓2 **4850** →18], 37
*ἀμοίβιμος **4848** 2
ἀμφί **4849** [→5], ↓8
Ἀμφιτρίτη **4848** 1
ἀμφότερος **4850** →9
ἄναξ **4849** ↓7
ἄνθρωπος **4850** →14
ἀνία **4852** →4
ἀοιδή **4850** ↓6
ἄρα **4849** ↓6
Ἄρειος **4853** 1
ἀρειότερος [**4850** ↓16?]
ἀρείων **4850** ↓17
ἀςτεροε- **4850** →3
ἄςτυ **4852** ↓4
Αὐςόνιος **4851** 7
αὐτάρ [**4846** 2]
Ἀχιλ(λ)εύς **4849** →5
ἄχρι [**4851** 5?]

γίγας **4847** 5
γυναι- **4850** →32
γνωτός **4851** 6

δάφνη **4849** ↓8
δέ **4846** 4 **4847** 4 **4849** ↓6, 8 **4850** →5, 8, 12, 13, 23?,
    ↓[9?], 14, 15
διαφε- **4850** ↓31
διηνεκ- ⟨διηνεκέως?⟩ **4852** ↓1

δινεῖν **4849** ↓1
δυςμ- **4847** 8

εἶναι [**4846** 5] **4850** ↓8
Ἕλενος [**4849** ↓5]
ἐμπλη- **4850** →22
ἐν **4846** 3
ἐνδεῖςθαι [**4850** →10?]
ἐνί **4849** ↓2 [**4850** ↓12?]
ἔντεα **4849** →1
ἐπαρήγειν [**4850** →21]
ἐπί **4847** 6
ἐπι- **4849** →1
ἔρις **4850** ↓5
Ἑρμῆς [**4851** 7?]
ἐρύκεςθαι [**4850** ↓6?]
ἕτερος **4850** →18
ἔϋςκοπ- **4851** 4
ἐϋςτεφής **4851** 2
ἐφιέναι [**4850** ↓5]
ἔχειν [**4850** →8?]

Ζεύς **4846** 4

ἠβαιός [**4850** ↓24]
ἠρεμεῖν [**4850** →20]

θέλειν **4850** →8
Θεογαμία **4853** 2
θεός **4851** 3
θεςπέςιος **4852** →1
θνητός **4846** 5
Θοῆρις **4851** 4

ἱδροῦν **4850** →11
ἴον **4849** ↓3?
ἵππος [**4850** →11]
ἱςτάναι **4849** ↓6

II. RHETORICAL TEXTS

ἀγγελία [**4854** ^B ↓7?]
ἀγρός **4855** i 17
ἀγορά **4855** i 17
ἀγωγή **4855** i 1, [4]
ἀγών **4854** ^C ↓7
ἄδηλος **4855** i 25
ἀδικία [**4854** ^C ↓3?]
ἄδικος **4855** i 27
αἰτεῖσθαι **4854** ^A ↓7
αἰτία **4855** i 12, [15]
ἀκούειν [**4854** ^A ↓8] **4855** iii 2
ἀλλά **4854** ^A ↓5, ^B →[7], [8], 10, [^C →6?]
ἄλληλος **4854** ^A ↓3
ἄλλος **4854** ^C ↓3 [**4855** i 5–6?]
ἄλλως [**4854** ^C →6?]
ἄν **4854** ^A ↓[3], 7
ἀναγκαῖος [**4854** ^B →5]
ἀνθιστάναι **4854** ^A →8
ἀντί **4854** ^A →5
ἀντίδικος [**4854** ^A ↓9]
ἄξιος **4854** [^A →10], ^B ↓3
ἀπαγγελία **4854** [^A →3], ^B ↓1
ἀπαλλάττεσθαι [**4854** ^B →10]
ἁπλός **4855** iii 7, 8
ἀπό [**4854** ^A →1] **4855** iii 17
ἀποδέχεσθαι **4854** ^A ↓9
ἀποδιωθεῖσθαι **4854** ^A ↓6
ἀποθνήσκειν **4855** i 23
ἀπορεῖσθαι [**4854** ^B →6]
ἀρετή **4854** ^A ↓1
ἀριστεύς [**4855** i 8]
ἄρρην **4855** i 4
ἀρχή **4855** i 10
ἄρχων **4855** i 7
ἀσαφής **4855** i 25
ἀτόπως [**4854** ^A →10]
αὐτός **4854** ^A [→12], ↓[4], [8], [9], 10, [11], ^C ↓5, 8
ἀφηγηματικός **4854** ^A →2

βίος **4855** iii 15 (*bis*)
βούλεσθαι **4854** ^B ↓2 [**4855** i 23–4]
βραχύτης **4854** ^B →[3], 4, [8]

γαμεῖν **4855** iii 6
γάρ (**4854** ^C →3, 4, 5, 8)
γένος **4855** i 1, 3
γεωργεῖν **4855** iii 6
γίνεσθαι **4854** ^A →3, [7], 13, 14, [↓3–4], ^B →4, (8) **4855** iii 17–18

γνήσιος [**4855** i 3–4]
γνώμη **4854** ^A →[7], (7), ^B →[4], 5 **4855** iii 2
γοῦν [**4854** ^A ↓2]

δέ **4854** ^A →(1), [3], [7], [10], (10), [11], [12], [13], [14], ↓(3), [3], 6, [11], ^B →(4), [7], (8) **4855** i 4, 11, [25], 27, iii 1, 4, 7, 10, 17
δεινός [**4854** ^A ↓10]
δεύτερος [**4854** ^A ↓5]
δή [**4855** i 24]
δηλοῦν **4854** ^A →4, ^B →10, ^C →4
διά **4854** ^C ↓3
διάθεσις **4855** i 2, 10
διαιρεῖσθαι **4855** i 11
διδάσκειν **4855** iii 5
διεξιέναι [**4854** ^A ↓6]
διιστάναι **4854** ^A ↓2
δίκαιος **4855** iii 14–15
δικαστη— **4854** ^C ↓2
δικαστής [**4854** ^A ↓7]
διοικεῖν **4855** iii 1
Διομη— **4854** ^B ↓3
δοκεῖν [**4854** ^A ↓5]
δύναμις [**4854** ^A ↓2]
δύνασθαι [**4854** ^A ↓3]
δυνατός **4855** iii 16
δύο **4855** iii 11

ἐάν **4855** i 5, 7, 8, 9, 10, 15, 18, 20, 22
ἑαυτός **4854** ^A ↓11
ἐγώ **4854** ^C ↓4, 6
εἰ **4854** ^A ↓2, ^B ↓3 **4855** i 8, 14, 21, 23, iii 1, 5, 6 (*bis*), 9
εἰδέναι **4854** ^A →10, ↓1
εἶδος **4854** ^C →3
εἰκάζειν [**4854** ^A →10]
εἶναι [**4854** ^A [→11, 12, 13], ↓4, 10, [10], [^C →3] **4855** i 8, 26, iii 7
εἰς **4855** i 11
εἰς **4855** iii 9
εἰσηγεῖσθαι **4855** i 26
ἐκ/ἐξ **4854** ^A →11 **4855** i 10, 22
ἐκεῖνος [**4854** ^A ↓10–11]
ἕκτος [**4854** ^A ↓9]
ἔμφασις [**4854** ^A ↓1]
ἐμφατικός **4854** ^B →2
ἐν **4854** ^A [→14–15?], ↓4, [7], ^B [→10], [↓5?], ^C →[3], 6, ↓8 **4855** i 13, [16], 21
ἐναντίος **4854** ^C ↓5 **4855** i 26, iii 17
ἐναργῶς **4854** ^A →4

χρᾶϲθαι **4854** ^A →[2], 2, [3], [4], 5, [14], 15, ^B →2, [7], [9]

χρεία [**4854** ^A ↓3]

χρή **4854** ^A →10, ↓1 **4855** iii 5, 6 (*bis*)

χρηϲτέοϲ **4855** iii 4

χρόνοϲ **4855** i 12, [17–18]

ὡϲ **4854** ^A [→12], ↓[4], 5, ^B →7, [7], [↓2?], [^C →6?]

ὥϲτε **4854** ^C ↓5

ὠφέλεια [**4854** ^A ↓11]

ὠφελεῖν **4855** iii 2–3

Citations of known authors

Demosth. 23.6 **4854** ^C →2–3

III. RULERS

HADRIANUS

Ἀδ[ριανοῦ **4868** 9 (year 7)

Ἀδριανοῦ τοῦ κυρίου **4856** 8, 11–12 (year 2) **4861** 13 (year 6) **4864** 6–7 (year 6), 11 (year 7) **4867** 6–7 (year 6) **4870** 7 (year 6 or 7) **4873** 6–7 (year 16) **4874** 7 (year 19)

Ἀδριανοῦ Καίϲαροϲ τοῦ κυρίου **4857** 12 (year 2) **4858** 4–5, 8–9 (year 3) **4859** 4–5 (year 4), 7 (year 5) **4860** 5 (year 6) **4861** 8–9 (year 6) **4862** 8–9, 11 (year 6) **4863** 3 (year 6) **4865** 5 (year 6) **4866** 4 (year 6), 6 (year 7) **4869** 4–5, 9–10 (year 7) **4872** 4, 12 (year 8), 7–8, 14–15 (year 9) **4875** 8–9 (year 19) **4876** 6 (year 19) **4877** 4–5 (year 19) **4878** 5 (year 19)

Αὐτοκράτοροϲ Καίϲαροϲ Τραϊανοῦ Ἀδριανοῦ Ϲεβαϲτοῦ **4860** 17–18 (year 6) **4863** 6 (year 7) **4865** 9–10 (year 7) **4867** 10–11 (year 7) **4873** 10–11 (year 17) **4874** 12–13 (year 19) **4875** 17–19 (year 19) **4876** 13–14 (year 19) **4877** 7–8 (year 20)

ANTONINUS PIUS

Ἀντωνίνου Καίϲαροϲ τοῦ κυρίου **4879** 4 (year 4) **4880** 5–6 (year 8) **4881** 7–8 (year 10) **4882** 5–6, 10 (year 16) **4883** 9–10 (year 16) **4884** 3–4 (year 20), 10 (year 21)

Αὐτοκράτοροϲ Καίϲαροϲ Τίτου Αἰλίου Ἀδριανοῦ Ἀντωνίνου Ϲεβαϲτοῦ Εὐϲεβοῦϲ **4879** 6–7 (year 5) **4881** 11–14 (year 11)

MARCUS AURELIUS AND VERUS

τῶν κυρίων Ϲεβαϲτῶν **4885** 6 (year 4)

Αὐρηλίων Ἀντωνίνου καὶ Οὐήρου τῶν κυρίων Ϲεβαϲτῶν **4885** 10–12 (year 5)

MARCUS AURELIUS

Αὐρηλίου Ἀντωνίνου Καίϲαροϲ τοῦ κυρίου **4886** 2–4 (year 15) **4887** 1–2 (year 15) **4888** 9–10 (year 16) **4889** 4–5 (year 16)

CARACALLA AND GETA

Μάρκου Αὐρηλίου Ἀντωνίνου καὶ Πουβλίου Ϲεπτιμίου Γέτα Βρεταννικῶν μεγίϲτων Εὐϲεβῶν Ϲεβαϲτῶν **4890** 2–4 (year 19)

SEVERUS ALEXANDER

Μάρκου Αὐρηλίου Ϲεουήρου Ἀλεξάνδρου Καίϲαροϲ τοῦ κυρίου **4891** 19–20 (oath formula)

Αὐτοκράτοροϲ Καίϲαροϲ Μάρκου Αὐρηλίου Ϲεουήρου Ἀλεξάνδρου Εὐϲεβοῦϲ Εὐτυχοῦϲ Ϲεβαϲτοῦ **4891** 22–4 (year 2)

MAXIMINUS THRAX AND MAXIMUS

Αὐτοκράτοροϲ Καίϲαροϲ Γαΐου Ἰουλίου Οὐήρου Μαξιμίνου Εὐϲεβοῦϲ Εὐτυχοῦϲ Ϲεβαϲτοῦ καὶ Γαΐου Ἰουλίου Οὐήρου Μαξίμου τοῦ ἱερωτάτου Καίϲαροϲ Ϲεβαϲτοῦ υἱοῦ τοῦ Ϲεβαϲτοῦ **4892** 1–5 (year 2?)

Tiberius II

βασιλείας τοῦ θειοτάτου καὶ εὐσεβεστάτου ἡμῶν δεσπότου μεγίστου εὐεργέτου Φλαουΐου Τιβερίου Κωνσταντίνου τοῦ αἰωνίου Αὐγούστου καὶ Αὐτοκράτορος **4922** 1–3 (year 8)

Heraclius

- - - - εὐεργέτου Φλαουΐου Ἡρακλείου τοῦ αἰωνίου Αὐγούστου καὶ Αὐτοκράτορος **4930** 1–2 (year 4 or 5)

IV. CONSULS

375 μετὰ τὴν ὑπατείαν τοῦ δεσπότου ἡμῶν Γρατιανοῦ αἰωνίου Αὐγούστου τὸ γ καὶ Φλαουΐου Εἰκυτίου τοῦ λαμπροτάτου **4893** 1–2

379 ὑπατείας Φλαουΐων Αὐσονίου καὶ Ὀλυβρίου τῶν λαμπροτάτων ἐπάρχων **4894** 5–6

380 ὑπατείας τῶν δεσποτῶν ἡμῶν Γρατιανοῦ τὸ ε καὶ Θεοδοσίου τὸ α τῶν αἰωνίων Αὐγούστων **4895** 1–4

386 ὑπατείας τοῦ δεσπότου ἡμῶν Ὁνωρίου τοῦ ἐπιφανεστάτου υἱοῦ τοῦ δεσπότου ἡμῶν Θεοδοσίου Αὐγούστου καὶ Φλαουΐου Εὐοδίου τοῦ λαμπροτάτου **4896** 1–3

391 μετὰ τὴν ὑπατείαν τοῦ δεσπότου ἡμῶν Οὐαλεντινιανοῦ αἰωνίου Αὐγούστου τὸ δ καὶ Φλαουΐου Νεωτερίου τοῦ λαμπροτάτου **4897** 1–3

    ὑπατείας Φλαουΐων Τατιανοῦ καὶ Συμμάχου τῶν λαμπροτάτων **4898** 1

393 μετὰ τὴν ὑπατείαν τοῦ δεσπότου ἡμῶν Ἀρκαδίου αἰωνίου Αὐγούστου τὸ β καὶ Φλαουΐου Ῥουφίνου τοῦ λαμπροτάτου **4899** 1–2

    ὑπατείας τοῦ δεσπότου ἡμῶν Θεοδοσίου αἰωνίου Αὐγούστου τὸ γ καὶ Φλαουΐου Ἀβουνδαντίου τοῦ λαμπροτάτου **4900** 1–2

408 μετὰ τὴν ὑπατείαν τῶν δεσποτῶν ἡμῶν Ἀρκαδίου (l. Ὁνωρίου) τὸ ζ καὶ Θεοδοσίου τὸ β τῶν αἰωνίων Αὐγούστων **4901** 1–2

415 ὑπατείας τῶν δεσποτῶν ἡμῶν Ὁνωρίου τὸ ι καὶ Θεοδοσίου τὸ ς τῶν αἰωνίων Αὐγούστων **4902** 2–3

417 μετὰ τὴν ὑπατείαν τοῦ δεσπότου ἡμῶν Θεοδοσίου αἰωνίου Αὐγούστου τὸ ζ καὶ Φλαουΐου Παλλαδίου τοῦ λαμπροτάτου **4903** 1–2

    ὑπατείᾳ τοῦ δεσπότου ἡμῶν Ὁνωρίου τοῦ αἰωνίου Αὐγούστου τὸ ια καὶ Φλαουΐου Κωνσταντίου τοῦ λαμπροτάτου τὸ β **4904** 1–2

419 ὑπατείᾳ Φλαουΐων Μοναξίου καὶ Πλίντα τῶν λαμπροτάτων **4905** 1

420 μετὰ τὴν ὑπατείαν Φλαουΐων Μοναξίου καὶ Πλίντα τῶν λαμπροτάτων **4906** 1–2

422 ὑπατείας τῶν δεσποτῶν ἡμῶν Ὁνωρίου τὸ ιγ καὶ Θεοδοσίου τὸ ι τῶν αἰωνίων Αὐγούστων **4907** 1–3

423 ὑπατείας Φλαουΐων Ἀσκληπιοδότου καὶ Μαρινιανοῦ τῶν λαμπροτάτων **4908** 1–2

444 μετὰ τὴν ὑπατείαν Φλαουΐων Μαξίμου τὸ β καὶ Πατερίου τῶν λαμπροτάτων **4909** 1–2

447 μετὰ τὴν ὑπατείαν Φλαουΐων Ἀετίου τὸ τρίτον καὶ Συμμάχου τῶν λαμπροτάτων **4910** 1

449 μετὰ τὴν ὑπατείαν Φλαουΐων Ζήνωνος καὶ Ποστουμιανοῦ τῶν λαμπροτάτων **4911** 1–2

450 μετὰ τὴν ὑπατείαν Φλαουΐων Πρωτογένους καὶ Ἀστουρίου τῶν λαμπροτάτων **4912** 2–3

462 ὑπατείας τοῦ δεσπότου ἡμῶν Φλαουΐου Λέοντος τοῦ αἰωνίου Αὐγούστου τὸ β **4913** 1–2

465 μετὰ τὴν ὑπατείαν Φλαουΐου Βιβιανοῦ τοῦ λαμπροτάτου καὶ τοῦ δηλωθησομένου **4914** 1–2

467 μετὰ τὴν ὑπατείαν τοῦ δεσπότου ἡμῶν Φλαουΐου Λέοντος τοῦ αἰωνίου Αὐγούστου τὸ γ καὶ τοῦ δηλωθησομένου **4915** 1–2

472 μετὰ τὴν ὑπατείαν τοῦ δεσπότου ἡμῶν Λέοντος αἰωνίου Αὐγούστου τὸ δ καὶ Φλαουΐου Προβινιανοῦ τοῦ λαμπροτάτου **4916** 1–3

473 ὑπατείας τοῦ δεσπότου ἡμῶν Φλαουΐου Λέοντος τοῦ αἰωνίου Αὐγούστου τὸ ε **4917** 1–2

494–6 μετὰ τὴν ὑπατείαν Φλαουΐου Εὐσεβίου τοῦ λαμπροτάτου τὸ β **4918** 1

501 ὑπατείᾳ Φλαουΐου Πομπηίου τοῦ ἐνδοξοτάτου **4919** 1

v/vi τοῖς μετὰ τὴν ὑπατείαν Φλαουΐου - - - **4920** 1

523 μετὰ τὴν ὑπατείαν Φλαουΐων Συμμάχου καὶ Βοηθίου τῶν λαμπροτάτων **4921** 2–3

582 ὑπατείας τοῦ αὐτοῦ (Tiberius II) εὐσεβεστάτου ἡμῶν δεσπότου ἔτους δ **4922** 3–4

V. INDICTIONS AND ERAS

(a) INDICTIONS

1st indiction **4913** 2 (= 462/3) **4921** 3 (= 522/3)
3rd indiction **4914** 2 (= 464/5) **4930** 3, 20 (= 614/15)
6th indiction **4907** [3], 10 (= 422/3) [**4915** 1–2 (= 467/8)]
7th indiction **4901** 11 (= 408/9) [**4915** 8 (= 468/9)]
10th indiction **4916** 3 (= 471/2) **4919** 2 (= 501/2)

12th indiction **4917** 2 (= 473/4) **4926** 5 **4927** 3, 5 **4928** 3 **4929** 4 (= 563/4)
14th indiction **4923** 2, 3 **4924** 3 (= 550/51)
15th indiction **4922** 4 (= 581/2) **4925** 3 (= 551/2)
n indiction [**4918** 2 (= 494–6)] [**4920** 2 (= v/vi)]

(b) ERAS

67/36= 390/91 **4897** 13
95/64= 418/19 **4904** 10
144/113= 467/8 [**4915** 8]

227/196= 550/51 **4923** 3 **4924** 3
228/197= 551/2 **4925** 3
240/209= 563/4 **4927** 5

VI. MONTHS

Θώθ **4863** 7 **4872** 8, 15 [**4877** 8] **4879** 9 **4880** 6 **4881** 14 **4911** 2 **4919** 2 **4923** 2, 3
Φαῶφι **4864** 11 **4865** 10 **4884** 10 **4885** 13 **4895** 5 **4900** 2 **4902** 4 **4905** 2 **4907** 3 **4909** 2 **4912** 3 [**4915** 2]
Ἀθύρ **4891** 25 **4917** 2 **4924** 2, 3 **4930** 18
Χοιάκ **4904** 2 **4913** 2
Τῦβι **4888** 10 **4907** 10
Μεχείρ **4914** 2

Φαμενώθ **4897** 3, 12 **4916** 3 **4918** 1 **4925** 3
Παχών **4893** 2 **4899** 2 [**4910** 2] **4922** 4 **4926** 4 **4927** 2, 5 **4928** 3
Παῦνι **4901** 2 **4929** 4
Ἐπείφ **4869** 10 **4892** 5 **4921** 3
Μεσορή **4856** 12 **4857** 13 (ἐπαγόμεναι) **4858** 9 **4860** 18 **4861** 14 (ἐπαγόμεναι) [**4874** 13] **4875** 20 **4876** 15 (ἐπαγόμεναι) **4882** 11 **4894** 6 **4901** 10 **4903** 2 **4906** 2 **4920** 2

VII. DATES

2 August 118 **4856** 11–12
26 August 118 **4857** 11–13
12 August 119 **4858** 7–9
120/21 **4859** 7
18 August 122 **4860** 17–18
28 August 122 **4861** 13–14
122 **4862** 11
26 September 122 **4863** 5–7
4 October 122 **4864** 10–11
6 October 122 **4865** 9–10
122/3 **4866** 6 **4867** 10–11 **4868** 9
28 June 123 **4869** 9–10
*c.*122–3? **4870** 6–7 [**4871**]
2 September 124 **4872** 7–8, 14–15
132/3 **4873** 9–12
25 July – 23 August 135 **4874** 11–13
23 August 135 **4875** 17–20
24–8 August 135 **4876** 13–15

13 September 135 **4877** 6–8
*c.*135 **4878** 4–5
29 August – 27 September 141 **4879** 7–9
2 September 144 **4880** 5–6
20 September 147 **4881** 10–15
13 August 153 **4882** 9–11
*c.*153 **4883** 9–10
14 October 157 **4884** 9–10
24 October 164 **4885** 10–13
175/6 **4886** 2–4 **4887** 1–2
16 January 176 **4888** 8–10
176/7 **4889** 4–5
211 **4890** 2–4
28 October – 26 November 222 **4891** 21–5
17 July 236 or 237 **4892** 1–5
26 April 375 **4893** 1–2
2 August 379 **4894** 5–6
14 October 380 **4895** 1–5

386 **4896** 1–3
5 March 391 **4897** 1–3
391 **4898** 1
27 April 393 **4899** 1–2
12 October 393 **4900** 1–2
1 June 408 **4901** 1–2
19 October 415 **4902** 2–4
1 August 417 **4903** 1–2
7 December 417 **4904** 1–2
16 October 419 **4905** 1–2
28 July 420 **4906** 1–2
28 September 422 **4907** 1–3
423 **4908** 1–2
15 October 444 **4909** 1–2
1 May 447 **4910** 1–2
24 September 449 **4911** 1–2
1 October 450 **4912** 2–3

2 December 462 **4913** 1–2
4 February 465 **4914** 1–2
10 October 467(?) **4915** 1–2
7 March 472 **4916** 1–3
13 November 473 **4917** 1–2
17(?) March 494–6 **4918** 1–2
30 August 501 **4919** 1–2
14 July 523 **4921** 2–3
4 May 582 **4922** 1–4
7 September 550 **4923** 3
21 November 550 **4924** 3
8 March 552 **4925** 3
21 May 564 **4926** 4–5
23 May 564 **4927** 5
16–24 May 564 **4928** 3
27 May 564 **4929** 4
29 August – 21 November 614 **4930** 1–3, 18–20

VIII. PERSONAL NAMES

Α—, f. of Aur. Ammon **4902** 8
Ἀβουνδάντιος see Index IV s.v. 393
Ἀβραάμιος, f. of Aur. Menas **4922** 8
Ἀγαθόκλεια, alias Apollonia, d. of Ischyrion **4870** 2
Ἀγαθὸς Δαίμων, s. of Dius **4877** 1, 3
Ἀδριανός see Index III s.vv. Hadrianus, Antoninus Pius
Ἀείων, f. of Aeatius **4899** 5
Ἀέτιος see Index IV s.v. 447
Ἀθηναῖος, f. of Theon, gr.f. of Didym— **4872** 13
Ἀθηνόδωρος **4889** 5–6
Αἰάτιος, s. of Aeion **4899** 5
Αἴλιος see Index III s.v. Antoninus Pius
Αἰῶν, Aur., s. of N.N. **4916** 7
Ἀκουσίλαος, f. of Dius, gr.f. of Acusilaus **4875** 1 **4876** 1
Ἀκουσίλαος, s. of Dius, gr.s. of Acusilaus **4875** 1–2
Ἀκύτης, s. of Haronnophris **4884** 1
Ἀκύτης, s. of Acytes, farmer **4884** 5, 7
Ἀκύτης, f. of Acytes **4884** 5
Ἄκωρις, s. of Hierax **4880** 3
Ἀλέξανδρος, f. of Sinthonis **4860** 12
Ἀλέξανδρος, s. of Demetrius **4874** 1
Ἀλέξανδρος, f. of Apollonius (**4889** 13)
Ἀλέξανδρος see Index III s.v. Severus Alexander; Index IX(*d*) s.v. Ἀλεξάνδρου (κλῆρος)
Ἄμμων, Aur., son of A— **4902** 8
Ἄμμων, f. of Aur. Maximinus **4906** 5
Ἀμμωνᾶς, s. of Ophelas **4889** 10
Ἀμμωνι—, Fl., soldier or veteran **4900** 4–5
Ἀμμώνιος, friend of Horus s. of Pausiris **4878** 1
Ἀμμώνιος, s. of Diogenes **4883** 6
Ἀμμώνιος, s. of Proculus **4888** 1

Ἀμμώνιος, f. of Tachnubis, h. of Harasis **4889** 7
Ἀμμωνοῦς, d. of Sarapammon, w. of Aur. Parion **4904** 3, [12]
Ἀμοιτᾶς, Dionysius alias, s. of Heron and Sinthonis, br. of Apollonius **4860** 11
Ἀμφίων, Faustus alias, *sitologus* **4860** 2
Ἀνίκητος, Aur. **4898** 4
Ἄννα, Aur., d. of Achilles **4911** 6
Ἀντι—, f. of Dionysis **4881** 1
Ἀντίοχος, f. of Sarapias **4890** 5
Ἀντωνῖνος see Index III s.vv. Antoninus Pius, Marcus Aurelius and Verus, Marcus Aurelius, Caracalla and Geta
Ἀντώνιος Δῖος **4861** 2, 6
Ἀντώνιος, Fl., *scrinarius* of the *officium* of the *comes Aegyptiaci limitis* **4902** 5
Ἀντώνιος, f. of Aur. Churus, h. of Philoxena **4921** 5
Ἄπ, f. of Aur. Thaesia **4920** 8
Ἀπίων, secretary of *praktores* **4864** 7
Ἀπίων, s. of —n **4867** 7
Ἀπίων, Heracles alias, s. of Apion **4875** 14
Ἀπίων, f. of Heracles alias Apion **4875** 14
Ἀπολλοφάνης, *sitologus* **4874** 3
Ἀπολλω— **4870** 8
Ἀπολλω—, *sitologus* **4878** 2
Ἀπολλωνία, Agathocleia alias, d. of Ischyrion **4870** 3
Ἀπολλώνιος, s. of Heron and Sinthonis, br. of Dionysius alias Amoitas **4860** 10
Ἀπολλώνιος, f. of Theon **4883** 1 **4885** 1
Ἀπολλώνιος, s. of Rufus, friend of Ammonius s. of Proculus **4888** 1–2

Εὐάγγελος, *sitologus* **4874** 3–4
Εὐδαίμων, s. of Theon **4886** 5
Εὐδαίμων, Apollonius alias, s. of Eudaemon **4889** 1
Εὐδαίμων, f. of Apollonius alias Eudaemon **4889** 1
Εὐθήριος, f. of Martyrius **4914** 5 [**4915** 4]
Εὐόδιος *see* Index IV s.v. 386
Εὐςέβιος *see* Index IV s.v. 494–6
Εὔφημος, steward of Agathocleia alias Apollonia **4870** 1
Εὐφράντιος, Aur., s. of Phoebammon, sausage maker **4903** 3, 11

Ζηνᾶς **4885** 8
Ζήνων *see* Index IV s.v. 449
Ζωίλος, s. of Geminus **4874** 10
Ζωίλος, s. of Heliodorus **4882** 8
Ζωίλος, f. of Theon **4888** 6

Ἡλιόδωρος, f. of Zoilus **4882** 8
Ἡλιόδωρος, Aur., s. of Muses, *systates* **4898** 2
Ἡλιόδωρος, f. of Aur. Parion **4904** 3
Ἡρ—, s. of Ptolemaeus **4860** 1
Ἡραΐς, d. of N.N., gr.d.(?) of Sarapion **4859** 5
Ἡραΐς, m. of Aur. Papnuthis, w. of Ioannes **4921** 4
Ἡρακλᾶς, Aur., s. of Nechthenibis **4891** 25
Ἡρακλείδης, s. of Heracleides **4882** 1
Ἡρακλείδης, f. of Heracleides **4882** 1
Ἡρακλείδης, alias Heras, *sitologus* **4890** 11
Ἡρακλείδης, Aur., s. of Heracleides **4891** 27–8
Ἡρακλείδης, f. of Aur. Heracleides **4891** 28
Ἡράκλειος *see* Index III s.v. Heraclius; Index IX(*b*) s.v. Ἡρακλείου
Ἡρακλῆς, alias Apion, s. of Apion **4875** 13
Ἡρᾶς, secretary of Iulius Theon **4872** 1, 9
Ἡρᾶς, farmer **4876** 10
Ἡρᾶς, Heracleides alias, *sitologus* **4890** 11–12
Ἡρωΐς, d. of Arch— **4889** 17
Ἡρῶς, d. of Ptolemaeus **4889** 14
Η . οῦτος (gen.), f. of Dionysius **4887** 8

Θαηςία, Aur., d. of Ap **4920** 8
Θεογένης, s. of Neoptolemus **4876** 9 n.
Θεοδόςιος *see* Index IV s.vv. 380, 386, 393, 408, 415, 417, 422
Θεόδωρος, Aur., s. of Demetrius **4895** 10/
Θέων *see* Ἰούλιος Θέων
Θέων, Diogenes alias, s. of Theon **4861** 10
Θέων, f. of Diogenes alias Theon **4861** 10
Θέων, s. of Sirion **4865** 6
Θέων, s. of Onnophris **4869** 7
Θέων, f. of Arsinoe **4872** 5
Θέων, s. of Athenaeus, f. of Didym— **4872** 13
Θέων, s. of Theon, cous. of Alexander s. of Demetrius **4874** 2

Θέων, f. of Theon **4874** 2–3
Θέων, s. of Apollonius, ex-gymnasiarch **4883** 1, 10 **4885** 1
Θέων, s. of Theon, friend of Acytes s. of Haronnophris **4884** 1
Θέων, f. of Theon **4884** 1
Θέων, alias Gaius, s. of Peteuris **4884** 4
Θέων, f. of Eudaemon (**4886** 6)
Θέων, s. of Zoilus **4888** 6
Θέων, f. of Aur. N.N. **4917** 5
Θῶνις, Aur., headman **4903** 6

Ἰέραξ, f. of Hacoris **4880** 4
Ἰούλιος *see* Index III s.v. Maximinus Thrax and Maximus
Ἰούλιος Θέων, gymnasiarch **4857** 1, 4–5 **4868** 1, 4 **4872** 1, 3, 9, 11
Ἰούλιος Cαραπίων, *hypomnematographus* **4869** 1, 5
Ἰούλιος, f. of Aur. N.N. **4904** 5
Ἰςάκ, Aur., s. of Nilus, Alexandrian tradesman **4918** 5
Ἰςαροῦς, d. of Diogenes **4857** 6
Ἰςχυρ—, f. of Ischyras **4889** 11
Ἰςχυρᾶς, s. of Ischyr— **4889** 10
Ἰςχυρίων, f. of Agathocleia alias Apollonia **4870** 3
Ἰωάννης, assistant of Fl. Antonius **4902** 7
Ἰωάννης, Aur., *lector*(?) **4902** 18
Ἰωάννης, Fl., soldier **4919** 3
Ἰωάννης, f. of Aur. Papnuthis, h. of Heraΐs **4921** 4
Ἰωάννης, Pileon, f. of Martinus **4922** 6
Ἰωςήφ, f. of Fl. Constantius [**4911** 5]

Καῖςαρ *see* Index III s.vv. Hadrianus, Antoninus Pius, Marcus Aurelius, Severus Alexander, Maximinus Thrax and Maximus
Κημ—, f. of Aur. Pieus, h. of Martha **4918** 3
Κλαυδία Πτολέμα **4879** 4–5
Κλαύδιος Γερμανός, steward of Claudius Munatianus **4862** 1
Κλαύδιος Μουνατιανός **4859** 1, 3–4 **4862** 2, 5–6 **4863** 1
Κλαύδιος Χαιρήμων **4879** 1, 10
Κολλοῦθος, f. of Aur. Phoebammon **4917** 7
Κορνήλιος **4890** 6
Κρονίων, f. of Aur. —on **4896** 4
Κρονοῦς, d. of Neoptolemus **4889** 9
Κυρία, Fl., *clarissima femina* and landowner [**4917** 3]
Κύριλλος, f. of Aur. Nicon **4897** 4
Κωνςταντῖνος *see* Index III s.v. Tiberius II
Κωνςτάντιος, Fl., s. of Ioseph, soldier **4911** 3
Κωνςτάντιος *see* Index IV s.v. 417

Λεοντᾶς, overseer of Claudius Munatianus **4863** 7
Λέων *see* Index IV s.vv. 462, 467, 472, 473
Λικινιανός *see* Λούκιος Λικινιανός Μαρτιᾶλις

Cαραπίων *see* Ἰούλιος Cαραπίων

Cαραπίων, f. of Saras(?) **4872** 5

Cαραπίων, secretary(?) of Agathus Daemon s. of Dius **4877** 1

Cαραπίων, f. of Diogenes **4882** 6–7

Cαραπίων **4889** 18

Cαραπίων, f. of Aur. —is **4916** 4–5

Cαρᾶc, s. of Sarapion **4872** 5 n.

Cαρᾶc, s. of Pausiris **4885** 7

Cεουῆρος *see* Index III s.v. Severus Alexander

Cεπτίμιος *see* Index III s.v. Caracalla and Geta

Cέργιος, Fl., s. of Victor, *vir spectabilis, comes* and *dioecetes* of the 'glorious household' **4930** 4

Cίνθωνις, d. of Alexander, w. of Heron, m. of Apollonius and Dionysius alias Amoitas (**4860** 11, 14)

Cίνθωνις, m. of Didym— (**4889** 12)

Cιρίων, f. of Theon **4865** 6

Cύμμαχος *see* Index IV s.vv. 391, 447, 523

Cυντύχη, freedwoman of Sarapias d. of Dionysius **4875** 9

Tαόννωφρις, alias Chaeremonis, d. of Dionysius **4884** 6

Tαπέκυcιc **4889** 16

Tατιανός *see* Index IV s.v. 391

Tαυcῖρις, m. of Sarapion, w. of Sarapion **4869** 6

Tάχνουβις, d. of Ammonius and Harasis **4889** 7

Tιβέριος *see* Index III s.v. Tiberius II

Tῖτος *see* Index III s.v. Antoninus Pius

Tραϊανός *see* Index III s.v. Hadrianus

Tρωcίλλα, d. of Harmiusis **4874** 8

Φανίας **4873** 7

Φαῦcτος, alias Amphion, *sitologus* **4860** 2

Φιλίcκος, f. of Dionysius **4877** 5

Φιλίcκος, Philoxenus alias **4887** 4

Φιλόνικος, Aur., s. of Dionysodorus **4895** 6

Φιλόξενα, m. of Aur. Churus, w. of Antonius **4921** 6

Φιλόξενος, alias Philiscus **4887** 4

Φλαουΐα *see* Κυρία

Φλάουϊος [**4893** 3] [**4910** 3]; *see also* Ἀμμωνι—, Ἀντώνιος, Ἄρων, Ἰωάννης, Κωνcτάντιος, Μάξιμος,

Μαρκιανός, Παμούθιος, Cέργιος, Φοιβάμμων; Index III s.vv. Tiberius II, Heraclius; Index IV s.vv. 375, 379, 386, 391, 393, 417, 419, 420, 423, 444, 447, 449, 450, 462, 465, 467, 472, 473, 494–6, 501, v/vi, 523

Φοιβάμμων, f. of Aur. Euphrantius **4903** 3

Φοιβάμμων, Fl., ex-*protector* and administrator of the *domus divina* [**4905** 3] **4906** 3

Φοιβάμμων, Fl., s. of E—, *devotissimus magistrianus* of the *sacra officia* **4909** 3

Φοιβάμμων, Aur., s. of Epimachus, tradesman **4910** 4

Φοιβάμμων, Aur., s. of Colluthus, guarantor of Aur. N.N. **4917** 7

Χαιρημονίς, Taonnophris alias, d. of Dionysius **4884** 7

Χαιρήμων *see* Κλαύδιος Χαιρήμων

Χαιρήμων, *sitologus*? **4886** 9

Χουροῦς, Aur., d. of Antonius and Philoxena, w. of Aur. Papnuthis, salt-fish seller **4921** 5

Χρ—, alias Fl. Maximus, soldier **4920** 3

Χωοῦς, f. of N.N. **4906** 7

Ψάμμις, s. of Psammis **4878** 5

Ψάμμις, f. of Psammis **4878** 5–6

Ὠρίων, alias Berenicianus **4890** 6–7

Ὧρος, s. of Pausiris **4878** 1

Ὧρος, f. of Demetria **4888** 6

Ὠφελᾶc, f. of Ammonas **4889** 10

. οττίων, f. of Didymus **4867** 1

] . υ . . . . , f. of Aur. N.N. **4913** 22

] . εῖc, Aur., d. of Sarapion **4916** 4

] . π . ννοc (gen.), m.(?) of Aur. Danielius **4921** 8

. α . εἴηc (gen.), m. of Aur. Menas **4922** 9

—άμμων, Aur. **4911** 6

—νοc, f. of Apion **4867** 7

—οc, Aur., s. of Apphus **4896** 6

—ων, f. of N.N. **4880** 1

—ων, Aur., s. of Cronion, assistant to the office of *exactor* **4896** 4

IX. GEOGRAPHICAL

(*a*) Countries, Nomes, Toparchies, Cities, etc.

Αἰγυπτιακός *see* Index XI s.v. κόμες τοῦ Αἰγυπτιακοῦ λιμίτου

Ἀλεξάνδρεια **4918** 7 **4922** fr. 2.1–2 n. **4930** 16, 30

Ἄνω Κυνοπολίτης (νομός) **4918** 4

Ἀρκαδία (ἐπαρχία) **4910** 3

Βρεταννικός *see* Index III s.v. Caracalla and Geta

Ἑρμοπολίτης **4903** 4

Ἡρακλεοπολιτῶν (πόλις) [**4896** 5]

(*b*) Villages, etc.

(*c*) Tribes and Demes

(*d*) Miscellaneous

X. RELIGION

XI. OFFICIAL AND MILITARY TERMS AND TITLES

XII. PROFESSIONS AND OCCUPATIONS

XIII. MEASURES

(a) Weights and Measures

(b) Money

Ἀλεξανδρείας (ζυγόν) **4930** 16, (30)

ἰδιωτικὸν (ζυγόν) **4921** 12

κεράτιον **4930** 14, 15, (30)

μυριάς **4903** 9

νόμιcμα **4907** 7, (8, 19) **4930** 13
νομιcμάτιον **4897** 10 **4902** 16 **4904** 8 **4918** 11, [(12)], (16) [**4921** 12] (**4930** 30)

XIV. TAXES

τέλεcμα **4891** 18

XV. GENERAL INDEX OF WORDS

ἅγιος *see* Index X
ἀγράμματος (**4930** 26)
ἀδελφός **4864** 4
ἀδικ- **4894** 4
Αἰγυπτιακός *see* Index XI s.v. κόμες τοῦ Αἰγυπτιακοῦ λιμίτου
αἰδέςιμος *see* Index XI
αἱρεῖcθαι **4861** 11 **4862** 7 **4873** 8
αἴρη **4891** 12–13
αἰτεῖcθαι **4907** 12
αἰώνιος *see* Index III s.vv. Tiberius II, Heraclius; Index IV s.vv. 375, 380, 391, 393, 408, 415, 417, 422, 462, 467, 472, 473
ἀκίνδυνος **4903** 10 **4904** 9 [**4921** 14]
ἀκόλουθος **4894** 3
ἀλληλεγγύη [**4904** 6] **4915** 7 **4921** 9
ἀλλήλων **4901** 7 [**4913** 8]
ἄλλος [**4898** 3] **4907** 12
ἅμα **4891** 17
ἄμφοδον [**4898** 3]
ἀμφότερος **4860** 11 **4897** 4 **4921** 6
ἀνά **4891** 5, 7, 10
ἀναγκαῖος **4897** 8–9 [**4903** 8] [**4904** 7] **4918** 10 [**4921** 11]
ἀναγνώcτης(?) *see* Index X
ἀναδέχεcθαι [**4917** 6]
ἀνάλωμα (**4923** 1) (**4924** 2) (**4925** 1)
ἀναφέρειν **4893** 3
ἀναφέρεcθαι *see* Index XI
ἄνευ **4897** 13 **4907** 11
ἀνεψιός **4874** 3
ἀντιλογία **4907** 11
ἀνυπερθέτως **4901** 11 **4907** 10–11 **4930** 20
ἄνω **4878** 2 **4890** 5; *see also* Index IX(a) s.v. Ἄνω Κυνοπολίτης
ἀξιοῦν [**4913** 23]

ἅπας **4917** 6
ἀπελευθέρα **4875** 10
ἀπελεύθερος **4881** 2, 15–16
ἀπέχειν **4899** 6
ἀπηλιώτης **4859** 2 **4860** 2, 6, 7 **4865** 2 [**4866** 1] **4868** 2 **4869** 2 **4871** 3 **4874** 4 [**4879** 1] **4882** 2 **4883** 4 **4884** 2 **4886** 4 **4891** 7, 10
ἁπλοῦς **4897** 17 [**4902** 13] **4904** 8 [**4913** 17] **4918** 11 **4930** 22
ἀπό **4856** 5 **4857** 3 **4859** 2 **4860** 1, 4 **4861** 4 **4862** 4 **4863** 2 **4865** 3 **4866** 2 **4868** 3 **4869** 3 **4871** 4 **4872** 3, [10] **4873** 4 **4874** 6 **4875** 5 **4876** 4 [**4877** 3] **4879** 2 **4883** 7 **4884** 1, 3 **4885** 4 **4887** 3 **4888** 3 **4889** 2, 3 **4891** 3, 6, 12 **4895** 7, 10 **4896** 4, 6 **4898** [2], 4 **4899** 3, 5 **4901** 4, 6 **4902** 9 **4903** 10 **4904** 4, 5, [9] [**4905** 3] **4906** 3, [6], 7, [8] **4910** 5 **4911** 5, [7] **4913** 3, [6] **4915** 5, [6], 7, 8 [**4916** 5, 8] **4917** 8 **4918** 3, 6, 16 [**4920** 8] **4921** 6, 8, [14] **4922** 6, 9 **4924** 2 **4926** 2, 3 **4927** 2 **4928** 2 **4929** 3 **4930** 7, 10, 15, 29, 30
ἀποδιδόναι **4891** 16 **4897** 11 **4902** 17 **4904** 10 **4907** 9 **4913** 12, [20]
ἀποκρότως **4930** 12
ἀποπληροῦν **4917** 6
ἀπότακτος **4917** 10
ἀργύριον **4903** 9
ἀρέςκειν [**4913** 9]
ἀρετή [**4918** 9]
ἀριθμός **4918** 12; *see also* Index XI
ἄριστος **4914** 4–5 [**4915** 4]
ἄρουρα *see* Index XIII(a)
ἀρτάβη *see* Index XIII(a)
ἀρτοπώλης *see* Index XII
ἀρχή **4915** 2
ἀρχιμανδρίτης *see* Index X
ἀcφάλεια **4910** 6 **4922** 10
Αὐτοκράτωρ *see* Index III s.vv. Hadrianus, Antoninus

XVI. CORRECTIONS TO PUBLISHED TEXTS

BGU I 102.5	**4885** 10 n.
CPR VII 23.5	**4913** 4 n.
P. Col. VII 183	**4900** 5 n.
P. Fouad 60.6, 8	**4889** 10 n.
P. Lips I 112.8	**4863** 7 n.
P. Lips I 113.8 & date; 9	**4878** 4 n.; **4869** 10 n.
P. Lips I 116 date	**4878** 4 n.
P. Lips II 141.3; 7	**4883** 4 n; **4882** 9 n.
P. Lips I 120.2	**4875** 1–2 n.
P. NYU II 52 (= *ZPE* 149 (2004 121 ff.))	**4889** 16 n.
P. Oxy. III 501.7–8	**4858** introd. (para. 1), 6–7 n.
P. Oxy. III 617 date	**4878** 4 n.
P. Oxy. XII 1444 date	**4878** 4 n.
P. Oxy. XII 1526 date	**4878** 4 n.
P. Oxy. XVI 1952.1 & date	**4926–4929** introd. (para. 1)
P. Oxy. XXXVIII 2866 date	**4878** 4 n.
P. Oxy. XXXVIII 2867.1; 10	**4872** 1 n.; 10 n.
P. Oxy. XLIV 3169.46	**4872** 10 n.
P. Oxy. L 3582.1–2	**4856** 9 n.
P. Oxy. LXII 4338.5; date	**4901** 3 n.; **4878** 4 n.
P. Petaus 57 date	**4878** 4 n.
PSI Congr. XX 9 date	**4878** 4 n.
P. Wash. Univ. I 24.2	**4905** 3–4 n., **4909** 3–4 n.
SB XII 11025.16	**4858** 10–11 n.
SB XII 11151 date	**4878** 4 n.
SB XII 11166.12 & date	**4878** 4 n.
SB XII 11167.5–6	**4879** 4–5 n.
SB XX 15171 date	**4898** 2–3 n.
SB XXII 15362 date	**4901** 4 n.

PLATE I

4844

4846

4847

4848

PLATE II

4845 ↓

→ **4849** ↓

PLATE III

4845 →

→ **4852** ↓

4853

PLATE IV

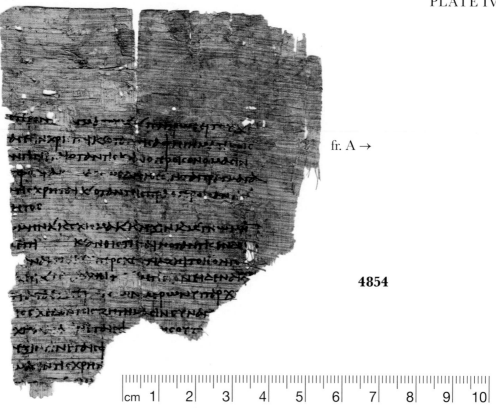

fr. A →

4854

fr. A ↓

PLATE V

fr. B   →   ↓

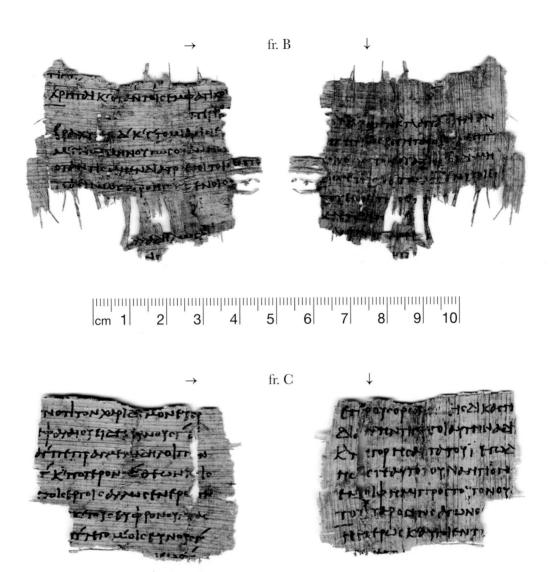

cm 1 2 3 4 5 6 7 8 9 10

fr. C   →   ↓

4854

PLATE VI

4855

fr. 1 (col. i)
(reduced)

PLATE VII

4855
fr. 2 (col. iii)
(reduced)

PLATE VIII

4850

4851

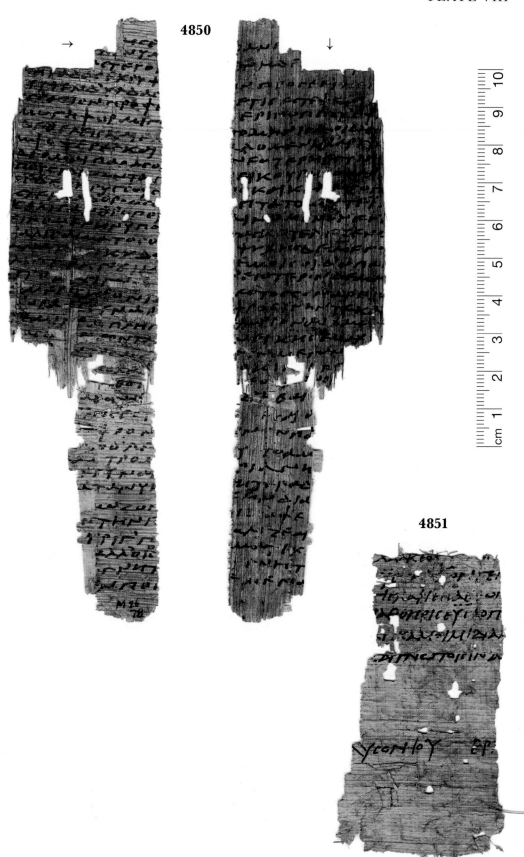

PLATE IX

4872

PLATE X

4885

4886

PLATE XI

4889

PLATE XII

4905

PLATE XIII

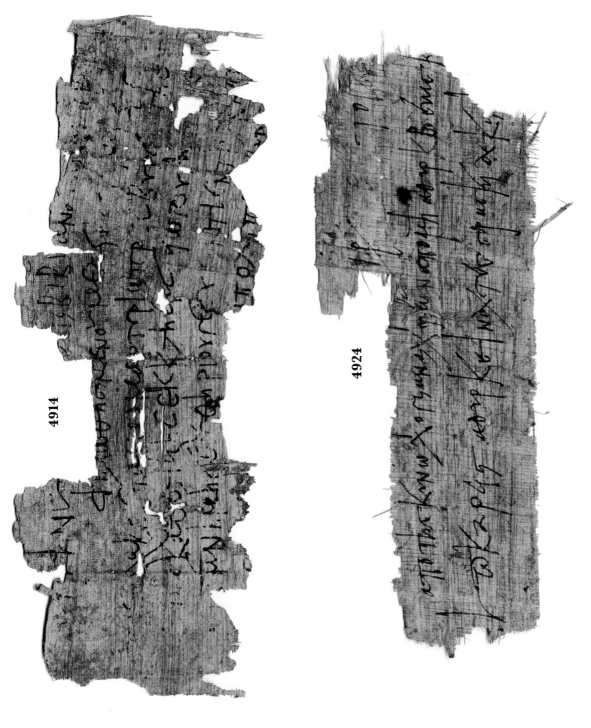

4914

4924

PLATE XIV

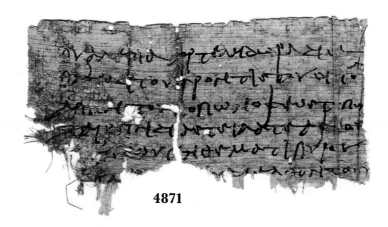

4871

4890

PLATE XV

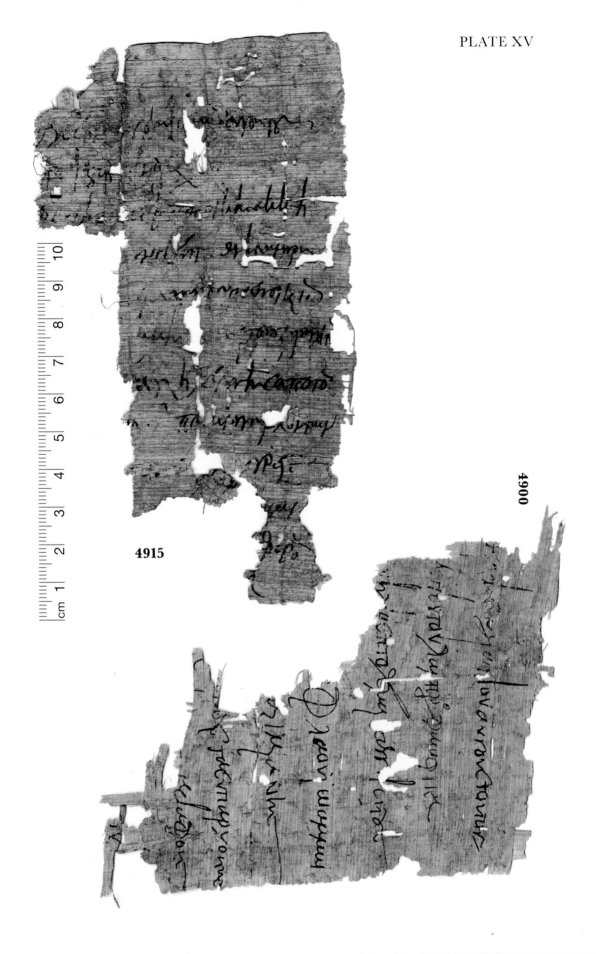

4915

4900

PLATE XVI

4930
(reduced)

2014. 10. 10   20. 04